The Write Start with Readings

PARAGRAPHS TO ESSAYS

The Write Start

with Readings

PARAGRAPHS TO ESSAYS

Lawrence Checkett

Gayle Feng-Checkett

St. Charles Community College

New York   San Francisco   Boston
London   Toronto   Sydney   Tokyo   Singapore   Madrid
Mexico City   Munich   Paris   Cape Town   Hong Kong   Montreal

Vice President and Editor-in-Chief: Joe Terry
Senior Acquisitions Editor: Steven Rigolosi
Development Editor: Marion B. Castellucci
Marketing Manager: Melanie Craig
Supplements Editor: Donna Campion
Production Manager: Ellen MacElree
Project Coordination, Text Design, and Electronic Page Makeup: Electronic Publishing Services Inc., NYC
Cover Designer/Manager: Wendy Ann Fredericks
Cover Illustration: © Jonathan Evans/Artville
Photo Researcher: Photosearch Inc.
Senior Manufacturing Manager: Dennis S. Para
Printer and Binder: Quebecor World/Taunton
Cover Printer: The Lehigh Press

For permission to use copyrighted material, grateful acknowledgment is made to the copyright holders on pp. 401 - 403, which are hereby made part of this copyright page.

Library of Congress Cataloging-in-Publication Data

Checkett, Lawrence.
    The write start with readings : paragraphs to essays / Lawrence Checkett, Gayle Feng-Checkett.
        p. cm.
    Includes bibliographical references and index.
    ISBN 0-321-06118-7
        1. English language—Rhetoric. 2. College readers. 3. Report writing. I. Feng-Checkett, Gayle. II. Title.

PE1408 .C444 2001
808'.0427–dc21   2001038397

Please visit our website at http://www.ablongman.com/checkett

ISBN 0-321-06118-7

1 2 3 4 5 6 7 8 9 10—QWT—04 03 02 01

To our children: Kitaro Lawrence,
Brian Yi Chuan, and
David Yi Shon. Knowledge is
life . . . pass it on.

BRIEF CONTENTS

DETAILED CONTENTS

PART 2

Moving Forward: Strategies for Developing Essays   55

Chapter 7

The Descriptive Essay   57

Chapter 8

The Narrative Essay   72

Chapter 9

The Example Essay   86

Chapter 10

The Classification Essay   98

Chapter 11

The Process Essay   111

Chapter 12

Chapter 15

The Persuasive Essay   178

PART 3

Special Writing Situations   203

Chapter 16

The Research Paper   205

Chapter 17

The Essay Exam   232

Chapter 18

The Writer's Resources   257

PREFACE

Colleges, especially two-year community colleges, are being challenged as never before. As the cost of attending four-year colleges and universities soars, enrollment at community colleges is increasing so dramatically that classrooms are bursting at the seams. These students seeking education at a more reasonable cost come from diverse cultures and have a wide range of learning abilities and learned basic skills. To respond to their varied needs, community colleges have had to reinvent basic course sequences in math, reading, and writing.

The Write Start Series

The Write Start is a two-book series designed to meet the needs of students taking developmental writing courses. The first text, *The Write Start with Readings: Sentences to Paragraphs,* addresses the most basic writing skills: grammar, sentence and paragraph structure, the integration of reading and writing, the special concerns of students for whom English is a second language, the various modes of developing topics, and an introduction to the essay. This text, *The Write Start with Readings: Paragraphs to Essays,* is the second book of the series. It continues the developmental writing sequence first by focusing on writing paragraphs that express thoughts about a topic by using the various modes of development, and then by expanding the topic by applying the techniques of the mode to the longer essay format. Grammar, sentence structure, and ESL concerns, while an integral part of writing, are embedded in the chapters in a less noticeable way in this text; instead, they are the primary focus of the *Writer's Resources* section at the end of the text.

Organization of the Text

We have organized the text in an effort to introduce the developing writer to the basic elements and skills necessary for writing effective essays in the academic environment. While these skills also will help students communicate more effectively in their personal and work correspondence, the primary focus is to ready developing writers for the rigors of their first college-level composition course (for credit) at the next level. Many developing writers are taking college courses requiring college-level writing skills while they are concurrently enrolled in developmental writing courses, and as a result they face problems doing the written work that is expected of them. Thus we have attempted to illustrate the processes and skills necessary for effective writing in as simple and straightforward a manner as possible, so students can immediately begin applying their new writing skills to their work in other courses.

Introduction: Chapters 1 and 2

Chapter 1 reinforces the idea that writing is important. The developing writer might at first resist this idea, but it is our belief, through years of experience, that the developing writer knows this to be true. This chapter stresses the idea that writing is difficult, but like other skills, can be developed with the proper attitude, information, and work ethic. It emphasizes the important link between reading and writing, the need for writing presentable papers without significant grammar, punctuation, and sentence structure errors, the mature writing and thinking that comes from writing about topics in a variety of modes, and the techniques for making the transition from paragraphs to essays.

Chapter 2 introduces the developing writer to the elements of reasoning that underpin the critical thinking processes for analyzing and evaluating reading and writing. At the end of each of the modes chapters, the developing writer is given a set of writing opportunities using critical thinking skills as the focus.

The Fundamentals: Chapters 3 through 6

Chapters 3 through 5 focus on the function of the introductory paragraph, the body paragraphs, and the concluding paragraph in an essay. Chapter 3, on the introductory paragraph, introduces the developing writer to lead-in techniques and the thesis sentence. Chapter 4 describes the body paragraphs, including the topic sentence and support sentences based on the six reporters' questions (who, what, where, when, why, how). Chapter 5 examines the concluding paragraph, focusing on several techniques to bring an essay to a successful end. Finally, Chapter 6 presents prewriting activities, such as listing, clustering, cubing, and cross examination. These chapters give an overview of the essay elements so the specific chapters dealing with the modes of development are understood in the context of the larger goal: writing the essay.

Some instructors will be more comfortable using Chapter 6 prewriting activities, before Chapters 3 through 5. Please feel free to do so. We like to explain the basic elements of the essay prior to students actually thinking, planning, and writing about specific topics. However, if you are more comfortable having your students explore topics prior to discussing the elements of the essay, *The Write Start* is flexible enough to allow you to do so.

Strategies for Developing Essays: Chapters 7 through 15

These nine chapters introduce the developing writer to the modes of development for examining topics. Each chapter begins by using the paragraph to explain the basic concepts and techniques of the mode; then the chapter shows students how to make the transition to the full essay. A list of transitional expressions is provided in each chapter to aid the developing writer in creating rhythm, connecting related ideas, and combining sentences. Student essays are used to model the concepts, techniques, and processes of each mode, as well as the thesis sentence with essay map approach. In addition, professional essays are provided in each chapter to give students exposure to writing that has a less structured format. Each chapter ends with a set of writing opportunities using specific critical thinking skills as the basis for the writing prompts, as well as a list of suggested topics for additional essays.

Special Writing Situations: Chapters 16 through 18

Because this textbook focuses on preparing the developing writer for the rigors of academic writing, specifically the first college composition course, these chapters focus on writing the research paper, the in-class essay examination, and the literary analysis essay.

Chapter 16 introduces the developing writer to the steps involved in writing a paper that requires research in primary and secondary sources and in documenting that research using the Modern Language Association format. The Chapter uses one student-written and one professionally written research paper to model the techniques and process for research writing.

Chapter 17 focuses on the key terms that developing writers should look for within the prompts they are given on examinations to help them organize an essay in just a few minutes. The thesis sentence with essay map is offered as a technique to quickly identify and organize subtopics into a clearly defined approach in response to the overall topic parameters. A number of prompts from various disciplines are illustrated with accompanying thesis sentences.

Chapter 18 examines the critical process involved in literary criticism. The elements of literary analysis (character, plot, setting, time, theme, and technique) are discussed as complements to the six reporter's questions (who, what, where, when, why, how), with which the developing writer is already familiar. Each of the elements of literary analysis is discussed in detail. Examples of the thesis sentence with and without the essay map are illustrated. The Chapter ends with two models of literary analysis essays: one for the poem "After Apple-Picking" by Robert Frost, and one for the novel *Sula* by Toni Morrison.

Additional Readings

The Additional Readings section contains two professional essays to accompany each of the modes covered in Chapters 7 through 15, in order to give students additional exposure to good writing. Each essay has its own apparatus, including vocabulary, writing technique questions, and writing opportunities.

The Writer's Resources

The Writer's Resources section is a veritable warehouse of information on parts of speech, usage, and spelling. Examples and exercises accompany the material for illustration, clarification, and additional practice. Material that is especially helpful to English as a second language (ESL) students is tagged by an ESL icon.

Limited Answer Key

At the end of *The Write Start*, an answer key contains half the answers to the in-chapter objective practices. Students can check their own work to see how their skills are developing. (A complete answer key is included in the Annotated Instructor's Edition.)

Special Features of *The Write Start*

The features embedded in *The Write Start with Readings: Paragraphs to Essays* have been carefully developed with the needs of developmental English students and instructors in mind.

- ■ **Clarity and Simplicity.** Concepts and techniques are simply described and illustrated, with key terms boldfaced and defined in each chapter as well as in the end-of-book glossary. The writing style is friendly, clear, and easy for students to understand. The topical presentation is logically sequenced and flows easily from chapter to chapter, yet all chapters are entirely modular, allowing instructors to determine their own order of presentation and structure their classes however they choose without having to worry about possible text usage problems. To support the clarity of the presentation, a simple, uncluttered, attractive design has been used.

- ■ **Smooth Flow of Concepts within Each Chapter.** In each chapter, concepts flow logically from the simple to the more complex. Students are presented with concepts in a fashion that allows them to understand a little at a time and build on what they have just learned.

■ **Examples.** One of the best ways for developmental students to learn is through example, and examples are used liberally to illustrate all the concepts presented. Examples are screened to make them pop out for clear emphasis and easier reference.

■ **Practices.** Numerous practices reinforce learning and help students apply what they've just read. The practices are narrowly focused on the content just covered, and they range from making lists, to writing sentences, to writing and rewriting paragraphs.

■ **Highly Structured Presentation of the Essay as a Form.** Writing a good essay is a complex undertaking. To help students develop their essay writing skills, *The Write Start* first presents a five-paragraph essay structure (introductory paragraph with thesis sentence and essay map, three body paragraphs, concluding paragraph) and then presents instruction on each essay mode (description, narration, etc.) using the five-paragraph essay as a structural model. Thus students can improve their organizational and writing skills within a highly structured form defined by the thesis sentence with essay map. All the model student essays use the essay map and are written in this five-paragraph form to reinforce the instruction.

A Word about the Thesis Sentence. Although this textbook uses the thesis sentence with essay map as the tool for organizing the essay, you are free to use whatever thesis sentence mechanism you feel comfortable with. Some writing teachers complain that the essay map forces the writer into a mechanical style. We believe this to be untrue. In writing this text, we have made two assumptions, one about the developing writer and one about writing. First, we believe that the developing writer, to be successful in academic work, needs structure. The essay map in the thesis sentence allows the developing writer to create a mini-outline of the essay, helping the writer to stay focused on the subtopic at hand and on the order in which the subtopics should be discussed. In fact, the feedback we have received from our students indicates that they rely on the thesis sentence in many of their other classes, particularly during in-class essay exams. Second, we believe that mechanical writing results from the failure to make good use of techniques that promote a fluid, rhythmical style. In each of the modes chapters we illustrate the transitional devices that help connect related ideas, foster rhythm in the paragraphs, and combine sentences to reduce choppiness and introduce variety, a hallmark of good writing. In fact, many professionals use the essay map as the organizing tool in their writing, yet one would hardly call the writing styles of professional writers Ernst Mayr and Barbara Ehrenreich—each of whom has used the essay map—stodgy, stolid, or mechanical.

■ **Focus on ESL.** The developmental writing market overlaps with the ESL market in that many ESL instructors need to use developmental texts and many developmental instructors have ESL students enrolled in their courses. One of us, Gayle Feng-Checkett, is a certified ESL instructor, and thus much of the text was written with ESL students in mind. This book uses ESL research and pedagogy to the benefit of all developmental English students.

■ **Critical Thinking Skills: The Connection between Reading and Writing.** Good writers are also good readers, and many of the skills used in reading are also used in writing. Chapter 2, on critical thinking, explains why critical thinking skills are important in today's information-overloaded society, provides students with an explanation of key critical thinking skills, and models the use of the skills on a reading. The skills covered in this introductory chapter are picked up in the later essay modes chapters. In each of these chapters, a critical thinking activity requires students to analyze the chapter's model essays using particular critical thinking skills and then to apply the same critical thinking skills to writing an essay.

■ **Model Essays.** Each of the essay modes chapters has two model essays. The first is a student essay written in the five-paragraph essay structure on which the instruction is built. The second is a professionally written essay that departs from the five-paragraph structure and gives students exposure to less structured, but excellent, writing. All essays have been chosen not only for their technical merit but because they are about high-interest topics.

■ **Writing Technique Questions.** Each model essay in the chapters (as well as in the Additional Readings) is followed by a series of questions that help students analyze the techniques used in the essay.

■ **Topics for Writing.** At the end of each of the essay modes chapters are suggested topics for essay writing. Students may choose a topic, or instructors may assign topics, as they prefer. In the Topics for Writing activity, at least one of the choices is a photo on which an essay can be based.

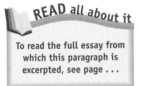

To read the full essay from which this paragraph is excerpted, see page . . .

■ **Read All About It.** Exercises in the Writer's Resources section are based on the readings that appear at the end of the text. An icon indicates the reading from which the exercise is excerpted so that students can refer to the complete essay for additional context.

The Teaching and Learning Package

Each component of the teaching and learning package has been crafted to ensure that the course is rewarding for instructors and students.

Annotated Instructor's Edition This book is a replica of the student text, but it includes answers printed directly on the fill-in lines provided in the text. 0-321-06119-5

Instructor's Manual with Transparency Masters. The Manual provides information on the following: *Using the Text, Syllabus Preparation, Answer Keys, Student and Professional Reading Selections, Thesis Sentences, Outlining, Proofreading Checklists, Peer Editing, English as a Second Language/English as a Foreign Language (ESL/EFL), Diagnostic Pre-Test, and Transparency Masters.* 0-321-06120-9

Test Bank These tests provide a wealth of printed quizzes and additional practice exercises for each Chapter in the text. The test bank is formatted in a way that simplifies copying and distribution. 0-321-06121-7

Electronic Test Bank for Writing The electronic test bank features more than 5,000 questions in all areas of writing, from grammar to paragraphing, through essay writing, research, and documentation. With this easy-to-use CD-ROM, instructors simply choose questions from the electronic test bank, then print the completed test for distribution. 0-321-08117-X. A printed version is also available.

[NEW] The Longman Writer's Warehouse. The innovative and exciting online supplement is the perfect accompaniment to any developmental writing course. Developed by developmental English instructors specially for developing writers, The Writer's Warehouse covers every part of the writing process. Also included are journaling capabilities, multimedia activities, diagnostic tests, an interactive handbook, and a complete instructor's manual. The Writer's Warehouse requires no space on your school's server; rather, students complete and store their work on the Longman server, and are able to access it, revise it, and continue working at any time. For more details about how to shrinkwrap a free subscription to The Writer's Warehouse with this text, please consult your Longman sales representative. For a free guided tour of the site, visit **http://longmanwriterswarehouse.com.**

The Longman Developmental English Package

In addition to the book-specific supplements discussed above, a series of other skills-based supplements is available for both instructors and students. All of these supplements are available either free or at greatly reduced prices.

For Additional Reading and Reference

The Dictionary Deal. Two dictionaries can be shrinkwrapped with *The Write Start* at a nominal fee. *The New American Webster Handy College Dictionary* is a paperback reference text with more than 100,000 entries. *Merriam Webster's Collegiate Dictionary*, tenth edition, is a hardback reference with a citation file of more than 14.5 million examples of English words drawn from actual use. For more information on how to shrinkwrap a dictionary with your text, please contact your Longman sales representative.

Penguin Quality Paperback Titles. A series of Penguin paperbacks is available at a significant discount when shrinkwrapped with this text. Some titles available are Toni Morrison's *Beloved*, Julia Alvarez's *How the Garcia Girls Lost Their Accents*, Mark Twain's *Huckleberry Finn, Narrative of the Life of Frederick Douglass*, Harriet Beecher Stowe's *Uncle Tom's Cabin*, Dr. Martin Luther King, Jr.'s *Why We Can't Wait*, and plays by Shakespeare, Miller, and Albee. For a complete list of titles or more information, please contact your Longman sales consultant.

100 Things to Write About. This 100-page book contains 100 individual assignments for writing on a variety of topics and in a wide range of formats, from expressive to analytical. Ask your Longman sales representative for a sample copy. 0-673-98239-4

Newsweek Alliance. Instructors may choose to shrinkwrap a 12-week subscription to *Newsweek* with any Longman text. The price of the subscription is 57 cents per issue (a total of $6.84 for the subscription). Available with the subscription is a free "Interactive Guide to *Newsweek*"—a workbook for students who are using the text. In addition, *Newsweek* provides a wide variety of instructor supplements free to teachers, including maps, Skills Builders, and weekly quizzes. For more information on the *Newsweek* program, please contact your Longman sales representative.

Electronic and Online Offerings

The Writer's ToolKit Plus. This CD-ROM offers a wealth of tutorial, exercise, and reference material for writers. It is compatible with either a PC or Macintosh platform, and is flexible enough to be used either occasionally for practice or regularly in class lab sessions. For information on how to bundle this CD-ROM FREE with your text, please contact your Longman sales representative.

The Longman English Pages Web Site. Both students and instructors can visit our free content-rich Web site for additional reading selections and writing exercises. From the Longman English pages, visitors can conduct a simulated Web search, learn how to write a resume and cover letter, or try their hand at poetry writing. Stop by and visit us at **http://www.ablongman.com/englishpages**.

The Longman Electronic Newsletter. Twice a month during the spring and fall, instructors who have subscribed receive a free copy of the Longman Developmental English Newsletter in their e-mailbox. Written by experienced classroom instructors, the newsletter offers teaching tips, classroom activities, book reviews, and more. To subscribe, visit the Longman Developmental English Website at **http://www.ablongman.com/basicskills**, or send an e-mail to **Basic Skills@ablongman.com**.

For Instructors

Competency Profile Test Bank, Second Edition. This series of 60 objective tests covers ten general areas of English competency, including fragments; comma splices and run-ons; pronouns; commas; and capitalization. Each test is available in remedial, standard, and advanced versions. Available as reproducible sheets or in computerized versions. Free to instructors. Paper version: 0-321-02224-6. Computerized IBM: 0-321-02633-0. Computerized Mac: 0-321-02632-2.

Diagnostic and Editing Tests, Third Edition. This collection of diagnostic tests helps instructors assess students' competence in Standard Written English for purpose of placement or to gauge progress. Available as reproducible sheets or in computerized versions, and free to instructors. Paper: 0-321-08382-2. CD-ROM: 0-321-08782-8.

ESL Worksheets, Third Edition. These reproducible worksheets provide ESL students with extra practice in areas they find the most troublesome. A diagnostic test and post-test are provided, along with answer keys and suggested topics for writing. Free to adopters. 0-321-07765-2

Longman Editing Exercises. Fifty-four pages of paragraph editing exercises give students extra practice using grammar skills in the context of longer passages. Free when packaged with any Longman title. 0-205-31792-8

80 Practices. A collection of reproducible, ten-item exercises that provide additional practices for specific grammatical usage problems, such as comma splices, capitalization, and pronouns. Includes an answer key, and free to adopters. 0-673-53422-7

CLAST Test Package, Fourth Edition. These two 40-item objective tests evaluate students' readiness for the CLAST exams. Strategies for teaching CLAST preparedness are included. Free with any Longman English title. Reproducible sheets: 0-321-01950-4 Computerized IBM version: 0-321-01982-2 Computerized Mac version: 0-321-01983-0

TASP Test Package, Third Edition. These 12 practice pre-tests and post-tests assess the same reading and writing skills covered in the TASP examination. Free with any Longman English title. Reproducible sheets: 0-321-01959-8 Computerized IBM version: 0-321-01985-7 Computerized Mac version: 0-321-01984-9

Teaching Online: Internet Research Conversation and Composition, Second Edition. Ideal for instructors who have never surfed the Net, this easy-to-follow guide offers basic definitions, numerous examples, and step-by-step information about finding and using Internet sources. Free to adopters. 0-321-01957-1

Teaching Writing to the Non-Native Speaker.   This booklet examines the issues that arise when non-native speakers enter the developmental classroom. Free to instructors, it includes profiles of international and permanent ESL students, factors influencing second-language acquisition, and tips on managing a multicultural classroom. 0-673-97452-9

For Students

[NEW] The Longman Writer's Journal.   This journal for writers, free with *The Write Start*, offers students a place to think, write, and react. For an examination copy, contact your Longman sales consultant. 0-321-08639-2

[NEW] The Longman Researcher's Journal.   This journal for writers and researchers, free with this text, helps students plan, schedule, write, and revise their research project. An all-in-one resource for first-time researchers, the journal guides students gently through the research process. 0-321-09530-8.

Researching Online, Fifth Edition.   A perfect companion for a new age, this indispensable new supplement helps students navigate the Internet. Adapted from *Teaching Online*, the instructor's Internet guide, *Researching Online* speaks directly to students, giving them detailed, step-by-step instructions for performing electronic searches. Available free when shrinkwrapped with this text. 0-321-09277-5

Learning Together: An Introduction to Collaborative Theory.   This brief guide to the fundamentals of collaborative learning teaches students how to work effectively in groups, how to revise with peer response, and how to co-author a paper or report. Shrinkwrapped free with any Longman Basic Skills text. 0-673-46848-8

A Guide for Peer Response, Second Edition.   This guide offers students forms for peer critiques, including general guidelines and specific forms for different stages in the writing process. Also appropriate for freshman-level course. Free to adopters. 0-321-01948-2

Thinking Through the Test, by D.J. Henry.   This special workbook, prepared specially for students in Florida, offers ample skill and practice exercises to help student prep for the Florida State Exit Exam. To shrinkwrap this workbook free with your textbook, please contact your Longman sales representative. Available in two versions: with and without answers. Also available: Two laminated grids (one for reading, one for writing) that can serve as handy references for students preparing for the Florida State Exit Exam.

Acknowledgments

Thanks to everyone at Longman for their steadfast effort in bringing *The Write Start: Paragraphs to Essays* to life.

Special thanks to Senior Editor Steven Rigolosi, who has shepherded the overall development of the *Write Start* series. His guidance, patience, understanding, and vision often sustained us in those times when deadlines and workload seemed overwhelming and goals too far down the road to seem attainable. His confident and enthusiastic nature is contagious and a welcome fuel for tired and overstressed engines. He has our undying admiration.

To our development editor, Marion Castellucci, we humbly offer our praise and thanks. Her title is simply insufficient to describe the contributions she made to this text. Marion not only added fresh approaches to age-old concepts, but her creativity put our initial ideas into a simple, clear, and comprehensible context. Having Marion as an editor was like having a third author. She has our unbounded gratitude.

To the staff at Longman...Kudos! Many thanks to Editorial Assistant Meegan Thompson, who sought the answers to all of our questions, even if the answers seemed obvious. A note of thanks to our Supplements Editor, Donna Campion, who kept her eye on a thousand details that make the text a whole, not just a series of unfinished and unrelated parts. And special thanks to Marketing Manager Melanie Craig, who masterminded the "marketing box" campaign (ask your sales representative for one if you haven't already received one!).

As always, thanks to our students, who contributed paragraphs and essays to the text and whose special needs and superlative successes have kept us on our toes and given us immeasurable rewards.

We also owe many thanks to our colleagues and other devoted English instructors around the country who reviewed the text in all stages of its development. Thank you to all of the following for your corrections, advice, and spirited encouragement:

Betty Bastankhah, San Jacinto College
Mary Anne Bernal, San Antonio College
Marianne Dzik, Illinois Valley Community College
Gene Fant, Mississippi College
Carlotta Hill, Oklahoma City Community College
Patsy A. Krech, University of Memphis
Irma Luna, San Antonio College
Margaret Murray, Western Connecticut State University
Raymond E. Mort, Oakland Community College
Andrew Nesset, Century College
Scottie Priesmeyer, St. Charles Community College
Linda C. Rollins, Motlow State Community College
John N. Thornburg, San Jacinto College Central
Peter Van Leunen, St. Charles Community College
Suzanne Weisar, San Jacinto College South

Lawrence Checkett
Gayle Feng-Checkett
St. Charles, MO

CHAPTER 1

To the Student

As a college student, you face multiple demands each day, and writing is an integral part of most of these challenges. This book has been written to help you, the developing college writer, in reaching your immediate and long-term goals. You have made the decision to go to college in an attempt to learn the skills that will help you succeed in your learning, as well as help you secure a rewarding career. Whether or not you already know what career path is the one for you, you will find that writing will play a large part in successfully completing your college work and in reaching your future work-related goals.

How This Book Can Help You Reach Your Goals

Good writing is hard, but good writing is achievable. People are not born good writers. With hard work, the right techniques, and helpful advice, you can master the skill of writing. This book will give you the tools, the strategies, and the advice that have been used successfully for years with students like you in classes just like yours.

This book will help you achieve your writing goals in the following ways.

■ **By emphasizing the important link between reading and writing.** The student and professional essays in this book are used to model the writing techniques demonstrated in the instructional chapters. By understanding how these techniques are used in the readings, you will improve your own writing skills.

■ **By helping you read and write with more depth and understanding through the use of critical thinking skills.** In Chapter 2, you will be introduced to the elements of reasoning, the underlying elements of critical thinking. The elements of reasoning will help you analyze and evaluate the information coming to you and the information you are communicating to others. At the end of each chapter, you will find a number of writing opportunities based on critical thinking skill elements.

■ **By helping you present your thoughts more professionally by eliminating errors in grammar, punctuation, and sentence structure.** Constructing logical and reasonable content is only half of the writing process. The other half has to do with proper presentation. For instance, you might have the most talented mind in the world, but if you show up

at a job interview wearing torn jeans, a shirt with food stains all over it, unwashed and uncombed hair, and a cigarette hanging out of the side of your mouth, you are not likely to get the job. You may have the right content, but your presentation is wrong. So it is with writing. If you have too many errors in punctuation or mechanics, your writing will not be successful, no matter how good the content is. The Writer's Resource at the end of the book is a complete guide to correct grammar, punctuation, and usage. It also contains information and helpful techniques for students whose first language is not English.

■ **By introducing you to a variety of methods you can use to develop your ideas about specific topics.** Not every topic can best be developed using the same approach. One piece of information might be best presented by using definition, while another might be clarified using example, and another might be best explained by comparing or contrasting it to something else. In this book, you will be introduced to the traditional methods used for developing topics.

■ **By teaching you a few techniques to develop a topic once it has been chosen.** In Chapter 6, you will be introduced to prewriting activities, such as clustering and cubing. These techniques can help you develop subtopics by which you can develop your ideas concerning the main topic. For instance, you may want to talk about investing (the main topic), but investing takes in a lot of possible areas (the subtopics): investing for immediate income as opposed to investing for retirement, investing in stocks versus investing in bonds, or whether or not to do your own investing or let a brokerage firm do it for you. Prewriting activities will help you map out a variety of subtopics so that you can focus on those you think will best develop the main topic.

■ **By showing you how to make the transition from writing the paragraph to writing the longer essay.** In Chapters 7 through 15, you will be introduced to different methods of developing a topic. At the start of each chapter, the method will be explained using the paragraph as the instructional model. The paragraph is used because it is short but still enables us to illustrate the key concepts of the method under discussion. Once the basic elements and techniques are demonstrated, the transition to a longer unit of writing, the essay, follows.

Writing Can Be Learned

People in academia and the business world view writing skills as essential, yet they have a growing concern about the writing abilities of the graduates they hire and work with. Teachers and executives have the same need for excellent communication skills on the part of their students and employees to foster increased productivity and enhanced performance. Whether it is a term paper or a business report you are asked to complete, good writing skills are a necessity. This book will help you establish and maintain the skills necessary for good writing. Once again, writing is a skill that can be learned with practice and dedication. In this way, good writing is no different from any other skill you want to learn and improve upon. There is an old joke that captures the essence of this undertaking:

A person carrying a violin case and walking along a street in New York City stops another person walking by and asks, "Excuse me, but how do I get to Carnegie Hall?" The second person answers sternly: "Practice, practice, practice."

Visit *The Write Start* Online!

For additional practice with the materials found in this chapter, visit our Website at

http://www.ablongman.com/checkett

The Website also features additional readings, quizzes, writing activities, and Internet links, as well as a bulletin board and interactive chat.

CHAPTER 2

Critical Thinking: The Connection between Reading and Writing

Not a day goes by without some individual, group, or organization wanting you to make a decision on their behalf. They ask for your time, your money, or both: "Vote for me." "Donate to my cause." "Become a member of our group." "Switch to our credit card." "Trade in that heap for one of our new vehicles." "Our insurance package will give you more coverage for less money." "Your teeth will be 37.5 percent brighter if you switch to our toothpaste."

It never seems to stop, does it? Each day, you are assaulted with information of every kind from every possible avenue of communication:

- political ads
- public service announcements
- advertisements on television and radio
- printed ads in newspapers, magazines, and mailings
- billboards
- ad banners and ad boxes on the Internet
- ads on movie screens
- charitable fund drives at the workplace

How are you to handle all this information? The silly stuff you can toss in the trash can, and the serious topics you can blindly accept or simply ignore. Of course, this allows whoever is putting out the information to be in control, and this may affect your life in many ways whether you like it or not. As a citizen living in a democracy, you are called on to make many decisions—sometimes frivolous, often serious. So it's important to be able to assess the information upon which you base your decisions.

Critical Thinking

Critical thinkers use their reasoning processes to question, judge, and evaluate the information that they hear, read, observe, discuss, and write about. They know that they need to understand information beyond the surface level so that hidden messages or agendas can be discovered and dealt with appropriately.

You need the ability to confront information, no matter what the format, and deal with it efficiently and intelligently. As a reasoning, thoughtful person, you need to be engaged in serious issues: international, national, regional, and local. These issues affect you and your family in your home, socially, in the workplace, and at school.

You need to learn how to listen, read, observe, evaluate, and communicate critically. Critical thinking encourages you to *analyze* (take apart), *synthesize* (put together), *evaluate* (come to conclusions), and *communicate* (via memos, letters, reports, papers, etc.) about the information you have studied. Critical thinking is a skill. People are not born intuitive, discerning, critical thinkers. Learning to think critically is a product of intellectual curiosity. It is a lifelong journey into the relationship that exists between you, the world around you, and your response to it.

The Elements of Reasoning

You often will be asked to write about information you have studied. In the academic world, this is the most common form of communication you will

A Critical Thinker Considers the Elements of Reasoning

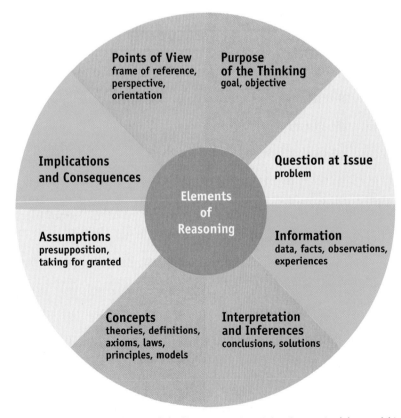

Points of View
frame of reference, perspective, orientation

Purpose of the Thinking
goal, objective

Implications and Consequences

Question at Issue
problem

Elements of Reasoning

Assumptions
presupposition, taking for granted

Information
data, facts, observations, experiences

Concepts
theories, definitions, axioms, laws, principles, models

Interpretation and Inferences
conclusions, solutions

Note: Dr. Richard Paul of the Center for Critical Thinking, Sonoma State University, permitted the use of this material.

have with your instructors. However, before you can write about what you have learned and the conclusions you have come to, you first must read and think critically. The *elements of reasoning* shown in the figure below will help you develop this skill. The elements of reasoning encompass eight questions that can be asked about the information you are assessing.

1. **Frame of reference.** What is the perspective of the writer?

2. **Purpose.** What is the writer's aim in writing the piece?

3. **Question at issue.** What question is being asked, or what problem is being solved?

4. **Information.** What facts, statistics, and personal experiences does the writer present to support his or her point of view?

5. **Interpretation and inferences.** How does the writer interpret the information, and are his or her inferences correct?

6. **Concepts.** What ideas and concepts are presented?

7. **Assumptions.** What does the writer take for granted is true?

8. **Implications and consequences.** What are the implications of what the writer says? What consequences follow from the facts and reasoning he or she presents?

Applying the Elements of Reasoning

As a student, you are often asked to argue for or against some topic. To argue effectively against someone else's ideas, however, you should first learn the specifics of the other side of the argument prior to developing your response.

Let's say your political science instructor hands out copies of an opinion piece, "Timing Now Right for Star Wars Missile Defense," written by syndicated columnist William Safire. Your assignment could be to read the article for a class discussion, a short essay quiz, or a team debate. Safire's opinion piece appeared in the *St. Louis Post-Dispatch* in 1998, and it was written a decade after former President Ronald Reagan (1981–1989) first brought up the need for a defensive shield against incoming nuclear missiles. Safire, by the way, was a speechwriter for President Reagan.

The proposed anti-ballistic missile (ABM) system was dubbed "Star Wars" by the press. Congress never passed legislation that would have brought the system into existence, and the issue hasn't been a serious consideration since the 1980s. However, when George W. Bush became president in the year 2001, he spoke out for the need for an anti-ballistic missile shield. He has had his Republican supporters in Congress pushing for funding to study the viability of an ABM system, much like the one President Reagan called for and Safire supported in his opinion piece.

First, read the Safire article below. Then, read the analysis that follows. In the analysis, each of the elements of reasoning is applied to the article. The paragraphs of the article are numbered for instructional purposes only.

Sample Article: TIMING NOW RIGHT FOR STAR WARS MISSILE DEFENSE

William Safire

St. Louis Post-Dispatch, Editorial Section, June 14, 1998

Timing Now Right for Star Wars Missile Defense

1   For years, when hawkish Republicans uttered the phrase "missile defense," dovish Democrats would respond with a derisive Bronx cheer: "Star Wars! Pie in the sky! Cost too much and would never work!"

2   Partisan positions froze and the debate was paralyzed. Tens of billions were spent on research just to keep our hand in but with no hope of actually defending the nation against incoming nuclear missiles.

3   Democrats asked, with some reason: How could we build a foolproof shield in the sky against 10,000 Soviet missiles? Wasn't it wiser to rely on the threat of mutual suicide that served us so well in the Cold War?

4   But circumstances changed. The threat is no longer an overwhelming rain of missiles from Russia, but only a dozen or 20 from rogue states or terrorist groups. That's more manageable.

5   Opponents of missile defense then tried a different argument: A shield in the sky would not stop a terrorist from sneaking a bomb into the United States in a suitcase.

6   True enough, and methods of detecting smuggled nuclear and germ weapons need refinement. But nations like China, Iran, Iraq, North Korea, India and Pakistan have not been investing heavily in suitcases. For some reason, they have been spending national treasure on long-range missiles, swapping know-how, importing hungry Russian scientists, buying or stealing American missile-guidance technology.

7   From this we may deduce that the preferred method of delivery is a missile, and that a monomaniacal dictator or a terrorist with little to lose would not be deterred, as soviet leaders were, by the assurance of massive retaliation.

8   As the nuclear club expands and as missiles become cheaper and rangier, the threat increases of an accidental launch—or of an unintended missile headed our way during a nuclear war among others.

9   What could we do about it? Now, nothing. Most Americans do not realize that our armed forces have no way of stopping the most likely weapon to be used against us. We spend a quarter-trillion dollars a year for defense and it buys the population of U.S. cities zero defense against missiles.

10   Why do we allow this terrible anomaly to exist? Some die-hard doves insist that our debatable 1972 ABM treaty with the defunct Soviet Union locks us in forever to "mutual assured destruction" (MAD)—even as Boris Yeltsin prepares to run for a third term on the theory that Russia is not the Soviet Union. President Bill Clinton, mired in decade-old rhetoric, still professes to see that treaty as the "cornerstone of strategic stability."

11   Sen. Carl Levin of Michigan argues, incredibly, that no defense is needed because the CIA would give us three years' warning of any threat. Those are

the same spooks who assured us in 1990 that Saddam Hussein was 10 years away from a nuclear device (postwar inspection showed it had been less than one year), and the same who were caught flatfooted by India's blasts.

12   But we are beginning to see evidence of a paradigm shift in the thinking of both sides about the threat of "incoming." Last week, as Levin led a filibuster against missile defense, only a bare minimum of 40 Democrats enabled him to block the will of a growing Senate bipartisan majority.

13   Even within the Clinton Defense Department, support is growing for deploying the Navy's Aegis fleet air defense system, a step toward serious missile defense. Secretary Bill Cohen's choice for chief technical adviser, the former NASA hand Hans Mark, was welcomed by Senate Armed Services as the harbinger of a new administration attitude toward countering missile dangers.

14   The center of gravity in the old "Star Wars" debate has moved. Ronald Reagan turns out not to have been deranged on defense—only ahead of his time. For those concerned about our new vulnerability the trick is not to adopt a nyah-nyah, told-you-so posture, but to give proponents of the old strategy a graceful exit citing changed circumstances.

15   "There is absolutely no question the nation will have missile defense in the future," Dr. Jaques Gansler, a top Clinton Defense official, has said. "The question is when. The threat is here. The money is there. The answer is now."

This article contains a lot of information presented in a variety of ways. Reading it without a strategy for analyzing it means you will miss a lot of what the author has to say. However, using the elements of reasoning can help you discover the topic of the article, the author's focus, the evidence used by the author to support his ideas, and any strengths or weaknesses in the author's argument.

Now, read the analysis based on the eight elements of reasoning. The number in the parentheses following each answer indicates the paragraph in the article where the information is found. More than one number in parentheses indicates that there is relevant information in more than one paragraph.

Using the elements of reasoning allows you to find specific quotations for in-class discussions, open-book exams, and for supporting your answers during debates.

Sample Analysis
1. Frame of Reference

Communication is written from someone's or some group's perspective: political, social, religious, ethnic, gender, etc. Identify the author's frame of reference.

> William Safire's frame of reference is from the position of the Republican Party. He is a strong political conservative. He was a speechwriter for President Ronald Reagan, and he usually supports right-wing positions. (We went online to find out some background about Safire.)

2. Purpose

Communication has purpose (a goal or objective). Identify the purpose clearly.

> Safire's purpose in writing the opinion piece is to support creation of a missile defense system. (7, 9, 14, 15)

3. Question at Issue

Communication is an attempt by a person or group to answer some question or to figure out the solution to some problem. Identify the question at issue.

> The question at issue is "Should the United States have a missile defense system?" (3, 4, 7, 9)

4. Information

Communication often contains data, facts, and personal experience as evidence to support a position. Identify these types of information.

> Safire uses many types of information to educate and persuade the reader. He makes observations about changing circumstance to argue against the opposition and for his own position (4, 6, 12, 13). He refers to a 1972 ABM treaty to argue against the opposition (10). He uses Senator Carl Levin as an opponent, and he argues against a statement that Levin made (11). He uses a quotation from Dr. Jacques Gansler, a Clinton Defense official, to support his argument (15).

5. Interpretation and Inferences

Most communication contains inferences or interpretations from which the author draws conclusions (an inference is a conclusion drawn from evidence not totally defined or stated). Make certain the author is inferring only what the evidence implies (imply means to suggest or convey a conclusion without stating it outright).

> Safire makes the interpretation that the "preferred method of delivery is a missile" (7). He also makes an inference that a missile pointed at the United States might be accidentally launched because of increasingly complex technology (8). He infers that the Star Wars plan should be implemented, and that the time is now (14, 15).

6. Concepts

Many communications are expressed through, and shaped by, concepts and ideas (special theories, definitions, laws, etc.). Identify key concepts.

> A concept that Safire uses is that of the *rogue enemy* launching a missile. He states that "a monomaniacal dictator or a terrorist with little to lose would not be deterred, as Soviet leaders were, by the assurance of massive retaliation" (7). He also mentions the concept of a Star Wars missile defense system, yet he mentions the term just briefly and never offers a definition as to what the system involves in either technology or cost (14). Using the term Star Wars to define the concept may be an easier way to involve the reader than by using highly technical terminology.

7. Assumptions

Communication often is based on assumptions (an assumption is a statement or conclusion accepted as true without proof). Clearly identify the assumptions that an author makes.

> Safire makes the assumption that the reader knows what the Star Wars plan includes because he says nothing about how it would operate (14). He also assumes that most dictators and terrorists will not be deterred by the assurance of a massive retaliation (7).

8. Implications and Consequences

When a communication draws conclusions, it often leads to implications and consequences. Point out any implications and consequences that follow from the reasoning. Search for negative as well as positive implications and consequences.

> The positive implication that Safire states is that the Star Wars missile defense system will save the United States from being attacked by missiles (2, 15), but nowhere in the article does he state any negative consequences. If a missile defense system is implemented, as Safire hopes, nothing is mentioned about the cost of implementing the plan, or testing that would have to be done, or even the long-term threats of nuclear waste storage.

After you learn to use the elements of reasoning as just modeled, you will be more confident when you analyze a piece of information. The elements of reasoning will help you become a more accomplished, organized thinker before you communicate your thoughts, especially when you are called upon to write in or out of class, on the job, or in many social situations.

Critical Thinking Writing Opportunities

At the end of Chapters 7 through 15, you will find a set of writing opportunities based on the critical thinking elements of reasoning you have studied in this chapter: frame of reference, purpose, question at issue, information, interpretation and inferences, concepts, assumptions, and implications and consequences.

By writing a short essay focusing on a particular element of reasoning, your reading comprehension will increase, and your communications will become clearer and more meaningful.

Chapter Review

■ *To cope with an information overload, critical thinking skills are needed.* Critical thinking involves analyzing (taking apart), synthesizing (putting together), evaluating (coming to conclusions), and communicating (via memos, letters, reports, papers, etc.) about information.

■ *Critical thinkers use the elements of reasoning as the process by which they understand information.* The elements of reasoning include frame of reference, purpose, question at issue, information, interpretation and inferences, concepts, assumptions, and implications and consequences.

■ *When analyzing information, you can ask key questions related to the elements of reasoning.* These will help you assess the information in an organized, thoughtful manner.

■ *Critical thinkers use the elements of reasoning to assess all information.* Whether communicating information to others or responding to the communications of others, the critical thinker should always be aware of the elements of reasoning. They determine the reasonableness, fairness, and intellectual standards necessary for thoughtful discussion.

Visit *The Write Start* Online!

For additional practice with the materials found in this chapter, visit our Website at

http://www.ablongman.com/checkett

The Website also features additional readings, quizzes, writing activities, and Internet links, as well as a bulletin board and interactive chat.

PART 1

Getting Started:
The Fundamentals

While sentences are good for expressing short pieces of information, a longer format is necessary for longer, more developed ideas. The following three chapters will enable you to discover, understand, and write the basic paragraphs that make up an even longer format called the essay. Writing paragraphs is good practice, because paragraphs contain many of the elements you will find in longer pieces of writing, such as letters, reports, essays, and research papers.

The Paragraph

A paragraph consists of a number of sentences that develop a single idea called a **topic.** In fact, you are reading a paragraph right now, and its topic is "the paragraph." Four to eight sentences is the length of most paragraphs, although they can be as short or as long as the topic or assignment demands. A good paragraph is long enough to develop the topic adequately but no longer.

On the page, a paragraph looks like this:

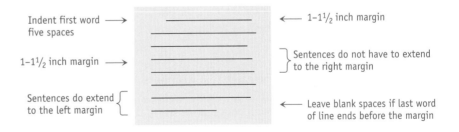

- The first sentence of a paragraph should be indented five spaces.
- Each line of the paragraph should begin at the left margin, but each line does not have to end exactly at the right margin. Your computer will automatically adjust end of line spacing for you.
- If the last word of a line comes before the right margin, leave the remainder of the line blank.

Types of Sentences

There are two basic types of sentences in a paragraph: the **topic sentence** and **support sentences.** The topic sentence tells the reader what the main idea, or topic, of the paragraph is. Although there is no set place in the paragraph for the topic sentence, making the topic sentence the first sentence in the paragraph will help you organize and develop the topic. The topic sentence is followed by support sentences that explain, clarify, and define the topic by using specific detail. Support sentences should demonstrate a variety of styles to show the relationship between the various pieces of information and to create rhythm.

To summarize the characteristics and elements of a paragraph:

- A topic sentence announces one main idea (the topic).
- Support sentences use specific detail to develop the topic.
- Sentence variety connects related ideas and adds rhythm.

Let's look at an example paragraph that exhibits the characteristics and elements you have been reading about.

Example Paragraph

Edward Kennedy "Duke" Ellington was an American composer, pianist, and conductor greatly admired for bringing jazz from nightclubs into mainstream concert halls. "Sophisticated Lady" and "Mood Indigo" were two of his most famous shorter jazz pieces, but his larger compositions, such as *Paris Blues* and *Far East Suite*, were styled after the classical concerto form, modified for his jazz stylizations. This creativity led to appearances on radio and television, in theaters and nightclubs, and on worldwide tours. Even though Duke Ellington was so prolific, his music won critical acclaim worldwide.

- The first sentence is the topic sentence, and it announces the topic (Duke Ellington) and the **controlling idea or attitude** toward the topic (Ellington was greatly admired for his ability to make jazz appreciated by the mainstream public).
- The following three support sentences develop the topic and controlling idea by naming his most famous compositions (sentence 2), by explaining that critics and the public enjoyed his music (sentences 3 and 4), and giving the vast numbers of venues in which he played his music (sentence 3).
- The sentences also exhibit variety. The second sentence is coordinated with the conjunction "but"; it also contains extra information between two commas. The third sentence is a simple sentence. The fourth sentence is subordinated by using an introductory dependent clause preceding the independent clause.

The Essay

Effective paragraph writing is useful for short pieces of communication, such as memos, short-answer exams, and brief writing assignments, but many business reports and longer college writing assignments require multiple paragraphs to explain many ideas.

Just as sentences are joined together to make paragraphs, paragraphs are used to make longer pieces of writing, including the **essay.** An essay is a number of paragraphs that develop a particular topic. Essays can be developed using many of the techniques for developing the paragraph.

Although an essay can have any number of paragraphs, this book will demonstrate the five-paragraph model to introduce the basic elements of the essay.

The Essay Title

Almost all essays should have a title. The title should pique the reader's interest. It should be a catchy or dramatic phrase, usually two to six words; longer titles can become wordy and cumbersome to read. If you cannot come up with something clever or dramatic, pick several key words from your thesis sentence and use them. It's a good idea to wait until your essay is finished before you create a title. In that way, you give yourself enough time to fully understand the point of your essay and create the most appropriate title for it.

When writing your title, do the following:

- Capitalize all words except articles (a, an, the) and prepositions (of, on, to, in) unless the article or preposition is the first word of the title. First words of titles are always capitalized.

- Center the title on the page and leave two line spaces between it and the introductory paragraph.

Essay Elements

Most essays begin with the **introductory paragraph.** Its purpose is to introduce the reader to the topic of the essay. The paragraph consists of **introductory sentences** and the **thesis sentence.**

After the introductory paragraph come the **body paragraphs.** Their purpose is to develop, support, and explain the topic idea stated in the thesis sentence. Body paragraphs consist of a **topic sentence** followed by **support sentences.**

The essay ends with the **concluding paragraph.** Its purpose is to bring the essay to a conclusion that gives the reader a sense of completeness.

These essay elements will be discussed in detail in the next three chapters. Chapter 3 examines the introductory paragraph, Chapter 4 discusses body paragraphs, and Chapter 5 discusses the concluding paragraph.

In Chapter 6 we'll look at prewriting technique strategies for getting started.

The Introductory Paragraph

The introductory paragraph introduces the reader to the essay's topic. It provides your first chance as a writer to engage your audience and set up the purpose of your essay. An introductory paragraph consists of a **thesis sentence** and a series of **introductory sentences.**

The Thesis Sentence

The thesis sentence is the most important element in any essay because it sets the tone for the entire essay. It also provides a roadmap for the entire essay. It states what you are going to clarify, explain, or argue for or against about the topic. Although there is no rule about where to place the thesis sentence in the introductory paragraph, it usually appears at the end. The thesis sentence:

- announces the overall topic
- has only one topic, never more
- states the importance of the topic (the controlling idea or the writer's attitude about the topic)
- limits the scope of the essay
- expresses the topic as an opinion that can be discussed
- does not express the topic as a fact
- does not express the topic as a question
- can outline the organizational structure of the essay

The Controlling Idea or Attitude in the Thesis Sentence

The **controlling idea or attitude** states what your focus is concerning the topic and how you feel about it. The verb usually starts to express your attitude about the topic. For this reason, the verb is sometimes called an **attitude word**. For example, the verbs *are/are not, is/is not, should/should not,* and *can/cannot* begin to tell the reader how you feel about the topic.

For instance, you might believe that reading to young children every day will make them more informed on a variety of subjects, thus making them better students. The thesis sentence might read: *Young children should become better students if their parents read to them every day.* The verb "should become" begins to express your attitude about the topic, and the words following the verb, "better students if their parents read to them every day," complete the controlling idea that will be used to develop the topic throughout the essay.

As a writer, your controlling idea or attitude not only expresses why the subject is important to you but why it should be important to the reader.

Examples

In each of the following sentences, the controlling idea or attitude is italicized. The attitude words are circled.

Lunch (is) *an important meal during the day.*

Psycho (is) *a scary movie because of the shower scene.*

Chevrolet (makes) *better trucks than Ford.*

Tanning beds (do) *less damage to your skin than the sun.*

Tanning beds (do) *as much damage to your skin as the sun.*

Providing readers with a thesis sentence containing a clearly defined controlling idea or attitude will help them understand your focus before they begin reading the body of the essay.

PRACTICE 1

In each of the following sentences, underline the attitude word or phrase once and the controlling idea twice.

Examples: The Rolls-Royce is considered by many as the finest car in the world.

The Lemonaire is not considered by anyone as the finest car in the world.

1. Reading a newspaper each day is important because it keeps you informed about current events.

2. Regular tune-ups can keep a car running efficiently for years.

3. Working while going to school should teach young people responsibility.

4. Laptop computers can make the workplace anywhere a worker happens to be sitting.

5. The Beatles remain popular, even after their breakup decades ago, because of their versatile musical style.

The Three-Item Essay Map

In this book, for ease and clarity of instruction, you will learn to write the five-paragraph model essay. All the student essays shown in the text are five-paragraph essays, although the professional essays vary in length. Each five-paragraph model contains an introductory paragraph, three body or development paragraphs, and a concluding paragraph.

Although this book uses the five-paragraph essay as a model, for the most part you will be writing longer essays in your course work as you continue your college life. There are as many methods of writing essays as there are different assignments. However, if you learn to write the five-paragraph essay, you will be able to expand this essay type into the longer, more complex formats.

One easy way to make sure that your essay is well organized is to include a **three-item essay map** in your thesis sentence. The three-item essay map lists the three topics that will support your thesis. Each of the three essay map items will become the topic for one of the three development paragraphs. The thesis sentence with essay map automatically organizes your essay and limits its scope.

In the following sentences, each element of the three-item essay map is identified by color. Notice that the essay map can be placed at the beginning, middle, or end of the thesis sentence.

Examples

1. To prevent fires in the home, people should *hide matches from children, never smoke in bed,* and *keep a fire extinguisher in the kitchen.*
2. *Practice, conditioning,* and a *proper diet* help athletes perform at a high level.
3. Communist countries worldwide, because of *insufficient international trade strategies, poor farming methods,* and *excessive military budgets,* have not been very successful.

PRACTICE 2

Underline the three-item essay map in each of the following sentences.

1. Airlines, trucking companies, and railroads are regulated by the federal government because they transport people and goods over state lines, safety regulations must be standardized, and the national economy depends on their remaining in business.

2. Getting older, talented newcomers, and constant travel make maintaining a sports career a difficult lifestyle.

3. Savings bonds, because of liquidity, safety, and interest, are a better investment vehicle than annuities.

4. A successful career often hinges upon hard work, dedication, and intelligence.

5. New York is an exciting city to visit because of its many points of historical interest, entertainment venues, and restaurants.

Checking Your Thesis Sentence

Your thesis sentence must be constructed properly. Without a good thesis sentence, the essay cannot succeed. To check your thesis sentence, ask yourself these questions:

■ Does the sentence introduce a single topic?

■ Is my attitude toward the topic clearly stated?

■ Have I included three supporting items in an essay map?

If the answer to any of these questions is "no," you need to rewrite your thesis sentence.

Examples

Poor	Voting and military service are important activities for all citizens. *(two topics with a clear attitude but no essay map)*
Better	Voting is an important responsibility for all citizens. *(one topic and clear attitude but no essay map)*
Good	Voting is an important responsibility for all citizens because it gives people a voice in how the government is run, removes ineffective politicians from office, and influences political decision making. *(one topic, clear attitude, three-item essay map that supports the attitude about the subject)*
Poor	Many students work while going to school. *(statement of fact, no attitude, no essay map)*
Better	Working while going to school can teach students valuable lessons. *(one topic, clear attitude, but no essay map)*
Good	Working while going to school can teach students responsibility, organizational skills, and teamwork. *(one topic, clear attitude, three-item essay map that supports the attitude about the subject)*
Poor	Are regular automobile oil changes really necessary? *(the sentence is in the form of a question, not a clearly stated opinion, no attitude, no essay map)*
Better	Regular oil changes can keep a car running better. *(one topic, a clearly stated opinion, but no essay map)*
Good	Regular oil changes can keep a car running more efficiently, improve gas mileage, and reduce long-term maintenance costs. *(one topic, clear attitude, three-item essay map that supports the attitude about the topic)*

The essay map in the thesis sentence is an easy and effective way to quickly organize thoughts about a topic developed in your essay.

PRACTICE 3

In each of the following thesis sentences, underline the topic once, the controlling idea or attitude twice, and the essay map three times. On the line provided, indicate if any element is missing.

1. Fruits are a good source for vitamin C.

The essay map is missing.

2. Fast serves, pinpoint lobs, and slice volleys make tennis an exciting sport to watch.

All the elements are present.

3. Many students make college a worthwhile experience by joining fraternities and sororities, playing intramural sports, and participating in student government.

All the elements are present.

4. Lightweight sleeping bags are good for camping trips.

The essay map is missing.

5. Styling, construction, and value make the Breitling a popular wristwatch for collectors.

All the elements are present.

6. Electric cars should be an industry priority because of skyrocketing fuel costs, environmental pollution, and diminishing fuel reserves.

All the elements are present.

7. Skydiving and bungee jumping are dangerous activities.

The essay map is missing.

8. The St. Louis Cardinals are a professional baseball team.

The controlling idea/attitude and essay map are missing.

9. *Star Trek* has been a long-running television series because of special effects, interesting characters, and fascinating stories.

All the elements are present.

10. Cruises are a popular form of vacationing because of good food, entertainment, and stops in exotic places.

All the elements are present.

PRACTICE 4

Answers will vary.

Rewrite the following thesis sentences if the essay map items do not explain, clarify, or support the controlling idea or attitude about the topic. If the essay map does explain, clarify, or support the controlling idea or attitude about the topic, write "Correct" in the space provided.

> **Example**
>
> San Francisco is an exciting city to visit because of highways, fences, and cats.
>
> *Problem:* The three essay map items do not provide "exciting" reasons to visit the city.
>
> *Revision:* San Francisco is an exciting city to visit because of the fantastic Fisherman's Wharf, the incredible Pacific Ocean, and the extraordinary restaurants.
>
> In the revised sentence, the essay map items explain why the city is exciting to visit. Additionally, the adjectives that accompany each essay map item, "fantastic," "incredible," and "extraordinary," help support the "exciting" attitude.

1. A new car is superior to a used car because of better viewing, colors, and the neighbors.

   _____

   _____

   _____

2. Reducing air pollution, expanding the economy, and supporting education are good reasons to vote for a political candidate.

   _____

   _____

   _____

3. A successful small business, built on spectacular vistas, aromatic candles, and U.S. Grade A ground beef, is easy to franchise.

   _____

   _____

   _____

4. Hiring a housecleaning crew can help cure your dizzy spells, make your pets happier, and cause your car to get better gas mileage.

   _____

   _____

   _____

5. A professional wrestling career can be easier to attain by studying classical music, ballet, and the opera.

   _____

   _____

   _____

Answers will vary.

Write thesis sentences for the following topics. Use the criteria for writing an effective thesis sentence that you have learned.

1. A book you have read.

_____

_____

2. A controversial movie you have seen.

_____

_____

3. Privacy on the Internet.

_____

_____

4. What makes a relationship work.

_____

_____

5. College drinking.

_____

_____

Introductory Sentences

In the introductory paragraph, the thesis sentence is introduced by **introductory sentences.** The purpose of introductory sentences is to catch the reader's attention and clarify your **tone** (for example, humorous, serious, or satiric). Some effective techniques for introducing the thesis sentence include using a shocking statistic or statement, posing a series of questions, or stating a common problem or misconception.

Examples

Shocking statistic or statement

One out of every three families is directly affected by alcoholism. Of the 50,000 people killed in automobile accidents each year, two-thirds have a direct link to drinking and driving. The trends are increasing each year. *(Place thesis sentence here.)*

Series of questions

When is the last time you enjoyed the process of buying a car? Are you tired of worrying about whether or not you are going to end up with a lemon? Do you resent smooth-talking sales people who are more interested in their commission than concerned with your satisfaction? *(Place thesis sentence here.)*

Common problem or misconception
Most people define welfare as money going to the poor living in the inner city. However, many corporations receive tax abatements when they move to a new city or town. Military dependents receive free medical and dental coverage and discounted food and merchandise at base stores. Many college students receive money for tuition and living expenses that they do not have to repay. *(Place thesis sentence here.)*

PRACTICE 6

Answers will vary.

Write a thesis sentence for each of the paragraph examples on pages 23–24. Don't forget to create an essay map that supports your controlling idea or attitude about the topic.

1. _____

2. _____

3. _____

PRACTICE 7

Answers will vary.

Write introductory sentences for each of the following thesis sentences. Try to create at least three sentences using one of the introductory sentence techniques you have learned.

1. _____

_____

_____

_____

_____

_____

_____

Traveling to foreign lands can make you appreciate your own country, allow you to understand other people's points of view, and broaden your knowledge of current international issues.

2. _____

_____

_____

_____

_____

_____

_____

Canning your own fruits and vegetables, keeping the thermostat set at 76° year-round, and making some of your own clothes can reduce your monthly bills by half.

3. _____

_____

_____

_____

_____

_____

_____

Senior citizens who continue learning, have a hobby, and exercise regularly can live longer and happier lives.

Putting It All Together

Exhibit 3-1
San Francisco
or Bust!

A five-paragraph essay using the thesis sentence with three-item essay map might be organized like this:

San Francisco or Bust! ←— Title

Introductory Paragraph
Introductory Sentences {

(The introduction may use a shocking statistic, state a

common problem, or pose a series of questions.)

Thesis Sentence {

San Francisco is an exciting city to visit because of the

fantastic Fisherman's Wharf, the incredible Pacific Ocean, ←— Essay Map

and the extraordinary restaurants.

1st Body Paragraph
[We'll learn more about
body paragraphs
in Chapter 4]

Fisherman's Wharf offers the visitor a wide array of ←— Topic Sentence

fascinating attractions.

Support Sentences {

2nd Body Paragraph

The Pacific Ocean, like an unbelievable expanse of ←— **Topic Sentence**

blue glass, is a boater's paradise.

Support Sentences

_____

_____

_____

3rd Body Paragraph

The city's restaurants serve a delectable variety of ←— **Topic Sentence**

international cuisines.

Support Sentences

_____

_____

_____

Concluding Paragraph
[We'll learn more about
concluding paragraphs
in Chapter 5]

(The conclusion can be a call to action, a warning,

a prediction, or an evaluation.)

_____

_____

_____

As illustrated in the schematic essay above, the three essay map items in the thesis sentence become the topics of the three body paragraphs. Each topic is introduced in the first sentence of the paragraph, called the topic sentence, and then developed in the support sentences that follow.

Sample Essay: SAN FRANCISCO OR BUST!

Patty Dubnau

The essay on page 28 demonstrates the techniques and illustrates the elements discussed in the essay schematic, Exhibit 3.1.

San Francisco or Bust!

1   Tired of looking at the same trees and hills year after year? Have you been going to the same time-share for so long that you have names for all the squirrels and chipmunks? Tired of hiking from museum to museum until you become lost in a faceless crowd shuffling from one overcrowded, stuffy room to another? Thinking of separate vacations just so you can be assured of "not seeing the same old thing"? Well, as famous American journalist Horace Greeley once said, "Go West, young man. Go West!" If you want a memorable vacation, one packed with new experiences and invigorating activities, run—don't walk—to San Francisco. San Francisco is an exciting city to visit because of the fantastic Fisherman's Wharf, the incredible Pacific Ocean, and the extraordinary restaurants.

2   Fisherman's Wharf offers the visitor a wide array of fascinating attractions. The fishing fleet docks along the Jefferson Street promenade. An early morning stroll along "Fish Alley" will allow you to see fishermen at work. Jefferson Street has a host of specialty shops and entertainment for the entire family. The Wharf has its share of museums, but they are a bit out of the ordinary. There's a wax museum, the Ripley's Believe It or Not! Museum, and a museum in the guise of a medieval dungeon. If you're not too claustrophobic, you can visit Pier 45 and tour the USS *Pampanito,* a retired WWII submarine. Also, you might want to visit Ghirardelli Square and pick a souvenir or two from the many specialty shops located there. Finally, before you leave the Wharf, make certain you take with you a loaf or two of San Francisco's famous sourdough bread. You'll probably want to visit Fisherman's Wharf several times before your vacation is over.

3   The Pacific Ocean, like an unbelievable expanse of blue glass, is a boater's paradise. In San Francisco, boating enthusiasts can participate in activities in and out of the water. The San Francisco Maritime National Historical Park contains four national landmark ships, including the famous square-rigger *Balclutha* and the ferryboat *Eureka,* which houses a collection of classic cars. The park's Maritime Museum houses a fascinating array of model ships, figureheads, paintings, photographs, and artifacts in an art deco building shaped to resemble a cruise ship. But, if it's the high seas you want, you can head for several marinas and rent a boat or take an excursion tour boat out into the bay. You can take a ferry to the infamous "Rock," Alcatraz Island. The former maximum-security prison now offers guided tours, a self-guided hiking trail, and a slide show illustrating the penitentiary's notorious history. Or sail or motor out into the bay to view the enormous expanse of the Pacific Ocean and the incredible Golden Gate Bridge. Even when the fog is clouding and shrouding the enormous structure, the sight of fog rolling over the 1.2-mile-long bridge is both spectacular and haunting.

4   The city's restaurants serve a delectable variety of international cuisines. The real difficulty is making a choice between so many savory and delicious options. The Richmond District is well known for Russian delis. Chinatown offers traditional Mandarin, Szechuan, and Hunan fare and an array of Asian restaurants, such as Cambodian, Laotian, Burmese, and Indian. The North Beach area is famous for Italian and California cuisines, while Central and South American food is the specialty in the Mission District. To borrow from the Swedish—what a *smorgasbord!* If you like dining out, San Francisco is the place.

5   As enjoyable as your vacation in San Francisco is likely to be, remember a few things. It's a big city, and it comes with the usual cautions. When you're in crowded places, keep your wallet in your front pocket, and hold onto your purse tightly. There are pickpockets in all large cities, and San Francisco is no different. Lock car doors, and don't leave anything in plain

sight. Discourage thieves from taking advantage of you. On a lighter but important topic, San Francisco, while blessed with a moderate climate, can get downright chilly at times. Remember, the city is quite far north, so always carry a windbreaker, and wearing shorts is only encouraged if you have listened carefully to the local weather before you go out. With just a bit of planning and precaution, your vacation to San Francisco, the "City by the Bay," will be an experience that you and your family will remember for years to come.

Essay Writing Technique Questions

1. What technique is used in the introductory sentences to introduce the thesis sentence?

   A series of questions.

2. Identify the thesis sentence, and write it on the lines below. Circle the subject. Underline each of the essay map items twice.

   (San Francisco) is an exciting city to visit because of the fantastic Fisherman's Wharf, the incredible Pacific Ocean, and the extraordinary restaurants.

3. Identify the topic sentence in each of the three body paragraphs, and write the sentences on the lines below. Circle the subject of each topic sentence. Are the subjects the same as the essay map items that you underlined twice in Question 2?

   (Fisherman's Wharf) offers the visitor a wide array of fascinating attractions.

   The (Pacific Ocean), like an unbelievable expanse of blue glass, is a boater's paradise.

   The city's (restaurants) serve a delectable variety of international cuisines.

   Yes, the subjects of the three topic sentences are the same as the three essay map items.

4. Identify the technique used in the concluding paragraph, and write your answer on the following lines. If you were thinking about traveling to San Francisco for a vacation, would the concluding paragraph affect your decision? Why, or why not?

   The concluding paragraph technique is a *warning* about pickpockets and thieves and about the surprisingly cool climate. (Remainder of answer will vary.)

Chapter Review

■ An essay's introductory paragraph consists of a series of introductory sentences and a thesis sentence.

■ The thesis sentence states what you are going to clarify, explain, or argue for or against about the topic of the essay. It usually appears at the end of the introductory paragraph.

■ In the thesis sentence, the controlling idea or attitude states your focus or feelings toward the topic of the essay.

■ The thesis sentence also presents the essay map. In an essay with three body paragraphs, the essay map states the three topics that are the subjects of the body paragraphs.

■ The thesis sentence has three elements: the topic, the controlling idea or attitude, and the essay map.

■ The thesis sentence of an essay is preceded by introductory sentences. These catch the reader's attention and establish the tone of the essay.

Visit *The Write Start* Online!

For additional practice with the materials found in this chapter, visit our Website at

http://www.ablongman.com/checkett

The Website also features additional readings, quizzes, writing activities, and Internet links, as well as a bulletin board and interactive chat.

CHAPTER 4

The Body Paragraphs

The purpose of the **body paragraphs** of an essay is to develop, support, and explain the topic stated in the thesis sentence in the introductory paragraph. Each body paragraph's topic is based on one of the items in the essay map of the thesis sentence. Body paragraphs follow the general organizational model for a paragraph as presented in Part 1: topic sentence and supporting sentences.

The Topic Sentence

The topic sentence has two parts: the **topic** (also called the subject) and the **controlling idea or attitude.** The topic is the subject of the body paragraph, and it is mentioned in the essay map located in the thesis sentence. The controlling idea or attitude limits what can be said about the topic, so new subjects or ideas cannot be introduced.

> **Example**
> In a book, description often creates a violent atmosphere.

In this example, the subject is "book." The controlling idea or attitude is "description often creates a violent atmosphere." In a paragraph with this subject, the controlling idea or attitude about the description is that it is violent. The writer cannot talk about other aspects of the book, such as romance, sales figures, or awards it might have won. The controlling idea or attitude forces the writer to talk only about those features of the description that develop the violent aspects of the book.

Topic sentences missing a controlling idea or attitude lack focus and specific direction. Without a controlling idea or attitude, the writer's thoughts or feelings about the subject can be unclear.

> **Examples**
> *Poor topic sentences*
>
> Sammy Sosa is a baseball player.
> (No controlling idea or attitude; this is simply a statement of fact)

Jogging is a popular form of exercise.

(No controlling idea or attitude; *popular* is too ambiguous)

Better topic sentences

Sammy Sosa's ability to hit home runs makes him an exciting baseball player.

(Controlling idea or attitude: *hitting home runs* makes Sosa exciting)

Jogging is a popular form of exercise because it promotes cardiovascular fitness.

(Controlling idea or attitude: *cardiovascular fitness* makes jogging popular)

PRACTICE 1

Answers will vary.

The following sentences are inadequate as topic sentences because they lack a controlling idea or attitude. Turn them into topic sentences by adding a controlling idea to each.

1. I drive my car each day.

2. Marathoners wear running shoes.

3. Many young people attend rock concerts.

4. Jonathan attends precalculus classes.

5. The World Series is played during October.

6. Most businesses use computers.

7. Millions diet each day.

_____

_____

8. Voting in presidential elections takes place every four years.

_____

_____

9. A relationship exists between farming and the rainforest.

_____

_____

10. The police respond to emergency situations.

_____

_____

PRACTICE 2

Answers will vary.

Write topic sentences for the following subjects. Don't forget to add a controlling idea or attitude.

1. Clothes

_____

2. Hurricanes

_____

3. Political Races

_____

4. Summer Jobs

_____

5. Exercising

_____

6. Soap Operas

_____

_____

7. Television Reruns

_____

_____

8. Rollerblading

_____

_____

9. Music

_____

_____

10. Astrology

_____

_____

PRACTICE 3

Answers will vary.

Write a topic sentence with a controlling idea or attitude for the support sentences in the following paragraphs.

1. _____

_____

First, the rafting trip down the river provided a thrill a minute as we hit the rapids. Next, the horseback ride along a winding trail took us through a dense forest filled with the sounds of many birds and other wildlife. After all the day's activities were complete, we sat around a roaring campfire and sang songs beneath a canopy of twinkling stars.

2. _____

_____

Monet's impressionistic paintings, with their muted colors and wispy, fog-like quality, seemed to be part of a dream. On the other hand, the shiny, brightly colored glass sculptures of Gilhooly appeared like fantastic clouds plunging from the sky, and the rigid, metallic armor suits of the knights seemed to stand guard over the earthly domain.

3. _____

_____

Uncle Morgan seemed about ten pounds heavier than the last time the family got together. Twins Marleena and Marlaana, first cousins from

Mom's side of the genealogy chart, were wearing their hair in long curls instead of their usual Peter Pan cut. The twinkle in Aunt Bessy's eyes had been replaced with a sad, almost mournful gaze.

4. _____

_____

China's population is already over 1 billion, and India's population will be over 1 billion in the near future. The total population for the United States, which has many well-advertised family planning organizations, has increased by 30 million in only a few decades. The rate at which the world's resources are being consumed is increasing at an alarming rate.

Support Sentences

Support sentences follow the topic sentence and help develop the subject by using specific facts, details, and examples. The supporting ideas must be consistent with the controlling idea or attitude. The controlling idea or attitude unifies the information in the paragraph by determining the kind of support ideas you can use in the support sentences.

Example

Teachers are most effective when helping students learn *how* to learn.

In this example, the topic is underlined once and the controlling idea is underlined twice.

Support sentences for this topic would focus on *what* teachers do to help students and might include teaching students the following activities:

a. what information to take down as notes during a lecture

b. what to identify as important information in reading assignments

c. what techniques help make for effective studying

The Six Reporters' Questions

Reporters often ask six questions when writing a story. The answers to the six questions provide the focus that allows them to select the details, facts, and examples to develop the story with specific information. The six questions are *who, what, where, when, why,* and *how.*

After selecting or being given a topic to write about, decide on the controlling idea. To help you do this, choose which of the reporters' questions allows you to write about the topic with the desired focus.

For instance, if your topic is an *important event,* the support sentences could focus on

Who: Who started the event?

Who attended, witnessed, or participated in the event?

Who was affected by the event?

What: What was the event?

What happened before, during, and after the event?

What was special about the event?

> **Where:** Where did the event occur?
>
> Did the location affect the event in any way?
>
> **When:** When did the event occur (a.m./p.m., day, month, year)?
>
> Did the time frame add any special significance to the event?
>
> Did the event coincide with a historically significant time?
>
> **Why:** Why did the event occur?
>
> Why was the event important?
>
> **How:** How did the event happen?
>
> How was the event funded?
>
> How was the event advertised?

You can add your own focus to these questions if other ideas come to you. There is no need to be limited to the list above.

> **Examples**
>
> 1. Investing can help people have a happier retirement. *(what?)*
> 2. Investing is best done in consultation with a financial expert. *(who?)*
> 3. Anyone interested in becoming a better investor should read as much as possible on the subject. *(how?)*

Although *investing* is the subject of each sentence in the preceding examples, the focus of the controlling idea is different. In Sentence 1, the focus is on "what" investing can do for people (help their retirement years); in Sentence 2, the focus is on "who" is consulted about investing (a financial advisor); in Sentence 3, the focus is on "how" to be a better investor (by reading material on the subject).

Creating a Working Outline

Before you begin writing, you may want to sketch out the major ideas that will appear in your paragraph. This can help you discover whether or not you have a topic, a controlling idea or attitude, and support ideas that work in unison for proper development. To create a working outline, list your topic, controlling idea or attitude, and support ideas in a ladder-like list. (For other prewriting techniques, see Chapter 6.)

> **Example**
>
> **Topic:** Smoking
>
> **Controlling idea or attitude:** can cause harmful effects
>
> **Support ideas:** lung cancer
>
> emphysema
>
> gum disease

The paragraph outlined in the example will discuss the harmful effects of smoking. This topic will be developed and supported by using lung cancer, emphysema, and gum disease as the negative outcomes that smoking can produce. The finished paragraph might look like this:

> Smoking can cause many harmful effects. It can lead to lung cancer, a potentially deadly condition for which cures are almost nonexistent. Emphysema, a chronic problem that worsens with time, is a disease wherein the air spaces in the lung increase, causing labored breathing and a susceptibility to infection. Additionally, smoking can cause excessive gum bleeding and gum cancer. Consult with your doctor for the best method for you to quit smoking.

PRACTICE 4

Answers will vary.

To practice creating working outlines, add a controlling idea for each of the topics listed below. Then, using one of the six reporters' questions for each topic, list three specific support details that develop the controlling idea or attitude. Do not use the same question for more than one topic. After you have finished, you will have a list of all the basic ideas that will go into a paragraph on the topic. This is called a *working outline* because the paragraph is still unfinished.

1. Topic: The *Mission Impossible* movies

Controlling idea or attitude:

_____

Reporters' question:

_____

Support ideas:

a. _____

b. _____

c. _____

2. Topic: Dating

Controlling idea or attitude:

_____

Reporters' question:

_____

Support ideas:

a. _____

b. _____

c. _____

3. Topic: School violence

Controlling idea or attitude:

_____

Reporters' question:

_____

Support ideas:

a. _____

b. _____

c. _____

4. Topic: Welfare

Controlling idea or attitude:

_____

Reporters' question:

_____

Support ideas:

a. _____

b. _____

c. _____

5. Topic: Recycling

Controlling idea or attitude:

_____

Reporters' question:

_____

Support ideas:

a. _____

b. _____

c. _____

PRACTICE 5

Write a paragraph for each of the working outlines you created in Practice 4.

Additional Writing Assignments

The following paragraph writing assignments will help you practice the techniques you have learned. Create a working outline before you write each paragraph.

1. *(Who)* Write about a person. This can be a person you know, such as a parent, sibling, relative, friend, teacher, co-worker, or a historical person with whom you are familiar. In your topic sentence, name the person, and write a controlling idea or attitude you wish to develop in the support sentences.

2. *(What)* Write about an event. This can be a public event such as an Olympic competition or an event from your own life, such as a religious ceremony, a birthday or graduation party, an operation, an athletic event, or an historical event with which you are familiar. In the topic sentence, name the event, and write a controlling idea or attitude you wish to develop in the support sentences.

3. *(Where)* Write about a location. This can be a place that you know, such as your room, house, school, workplace, or an historical location with which you are familiar. In your topic sentence, name the location, and write a controlling idea or attitude you wish to develop in the support sentences.

4. *(When)* Write about an important time. This can be a time in your life, such as your childhood or teenage years, or a well-known time in history with which you are familiar. In your topic sentence, name the time frame, and write a controlling idea or attitude you wish to develop in the support sentences.

5. *(Why)* Write about why something happened. This can be about why something happened to you or to someone you know, or the reason something happened in history. In your topic sentence, name the reason, and write a controlling idea or attitude you wish to develop in the support sentences.

6. *(How)* Write about how something happens or is done. This can be something you have accomplished or were witness to or something that occurs in nature or happened historically. In your topic sentence, name the process, and write a controlling idea or attitude you wish to develop in the support sentences.

Chapter Review

◼ The body paragraphs of an essay develop and support the essay's topic as set forth in the essay map of the thesis sentence.

◼ The topic sentence of a body paragraph states the topic and the controlling idea or attitude toward the topic.

◼ Support sentences follow the topic sentence and help develop the topic by using specific facts, details, and examples.

◼ Asking the six reporters' questions—who, what, where, when, why, and how—can provide a focus and details for the body paragraphs.

◼ A working outline that states the topic, controlling idea or attitude, and support ideas can help you organize your paragraph.

Visit *The Write Start* Online!

For additional practice with the materials found in this chapter, visit our Website at

http://www.ablongman.com/checkett

The Website also features additional readings, quizzes, writing activities, and Internet links, as well as a bulletin board and interactive chat.

CHAPTER 5

The Concluding Paragraph

Essays should not simply stop abruptly after the final body paragraph. Instead, you should leave your reader with a sense that your essay is complete. Use a **concluding paragraph** to bring a sense of completion to your essay and to reemphasize the central thesis. A concluding paragraph can simply be a summation of the points you've made, but it can also urge your readers to action, predict an outcome, or provide a warning based on the information in your essay. There are some things, however, that a concluding paragraph should *not* do.

- The concluding paragraph is not used to introduce new points; developing new points is the function of the body paragraphs.

- A concluding paragraph in a short essay should not simply restate your thesis sentence. Your reader is not likely to have forgotten the points you have developed in your body paragraphs. (In a longer, more complex essay, restating the thesis in the concluding paragraph can be helpful, because doing so reminds the reader of the major points that were used to support your ideas about the essay's topic.)

There are several techniques you can use in the concluding paragraph to place emphasis on the points you have made throughout the essay. These include:

- call to action
- warning
- prediction
- evaluation

Call to Action

In a concluding paragraph that uses a call to action, the reader is asked to take some action—to do something based on the essay's content.

Example

Call to Action →

New procedures are necessary to handle the burgeoning number of yearly visitors to our national parks, but simply increasing entrance fees to generate more revenues is not an acceptable answer. <u>Write your senators and representatives and suggest that they need to hold hearings to determine what can be done to save these treasures.</u> If we can stem the destruction of our national parks, future generations will be able to enjoy the natural beauty of America's great outdoors.

Warning

In some concluding paragraphs, the reader is warned that negative events might occur.

Example

Warning →

Buying insurance on the Internet is becoming a commonplace practice. The amount of money spent online for insurance is doubling every year. The main reason for the popularity of buying insurance on the Internet is convenience. However, you should be careful when purchasing insurance online. <u>Make certain the company you are doing business with has an A⁺ Superior rating by a reputable rating service.</u> There have been cases where consumers paid for policies that didn't exist because the companies that sold the policies weren't actual insurance companies.

Prediction

A concluding paragraph may predict potential outcomes stemming from the discussion of the essay's topic. The writer looks into the future, so to speak.

Example

Prediction →

The new SUV family vans are becoming larger every year. They look like military hum-vee rejects. Families love the extra room, great for all kinds of shopping around town and vacationing with the children (pets included). However, handling the bigger vehicles can become a problem. Also, because their bumper height causes more damage to smaller cars, insurance companies are charging their owners higher premiums. <u>With the increasing popularity of SUVs, insurance rates will rise for all vehicles over the next few years.</u> It is incumbent upon the manufacturers of suburban vans to plan for ways to reduce the spiraling insurance costs associated with these vehicles.

Evaluation

The importance of the overall topic may be summarized and judged in a concluding paragraph.

> **Example**
>
> Many bacteria that cause diseases are becoming resistant to antibiotics used to treat them. The rainforest provides many of the plants from which these antibiotics are made. But with so much of the rainforest being destroyed each year, a different method of producing antibiotics is necessary. New synthetic drugs can be effective in combating diseases currently resistant to natural drugs. Additionally, new synthetic derivatives can be created by studying both natural and existing synthetics. With assistance from the government, pharmaceutical companies should find new synthetic drug research a lucrative endeavor.

Evaluation →

Evaluation →

PRACTICE 1

The "San Francisco or Bust!" essay from Chapter 3 is reprinted below. Reread the essay. You will find that the concluding paragraph, which uses the warning technique, is missing. Choose two concluding techniques other than warning (call to action, prediction, or evaluation), and write two different concluding paragraphs for the essay.

San Francisco or Bust!

1   Tired of looking at the same trees and hills year after year? Have you been going to the same time-share for so long that you have names for all the squirrels and chipmunks? Tired of hiking from museum to museum until you become lost in a faceless crowd shuffling from one overcrowded, stuffy room to another? Thinking of separate vacations just so you can be assured of "not seeing the same old thing"? Well, as famous American journalist Horace Greeley once said, "Go West, young man. Go West!" If you want a memorable vacation, one packed with new experiences and invigorating activities, run—don't walk—to San Francisco. San Francisco is an exciting city to visit because of the fantastic Fisherman's Wharf, the incredible Pacific Ocean, and the extraordinary restaurants.

2   Fisherman's Wharf offers the visitor a wide array of fascinating attractions. The fishing fleet docks along the Jefferson Street promenade. An early morning stroll along "Fish Alley" will allow you to see fishermen at work. Jefferson Street has a host of specialty shops and entertainment for the entire family. The Wharf has its share of museums, but they are a bit out of the ordinary. There's a wax museum, the Ripley's Believe It or Not! Museum, and a museum in the guise of a medieval dungeon. If you're not too claustrophobic, you can visit Pier 45 and tour the USS *Pampanito*, a retired WWII submarine. Also, you might want to visit Ghirardelli Square and pick a souvenir or two from the many specialty shops

located there. Finally, before you leave the Wharf, make certain you take with you a loaf or two of San Francisco's famous sourdough bread. You'll probably want to visit Fisherman's Wharf several times before your vacation is over.

3   The Pacific Ocean, like an unbelievable expanse of blue glass, is a boater's paradise. In San Francisco, boating enthusiasts can participate in activities in and out of the water. The San Francisco Maritime National Historical Park contains four national landmark ships, including the famous square-rigger *Balclutha* and the ferryboat *Eureka,* which houses a collection of classic cars. The park's Maritime Museum houses a fascinating array of model ships, figureheads, paintings, photographs, and artifacts in an art deco building shaped to resemble a cruise ship. But, if it's the high seas you want, you can head for several marinas and rent a boat or take an excursion tour boat out into the bay. You can take a ferry to the infamous "Rock," Alcatraz Island. The former maximum-security prison now offers guided tours, a self-guided hiking trail, and a slide show illustrating the penitentiary's notorious history. Or sail or motor out into the bay to view the enormous expanse of the Pacific Ocean and the incredible Golden Gate Bridge. Even when the fog is clouding and shrouding the enormous structure, the sight of fog rolling over the 1.2-mile-long bridge is both spectacular and haunting.

4   The city's restaurants serve a delectable variety of international cuisines. The real difficulty is making a choice between so many savory and delicious options. The Richmond District is well known for Russian delis. Chinatown offers traditional Mandarin, Szechuan, and Hunan fare and an array of Asian restaurants, such as Cambodian, Laotian, Burmese, and Indian. The North Beach area is famous for Italian and California cuisines, while Central and South American food is the specialty in the Mission District. To borrow from the Swedish—what a *smorgasbord!* If you like dining out, San Francisco is the place.

Write your concluding paragraph #1.

Which technique did you use?

Answers will vary

_____

_____

_____

_____

_____

_____

_____

_____

_____

Write your concluding paragraph #2.
Which technique did you use?

Answers will vary

_____

_____

_____

_____

_____

_____

_____

_____

_____

_____

Chapter Review

■ The concluding paragraph of an essay brings a sense of completion to the essay and reemphasizes its general thesis.

■ Techniques for writing a concluding paragraph include call to action, warning, prediction, and evaluation.

Visit *The Write Start* Online!

For additional practice with the materials found in this chapter, visit our Website at

http://www.ablongman.com/checkett

The Website also features additional readings, quizzes, writing activities, and Internet links, as well as a bulletin board and interactive chat.

Copyright © 2002 by Addison-Wesley Educational Publishers Inc.

Prewriting Activities

Ask almost any writer what is the hardest part of the writing process and the typical response will be "Getting started!" You've probably had problems getting started with some of your own writing assignments. Coming up with a topic is usually easy enough, but deciding what to write and how to say it can be paralyzing.

Over the years, writers have developed numerous methods for getting started with a piece of writing. Some of the more popular prewriting methods include listing, clustering, cubing, and cross examination.

In this chapter, you will be introduced to these four strategies to help you develop your topic. Your teacher can probably suggest several others. You might find that using one single method will work very well, or you might find it effective to use more than one strategy each time you write. The key is to experiment with as many prewriting methods as you need to get started writing.

Listing

Listing is exactly what it sounds like—making a list. Here's how it works. Take a blank piece of paper and write the topic at the top. If you are using a computer, write the topic at the beginning of the document. Next, write down any idea that pops into your head as quickly as possible. Don't stop to think about how to develop each idea. This thinking technique is called *free association*. Let the words come fast, and write them down as they come. Remember, don't revise, correct, or edit your thoughts—just let them flow. A list of ideas on the topic of writing might look like this:

Example

Writing

assignment	thesis	paragraphs	content
grammar	topic	punctuation	analysis
sentences	spelling	development	conclusion
subtopics	coordination	essay	research
facts	opinion	title	body paragraphs

Continue listing for at least ten minutes, because one idea often inspires another. The act of writing helps the thinking process for most writers. When you have finished listing, see which ideas are related, and rearrange the items into groups. Your new page might look something like this:

Example

Writing

Group 1	**Group 2**	**Group 3**
grammar	sentences	thesis
spelling	paragraphs	topic
punctuation	conclusion	subtopics
	body paragraphs	

After you have put the ideas into lists of related terms, try to find a logical order for them, perhaps by chronology (what you would do first, then second, third, etc.) or by priority or importance (most important to least important, or vice versa). This step can help you outline your topic.

PRACTICE 1

Answers will vary.

List at least ten words that come to mind about each of the following topics.

1. Your favorite vacation spot.

_____

_____

_____

2. A sport or sporting event.

_____

_____

_____

3. Ending a relationship.

_____

_____

_____

4. A memorable person.

_____

_____

_____

5. A phobia or fear (snakes, heights, spiders, enclosed spaces).

_____

_____

_____

_____

Clustering (Mapping)

A technique similar to listing but more visual is **clustering,** or **mapping.** Clustering can help you see relationships among possible ideas more clearly. First, draw a circle at the center of your paper and write the topic inside it. Then, think of related topics and write them in circles around it. Link these to the topic circle by lines. Next, focus on the new circles, one by one. Think of topics related to these, and put them in another layer of circles. Note the diagram that follows. The main topic is educational television.

After studying the individual clusters, select the group that best develops the topic. You can expand on your options by continuing to add to the groups you have chosen. For instance, you could add Polynesian and Tex-Mex circles to the Cooking cluster. You could add Northern and Southern to the Italian circle. Then, you could write a paper about Northern Italian cooking versus Southern Italian cooking. The possibilities are as endless as the number of circles you can add to the clusters.

Place each of the following topics in the middle of a piece of paper. As related ideas come to you, make clusters with lines connecting them to one another if the ideas are also related.

The Internet

Video games

Parenting

Cubing

Another method to generate new approaches to a topic is called **cubing.** To do this, imagine a cube with six sides with the following questions on each side:

1. *Describe the topic:* What does the subject look like? What is the size, color, shape, texture, smell, and sound? Which details are unique?

2. *Compare or contrast the topic:* What is your subject like? How does it differ from other subjects? How is it similar? Give details.

3. *Free associate about the topic:* What does your subject remind you of? What further ideas can you think of?

4. *Analyze the topic:* What are the parts of the topic? How does each part function? How are the parts connected? What is the significance of the subject?

5. *Argue for or against the topic:* What are the arguments for and against your topic? What are its advantages and disadvantages?

6. *Apply the topic:* How can the topic be used?

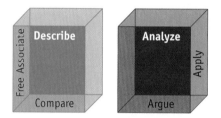

Approach your topic from each of the six perspectives, freewriting your answers as with listing or clustering. Give yourself ten minutes to explore your ideas. Do not worry about topic development at this point. Just get your ideas down. Finally, review your responses. See if any are appropriate to your assignment. Sometimes, doing this will generate ideas for your writing assignment.

Answers will vary.

Choose one of the following topics. Answer the questions on each side of the cube to develop ideas for the topic.

Ways to relax	A favorite room
A theatrical play	A type of music
An exciting city	Advertising a new product

1. Describe

_____

_____

_____

_____

2. Compare or contrast

_____

_____

_____

_____

3. Free associate

_____

_____

_____

_____

4. Analyze

_____

_____

_____

_____

5. Argue for or against

_____

_____

_____

_____

6. Apply

_____

_____

_____

_____

Cross Examination

You can use cross examination on your own or with a partner. Cross examination is a variation on the six reporter's questions discussed in Chapter 4. Depending on the type of essay assignment or the type of essay you would like to write, the questions can be grouped differently. You can interview yourself or your partner regarding the topic, using the following sets of questions:

Definition

How is the subject defined or explained by the dictionary or encyclopedia?

How do most people define the topic informally?

How do I define the subject?

What is the history, origin, or background of the topic?

What are some examples of the topic?

Relationship

What is the cause of the topic?

To what larger group or category does the subject belong?

What are the values or goals of the subject?

What are the effects of the subject?

Comparison and Contrast

What is the subject similar to?

What is the subject different from?

What is the subject better than?

What is the subject worse than?

What is the subject opposite to?

Testimony

What do people say about the topic?

What authorities exist on this topic?

Has anything been written on this topic?

What are the important statistics?

Is there any further research on the topic?

Have I had any personal experience on this topic?

Circumstance

Is this subject possible?

Is the subject impossible?

When has this subject happened before?

What might prevent it from happening?

Why might it happen again?

Who or what is associated with the topic?

Of course, not all of these questions will apply to every topic. Choose those that help you develop your topic most thoroughly and effectively.

PRACTICE 4

Answers will vary.

For one of the following topics, quickly write down answers for as many of the questions in each category as you can. Don't hesitate to write down answers for questions that come to you that are not listed in the categories provided here.

Mandatory handgun registration   Parental control lockouts for the Internet
A prison without guards   Commercial-free television

1. Definition

_____

_____

_____

_____

2. Relationship

_____

_____

_____

_____

3. Comparison and contrast

_____

_____

_____

_____

4. Testimony

_____

_____

_____

_____

5. Circumstance

_____

_____

_____

_____

A Final Word about Prewriting

If you practice a variety of prewriting strategies, you are likely to find one or two with which you are most comfortable and that allow you to write with a sense of confidence. You'll probably learn which strategies best apply to different topics. Getting started on a writing project can be the most difficult part of the assignment, but using prewriting strategies can make the entire process get off the ground with less frustration and more success. Never forget that the goal of prewriting is *discovery*, not completion. Progress through your writing assignment step by step, don't get ahead of yourself, and you'll find the total experience much more enjoyable and worthwhile.

Chapter Review

- Prewriting techniques are methods that writers use to get the writing process started. They include listing, clustering, cubing, and cross examination.
- In the listing method, you make a list of ideas that you free associate about a topic.
- In the clustering or mapping method, you write your topic in a circle at the center of a piece of paper and then place related topics in connected circles.
- In the cubing method, you approach a topic from each of six perspectives on the six sides of a cube: describe, compare or contrast, free associate, analyze, argue for or against, and apply.
- In cross examination, you interview yourself or a partner, asking questions about definition, relationship, comparison and contrast, testimony, and circumstance.

Visit *The Write Start* Online!

For additional practice with the materials found in this chapter, visit our Website at

http://www.ablongman.com/checkett

The Website also features additional readings, quizzes, writing activities, and Internet links, as well as a bulletin board and interactive chat.

PART 2

Moving Forward: Strategies for Developing Essays

Now that you have studied how to write introductory, body, and concluding paragraphs, it is time to put them together and construct a longer unit of writing called an essay, theme, paper, or composition. Essays are an important part of the college learning process because the essay helps you in three important respects: (1) writing an essay helps you to learn, (2) writing an essay helps you to learn about a topic from a variety of viewpoints, and (3) your essay tells your instructor what you have learned.

The Modes of Development

The different viewpoints from which you can write about a topic are called **modes of development.** *Mode* simply means method or process. You can develop a topic in more than one way, thereby learning something different about it each time, depending upon the mode of development you use.

In Part 2 of the text, you will be exploring, in order, the following modes of development:

Description: developing a topic through the use of vivid detail.

Narration: developing a topic through a recounting of events.

Example: developing a topic by using illustrations as clarification.

Classification: developing a topic by categorizing its characteristics.

Process: developing a topic by explaining how to do something or how something operates.

Comparison and Contrast: developing a topic by focusing on similarities and differences.

Definition: developing a topic by explaining what it is and, at times, is not.

Cause and Effect: developing a topic by focusing on why it occurs or the consequences or results of it occurring.

Persuasion: developing a topic by convincing the audience to agree with a particular point of view.

For instance, in an engineering course, your instructor might ask you to write an essay about a piece of machinery. The modes of development can guide you in making choices about your approach to the assignment. You can use *description* to tell about the physical dimensions and visual characteristics of the machine, or you can use *description* to give your reader an emotional sense of the machine: what it sounds like and feels like when you use it. You can use *process* to explain how the machine works. You can *compare* or *contrast* the machine to other machines with similar or different characteristics. A *cause and effect* essay might explore what effects the machine has had on product development, company profitability, or later developments in technology or commerce.

Of course, you can increase your essay's depth and vision by combining one or more of the modes of development. In fact, you will do this to some degree whether you plan to do it or not. That is, you cannot *describe, compare,* or show *cause and effect* about a person, place, or thing without *defining* it; likewise, it is difficult to *compare, contrast, define, describe,* or show *cause and effect* without using *examples.*

The modes of development are tools to assist you in writing your paper by helping you to choose your approach to the topic. By learning to use these techniques, your writing will become more developed in content and more varied in style—both signs of a mature, intelligent thinker and communicator.

CHAPTER 7

The Descriptive Essay

All essays develop a topic. One method to build on a topic is by describing it in detail. Effective **description** creates images in the reader's mind by using specific details. Like a painter using color on a canvas, the writer uses words (the color) to create pictures in the reader's mind (the canvas).

Instead of merely writing

> The bowl contained three scoops of ice cream.

A writer using effective description might write

> The glistening white bowl, decorated with bright blue spirals, overflowed with three gigantic mounds of vanilla, chocolate, and strawberry ice cream covered by a thick layer of whipped cream and garnished with a bright red cherry.

The specific details help develop the word-painting that describes persons, places, things, and emotions.

Identifying Your Purpose

All writing has purpose, and the purpose of writing a descriptive essay is to clarify, explain, or create a particular mood about a person, place, or thing. Sometimes you want to be objective (factual) in your description. For instance, **objective description** can be useful in describing a medical procedure, a legal concept, or a new piece of technological hardware.

Most of the time, you will use **subjective description** to create a more emotionally charged impression. For instance, a subjective (or impressionistic) description may relate how a medical advance will affect the lives of patients and their families, how a legal concept can affect an entire population, or how a technological advance can change the economic outlook of an entire industry.

At times, you will want to convey a feeling of sadness. At other times, you might want to evoke a feeling of happiness, or frustration, or hope, or sarcasm. Effective description evokes emotion and adds clarity and depth to your writing.

Objective versus Subjective Description

Objective description relies on factual detail without much embellishment. You write down what you see, hear, taste, smell, or touch without any emotional response or interpretation.

> The old mansion sat in the middle of the unkempt property.

From this objective description, it is difficult to recognize what emotion or impression the writer wants the reader to understand.

In contrast, subjective description creates an easily identifiable emotion or impression.

> The hulking, old mansion, its insides hidden by windows covered with broken spider webs and darkened by a thick covering of dust, sat like some lurking beast hiding in a yard overgrown with weeds and creeping vines.

From this subjective description, it is clear that the writer wants the site of the mansion to evoke a mysterious or dreadful emotion. Objective description describes what the writer actually perceives. Subjective description describes the writer's emotional response to what he or she encounters.

PRACTICE 1

On a separate piece of paper, write a paragraph about the room you are now sitting in. Describe the room objectively by simply writing down, in four or five sentences, what you see, hear, smell, or touch.

Dominant Impression

Your descriptive writing will be clearer and more enjoyable if you focus on just one **dominant impression** (sometimes identified as the DI). The dominant impression is the overall feeling or emotional response you want the reader to take away from the description. When you write a descriptive paragraph, each support sentence should build on the dominant impression you create in the topic sentence. Be careful to add only those details that support the dominant impression. Do not add details that suggest a different impression, as in the following example.

Examples

Poor dominant impression
On a bright, sunny day, Meiling played joyously with her frisky, new puppy until it fell into a drainage ditch full of sewage.

Better dominant impression
On a bright, sunny day, Meiling romped joyously with her frisky, new puppy, and she could not contain herself from laughing out loud at the cute little dog's frolicking antics.

In the first example above, the reader will not know what dominant impression the writer is attempting to convey. Is the writer trying to convey a positive impression (Meiling playing joyously with her puppy) or a negative impression (the puppy falling into a ditch full of sewage). The second example is more convincing and focused on the writer's intentions. The descriptions of the dog, its actions, and Meiling's responses are consistent with the same happy mood. The positive dominant impression is clear, supported by such word choices as "bright," "sunny," "romped," "joyously," "frisky," "laughing," and "frolicking."

Dominant Impression Words				
aggressive	angry	bitter	boisterous	bumbling
cheerful	clumsy	cluttered	comfortable	cozy
crowded	dazzling	depressing	drab	dreadful
eerie	fierce	friendly	gaudy	generous
gigantic	inviting	peaceful	pessimistic	placid
restful	restless	romantic	rustic	shy
silent	snobbish	spacious	stuffy	sullen
tasteless	tense	ugly	uncomfortable	unfriendly

PRACTICE 2

In Practice 1, you wrote an objective description of a room. On a separate piece of paper, rewrite your paragraph subjectively. Focus on the dominant impression the room suggests to you, perhaps because of the room's color scheme, some object in the room, or the type of activity that happens in the room. After you have finished, compare the two paragraphs. Which one do you think paints a sharper, clearer image in the reader's mind? You can choose one of the dominant impression words from the list above if you cannot think of one.

Writing the Descriptive Paragraph

A descriptive paragraph has a topic sentence that conveys the dominant impression. It also includes details that describe sensory images, sometimes using figurative language to make comparisons.

The Topic Sentence in a Subjective Description Paragraph

The topic sentence in a subjective description paragraph states the topic to be discussed and clearly states the dominant impression that will be developed in the supporting sentences that follow. Topic sentences without a dominant impression are usually statements of fact; in other words, they are too objective for a subjective description paragraph.

Examples

Topic sentences without a dominant impression:

The parade passed down the street.

Sareena wore a dress to the prom.

The hockey game was played Saturday night.

Yoshi had an interesting personality.

Topic sentences with a dominant impression:

The parade passing down the street was **dazzling.**

The dress Sareena wore to the prom was **tasteless.**

The hockey game played Saturday night was **exciting.**

Yoshi's personality was **bitter.**

Resource Note: A useful type of book to help you select better dominant impression words is a *thesaurus.* This type of reference book contains lists of synonyms, homonyms, and antonyms for almost any word you can think of. You can find an inexpensive paperback thesaurus at any bookstore or from an online book source, and some computer programs have a thesaurus built in.

PRACTICE 3

Answers will vary.

Rewrite the following topic sentences by adding a dominant impression to each one.

1. William Jefferson Clinton was President of the United States.

_____

_____

2. Students use the Internet to find information.

_____

_____

3. Ecstasy is a drug used mostly by young people.

_____

_____

4. Security police help keep order on campuses.

_____

_____

5. Date rape is a new crime.

_____

_____

Supporting Details: Sensory Images

Once you have decided on the dominant impression you wish to create, you need to choose language and details to develop that impression. Writers can choose from a rich array of language to create and support description, including **sensory images.** These sensory images are based on the five senses we are all familiar with: sight, touch, smell, sound, and taste. Because description creates images, it can tell the reader what a person, place, or thing

- looks like
- feels like
- smells like
- sounds like
- tastes like

By using sensory images, writers can draw a more fully developed picture of what they are describing. Good description actually causes readers to remember similar persons, places, or things from their own experiences. This personal interaction between the reader and the writing is a wonderful and powerful process.

Examples

Sight

Nondescriptive: The sky was blue.

Descriptive: The sky was a **deep, azure blue, dotted** by **fluffy, white clouds.**

Touch

Nondescriptive: The hospital bedsheets were uncomfortable.

Descriptive: The hospital sheets were **stiff** and **scratchy,** like **sandpaper scraping** against my skin.

Smell

Nondescriptive: The cab of Miguel's truck smelled awful.

Descriptive: The cab of Miguel's truck smelled like a **gym locker stuffed** with a year's worth of **dirty socks.**

Sound

Nondescriptive: The jetliner was loud as it took off.

Descriptive: As it took off, the jetliner was so loud that it **made your teeth vibrate, as if a dozen motorcycles were passing by.**

Taste

Nondescriptive: The bagels tasted old.

Descriptive: The bagels **tasted musty, like moldy cheese** I remember eating at my brother-in-law's house last New Year's Eve.

PRACTICE 4

Using the subjective paragraph you completed in Practice 2, add sensory description to some of the sentences. Try to use at least two different sensory techniques. After you are finished, compare this new paragraph to your previous version. Are the images more vivid in your mind?

Supporting Details: Comparisons Using Figurative Language

Another device that writers can use to describe something is comparison. Comparisons to well-known or everyday objects or images provide descriptions that readers can immediately recognize. Many writers find comparison the easiest descriptive tool because comparisons allow writers to provide clear ideas to the reader by tapping into images and emotions that the reader has already experienced.

Figurative language is one tool writers use to make comparisons. Figurative language describes a person or thing in terms usually associated with something very different. The three most effective figurative language devices are **similes, metaphors,** and **personification.**

A *simile* is a comparison using either "like" or "as" to show a similarity between two dissimilar things. Notice how similar the words "simile" and "similarity" are.

> **Examples**
>
> The huge, football lineman is **like** a mountain.
> The clouds covered the city **like** a thick, wool blanket.
> The workman is **as** strong **as** a bull.
> The gymnast is **as** agile **as** a monkey.

A *metaphor* is a stronger comparison between two things without using "like" or "as." The implication is that one thing "is" the same as the other.

> **Examples**
>
> The huge football lineman **is** a mountain.
> The cloud cover **is** a thick blanket smothering the city.
> The workman **is** a bull.
> The gymnast **is** an agile monkey.

Personification gives human emotions or characteristics to animals, objects, or ideas.

> **Examples**
>
> The wind **howled** past my ears.
> Love **danced** in their eyes.
> The fox **cheated** the farmer by **stealing** eggs from the henhouse.
> The candle in the window **winked** at the passing cars.
> The sun **slept** as the moon **kept watch** over the campers.

PRACTICE 5

Using the completed paragraph from Practice 4, add several figurative language techniques to several ideas. After you are finished, compare the paragraph to the previous ones. Quite a difference, isn't there? Your paragraph illustrates the creative power of effectively written description.

Moving from Paragraph to Essay

Now that you have studied and practiced the techniques to create effective subjective description paragraphs, it is time to expand your ideas to a larger writing unit: the descriptive essay. The descriptive essay is a union of the paragraph techniques you learned in Part 1 regarding developing the essay and the subjective description techniques you have just learned. This might be a good time to return to Part 1 and review the techniques for developing the full essay.

Creating the Introductory Paragraph

Description often can seem free-flowing and without purpose. But a descriptive essay is a piece of writing—and all good writing has a purpose and a clearly defined organization. The thesis sentence of the introductory paragraph should clearly state the purpose of the essay and how the essay will develop.

The thesis in a descriptive essay should blend naturally into the rest of the introductory paragraph. In the following example, notice how the thesis announces the topic *(storms)*, the writer's controlling attitude—the dominant impression—toward the topic *(devastation)*, and the essay map containing the body paragraph subtopics *(lightning, winds, and flooding)*. The thesis sentence is underlined for instructional purposes only.

> **Example**
> The sky darkened like a ceiling scorched by fire. Raindrops as big as marbles began to pelt the ground, hurling bits of mud and grass into the air as the banks of creeks began to overflow. The wind swirled and muscled trees into spaghetti-like shapes. Brilliant flashes of light split the air like a hot knife through butter. <u>Lightning, raging winds, and flooding all added to the storm's devastation.</u> Such was the storm's vengeance; all in its path was destroyed.

Notice how the specific detail and the figurative language all support the dominant impression of devastation. There are specific sensory details: *darkened, scorched, hurling, swirled, muscled, flashes, split, raging, vengeance, destroyed.* There are similes: *sky darkened like a ceiling scorched by fire; raindrops as big as marbles; flashes of light split the air like a hot knife through butter.* There is also personification: *the wind…muscled; such was the storm's vengeance.*

Creating the Body Paragraphs

For a paper describing a storm's devastation, the focus of the body paragraphs will be the paragraph topics listed in the thesis sentence's essay map. The first body paragraph's topic will be about *lightning*, the second body paragraph's topic will be about *raging winds*, and the third body paragraph's topic will be about *flooding*. Remember, as you write about each of these topics, your focus should be that these elements *added to the storm's devastation*. Your focus should not be on how the National Weather Service tracks storms, or how local authorities marshal their forces to help victims, or how people take precautions when preparing for severe weather. Keep your focus on the controlling idea or attitude as stated in your thesis sentence.

Creating the Concluding Paragraph

The approach of the concluding paragraph should flow naturally from the essay's main topic. Because the essay's focus is on how various elements can make a storm devastating, *evaluating* each element that might be part of a devastating storm would seem an appropriate choice. You might describe how each different element (lightning, wind, and flooding) can affect people's lives and property. Whereas the body paragraphs were used to describe the effects of the elements, you can use the concluding paragraph to present the more personal effects of the storm on its victims.

Sample Student Essay: WARNING: BIOHAZARD!

Angie Bunch

The following essay, "Warning: Biohazard!" by student writer Angie Bunch, is a humorous look at a younger sibling by describing his messy room. The essay relies on exaggeration to achieve its tone. The numerous description techniques create images that are both funny and recognizable to anyone with brothers or sisters who are less than neat.

Vocabulary

Meaning comes primarily from words. Before you start reading, use a dictionary to look up the definitions of the following words that appear in the essay.

accessory	biohazard	futon	disarray
garish	penetrate	shrivel	stench
stereotype	strewn	traumatize	unique

Warning: Biohazard!

1   It's not hard to find my little brother's room. Just follow the smell, or the radioactive cloud hovering just above his door. By the way, you can't see the door. It's covered with garish photos of teenybopper rock stars and assorted pictures of gross-looking monsters—the stars of his unique collection of violent and bloody computer games. Through the open door, the piles of clothes, the foul stench, and scattered debris prove the room belongs to an owner as equally disarrayed.

2   With a flip of the light switch, you enter a world of expertly strewn clutter. Through the window, the sun's rays scream after being devoured by mounds of menacing clothes. On the opposite wall, the contents of a small bookshelf are hidden by a variety of dirty hand towels and dingy, white socks thrown with total disregard for place or space. The child's twin bed has been replaced by a futon, although you would never know it; unfortunately, it is hidden somewhere beneath a collection of wet bath towels, rumpled jackets, sweaty caps, and unmentionable underwear. The Salvation Army would reject such a donation.

3   The smell of leftover late night snacks mixed with the dirty laundry creates a smell that reminds you of four-year-old gym shoes left in the trunk of a car during a ninety degree summer day. The smell of the aquarium, filled with green water, penetrates even the thick, plaster walls. Five or six soda cups with

mold floating on the surface of the remaining liquid are buried beneath the trash like little landmines ready to expel their contents on an unwary victim. The tops of the dresser and chest of drawers are covered with a thick layer of dust that gives off a musty odor like that of a moldy swamp. Flowery deodorizing sprays are defused by the overpowering stench. Rats from the city dump refuse to live here.

4   It appears as if a tornado has ripped through the room. A dizzying patchwork of schoolbooks and accessories, comic books, CDs, discarded candy wrappers, and scraps of paper has consumed and replaced the carpet. In the corner, a bean bag chair is a mutant grape jellybean, and the inflatable footrest is like a shriveled plum. The closet door refuses to close, as if it might injure the shoes spilling out from within, and the window blind cannot reach the sill because an old phone book, bent and ripped, lays on it like a wounded accordion. Passersby shield their eyes rather than risk looking inside and possibly being traumatized for life.

5   Older sisters often see young boys as stereotypical slobs. While boys consider their bedrooms their own private worlds, others consider the offensive cubicles health hazards. In the future, if a young boy is not severely punished for polluting the household environment for everyone else, especially an older sister, the fall of Western Civilization cannot be too far off.

Descriptive Technique Questions

1. Identify the thesis sentence by listing the topic, the controlling idea or attitude, and the three-item essay map.

Topic:

the room

Attitude:

disarrayed

Essay Map Items:

piles of clothes

foul stench

scattered debris

2. How serious do you think the author is in suggesting that young boys should be severely punished if they don't keep their rooms neat? Point out some passages that might suggest an answer.

The author often uses humorous hyperbole (exaggeration) to end each of

the body paragraphs: "The Salvation Army would reject such a donation";

"Rats from the city dump refuse to live here"; "Passersby shield their eyes

rather than risk looking inside and possibly being traumatized for life."

3. Underline as many similes and metaphors as you can find. How do they help support the writer's attitude about young boys and their rooms?

Answers will vary.

_____

_____

_____

_____

4. Point out as many sensory images as you can. How do they help develop the writer's attitude about boys and their rooms?

Answers will vary.

_____

_____

_____

_____

5. Sentence variety helps to create rhythm and to connect related ideas. Identify different types of coordinated and subordinated sentences.

Answers will vary.

_____

_____

_____

_____

Sample Professional Essay: EL HOYO

Mario Suarez

Although written in his first year of college at the University of Arizona, this essay by Mario Suarez is as professional as any you will ever read. It was published in the _Arizona Quarterly_. Suarez's audience was probably not very familiar with the Latino culture and some of the words he uses. Also, some of the words, like _barrio_, probably had negative connotations for the reader. To create a more positive image of the Latino culture, Suarez builds one positive event upon another with unrelenting descriptive imagery until the dignity of the chicano shines through the rubble and the squalor.

Vocabulary

Meaning comes primarily from words. Before you start to read, use a dictionary to look up the definitions for the following words appearing in the essay.

benevolent	bicker	conquistador	famine
imply	inundated	solace	solicited

See the Glossary at the end of the story for an explanation of words marked with an asterisk (*).

El Hoyo

1   From the center of downtown Tucson the ground slopes gently away to Main Street, drops a few feet, and then rolls to the banks of the Santa Cruz River. Here lies the section of the city known as El Hoyo. Why it is called El Hoyo is not very clear. In no sense is it a hole as its name would imply; it is simply the river's immediate valley. Its inhabitants are chicanos who raise hell on Saturday night and listen to Padre Estanislao on Sunday morning. While the term chicano is the short way of saying Mexican, it is not restricted to the paisanos who came from old Mexico with the territory or the last famine to work for the railroad, labor, sing, and go on relief. Chicano is the easy way of referring to everybody. Pablo Gutierrez married the Chinese grocer's daughter and now runs a meat department; his sons are chicanos. So are the sons of Killer Jones who threw a fight in Harlem and fled to El Hoyo to marry Cristina Mendez. And so are all of them. However, it is doubtful that all these spiritual sons of Mexico live in El Hoyo because they love each other—many fight and bicker constantly. It is doubtful they live in El Hoyo because of its scenic beauty—it is everything but beautiful. Its houses are simple affairs of unplastered adobe, wood, and abandoned car parts. Its narrow streets are mostly clearings which have, in time, acquired names. Except for some tall trees which nobody has ever cared to identify, nurse, or destroy, the main things known to grow in the general area are weeds, garbage piles, dark-eyed chavalos,* and dogs. And it is doubtful that the chicanos live in El Hoyo because it is safe—many times the Santa Cruz has risen and inundated the area.

2   In other respects living in El Hoyo has its advantages. If one is born with weakness for acquiring bills, El Hoyo is where the collectors are less likely to find you. If one has acquired the habit of listening to Octavio Perea's Mexican Hour in the wee hours of the morning with the radio on at full blast, El Hoyo is where you are less likely to be reported to the authorities. Besides, Perea is very popular and sooner or later to everyone "Smoke in the Eyes" is dedicated between the pinto beans and white flour commercials. If one, for any reason whatever, comes on an extended period of hard times, where, if not in El Hoyo, are the neighbors more willing to offer solace? When Teofila Malacara's house burned to the ground with all her belongings and two children, a benevolent gentleman carried through the gesture that made tolerable her burden. He made a list of 500 names and solicited from each a dollar. At the end of a month he turned over to the tearful but grateful señora* $100 in cold cash and then accompanied her on a short vacation. When the new manager of a local store decided that no more chicanas were to work behind the counters, it was the chicanos of El Hoyo who, on taking their individually small but collectively great buying power elsewhere, drove the manager out and the girls returned to their jobs. When the Mexican Army was en route to Baja California and the chicanos found out that the enlisted men ate only at infrequent intervals, it was El Hoyo's chicanos who crusaded across town with pots of beans and trays of tortillas to meet the train. When someone gets married, celebrating is not restricted to the immediate

friends of the couple. Everybody is invited. Anything calls for a celebration and a celebration calls for anything. On Memorial Day there are no less than half a dozen good fights at the Riverside Dance Hall. On Mexican Independence Day more than one flag is sworn allegiance to amid cheers for the queen.

3   And El Hoyo is something more. It is this something more which brought Felipe Suarez back from the wars after having killed a score of Vietnamese with his body resembling a patchwork quilt to marry Julia Armijo. It brought Joe Zepeda, a gunner, …back to compose boleros.* He has a metal plate for a skull. Perhaps El Hoyo is proof that those people exist, and perhaps exist best, who have as yet failed to observe the more popular modes of human conduct. Perhaps the humble appearance of El Hoyo justifies the indifferent shrug of those made aware of its existence. Perhaps El Hoyo's simplicity motivates an occasional chicano to move away from its narrow streets, babbling comrades, and shrieking children to deny the bloodwell from which he springs and to claim the blood of a conquistador while his hair is straight and his face beardless. Yet El Hoyo is not an outpost of a few families against the world. It fights for no causes except those which soothe its immediate angers. It laughs and cries with the same amount of passion in times of plenty and of want.

4   Perhaps El Hoyo, its inhabitants, and its essence can best be explained by telling a bit about a dish called capirotada. Its origin is uncertain. But, according to the time and the circumstance, it is made of old, new or hard bread. It is softened with water and then cooked with peanuts, raisins, onions, cheese, and panocha.* It is fired with sherry wine. Then it is served hot, cold, or just "on the weather" as they say in El Hoyo. The Sermenos like it one way, the Garcias another, and the Ortegas still another. While it might differ greatly from one home to another, nevertheless it is still capirotada. And so it is with El Hoyo's chicanos. While being divided from within and from without, like the capirotada, they remain chicanos.

Glossary of Terms

chavalos = young man; lad   boleros = a type of dance
señora = Mrs.; woman   panocha = corn

Descriptive Technique Questions

1. Suarez describes *what* El Hoyo is by examining many aspects of the community. Point out examples of *where* El Hoyo is, *who* lives there, *how* the inhabitants live there, and *why*.

   It's located in Tucson near the banks of the Santa Cruz River (¶ 1); predominantly chicanos, with some African Americans, and some Chinese (¶ 1); they live in small houses made from unplastered adobe, wood, and abandoned car parts (¶ 1) amid the loud radios (¶ 2) and screaming children (¶ 3); not because it is beautiful or they love each other (¶ 1) but perhaps to escape bill collectors and to live by others willing to help because they all know what hard times are like (¶ 2).

2. In the last paragraph, Suarez describes chicanos by comparing them to something else. Describe the details of the comparison. In what other parts of the essay do you find details to support your answer?

He compares chicanos to a food dish called capirotada because its origins

are uncertain, it is comprised of ingredients both old, new, and hard, and

it often absorbs alcohol. No matter how it is prepared, often different in

each household, it is still capirotada. Other answers will vary.

3. What do you think Suarez's purpose is for writing the essay? Is his thesis implied, or can you find a sentence that states his thesis?

Answers will vary.

4. Considering all the description about El Hoyo, what dominant impression do you think Suarez is trying to create in the reader's mind?

Answers will vary.

5. How do you think Suarez feels about El Hoyo? Is the image he creates positive or negative? Support your answer with specific details from the essay.

Answers will vary.

6. Create a thesis sentence with a three-item essay map for "El Hoyo." Use the dominant impression you chose for your answer in Question 4 above as the attitude in the thesis sentence.

Answers will vary.

Critical Thinking Writing Opportunities

1. In "Warning: Biohazard!" student writer Angie Bunch's *point of view* or *frame of reference* (the big sister to what she considers a slovenly younger brother) influences how she feels about her brother's room, and it provides her with intimate insight and detail about the room she describes in the essay. The depth of her knowledge and familiarity with her brother's room also allow her to create many wonderful metaphors, similes, and personifications (figurative language devices) that help establish the humorous quality of the essay.

Write an essay describing a room that is not yours but about which you have considerable knowledge. Create metaphors, similes, and personifications to explore your feelings about the room and its inhabitant.

2. One of the important elements in thinking critically is to have a *purpose* to your writing. Suarez's essay is not simply a description of a neighborhood with which he is familiar. For instance, he may be attempting to familiarize his readers with an environment they might not be familiar with or about which they may have a misunderstanding. He might be describing the neighborhood with an eye toward convincing his readers that this environment is not one we need to fear but one that could use our financial help or some other kind of understanding.

Write an essay describing a neighborhood or area with which you are familiar. This can be a place where you once lived or the one in which you currently reside. You will most likely want to include descriptions of the houses or apartment buildings, the businesses, the surrounding neighborhood and environs, and the people living there. After you have completed your prewriting techniques, create a thesis sentence that expresses the underlying purpose for writing your descriptive essay.

Topics for a Descriptive Essay

Here are some possible topics for descriptive writing assignments. Remember, descriptive writing has purpose, so don't forget to create a thesis sentence with an appropriate attitude. Use an essay map to organize the topics for your body paragraphs. Be certain that all specific information supports your topic sentences.

1. A spectacular event, such as a fireworks display or a lightning storm, or a famous event in history (the attack on Pearl Harbor or the marriage of Britain's Prince Charles and Diana).

2. A messy desk.

3. A piece of art, such as a painting or sculpture.

4. A holiday event, such as Christmas or Thanksgiving.

5. A bustling office.

6. An ethnic restaurant.

7. A busy street or intersection (this can be a famous location, such as London's Piccadilly Circus or New York's Times Square).

8. A nature setting.

9. A famous building or monument.

10. An interesting or unusual person (this can be a famous historical person).

11. Describe what you have seen under a microscope in a biology class (for example: blood cells, amoebae or paramecia, a strand of hair, or an insect's wing).

Chapter Review

■ Description is a technique that creates images in the reader's mind by using specific details. Description can be objective or factual, or it can be subjective, evoking an emotion or mood. Good descriptive writing makes a dominant impression, creating a single mood or emotion.

■ The topic sentence of a subjective description paragraph states the dominant impression, and all the details support the dominant impression. Supporting details in descriptive writing include sensory images and figurative language—similes, metaphors, and personification.

■ In the introductory paragraph of a descriptive essay, the dominant impression is the controlling idea or attitude to the topic as a whole, and the body paragraphs focus on the items in the essay map. Evaluation is often used as the approach to the concluding paragraph.

Visit *The Write Start* Online!

For additional practice with the materials found in this chapter, visit our Website at

http://www.ablongman.com/checkett

The Website also features additional readings, quizzes, writing activities, and Internet links, as well as a bulletin board and interactive chat.

CHAPTER 8

The Narrative Essay

To use **narration** is to tell a story, either to entertain or to inform. Narration can be made up, like a fictional short story or novel, or it can be nonfiction, the retelling of an incident that actually happened. When you listen to a news program, the anchor narrates the day's events to you, perhaps reporting how an airplane disaster was averted, or explaining the background of the Supreme Court's latest legal decision. If you read a novel, you are reading a narrative.

Identifying Your Purpose

In college, you will be asked to write narrative essays quite frequently. In English classes, your instructor might ask you to retell an incident from your own life. In a science class, you might be asked to recount how a famous experiment led to an important discovery, such as Marie and Pierre Curie's discovery of radium. In a history course, you might be asked to write about a famous event, such as Germany's invasion of Poland that started World War II. Whatever the writing assignment, the narrative, like all writing, must have a purpose.

Writing the Narrative Paragraph

In addition to recounting events, the narrative paragraph must indicate why the events are important. Techniques for writing an effective narrative paragraph include using the six reporters' questions to focus the narrative and using transitional expressions to sequence the events being recounted.

The Topic Sentence and the Point of the Story

There must be a point to every narrative paragraph; otherwise, the reader will lose interest in it. Narrative writing, then, must have a clear point or purpose. This might seem obvious, but too many writers lose sight of it. The topic sentence of a narrative paragraph should announce the subject and clarify what is interesting about the subject. That interest is the **point of the story.**

Exhibit 8.1
The Point of the Story

Topic Sentence ⟶

Subject: abuse
Point of the story: abuse can change the victim's life

The Paragraph:

From the first moment I felt his large, cold hand strike my face, my life changed forever. For the first six months of our marriage, I truly believed he was my dream partner for a lifetime. I had done nothing wrong—I thought I was the perfect wife. I worked a 40-hour-a-week job, did the food shopping, house cleaning, cooking, and even made snacks for his weekly poker parties. He was tall, dark, blonde with blue eyes, and at first he seemed as perfect as a person could be but, at the end of six months, he was the devil in disguise. I have never been able wholly to trust another person since.

PRACTICE 1

Answers will vary.

Write a narrative topic sentence for each of the following subjects. Be certain that the sentence expresses the point of the story, the idea that will keep the reader's interest. You will have to make up the point of each story.

1. Visiting a new place

_____

_____

_____

2. An important event

_____

_____

_____

3. An important person

_____

_____

_____

Supporting Details: The Six Reporters' Questions

Once you have chosen the subject and the point of the story, you must decide how to develop the subject. What details, facts, and examples will develop the ideas and get the point of the story across? The simplest method to develop the subject and maintain focus is to use the six reporters' questions: who, what, where, when, why, and how. (See Chapter 4 for a review of the six reporters' questions.)

For the topic sentence example in Exhibit 8.1, the developing focus could be any of the following.

Examples

Who: Who was affected by the abuse?

As the topic sentence states, the writer was.

What: What was the abuse?

The abuse was physical, but the paragraph might also detail emotional abuse.

Where: Where did the abuse take place?

Although the inference is "in the home," abuse at other locations might be explored.

When: When did the abuse take place?

In this paragraph, the abuse took place early in the marriage.

Why: Why did the abuse take place?

The writer states that she did not do anything to cause the violence. Something in the husband's experience may have to be examined.

How: How did the abuse happen?

The abuse may have happened spontaneously, or a pattern of behavior may have preceded it.

From the list of examples, the answers to *who, where,* and *when* may be fairly obvious or they may be the least important of the factors. Thus, they probably do not need to be developed. The most important factors to develop would be *what* (the emotional abuse might be even more damaging over the long run than the physical abuse), *why* (why did the abuse occur), and *how* (what were the patterns of behavior that led up to the abuse). Other ideas might come to your mind as you ask these questions, and you can pick and choose depending upon your own experience.

Model Paragraphs

The three model paragraphs that follow were developed for the topic sentence in Exhibit 8.1 on page 73 using the three focus questions *what, why,* and *how.*

Focus on What: developing the emotional effects stemming from the physical abuse.

Topic Sentence ⟶ The daily physical beatings took their toll. Their effects were short-lived compared to the devastating emotional effects that remain with me till this day. I used to be a very trusting individual.

> I would lend my car or give money to almost anyone if they were in need. My first thoughts about people were that they were as kind and generous as I was. If I showed kindness to someone, I expected the same in return. Now I am suspicious of everyone. It doesn't matter how good or nice they are to me. In the back of my mind there is a fear of what monster might crouch hidden behind the friendly mask looking at me. People have become like the famous creature of literature—Dr. Jekyll and Mr. Hyde.

In this paragraph, the topic is developed by those details that support the "what" focus question: the narrator used to be trusting; she would lend her car or money; she thought people were as kind and generous as she was; but now she is suspicious of people; she sees everyone as having a hidden personality.

Focus on Why: developing the reasons for the abuse.

Topic Sentence →
> <u>From the beginning, I couldn't figure out why he was abusing me.</u> I had done everything possible to please him and to keep a good home. It wasn't until after the divorce that his sister confided in me. My husband had been physically abused when he was a child. It turns out that his father was an alcoholic who had trouble keeping a job. He took his troubles out on Dennis. I have since learned that almost all abusers were abused as children—a terrible cycle of pain for everyone involved.

In this paragraph, the topic is developed by those details that support the "why" focus question: at first, the narrator could not figure out why the abuse was occurring; later she learned that her husband had been abused by an alcoholic father and that abused children grow up to be adults who abuse.

Focus on How: developing the patterns of behavior that led up to the abuse.

Topic Sentence →
> <u>Thinking back about how each of the horrible attacks occurred, I have come to the conclusion that each encounter was preceded by my husband being angry about something else, not me.</u> He struck me when we had been discussing what bills to pay immediately and what bills could wait. He was angry that we couldn't pay them all at once. An attack came immediately after he had returned home from work. His boss had chewed him out because he had shipped some materials to the wrong buyer. Each time something made him angry, he took his anger out on me. It could be something as big as his boss threatening to fire him or something as small as bird droppings on his car. It didn't matter. I became the object of his anger.

In this paragraph, the topic is developed by those details that support the "how" focus question: the attacks were preceded by the husband being angry at things other than his wife, such as not being able to pay all the bills, his boss getting angry at him, and bird droppings on his car.

The important thing to remember is that each paragraph develops the same general topic—abuse—yet the topic is developed using information that places emphasis on a different aspect of the abuse.

Using the narrative topic sentences you created in Practice 1, write a narrative paragraph for each. Choose one of the six reporters' questions (who, what, where, when, why, and how) to develop the topic for each paragraph.

Using Transitional Expressions to Order Events

Narrative writing tells a story. Therefore, it is important to present the events of the story in proper order so that the reader can remain focused without being confused about the sequence of how things happened. To help keep track of the chronological order of events, you need to use **transitional expressions.** Transitional expressions connect related ideas appropriately, and they also add rhythm to your writing.

Transitional Expressions for Narration		
after	first, second,…	soon
afterward	last(ly)	then
as	later	thus
as soon as	meanwhile	upon
before	next	when

Transitional expressions are simply words and phrases that indicate when one event happens in relation to another. When transitional expressions are added to the Focus on How paragraph, they help keep the events in chronological order, add rhythm, and connect related ideas.

Example

Thinking back about how each of the horrible attacks occurred, I have come to the conclusion that each encounter was preceded by my husband being angry about something else, not me. The **first** time he struck me was **when** we had been discussing what bills to pay immediately and what bills could wait. He was angry that we couldn't pay them all at once. The **next** attack came immediately **after** he had returned home from work. **Upon** arriving at work, his boss had chewed him out because he had shipped some materials to the wrong buyer. **Afterward,** each time something made him angry, he took his anger out on me. It could be something as big as his boss threatening to fire him, or something as small as bird droppings on his car. It didn't matter. I always became the object of his anger.

Add at least three transitional expressions to each of the paragraphs you wrote in Practice 2. Choose the expressions that help order the events chronologically and connect related ideas appropriately.

Moving from Paragraph to Essay

Now that you have studied and practiced the techniques to create effective narration, it is time to expand your ideas by writing a narrative essay. The narrative essay is a union of the techniques you learned in Part 1 regarding developing the essay paragraphs and the narration techniques you have just learned. Return to Part 1 if you need to review the instruction concerning writing the essay.

Creating the Introductory Paragraph

Even though narration is the retelling of an event, don't let the reader become lost in a myriad of details, facts, and examples. Be certain that the purpose of the story remains the focus of the story. Your story should have a thesis around which the events unfold.

The thesis in the narration essay should blend naturally into the rest of the introductory paragraph. In the following introductory paragraph for a narrative essay, the thesis identifies the topic (drinking and driving), the writer's attitude about the topic (negative consequences arise from this activity), and the essay map containing the subtopics that will be developed in the body paragraphs (risking your life, risking the lives of others, and the possibility of a lifelong injury). The thesis sentence in the example is underlined for instructional purposes only.

> **Example**
>
> It started out as a night full of anticipation. My four best friends and I were driving to a high school graduation party. We knew there would be some drinking at the party, but we never suspected how it would impact our lives. Why would we? We were young and fearless—invincible! We had all of our lives ahead of us. At least that's what we thought as we began the evening looking forward to another rite of passage. But risking your life, risking the lives of others, and the possibility of a lifelong injury are negative consequences of drinking and driving.

Notice that while the story will be about the night of revelry by the group of graduating high school seniors, the point of the story (the story's purpose) will be the negative consequences of drinking and driving.

Creating the Body Paragraphs

For an essay on drinking and driving, the focus of the body paragraphs will be the paragraph topics listed in the thesis sentence's essay map. The first body paragraph's topic will be "risking your life," the second body paragraph's topic will be "risking the lives of others," and the third body paragraph's topic will be "the possibility of a lifelong injury." Remember, as you write about each of these topics, your focus should be that these are the *negative consequences of drinking and driving*. Your focus should not be on medical expenses or the need for tougher national drunk driving laws. Keep your focus on the point of the story: the negative *physical* possibilities stemming from driving drunk.

Creating the Concluding Paragraph

The approach of the concluding paragraph should flow naturally from the essay's main topic. Because this essay's focus is the negative consequences stemming from drinking and driving, a *warning* would seem an appropriate choice for the concluding paragraph. You might identify other negative consequences that might come from driving under the influence. Unlike the body paragraphs, the concluding paragraph is the proper place to mention medical expenses, the effects on family and friends should you be killed, or the potential legal problems that can occur if you are convicted of a related crime in a court of law. Other, more positive narrative essay topics might lend themselves to *prediction* rather than warning in the concluding paragraph. (Refer to Chapter 5 for other approaches for concluding paragraphs.)

Sample Student Essay: SMALL-TOWN VIEWS

Matt Grant

The following essay, "Small-Town Views," by student writer Matt Grant, recounts the author's trip to a small town on the U.S.-Canada border. Having lived his entire life in large cities, the author, like most Americans, believed that small towns were very different from large ones. Instead of vast differences, what he found were many similarities making the differences more exaggerated than they would otherwise seem.

Vocabulary

Meaning comes primarily from words. Before you begin reading, use a dictionary to look up the definitions of the following words that appear in the essay.

majestic	obscurity	perception
propane	quaint	sprawl

Small-Town Views

1   Perceptions of a small town all too often are the same. Moviemakers create the ideal vision of what a rural American town should look like, and society believes what moviemakers create: a single, white, steepled church in the middle of town surrounded by a few streets, mostly named for the trees that front small brick and clapboard houses. No brightly lit neon signs, no high-rise office buildings, and no multiplex cinema showing twelve movies almost twenty-four hours a day. I've lived in a large town most of my life; my experience with small towns only involves driving by them on vacation. What I've seen during my "passerby" trips has given me the same perception as most of society. However, all that would change after I made my first extended visit to a small town on the U.S.-Canada border. The buildings in the town, my relative's house where I stayed, and the streets and roads in and around town forever altered my view of the small town.

2   The town of Sault Ste. Marie (pronounced Soo Saint Marie) appeared small, at first. But soon, a drive down the main four-lane road through town revealed a McDonalds, a Burger King, a Wendy's, an Arby's, an Applebees, and a Cracker Barrel. Then, as I continued on, I saw separating the national restaurant chain outlets a variety of stores and businesses, including four car and two boat dealerships. So far, I could be back home, driving down any main drag in

any suburban area. Next, a fairly new Wal-Mart stood out as one of the larger buildings. On top of a large, grassy hill, Lake Superior State College sat facing the divided highway that passed by the edge of town. Meanwhile, to the north, the Soo Locks controlled the busy and bustling river port traffic on the St. Mary River. The town was as cosmopolitan as St. Louis or Cincinnati.

3   Later, I drove from the center of town to my aunt and uncle's house, where I would be staying for the week. Their "house" turned out to be a quaint two-bedroom trailer among a whole subdivision of trailers. Not exactly the turn-of-the-century, solidly built homes one would expect from looking at movies depicting small-town America. After dinner, they took me for a walk. The homes lined a white rock road, and each house sat on a small lot set back a little ways into the woods that surrounded the trailer park. Gas lines were unavailable, so a large propane gasoline tank flanked each home. Without cable television, satellite dishes sprouted in the back yards like some strange, mutant plant. Upon returning to their house, we sat on the small, concrete patio and watched as millions of stars twinkled brightly without the obscurity of city lights; moreover, the silence was deafening. Suddenly, I wasn't in Kansas City anymore, Toto.

4   As soon as I awoke, I went for a drive. Unlike objects in your rearview mirror, objects at a distance appear smaller and, at fifteen miles out, the town seemed to disappear. I began to notice things that would not be seen in a large town. The roads leading away from the highway, like "6 mile," were named for the number of miles the road was from the town center. Subdivisions with miles of winding concrete streets did not exist. The homes were either located on acres of land out by the highway or, like my aunt and uncle's place, cramped together on small lots no bigger than half a basketball court lining a gravel strip that looked more like a dried-up creek bed than a thoroughfare. Traffic did not seem to exist at any time of day or night even though there were only two roads leading in and out of town.

5   When my week's stay was up, I said my good-byes and headed toward town. I grabbed lunch at one of the fast food drive-thrus and parked alongside the river. I watched as the lake freighters locked down and passed through the narrow channel as they headed up river. As I drove away on the southbound highway, Sault Ste. Marie seemed a bit of a puzzle to me. When I was driving through the town, it seemed fairly large, but the more I drove away from it, the smaller it seemed. I guess that's the magic of illusion. It all depends on your perspective.

Narrative Technique Questions

1. What do you think is the point of the story?

Often, our initial or long-held beliefs and perceptions are changed when

our involvement becomes more intimate. (Other similar ideas may be

expressed.)

2. Which of the six reporters' questions does the writer use most often to develop the story? Give examples.

***Where*: the author uses specific locations to compare small and large**

towns. For example, "main four-lane road through town," "back home,"

"main drag," "suburban area," "On top of a large, grassy knoll," "edge of

town," "to the north," (¶ 2); "the center of town," "a whole subdivision,"

"small-town America," "a white rock road," "small lot set back a little ways

into the woods," (¶ 3); "fifteen miles out," "the town," "roads leading away

from the highway," "a number of miles...from the town center," "land out

by the highway," "a dried-up creek bed" (¶ 4).

3. Identify the three essay map subtopics in the thesis sentence. Are they clearly stated in the topic sentence of each body paragraph?

"The buildings in the town," "my relative's house where I stayed," and "the

streets and roads in and around the town." Not in the first body paragraph;

the town buildings begin to be mentioned in the second and subsequent

sentences. In the second body paragraph the answer is yes. Not in the

third body paragraph; the roads are not mentioned until the fourth

sentence.

4. The writer uses many transitional expressions. List at least five of them. How does each transitional expression help order the events chronologically?

Answers will vary.

5. Sentence variety helps to create rhythm and to connect related ideas. Identify different types of coordinated and subordinated sentences.

Answers will vary.

Sample Professional Essay: I HAVE A GUN

Tania Nyman

> This essay was written in 1989 when New Orleans was becoming the murder capital of the United States. The *Times-Picayune* newspaper published this essay by Tania Nyman, a young, single woman living in New Orleans, because excessive violence makes many people feel exactly as she does. The essay also presents a paradox (a seeming contradiction) in that the author felt just as frightened when she had the ability to defend herself as she felt when she was defenseless.

Vocabulary

Meaning comes primarily from words. Before you start to read, use a dictionary to look up the definitions for the following words appearing in the essay.

capable	confrontation	immune	intimidating
nonchalantly	omitted	paranoid	scenario

I Have a Gun

1   I have a gun, a .38 caliber that holds five bullets. It is black with a brown handle and it stays by my bed.

2   I don't want a gun. I don't even like guns. But it seems I need one.

3   I've always believed in gun control, and the funny thing is I still do. But my gun is loaded next to my bed.

4   It wasn't ignorance of crime statistics that previously kept me from owning a gun. Nor was it the belief that I was immune to violence.

5   I thought that because I didn't believe in violence, that because I wasn't violent, I wouldn't be touched by violence. I believed that my belief in the best of human nature could make it real.

6   I want to believe in a world where people do not need to protect themselves from one another. But I have a gun, and it stays by my bed.

7   I should carry the gun from my house to my car, but I don't. What the gun is capable of, what the gun is for, still frightens me more than what it is supposed to prevent.

8   If I carry my gun and I am attacked, I must use it. I cannot shoot to injure. I must shoot to kill.

9   I have confronted an attacker not in reality but in my imagination. The man is walking down the street. To prove I am not paranoid, I lock my car and walk to my door with house key ready.

10   Before I reach the steps, I think I hear a voice. "Money." I turn to see the man with the gun.

11   He is frightened. I am frightened. I am frightened that I will scare him and he will shoot. I am frightened that I will give him my money and he will shoot.

12   I am frightened, but I am angry. I am angry because there is a gun pointed at me by someone I've never met and never hurt.

13   There is something that bothers me about this robbery I have created in my head. It is something that makes me uncomfortable with myself. It is something I don't want to admit, something I almost intentionally omitted because I am ashamed.

14   I guess I understand why I imagine being robbed by a man. They're physically more intimidating and I've never heard of anyone being robbed by a woman, though I'm sure it happens. But I'm being robbed by a man.

15   But why is he a black man? Why is he a black man with a worn T-shirt and glassy eyes? Why do I not imagine being robbed by a white man?

16   I am standing in a gas station on Claiborne and Jackson waiting to pay the cashier when a black man walks up behind me. I do not turn around. I stare in front of me waiting to pay. I try not to admit that I am nervous because a black man has walked up behind me in a gas station in a bad neighborhood and he does not have a car.

17   There is another scenario I imagine. I am walking to my door with my gun in my hand and I hear the voice. The man mustn't have seen my gun. I get angry because I am threatened, because someone is endangering my life for the money in my pocket.

18   I turn and without really thinking, angry and frightened, I shoot. I kill a man for $50. Or it could be $100. It does not matter that he was trying to rob me. A man has died for money. Not my money or his money, just money. Who put the price on his life, he or I?

19   I remember driving one night with my friend in her parents' car. We stop at a red light at Carollton and Tulane and a black man is crossing the street in front of us. My friend quickly but nonchalantly locks the doors with the power lock.

20   I am disgusted that she sees the man as a reminder to lock her doors. I wonder if he noticed the two girls nonchalantly lock their doors. I wonder how it feels to have people lock their doors at the sight of you.

21   I imagine again a confrontation in front of my house. I have my gun when the man asks for money. I am angry and scared, but I do not use the gun. I am afraid of what may happen to me if I don't use it, but I am more afraid of killing another human being, more afraid of trying to live with the guilt of murdering another person. I bet my life that he will take my money and leave, and I hope I win.

22   I am in a gas station on St. Charles and South Carollton near my house and there is a black man waiting to pay the cashier. I walk up behind him to wait in line and he jumps and turns around.

23   When he sees me, he relaxes and says I scared him because of the way things have gotten in this neighborhood.

24   "Sorry," I say and smile. I realize I am not the only one who is frightened.

Narrative Technique Questions

1. Even though there is no thesis sentence in this essay, state what you think the point of the story is. Which of the author's statements leads you to this conclusion?

Answers will vary.

_____

_____

_____

_____

2. The paragraphs in the essay are very short, unlike those you find in most essays. In order to give the reader a clearer sense of the topic and the author's attitude about the topic, which paragraphs would you combine to make an introductory paragraph?

Answers will vary. However, good candidates would be the first six

paragraphs because they set up the main problem at the heart of the

essay: a person who believes in nonviolence feels forced to carry a

weapon.

3. Which of the six reporters' questions does the author use most frequently to develop the supporting detail of the essay?

Why: **why she carries a gun when she believes in nonviolence. She relates**

two imaginary incidents in which she confronts an attacker. These images

frighten her because in both imaginary events, the attackers are males

who are physically intimidating.

4. Most of the sentences are very short and begin with "I." Would the essay have been more effective if the author had used longer paragraphs with transitional expressions to add rhythm and connect related ideas? Point out some examples where this would have added to the essay's effectiveness.

Answers will vary.

5. Is the author racially prejudiced? If so, what do you think has influenced her to feel this way? If your answer is no, point out instances in the narrative that suggest she is not prejudiced.

Answers will vary.

Critical Thinking Writing Opportunities

1. In Matt Grant's essay, "Small-Town Views," his *assumption* leads him to believe that when he visits a small town, he will find it much different from the large city he has grown up in. Write an essay explaining an assumption that you had about a place you visited and whether or not that assumption held true.

2. In the essay "I Have a Gun," by Tania Nyman, the author feels so afraid of the excessive violence in the city where she is living that she comes to the *conclusion* that she must carry a gun to defend herself. However, the *consequences* arising from her decision were unexpected. Rather than feel safe, she feels just as vulnerable and afraid as when she perceived herself as defenseless. Write an essay about an event in your life wherein you came to a conclusion, took action, but the results you expected never came to pass.

Topics for a Narrative Essay

Here are some possible topics for narration writing assignments. Remember, your narrative essay should have a clearly defined point or purpose to it.

1. Being different from those around you (at work, school, or in your neighborhood).

2. A friend or loved one not sensitive to your needs.

3. An incident that challenged your opinion about something or someone.

4. A trip where you discovered something about yourself or the place you visited that you weren't aware of.

5. What a pet meant to you or your family.

6. A time when you were very lonely or very happy.

7. An event at which you or someone else were heroic.

8. A medical procedure or problem and its effects on you or your loved ones.

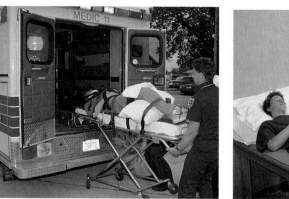
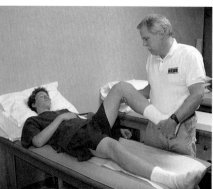

9. How a story you read or a movie or play you went to affected your view of life.

10. How the life of someone you know, or know of, affected your view of yourself.

Chapter Review

■ A narrative essay tells a story, fictional or true. An effective narrative has a point, a reason that the story is important.

■ Techniques for writing narrative paragraphs include stating the point of the narrative in the topic sentence, using the six reporters' questions to focus the narrative, and using transitional expressions to order events.

■ In a narrative essay, the thesis sentence should state the point of the story as well as lay out the essay map. The body paragraphs pick up the topics of the essay map. The last paragraph can use any of the techniques for concluding paragraphs, but warning and prediction are often suitable for concluding a narrative essay.

Visit *The Write Start* Online!

For additional practice with the materials found in this chapter, visit our Website at

http://www.ablongman.com/checkett

The Website also features additional readings, quizzes, writing activities, and Internet links, as well as a bulletin board and interactive chat.

CHAPTER 9

The Example Essay

Using **example** is one of the most popular and effective methods for developing an essay topic. Good examples can help focus the reader's attention and illustrate a topic quickly and clearly. Maybe you've heard a friend say, "School isn't any fun!" Your first thought might be to ask why your friend feels this way. You might ask her what specifically makes her feel the way she does. Your friend will probably respond by giving you examples: the teachers are uncaring, there's too much homework, the tests are too difficult, and the teachers assign too many papers. By giving you specific examples, your friend supports and clarifies her general critical view about her school experience.

Identifying Your Purpose

Detailed examples are used to illustrate, clarify, convince, or make concrete a general idea about a subject. Most people find specific, concrete examples easier to understand than general concepts. For instance, the topics in Exhibit 9.1 are accompanied by a list of examples that can be used to develop the subject.

**Exhibit 9.1
Detail through
Examples**

Topic	Examples
clothing	formal, casual, athletic
food	ethnic, holiday, diet
airplanes	acrobatic, commercial, military
politicians	mayors, presidents, senators
glasses	reading, bifocals, sun

**Exhibit 9.2
The Adaptable
Airplane**

Exhibit 9.2 is an example paragraph using one of the topics and specific examples taken from Exhibit 9.1.

Topic Sentence ⟶

Airplanes have many uses besides transporting travelers. At county fairs

and Fourth of July celebrations, the festivities often include a demonstration of aerial acrobatics. Usually, either a single biplane or a team of biplanes will dive and tumble their way through a series of flight patterns designed to bring "oohs" and "aahs" from the crowd below. Airplanes, since early in the 20th century, have been used to deliver mail. Big companies, such as FedEx and UPS, owe much of their success to the airplane because it allows them to deliver mail overnight, instead of the normal three to five days. Of course, no one uses the airplane more extensively than the military. Fighters, bombers, refueling tankers, cargo transports, and communication jets are only a few of the planes the armed services use to complete their varied missions.

PRACTICE 1

Using one of the other topics in Exhibit 9.1, make a list of three examples that you could use to develop the subject you have chosen. Next, write a paragraph using your chosen examples to develop the topic.

Writing the Example Paragraph

An example paragraph should include both the general topic under discussion as well as the examples that develop the topic. The six reporters' questions can be used to focus the discussion, and transitional expressions can help identify examples.

The Topic Sentence in an Example Paragraph

The topic sentence in an example paragraph states the general topic to be discussed and the controlling idea or attitude that will guide the development of the paragraph.

The controlling idea is a statement that tells the reader what your focus will be as you develop the topic and how you feel about it (your attitude). In Exhibit 9.2, the topic is *airplanes*, and the controlling idea is that *they have many uses besides transporting travelers.*

PRACTICE 2

Underline the topic once and the controlling idea or attitude twice in the topic sentences that follow.

1. Cybersex is becoming a popular activity.

2. Religion is an important aspect of most people's lives.

3. Binge drinking at parties is increasing.

4. Date rape is hard to prove in court.

5. A positive attitude can help fight illness.

6. Plagiarism defeats the purpose of writing assignments.

Supporting Details: The Six Reporters' Questions

To develop the controlling idea, use one of the six reporters' questions (who, what, where, when, why, and how). The reporters' questions will help you focus on how you will develop the topic through developing the controlling idea. In Exhibit 9.2, the controlling idea that airplanes *have many uses* focuses on *what* the airplanes are used for: acrobatic exhibitions, delivering mail, and military missions. Acrobatic exhibitions, delivering mail, and military missions are, therefore, the **examples** used to develop the topic.

PRACTICE 3

Using one of the topic sentences in Practice 2, select one of the six reporters' questions you will use to develop the controlling idea. Second, make a list of three examples that explain the focus you've chosen for developing the controlling idea. Third, write one or more sentences for each of the examples you have chosen. Finally, rewrite your sentences into standard paragraph form.

Using Transitional Expressions to Connect Examples to the Topic

While each example helps to clarify, explain, and develop the topic, **transitional expressions** help to connect the examples to the topic, and they add rhythm to the paragraph. Use transitional expressions so that the examples don't appear merely as a list. Examples should act in unison to develop the subject expressed in the topic sentence.

Transitional Expressions for Example	
a case in point is	for example
another example of	for instance
another instance of	to illustrate
another illustration of	specifically

Look how using transitional expressions can help identify examples, connect related ideas, and add rhythm to the paragraph from Exhibit 9.2.

Airplanes have many uses besides transporting travelers. **For instance,** at county fairs and Fourth of July celebrations, the festivities often include a demonstration of aerial acrobatics. Usually, either a single biplane or a team of biplanes will dive and tumble their way through a series of flight patterns designed to bring "oohs" and "aahs" from the crowd below. Airplanes, since early in the 20th century, have been used to deliver mail. **To illustrate,** big companies, such as FedEx and UPS, owe much of their success to the airplane because it allows them to deliver mail overnight, instead of the normal three to five days. Of course, no one uses the airplane more extensively than the military. **For example,** fighters, bombers, refueling tankers, cargo transports, and communication jets are only a few of the planes the armed services use to complete their varied missions.

In the example paragraph above, the transitional expressions "for instance," "to illustrate," and "for example" are used to announce to the reader that an example is forthcoming. This technique helps to keep the reader focused on the specific example you are using to explain, clarify, and develop the topic.

PRACTICE 4

Using the paragraph you wrote for Practice 3, add at least three transitional expressions to connect related ideas, add rhythm, and announce upcoming examples. After you have finished, compare the two paragraphs. The paragraph with the transitional expressions should be easier to read and understand.

Moving from Paragraph to Essay

Now that you have studied and practiced the techniques to create effective example paragraphs, it is time to expand your ideas to a larger writing unit: the example essay. You will use the techniques you learned in Part 1 regarding developing the essay paragraphs and the example techniques you have just learned to create the example essay. This might be a good time to return to Part 1 and review the techniques for developing the full essay.

Creating the Introductory Paragraph

Because examples are such good devices to clarify ideas, it is easy for a writer to think that there needn't be any special concern regarding the organization and focus of an example essay. However, an example essay is writing, and all writing has specific purpose. Therefore, an example essay needs clearly defined purpose and organization. The thesis sentence in an example essay should state the essay's purpose and organization.

The thesis in an example essay should blend naturally into the rest of the introductory paragraph. In the following introductory paragraph, notice how the thesis sentence announces the topic (*required courses*), the writer's controlling idea about the topic (*are essential to a student's education*), and the essay map containing the body paragraph topics (*refining communication skills, developing a wide range of interests,* and *building practical skills*). The thesis sentence in the example is underlined for instructional purposes only.

Freshman students attending college each fall soon discover that they have few choices in putting together their class schedule. Regardless if they have declared a major field of study, all students find out that they are required to take a minimum number of hours in general course work (introductory courses in history, civics, sociology, and writing, for example) before they can receive a degree. Many students think taking these courses is a waste of time because they have already taken these courses in high school. However, the amount of material covered and the specialized knowledge of college professors makes these courses valuable assets to college students as they prepare themselves for life in college and beyond. Required courses are essential to a student's education because they help refine communication skills, develop a wide range of interests, and build practical skills.

While this essay's topic is *required courses,* the focus of the essay is the idea that the required courses are essential to a student's education.

Creating the Body Paragraphs

For a paper on the "required courses" topic, the focus of the body paragraphs will be the topics listed in the thesis sentence's essay map. The first body paragraph's topic will be "they help refine communication skills," the second body paragraph's topic will be "they help develop a wide range of interests," and the third body paragraph's topic will be "they help build practical skills." Remember, as you write about each of these topics, giving examples, your focus should be that required courses *are essential to a student's education.*

Creating the Concluding Paragraph

The concluding paragraph should flow naturally from the essay's main topic. Because the essay's focus is that required courses are essential for a student's education, a *prediction* would seem an appropriate choice. You might point out that students should not resent taking required courses; rather, if they apply themselves to their required course work, their educational development will be substantially rewarded. The concluding paragraph is the proper place to mention rewards other than those mentioned in the body paragraphs, such as nomination to honor societies, reference letters from teachers, and teaching assistantships during graduate studies.

Sample Student Essay: OPPORTUNITIES IN THE ARMED FORCES

Jennifer Staggs

In today's world of corporate downsizing and job insecurity, many young people are not prepared for the competitive world of job hunting and retention. Even college graduates can find it difficult to find employment because they lack specific skills. In this essay, student writer Jennifer Staggs, who spent four years in the Air Force immediately following high school, suggests that many young people would benefit from a tour in the armed forces. While this particular essay uses many examples to support the thesis, it also uses many descriptive adjectives to help bring the examples to life.

Vocabulary

Meaning comes primarily from words. Before you start reading, use a dictionary to look up the definitions of the following words that appear in the essay.

acquiring	apprehension	burden
distinct	encounter	impeccable
initial	invigorating	propel
rigorous	sculpting	sufficient

Note: Icarus, in Greek mythology, was the son of Daedalus. Trapped in a labyrinth, Icarus attempted to escape by flying out of the labyrinth with wax wings. Although he thought he was properly prepared to be successful, he flew too close to the sun, the wax wings melted, and he fell into the ocean and was drowned.

Opportunities in the Armed Forces

1   Since the days of Icarus, young people have awaited the day to spread their wings and gain freedom and independence; however, although the future may seem sunny and bright, dark clouds can quickly appear on the horizon. An uncertain unemployment environment and the economic burden of college can also create apprehension in both student and parent. Even college graduates have difficulty acquiring employment because they may lack specific skills. Many of these young people do not have the proper advice and guidance from more experienced adults, and they also are unaware of an exciting world awaiting discovery. Because of discipline, travel, and work experience, young people should consider enlisting in the military.   ←— **Thesis with Essay Map**

Topic Sentence ⟶ 2   In the armed forces, a new recruit will encounter many forms of discipline. During basic training, lasting eight to 13 weeks, trainees learn rigorous, invigorating exercises for achieving fitness and sculpting the body's shape. Maintaining a nutritious diet helps to fuel the vigorous routine that the trainee meets with each new day. The recruit will eat three balanced meals each day, including plenty of fruit and fresh vegetables—no more junk food! Most important, the trainee will learn to respect authority and to understand the life-saving elements of teamwork. There is no "I" in "team."

Topic Sentence ⟶ 3   After initial training, overseas assignments or other travel opportunities often become available. Imagine experiencing the mysteries of the Far East, the breathtaking landscapes of Ireland, or the magnificent Rhineland castles of Germany! Gourmet foods, exotic dress, and colorful arts and crafts are just some of the many aspects that make other cultures so fascinating. All the branches of the armed forces have duty stations worldwide that broaden the horizons of military personnel.

Topic Sentence ⟶ 4   The armed forces have an impeccable record of sending veterans out into the civilian world with superior work experience and skills. Because of sufficient funding, the military has some of the best equipment and training in the world. Many veterans return to civilian businesses with the knowledge and experience to operate or repair some of the most up-to-date and sophisticated machinery and electronic equipment in existence. Veterans of the military, because of their operating within a distinct chain of command, bring excellent communication abilities, organization strengths, and teamwork readiness to be successful in whatever work environment they enter. Employers find these "ready-to-work" veterans an invaluable resource for their companies.

5   Following a successful enlistment period, men and women are better prepared for the future. In addition to receiving the best education, honor is

bestowed upon those serving the people of the United States. In the past, many young people have used their military experience to propel themselves into careers in business, industry, and politics. Most of our past and present congresspersons, senators, and presidents have served honorably and proudly in the military. All in all, from any employer's perspective, a veteran is a well-rounded person, an outstanding worker, and a trustworthy citizen.

Example Technique Questions

1. How does the reference to Icarus help the writer establish the seriousness of the topic?

   It exemplifies the idea that young people often have the right spirit and

   enthusiasm, but they often do not have the right skills to be successful.

   Dire consequences can occur.

2. The writer's attitude toward military service is that young people "should consider" it. What are some of the examples the writer uses in the body paragraphs to develop and support this attitude?

   In paragraph 2: "trainees learn rigorous, invigorating exercises for

   achieving fitness," "maintaining a nutritious diet helps fuel the vigorous

   routine," "no more junk food," and "the trainee will learn to respect

   authority and to understand the life-saving elements of teamwork." In

   paragraph 3: "overseas assignments or other travel opportunities," "the

   mysteries of the Far East," "the breathtaking landscapes of Ireland," "the

   magnificent Rhineland castles of Germany," "Gourmet foods," "exotic

   dress," and "many aspects that make other cultures so fascinating." In

   paragraph 4: "The armed forces have an impeccable record of sending

   veterans out into the civilian world with superior work experience and

   skills," "the military has some of the best equipment and training in the

   world," "many veterans return to civilian businesses with the knowledge

   and experience to operate or repair some of the most up-to-date and

   sophisticated machinery and electronic equipment in existence," and

   "Veterans...bring excellent communications abilities, organization

   strengths, and teamwork readiness to be successful in [any] work

   environment."

3. Underline the adjectives in the essay. How do they enhance and support the writer's attitude that serving in the military can be a rewarding experience for young people?

Adjectives such as "rigorous," "invigorating," "nutritious," "vigorous," "balanced" (¶ 2); "breathtaking," "magnificent," "exotic," "colorful," "fascinating" (¶ 3); "impeccable," "superior," "best," "up-to-date," "sophisticated," "excellent," "successful," "invaluable" (¶ 4) are all positive in the attitude that they suggest. This positive attitude supports the idea that serving in the military can be a rewarding experience.

4. List some occupations that young people not going to college might consider exploring. What examples does the writer point out that could help young people have a better chance at success in these occupations?

Occupations will vary. The examples will be the same as expressed in Question 2.

Sample Professional Essay: DARKNESS AT NOON

Harold Krents

> The following article originally appeared in the *New York Times* in 1978. Author Harold Krents, blind from birth, was a lawyer and writer who never allowed his "handicap" to stand in the way of his accomplishments. In the article, Krents points out many examples of discrimination that he had to endure as a result of his being blind.

Vocabulary

Meaning comes primarily from words. Before you start reading, use a dictionary to look up the meanings of the following words that appear in the essay.

converse	cum laude	dependent
disposition	enunciating	graphically
intoned	invariably	narcissistic

Darkness at Noon

1   Blind from birth, I have never had the opportunity to see myself and have been completely dependent on the image I create in the eye of the observer. To date it has not been narcissistic.

2   There are those who assume that since I can't see, I obviously cannot hear. Very often people will converse with me at the top of their lungs, enunciating each word very carefully. Conversely, people will also often whisper, assuming that since my eyes don't work, my ears don't either.

3   For example, when I go the airport and ask the ticket agent for assistance to the plane, he or she will invariably pick up the phone, call a ground hostess and whisper: "Hi, Jane, we've got a 76 here." I have concluded that the word "blind" is not used for one of two reasons: Either they fear that if the dread word is spoken, the ticket agent's retina will immediately detach, or they are reluctant to inform me of my condition of which I may not have been previously aware.

4   On the other hand, others know that of course I can hear, but believe that I can't talk. Often, therefore, when my wife and I go out to dinner, a waiter or waitress will ask Kit if "*he* would like a drink" to which I respond that "indeed *he* would."

5   This point was graphically driven home to me while we were in England. I had been given a year's leave of absence from my Washington law firm to study for a diploma in law degree at Oxford University. During the year I became ill and was hospitalized. Immediately after admission, I was wheeled down to the X-ray room. Just at the door sat an elderly woman—elderly I would judge from the sound of her voice. "What is his name?" the woman asked the orderly who had been wheeling me.

6   "What's your name?" the orderly repeated to me.

7   "Harold Krents," I replied.

8   "Harold Krents," he repeated.

9   "When was he born?"

10   "When were you born?"

11   "November 5, 1944," I responded.

12   "November 5, 1944," the orderly intoned.

13   This procedure continued for approximately five minutes, at which point even my saint-like disposition deserted me. "Look," I finally blurted out, "this is absolutely ridiculous. Okay, granted I can't see, but it's got to have become pretty clear to both of you that I don't need an interpreter."

14   "He says he doesn't need an interpreter," the orderly reported to the woman.

15   The toughest misconception of all is the view that because I can't see, I can't work. I was turned down by over forty law firms because of my blindness, even though my qualifications included a cum laude degree from Harvard college and a good ranking in my Harvard Law School class.

16   The attempt to find employment, the continuous frustration of being told that it was impossible for a blind person to practice law, the rejection letters, not based on my lack of ability but rather on my disability, will always remain one of the most disillusioning experiences of my life.

17   I therefore look forward to the day, with the expectation that it is certain to come, when employers will view their handicapped workers as a little child did me years ago when my family still lived in Scarsdale.

18   I was playing basketball with my father in our backyard according to procedures we had developed. My father would stand beneath the hoop, shout, and I would shoot over his head at the basket attached to our garage. Our next-door neighbor, aged five, wandered over into our yard with a playmate. "He's

blind," our neighbor whispered to her friend in a voice that could be heard distinctly by Dad and me. Dad shot and missed; I did the same. Dad hit the rim; I missed entirely; dad shot and missed the garage entirely. "Which one is blind?" whispered back the little friend.

19 I would hope that in the near future when a plant manager is touring the factory with the foreman and comes upon a handicapped and nonhandicapped person working together, his comment after watching them work will be, "Which one is disabled?"

Example Technique Questions

1. The author uses humor to describe the situations that he found himself in. Point out some examples, and relate how the humorous tone affects your feelings toward the essay.

> Paragraphs 2–3: people either shouting or whispering because since he is blind, he also cannot hear; paragraphs 4–7: people assume he can hear, but they then assume he cannot talk. The author's recognition of the humor in these situations shows that, despite how he is treated, he accepts his situation because he is often smarter, more perceptive, and more rational than those people around him who have no disability (except, perhaps, lacking the obvious intelligence and sensitivity that the author demonstrates).

2. Krents expresses that there are many common misconceptions about blind people. Point out three examples.

> Blind persons cannot hear (¶ 2); blind persons cannot speak (¶ 4); blind persons cannot work (¶ 15).

3. Examples sometimes are expressed in the form of dialogue. Explain why this is an effective method to develop Krents's main points.

> Answers will vary, but dialogue, because it is directly associated with specific people or characters, makes the points more personal and authentic.

4. Even though the author uses humor throughout the essay, how do you know his attitude about being handicapped is serious?

> **By statements such as "I was turned down by over forty law firms because**
>
> **of my blindness" (¶ 15); and "the continuous frustration of being told that**
>
> **it was impossible for a blind person to practice law, the rejection letters,**
>
> **not based on my lack of ability but rather on my disability" (¶ 16).**

Critical Thinking Writing Opportunities

1. In her essay "Opportunities in the Armed Forces," student writer Jennifer Staggs points out a *problem* that she notices about many young people (a lack of proper advice and guidance from adults and a lack of awareness of an exciting world around them). Her attempt to answer the problem is to introduce young people to the opportunities in the armed forces that help solve the problem. Write an example essay that explains how to solve a problem you see in your group of friends or in your general age group. Some problems might be voting apathy, distrust in working for a large corporation, or a feeling that a high school or college degree is not important.

2. In his essay "Darkness at Noon," writer Harold Krents points out an *inference* people have about blind persons—that they cannot work. This inference also happens to be a misconception and, therefore, a *problem*. Have you ever been in a situation in which you were temporarily handicapped? Have you ever been confined to a wheelchair, had an arm in a sling or a leg in a cast? Have you ever had your eyes dilated at the optometrist's so that someone else had to drive you home? Write an essay relating how you felt being disabled. Give examples of how the handicap affected your daily life and if it made you empathize with those that are truly handicapped.

Topics for an Example Essay

Here are some possible topics for example writing assignments. Remember, you must use examples for a purpose, so don't forget to create a thesis sentence with an appropriate controlling idea or attitude. Use the essay map to organize the subtopics for your body paragraphs. Be certain that all specific information supports your topic sentences.

1. Tattooing.
2. Dropping out of high school.
3. Role models.
4. Premarital sex.
5. Violence in video games, movies, or television.
6. Working for a large corporation.
7. Male and female homosexuality.
8. Interracial marriage.
9. Fraternities and sororities.
10. Body piercing.

Chapter Review

■ In an example essay, detailed examples are used to illustrate, clarify, convince, or make concrete a general topic.

■ The topic sentence of an example paragraph states the general topic and the controlling idea that guides the development of the paragraph. The six reporters' questions can be used to focus the discussion. Transitional expressions help identify examples, connect related ideas, and add rhythm to the paragraph.

■ In an example essay, the thesis sentence states the general topic, the controlling idea, and the essay map with subtopics. All the examples given in the body paragraphs should support the controlling idea of the essay.

Visit *The Write Start* Online!

For additional practice with the materials found in this chapter, visit our Website at

http://www.ablongman.com/checkett

The Website also features additional readings, quizzes, writing activities, and Internet links, as well as a bulletin board and interactive chat.

chapter 10

The Classification Essay

Some topics you will be assigned to write about are very complex because they have many aspects. A simple definition or description of these topics often is not sufficient to adequately explain them. How, then, do you approach a large, complex subject so your reader has a full understanding of the point you are trying to make? One possibility is **classification,** the separation of smaller points from a larger concept and the arrangement of these smaller concepts into easily recognized groups.

These groups can be based on shape, kind, color, function, or any other category your reader will easily understand. For example, you can classify chefs as specializing in regional cooking: French, Southwest American, Northern Italian, Cajun; you can categorize birds by color: blue, red, yellow; you can group geometric figures by shape: rectangles, circles, triangles, hexagons.

Identifying Your Purpose

The purpose of classification, as for all writing, is to either inform, entertain, or persuade. When the subject is sufficiently complicated, classification is one method of making a complex subject easier to write about and easier for your reader to understand.

Suppose you were to write about William Shakespeare and that your focus was his genius. You would not be able to find out his IQ and his SAT scores because such testing did not exist in the 16th and 17th centuries. You could try to find out what his contemporaries and later critics said about him. Unfortunately, not many comments from his contemporaries have survived, and the analyses of later critics are too numerous for you to read every one.

You might look at Shakespeare's writings. He was a prolific writer, and we have plenty of his works. In fact, because so many of his plays have survived and are still produced and studied worldwide, this might give you your focus.

Example

William Shakespeare can be considered a genius because of his prolific writings in so many forms. Shakespeare wrote sonnets, histories, comedies, tragedies, dark comedies, and romances. Many of his plays are still produced both on the stage and in films. Courses of study in Shakespeare's writings remain a staple in colleges and universities worldwide.

Answers will vary.

Separate each of the following topics into three classifications or groups. They can be based on shape, color, size, kind, or any other category that helps explain the topic. The first one is done as a sample.

Fish:	arctic	tropical	oceanic
Clothes:			
Music:			
Movies:			
Storms:			
Dates:			
Ice cream:			

Writing the Classification Paragraph

A classification paragraph should indicate the general topic being discussed as well as explain the categories into which it is divided. The six reporters' questions can be used to focus the discussion, and transitional expressions can provide signposts for the reader's guidance.

The Topic Sentence in a Classification Paragraph

In a classification paragraph, the topic sentence must state the subject, how the subject will be divided, and why classifying the subject is important. Here is an example of a topic sentence for a classification paragraph:

Exhibit 10.1 Classification Topic Sentence

> **Topic Sentence:** The negative effects of discrimination can be more easily understood if its targets are classified by race, gender, and age.
>
> **Subject:** discrimination
> **Categories:** race, gender, age
> **Controlling idea or attitude:** to learn about discrimination's negative effects

Write a topic sentence for each of the subjects you classified in Practice 1. Remember, your topic sentence must state the subject, the classification categories, and why it is important to divide the topic into groups.

Supporting Details: The Six Reporters' Questions

To develop the controlling idea, use the six reporters' questions: who, what, where, when, why, and how. The reporters' questions will help you focus on how you will develop the categories in which you have divided the subject. In Exhibit 10.1, the controlling idea or attitude that discrimination has negative effects focuses on *who* (people of color, women, and older adults) receive the effects of discrimination. While other aspects might be expressed in the paragraph, such as *what* happens and *why*, *who* will be the main focus.

A paragraph based on the categories of race, gender, and age might look like the following.

Exhibit 10.2 Supporting Details

> The negative effects of discrimination can be more easily understood if its targets are classified by race, gender, and age. Although some progress has been made, racial discrimination is still evident in our culture. Hate groups still march in parades on Main Street, and with the advent of the Internet, they have filled cyberspace with their special brand of hatred against all people of color. Women are still expected by many men to stay home and take care of the house and the children (and of the husband's needs). In the workplace, men still get promoted faster, and men are still paid more for the same work as women. Older adults often are not hired because they are perceived as less dynamic and less willing to learn since they are set in their ways. Additionally, many older adults are downsized because younger workers can take their place at a lower salary rate. Discrimination knows no limits. It can strike almost anyone, anytime, and anywhere.

PRACTICE 3

Using one of the topics from Practice 1, write a classification paragraph. Develop the paragraph by focusing on the three categories into which you divided the subject. Use the topic sentence you created in Practice 2 as the first sentence of the paragraph.

Using Transitional Expressions to Identify Classifications

While developing each category or group helps to inform, entertain, or persuade the reader, **transitional expressions** help to connect related ideas and add rhythm to the paragraph. Use transitional expressions in your classification paragraph so that the categories don't appear merely as a list. The groups or categories should work together to develop the subject and the controlling idea.

> **Transitional Expressions for Classification**
>
> | | | |
> |---|---|---|
> | can be categorized | can be classified | can be divided |
> | can be grouped | the first/second category | the first group |
> | the first/second kind | the first/second type | the last |

See how adding transitional expressions can help make the paragraph in Exhibit 10.2 more readable and understandable.

> The negative effects of discrimination can be more easily understood if its targets are **classified** by race, gender, and age. Although some progress has been made with the **first group,** people of color, racial discrimination is still evident in our culture. Hate groups still march in parades on Main Street, and with the advent of the Internet, they have filled cyberspace with their special brand of hatred against all people of color. **The second group** targeted by discrimination is women. Women are still expected by many men to stay home and take care of the house and the children (and of the husband's needs). In the workplace, men still get promoted faster, and men are still paid more for the same work as women. Members of **the last category,** the elderly, are often downsized because younger workers can take their place at a lower salary rate. Discrimination knows no limits. It can strike almost anyone, anytime, and anywhere.

In the classification paragraph above, the transitional expressions "are classified," "the first group," "the second group," and " the last category" also are used to announce that the next group to be discussed is forthcoming. The technique helps to keep the reader focused on the specific categories being used to develop the topic and the controlling idea or attitude.

PRACTICE 4

Using the paragraph you wrote in Practice 3, add at least three transitional expressions to connect related ideas, add rhythm, and announce upcoming categories. After you have finished, compare the two paragraphs. The paragraph containing the transitional expressions should be easier to read and understand.

Moving from Paragraph to Essay

Now that you have studied and practiced the techniques to create effective classification, it is time to expand your ideas to a larger writing unit: the classification essay. Using the techniques you learned in Part 1 regarding developing the essay paragraphs and the classification techniques you have just learned, you can write a classification essay. This might be a good time to return to Part 1 and review the techniques for developing the full essay.

Creating the Introductory Paragraph

Some writers think that once they have divided their topic into distinct categories their job is complete. Nothing could be further from the truth. All writing has to have a purpose, and that purpose must be clearly expressed. The thesis sentence of a classification essay must state the topic, announce the controlling idea or attitude that the writer has toward the topic, and clarify the organizational format of the essay.

The thesis in a classification essay should occur naturally as the introductory paragraph unfolds. In the following introductory paragraph, taken from the sample student essay to follow, notice how the thesis sentence announces the subject (selecting beneficiaries in a will), the writer's controlling idea about the topic (categorizing the beneficiaries makes the process easier), and the essay map containing the categories to be developed in the body paragraphs (the disorderly, beggars, and friends). The thesis sentence is underlined for identification purposes only.

Example

Year after year, many Americans go through the dreadful task of preparing a will. Whether using the family attorney or the family computer, the question of who gets the house and who gets the loot needs to be answered clearly in black and white. Documents of this nature can get very complex and detailed, needing a linguist for translation, but choosing kin for determining who's in and who's definitely out of the legal instrument shouldn't be difficult at all. Placing relatives into three categories, the disorderly, the beggars, and the friends, eases the process of selecting beneficiaries.

Using the thesis sentence with an essay map makes the contents and organizational structure clear for both writer and reader. As we shall see below, the essay will continue by developing the essay map items in their respective body paragraphs.

PRACTICE 5

Create a thesis sentence with a controlling idea or attitude and a three-item essay map using the topic idea in the paragraph you created for Practice 3. Make certain that the three essay map items you choose will be able to develop the topic as the controlling idea suggests. (See the section titled "The Controlling Idea or Attitude in the Thesis Sentence" in Chapter 3 if you need to review this information.)

Creating the Body Paragraphs

For an essay on preparing a will, the focus of the body paragraphs will be the paragraph topics listed in the thesis sentence's essay map. The first body paragraph's topic will be about the "disorderly" relatives, the second body paragraph's topic will be about the "beggars," and the third body paragraph will be about "friends." Thus each of the body paragraphs in a classification essay focuses on one of the categories into which the topic has been divided. Remember, as you write about each of the topics, your focus should be on the controlling idea or attitude; in this case, the controlling idea is that *classifying potential beneficiaries makes the process of writing the will easier.*

Creating the Concluding Paragraph

The approach of the concluding paragraph should flow naturally from the essay's main topic. Because the essay's focus is placing potential beneficiaries into categories in order to make the overall process of selecting the actual beneficiaries easier, an evaluation of the main points in each category would seem appropriate. You might discuss how to be more precise in the classification of the disorderly, the beggars, and the friends. You could classify them further by age, schooling, how many times they've been arrested, or how distant they are on the branches of the family tree. You could further classify them by how many family functions they've attended, how many times they've asked for money, or how many times they've sued members of the family over property, possessions, or money. (Refer to Chapter 5 for other approaches for concluding paragraphs.)

Sample Student Essay: LEFT OUT

Randy Raterman

In the essay "Left Out," student writer Randy Raterman takes a humorous and somewhat sarcastic look at making a will. The problem isn't so much a question of whether or not to leave possessions to relatives; the problem turns out to be deciding which relatives should be mentioned in the will. Raterman divides the potential recipients into three groups, two of which are decidedly on the "left out" list, making it easier to identify those on the "in" list. Notice how many adjectives the author attaches to nouns in order to bring them to life.

Vocabulary

Meaning comes primarily from words. Before starting to read, use a dictionary to look up the definitions of the following words that appear in the essay.

beneficiaries	commendable	inanimate	linguist
mendicant	ominous	proverbial	riffraff

Left Out

1   Year after year, many Americans go through the dreadful task of preparing a will. Whether using the family attorney or the family computer, the question of who gets the house and who gets the loot needs to be answered clearly in black and white. Documents of this nature can get very complex and detailed, needing a linguist for translation, but choosing kin for determining who's in

and who's definitely out of the legal instrument shouldn't be difficult at all. Placing relatives into three categories, the disorderly, the beggars, and the friends, eases the process of selecting beneficiaries. ←— **Thesis sentence with essay map**

Topic Sentence → 2   The first group to be eliminated from the selection of beneficiaries is the disorderly. Almost every family has individuals fitting this category. Kinfolk of this kind should include the uncontrollable creatures hanging from the branches of the family tree. This prevents the disobedient, undisciplined, unruly, rebellious, and violent souls from inheriting one red cent. If an entire branch is infested with precarious parasites, pruning is essential. Additionally, the pesky rodents burrowing in the tree roots may fill the void left by the branchless trunk. Tending to legalities is imperative because related riffraff have no problem dragging heirs through the legal system in search of a gold mine. Even though the timid and light of heart may be hesitant, constructing this category is highly effective for excluding unworthy, vulture-like inheritors.

Topic Sentence → 3   The second category, the beggars, also needs to be eliminated from consideration. Recording names of kinfolk in this second group may be the most challenging; numerous leeches will befriend the benefactors while simultaneously desiring particular heirlooms. Nonetheless, some mendicant pests are easy to identify. If receiving inescapable phone calls from long-lost family members gives rise to the question: "What did that misfit want? We haven't heard from him in years," simply jot down the callers' names. If several members possess a needy personality that seems only satisfied if they amass more objects than those listed in the will, put them on the list. Members of the proverbial family tree exhibiting sponge-like characteristics (never losing absorbency for family possessions) appropriately fit the category as well. Consequently, individuals in this group are notorious for dragging legitimate recipients to court, so double check all legal documents for erroneous entries. Unmentioned kin clearly belong with the uncontrollable creatures, parasites, and pesky rodents, or they (and their legal team) will think they are rightful recipients.

Topic Sentence → 4   The final category of potential, worthwhile inheritors contains the names of preferable kin. When composing the list, focus on relatives having friendly traits. Jot down the names of those who are truly close and dear; immediate loved ones would be devastated if they were accidentally left out or inherited the dirty sock collection, so double check to make sure these names have been inscribed. A truly considerate benefactor would include names of kin who have come to the rescue in time of need, no questions asked. Many relatives may at first seem helpful, but excluding those who want a crispy, new Ben Franklin for a couple hours of babysitting will leave just a handful of good-natured, kindhearted, and loving souls. Obviously, the most difficult task is still at hand. Who from the roster will be the recipients, and what will the recipients receive? Nonetheless, legally protecting the beneficiaries from the leeches, sponges, parasites, pesky rodents, and uncontrollable creatures inhabiting the family tree would be commendable.

5   Unfortunately, most Americans pass away each year having not completed a will or any other legal instrument that indicates how they want their possessions distributed to family. Occasionally, the goods get turned over to the state, leaving opportunities for the unworthy, ominous family members to inherit entire estates. Unpleasant as it may be, a few affectionate, kindhearted kin will be grieving the loss of a family member, so don't amplify the grief by not having a will or estate plan. Numerous little family squabbles may break out after the departure of the benefactor if legalities haven't been resolved, so heed the warning to exclude wicked, unworthy family members from the list of recipients.

Classification Technique Questions

1. How does the writer categorize potential beneficiaries?

Into three categories: the disorderly, the beggars, and the friends.

2. What do you think is the writer's purpose for writing the essay?

Possible answer: To make the usually difficult task of choosing benefi-

ciaries easier but with a humorous tone. (Other answers may be posited.)

3. What other categories can you think of that might fit in the essay?

Answers will vary.

4. Underline as many of the classification transitional expressions that you can find, and list them below.

The topic sentence in each of the three body paragraphs begins with a

classification transitional expression: "The first group," "The second cat-

egory," and " the final category."

5. How do the transitional expressions help create a more effective essay?

They help by organizing and ordering the essay's paragraph topics, and

they help identify the various categories into which the author divides

the beneficiaries.

6. One form of alliteration is the intentional repetition of consonant sounds at the beginning of words or in stressed syllables (*p*etulant *p*uppies, *w*ithering *w*illows). Point out some examples of alliteration in the essay. How does Raterman's use of alliteration support the humorous aspect of the essay?

Paragraph 2: "precarious parasites," "related riffraff," and "timid and light

of heart"; paragraph 3: "befriend the benefactors," "uncontrollable crea-

tures," and "parasites, and pesky"; paragraph 4: "kindhearted kin." The

repetitive sounds add a quick rhythm and a light, funny sound quality

that supports the light, humorous tone.

Sample Professional Essay: WHY I WANT A WIFE

Judy Brady-Syfers

The following essay, first published in *Ms.* magazine under the name Judy Syfers, is a satiric look at a woman's traditional, social role as a servant to her husband's needs. The author divides this major role into distinct categories as she comments on the female situation in respect to her husband, herself, and the society at large.

Vocabulary

Meaning comes primarily from words. Before you start reading, use a dictionary to look up the definitions of the following words that appear in the essay.

adherence	dependent	entail	hors d'oeuvres
monogamy	nurturant	rambling	replenished

Why I Want a Wife

1   I belong to that classification of people known as wives. I am a Wife. And, not altogether incidentally, I am a mother.

2   Not too long ago a male friend of mine appeared on the scene fresh from a recent divorce. He had one child, who is, of course, with his ex-wife. He is looking for another wife. As I thought about him while I was ironing one evening, it suddenly occurred to me that I, too, would like to have a wife. Why do I want a wife?

3   I would like to go back to school, so I can become economically independent, support myself, and, if need be, support those dependent upon me. I want a wife who will work and send me to school. And while I am going to school I want a wife to take care of my children. I want a wife to keep track of the children's doctor and dentist appointments. And to keep track of mine, too. I want a wife to make sure my children eat properly and are kept clean. I want a wife who will wash the children's clothes and keep them mended. I want a wife who is a good nurturant attendant to my children, who arranges for their schooling, makes sure that they have an adequate social life with their peers, takes them to the park, the zoo, etc. I want a wife who takes care of the children when they are sick, a wife who arranges to be around when the children need special care, because, of course, I cannot miss classes at school. My wife must arrange to lose time at work and not lose the job. It may mean a small cut in my wife's income from time to time, but I guess I can tolerate that. Needless to say, my wife will arrange and pay for the care of the children while my wife is working.

4   I want a wife who will take care of *my* physical needs. I want a wife who will keep my house clean. A wife who will pick up after my children, a wife who will pick up after me. I want a wife who will keep my clothes clean, ironed, mended, replaced when need be, and who will see to it that my personal things are kept in their proper place so that I can find what I need the

minute I need it. I want a wife who cooks the meals, a wife who is a *good* cook. I want a wife who will plan the menus, do the necessary grocery shopping, prepare the meals, serve them pleasantly, and then do the cleaning up while I do my studying. I want a wife who will care for me when I am sick and sympathize with my pain and loss of time from school. I want a wife to go along when our family takes a vacation so that someone can continue to care for me and my children when I need a rest and change of scene.

5   I want a wife who will not bother me with rambling complaints about a wife's duties. But I want a wife who will listen to me when I feel the need to explain a rather difficult point I have come across in my course of studies. And I want a wife who will type my papers for me when I have written them.

6   I want a wife who will take care of the details of my social life. When my wife and I are invited out by my friends, I want a wife who will take care of the babysitting arrangements. When I meet people at school that I like and want to entertain, I want a wife who will have the house clean, will prepare a special meal, serve it to me and my friends, and not interrupt when I talk about things that interest me and my friends. I want a wife who will have arranged that the children are fed and ready for bed before my guests arrive so that the children do not bother us. I want a wife who takes care of the needs of my guests so that they feel comfortable, who makes sure that they have an ashtray, that they are passed the hors d'oeuvres, that they are offered a second helping of the food, that their wine glasses are replenished when necessary, that their coffee is served to them as they like it. And I want a wife who knows that sometimes I need a night out by myself.

7   I want a wife who is sensitive to my sexual needs, a wife who makes love passionately and eagerly when I feel like it, a wife who makes sure that I am satisfied. And, of course, I want a wife who will not demand sexual attention when I am not in the mood for it. I want a wife who assumes the complete responsibility for birth control, because I do not want more children. I want a wife who will remain sexually faithful to me so that I do not have to clutter up my intellectual life with jealousies. And I want a wife who understands that *my* sexual needs may entail more than strict adherence to monogamy. I must, after all, be able to relate to people as fully as possible.

8   If, by chance, I find another person more suitable as a wife than the wife I already have, I want the liberty to replace my present wife with another one. Naturally, I will expect a fresh, new life; my wife will take the children and be solely responsible for them so that I am left free.

9   When I am through with school and have a job, I want my wife to quit working and remain at home so that my wife can more fully and completely take care of a wife's duties.

10   My God, who *wouldn't* want a wife?

Classification Technique Questions

1. What is the purpose of Brady's essay?

Possible answer: To point out how many skills the role of wife entails, and

to offer a sarcastic commentary on what is expected of a wife by men and

by the larger society. (Other answers may be posited.)

2. This essay was written in 1972. Is it still relevant today? Why or why not?

Answers will vary.

3. Most sentences begin with "I want a wife." Is this repetitious form effective? Why or why not?

Answers will vary.

4. The author lists a staggering number of wife-duty categories. Are they related in any particular way? Explain.

Answers will vary.

5. What is the effect of the author's continual use of "my" in the essay?

Although the "my" repetition suggests that the duties belong to the wife,

they are actually duties she performs for the benefit of others.

6. In the last line of the essay, Brady-Syfers asks, "My God, who *wouldn't* want a wife?" How would you answer this question, and why?

Answers will vary.

Critical Thinking Writing Opportunities

1. In his essay "Left Out," student writer Randy Raterman states that the *question at issue* for will-makers is not whether to leave an inheritance, but to identify those people who will not be left out. To help identify potential heirs, he places friends and relatives into a variety of categories. Whether or not making a will is in your immediate future, write an essay classifying your friends and relatives into distinct categories that would help you decide who gets what or who gets nothing.

2. In her essay "Why I Want a Wife," Judy Brady-Syfers's *frame of reference* (a wife divorced by her husband) affects her feelings about the many roles that wives have to assume and how those roles are perceived by husbands and society. Examine the roles you play in your own life, such as student, friend, parent, worker (your frame of reference) and how the various roles make you feel about yourself. Take one of the roles, break it into distinct categories, and write an essay explaining how others respond to you differently as you act out the various parts.

Topics for a Classification Essay

Here are some possible topics for classification writing assignments. Remember, your essay must have a purpose, so don't forget to create a thesis sentence with an appropriate attitude. Use the essay map to organize the subtopics for your body paragraphs. Be certain that all specific information supports your topic sentences.

1. Thrill-seeking activities
2. Television sit-coms
3. Sports
4. Movies
5. Pets
6. Summer jobs
7. Dates you've had
8. Types of discipline
9. Phobias
10. Parties

Chapter Review

- In a classification essay, a large, complex topic is approached by breaking it into categories that the reader can easily grasp.

- The six reporters' questions can be used to help develop the categories into which the topic is divided, and transitional expressions can identify the classifications.

- In the five-paragraph classification essay, the introductory paragraph introduces the topic, states the categories that frame the discussion, and indicates the controlling idea or attitude. Each of the body paragraphs expands on one of the categories presented in the thesis sentence.

Visit *The Write Start* Online!

For additional practice with the materials found in this chapter, visit our Website at

http://www.ablongman.com/checkett

The Website also features additional readings, quizzes, writing activities, and Internet links, as well as a bulletin board and interactive chat.

CHAPTER 11

The Process Essay

Have you ever had to explain how something works or how you did something? Perhaps you had to explain how to install a computer program or how you made chocolate fudge. Think about how you would explain these activities in writing. You would have to describe a step-by-step **process** to develop these topics.

Identifying Your Purpose

Explaining the steps involved in completing an operation, a procedure, or an event is called process writing. Process is an important method in developing ideas for science, history, sports, medicine, and business. Think of how such a set of instructions might apply to your writing for school or work. In a science class, you might be assigned to explain how you did a specific experiment. In a history class, you might have to explain how an historical event happened. In a business class, you might have to explain how a product's advertising campaign was planned. All of these writing situations involve explaining a process. The following paragraph outlines some steps necessary to the process of becoming a better college student.

Example

In order to use time more effectively, the student should buy a schedule-planner. Write the subjects for each day in the planner, and then add the time it will take to study each subject per day. Studying immediately after class can be an effective method for remembering information because it already is fresh in the mind. Don't forget to schedule a 15 to 20 minute break between studying each subject, or take a break if you are having a hard time with a particular problem or in understanding a passage you have been reading. Studying a topic should be scheduled well in advance of the class in which it is supposed to be discussed. This will give you the time to think about what you have read and formalize answers to the questions the instructor might ask you. It also will allow you time to prepare questions for the instructor about anything you do not understand.

Write a paragraph explaining, step-by-step, how you do one of the following activities.

■ fix a meal

■ study for a test

■ plant a garden

■ purchase a car

■ plan a party

Directional Process

There are two methods to develop a topic using process: directional and informational. **Directional process** explains how to do something: how to bake a cake, how to tune a car engine, or how to write a process essay. The intent, or goal, of directional process writing is to enable the readers to do something (to duplicate some process) after they have followed the directions. Recipes, assembly instructions, how-to books, and manuals are all examples of directional process writing. The following directional process paragraph explains, in part, how to plan for an inexpensive vacation.

Example

Setting a budget not only helps you plan your trip but can save you money. Decide how much money you have available, and plan your trip around places that fit your budget. Now that the budget is set, look on the Internet for sites offering discount vacation plans. If you cannot find a suitable package deal, then you can call hotels in the area where you are planning to stay. Inquire if they have discounts for the time of year that you will be arriving. Discounted tickets for events and places of interest are usually available for cities that promote tourism. The Internet is a great place to look for deals. Also, stop by travel agencies to get brochures on the locations and discount packages.

Informational Process

Informational process explains how something was made, how an event occurred, or how something works: how a treaty between two or more countries was finalized, how the Panama Canal was built, or how an industrial laser is used in medical procedures. After reading informational process writing, readers should understand the process, but they usually do not repeat it. Duplication is not the intent of informational process. After all, you might understand how the Panama Canal was built, but you would never be able to duplicate its construction. Look at the following informational process paragraph that describes the process a patient suffering from GERD (Gastroesophageal Reflux Disease) must undergo to determine if surgery is necessary.

Example

When the doctor suggests that an operation is necessary, a GERD sufferer may be referred to a gastroenterologist or gastrointestinal surgeon. The patient will undergo a series of upper gastrointestinal X-rays that involve swallowing a chalky substance called barium and watching the substance go down the esophagus into the stomach for diagnosis of a hiatal hernia that may demonstrate gastroesophageal reflux. The specialist may recommend endoscopy, wherein a small tube with a microscopic camera attached to the end is placed into the esophagus, helping the doctor visualize the damage done to the lining of the esophagus by gastric juices. If GERD is confirmed, the surgeon will help the patient make the decision of whether or not to have the surgery.

Writing a Process Paragraph

A process paragraph introduces the process under discussion and outlines the steps in the process. Transitional expressions relate the steps in the process to one another to help the reader orient himself or herself.

The Topic Sentence in a Process Paragraph

Directional and informational process paragraphs begin with a topic sentence that clearly states what the reader should be able to do or to understand after reading the steps of the process. The topic sentence also should point out why the process is important. Read the following topic sentence for an informational process paragraph.

Example

A series of dubious events led to the outbreak of the Spanish-American War.

The entire paragraph might read this way:

A series of dubious events led to the outbreak of the Spanish-American War. Cubans had long attempted to overthrow Spanish rule in their country. The rebellion began in 1885 and lasted for many years. William Randolph Hearst, owner of the *New York Journal,* falsely reported on the war; his reporters made the conflict seem as if the Spanish were massacring the Cubans. Such a wave of propaganda caused a wave of anti-Spain feelings to sweep across America. In late February 1898, the American vessel *Maine,* sent to Cuba to protect American people and property, blew up in Havana harbor, killing more than 260 people. Consequently, Americans instantly assumed that the Spanish had blown up the *Maine* by means of a submarine. War frenzy broke out in the United States, and Americans wanted war more than ever. "To hell with Spain, remember the *Maine!*" was a popular chant shouted by war enthusiasts.

In the example above, the process described that led to the Spanish-American War is as follows: the Cubans rebel against the Spanish, the *New York Journal* prints false reports of the treatment of Cuban rebels by the Spanish, the vessel *Maine* is sent to Havana, the *Maine* blows up, Americans think the Spanish are responsible. All of these steps eventually led to the war between Spain and the United States. The reason the writer thinks the topic is important is expressed in the word *dubious.* This attitude suggests that some of the events that led to the war were less than genuine. The writer uses words like "falsely," "propaganda," and "frenzy" to suggest that Americans were, in many ways, tricked into their anti-Spain attitude.

Organizing the Process Paragraph

Directional and informational process paragraphs are developed according to the order in which the steps of the process occur. Sticking to chronological order avoids confusion. For example, in describing how to save information to a floppy disk using a computer, you would not give the instructions as suggested in the list on the left; rather, you would follow the chronological order as listed on the right.

Wrong	**Right**
1. Click on the Save icon	1. Click on the File icon
2. Move cursor to down arrow	2. Move cursor to "Save As"
3. Click on "3½ Floppy (A:)"	3. Click on "Save As"
4. Move cursor to "Save As"	4. Open Menu by clicking on arrow
5. Open Menu by clicking on arrow	5. Click on "3½ Floppy (A:)"
6. Click on File icon	6. Click on the Save icon

PRACTICE 2

Using the paragraph you wrote for Practice 1, go through the paragraph and make a numbered list of the steps in the process. Are they out of chronological order? Are any important steps missing? If so, rewrite the paragraph so that all relevant steps are included in the proper chronological order. If your paragraph for Practice 1 did not need to be rewritten, choose another of the topics from Practice 1, create a numbered list of relevant steps in the process, and write a paragraph following the correct chronological order for the steps.

Transitional Expressions: Connecting the Steps

Once you have the steps of your process in the correct order, you have to connect them so that they follow each other chronologically. Using transitional expressions will help you connect the steps of the process, and they will announce to the reader that a step is forthcoming. Of course, transitional expressions will also add rhythm to the paragraph, making it easier to read.

Transitional Expressions for Process

afterwards	before	initially	to begin
as	begin by	later	until
as soon as	during	meanwhile	upon
at first	finally	next	when
at last	first, second	now	while
at this point	following	then	

Using the paragraph you wrote for Practice 1, add at least three appropriate transitional expressions. When you have finished, compare the two paragraphs. The paragraph containing the transitional expressions should be easier to understand and easier to read.

Moving from Paragraph to Essay

Now that you have studied and practiced the techniques to create effective process paragraphs, it is time to expand your ideas to a larger writing unit: the process essay. Using the techniques you learned in Part 1 regarding developing the essay paragraphs and the process techniques you have just learned, you can write a process essay. This might be a good time to return to Part 1 and review the techniques for developing the full essay.

Creating the Introductory Paragraph

Because process writing uses chronological order to organize its development, writers sometimes think that they needn't be concerned about overall organization and focus. But a process essay is writing, and all writing has specific purpose. The thesis sentence in a process essay should state the essay's overall purpose and organizational structure.

The thesis for directional and informational process essays should blend naturally into the introductory paragraph. The following example of an introductory paragraph for a process essay was written by a student. You will see the full essay a bit later. Notice how the thesis sentence announces the topic (*photography*), the writer's controlling idea about the topic (*certain steps are necessary for photographs to be successful*), and the essay map containing the body paragraph subtopics (*techniques of adjusting the camera while taking photographs, correctly developing the negative, and creatively enlarging the print*). The thesis sentence in the example is underlined for identification purposes.

Example

In photography, many steps must be completed properly for the final results to be worthwhile. Many photographs have flaws that detract from their overall presentation. By using creative techniques while shooting photos and processing film and prints, the photographer can enhance prints from their original negatives. These steps are crucial to the final results, for they determine the quality of the negative and the finished print. A photographer must adjust the camera settings while shooting, correctly develop the negative, and creatively enlarge the print to achieve a successful photograph.

This essay will continue by developing in the body paragraphs each of the sub-topics contained in the essay map. Using the thesis sentence with the essay map makes the content and organizational structure clear for both writer and reader.

Create a thesis sentence with a controlling idea or attitude and a three-item essay map using the topic idea in the paragraph you wrote for Practice 3. Make certain that the three essay map items you choose are suitable for developing the topic as the controlling idea or attitude suggests. (See "The Controlling Idea or Attitude in the Thesis Sentence" in Chapter 3 if you need to review this information.)

Creating the Body Paragraphs

For a paper on the topic of creating a successful photograph, the focus of the body paragraphs will be the topics listed in the thesis sentence's essay map. The first body paragraph's topic will be "adjusting the camera setting while shooting," the second body paragraph's topic will be "correctly developing the negative," and the third body paragraph's topic will be "creatively enlarging the print." Remember, as you write about each of these topics, your focus should not be on film speed, types of cameras, or lighting equipment. Keep the focus on the controlling idea: the steps necessary *to achieve a successful photograph.*

Creating the Concluding Paragraph

The approach of the concluding paragraph should flow naturally from the essay's main topic. Because the essay's focus is the steps necessary to create a successful photograph, an *evaluation* of the importance of the essay's subject seems appropriate. You might mention that photographic equipment and supplies are not inexpensive, so you will want to maximize your successes. You might remind the readers that they probably will put a lot of time and thought into the photographs they are taking, so care and patience during the shooting and developing stages are critical. (Refer to Chapter 5 for other approaches for concluding paragraphs.)

Sample Directional Process Student Essay: A STEP-BY-STEP GUIDE TO PHOTOGRAPHY

Stephanie Weidemann

Photography is a popular activity for millions of people. But with today's automatic cameras that promise to do everything but ensure a smile on the subject's face, there comes a price. The photographs taken with these technological marvels don't always live up to the expectations of the amateur picture-taker. Many people therefore buy a more sophisticated and expensive camera, thinking that cost and complexity will solve their problems. This, of course, only leads to more costly photographs that exhibit many of the same shortcomings as those produced with the earlier, cheaper camera. In this essay, "A Step-by-Step Guide to Photography," student writer Stephanie Weidemann explains the process for producing worthwhile prints. The writer uses many transitional expressions to help connect relevant ideas and keep the steps in the process in chronological order.

Vocabulary

Meaning comes primarily from words. Before starting to read, use a dictionary to look up the definitions of the following words appearing in the essay.

acidic	aperture	enhanced	manipulating
neutralize	proficiency	residual	resin
scale	sensitized	solution	vantage

A Step-by-Step Guide to Photography

1   In photography, many steps must be completed properly for the final results to be worthwhile. Many photographs have flaws that detract from their overall presentation. By using creative techniques while shooting photos and processing film and prints, the photographer can enhance prints from their original negatives. These steps are crucial to the final results, for they determine the quality of the negative and the finished prints. A photographer must adjust the camera settings while shooting, correctly develop the negative, and creatively enlarge the print to achieve a successful photograph.

Thesis sentence with essay map →

Topic Sentence →

2   Before taking each shot, adjusting the aperture is necessary. First, using a gray card, measure the light that the camera is reading from the scene. Adjust the aperture so that the light meter indicator (usually a needle or pointer) is floating in the center of its scale; this insures the picture will not be under or over exposed. Due to circumstances unseen by the human eye, light and dark fluctuations can affect what the picture will ultimately look like. Therefore, it is important to vary the aperture settings, and then take more than one photo of the scene. This will allow for variations in light and dark that you might not be aware of.

Topic Sentence →

3   Developing is by far the most technical processing in creating a print. First, the film is placed into a liquid developer. This solution reactivates the process begun by the action of light when the film was exposed during the shoot. Great care must be given to light sensitivity during the development. Next, be certain that no light ever reaches the negative during the developing process. Be sure the door to the darkroom is locked and cannot be opened while you are working. Red light can be used in the darkroom because red light will not affect the negative. Next, load the film onto a developing reel. As soon as you have completed this task, immerse the reel into the developer solution. After this, stop the development by placing the reel into the stop liquid to neutralize the developer. Upon completing this step, put the film into the fixing solution to stop all chemical reactions. Finally, the film must be thoroughly rinsed in water to remove all residual chemicals. This also promotes uniform drying and prevents formation of water spots and streaks.

Topic Sentence →

4   After this, the negative is used to enlarge the print. First, place the negative in the enlarger projector. Next, allow light from the enlarger to pass through the negative to the lens. Then, as soon as the image is projected, enlarge or reduce the image to the desired size. After completing this task, project the image onto the sensitized printing material. Next, adjust the light source to bring out light areas or create darker areas to enhance the scene. Finally, develop the print as you did in the developing process.

5   Photography requires technical proficiency; consequently, many potentially interesting prints do not turn out well. Unlike many art forms, photography is an exact science. However, it is the science that is the art. A print can be made visually effective by making adjustments to the light allowed to strike the film negative during the shooting and by the creative effects done in the darkroom.

Process Technique Questions

1. How many steps are there in the process? List them below.

   Three: adjust camera settings while shooting, correctly develop the neg-

   ative, and creatively enlarge the print.

2. Identify the transitional expressions the writer uses. How do they help organize the steps chronologically?

   Paragraph 2: "First," "and then"; paragraph 3: "First," "Next (twice)," "As

   soon as," "After this," and "Finally"; paragraph 4: "After this," "First," "Next

   (twice)," "Then," "After," and "Finally." They announce to the reader what

   steps are coming next and whether the step is first, second, third, etc.

3. Which of the steps is explained in the most detail? Why do you think the writer chose to focus more on that step than the others? Did this add or detract from the essay's effectiveness? Explain.

   The second step, developing, is given the most detail because, as the

   writer states, it is the most technical step in the process. (Other answers

   will vary.)

4. Identify any steps that, in your opinion, were not clearly expressed or needed more explanation. Can you suggest any additional information that would make the process clearer and more understandable?

   Answers will vary.

Sample Informational Process Student Essay: HOW TO BE SUCCESSFUL AT KICKING THE SMOKING HABIT

Stephany K. Higgs

With the advent of so many advances in medical technology, the negative effects of smoking have been known for a long time. The depth and breadth of smoking's short- and long-term effects on the body, and even fetuses in the womb, has caused millions to quit the habit and prevented millions more from beginning the activity in the first place. Yet despite educational programs, the surgeon general's warning on each pack of cigarettes, and continual public service announcements in all the media, millions more find it next to impossible to kick the habit. In this essay, "How to Be Successful at Kicking the Smoking Habit," student writer Stephany K. Higgs outlines the steps necessary to stop smoking. Notice how the writer mixes both tangible activities that can help the smoker quit with the psychological motivations that must be understood to make the process of quitting effective.

Vocabulary

Meaning comes primarily from words. Before you begin reading, use a dictionary to look up the definitions for the following words appearing in the essay.

cessation	counsel	designated	empowered
induced	resolve	skepticism	tenacity

How to be Successful at Kicking the Smoking Habit

1   On New Year's Eve, millions of people resolve to quit smoking during the upcoming year. Unfortunately, many people fail before they even get started because smoking is both a physical and psychological addiction. Quitting will require commitment and tenacity. Quitting smoking can be done if smokers **Thesis sentence with essay map →** explore the reasons why they smoke, develop a plan with a method for stopping smoking, and obtain support from friends and family.

Topic Sentence → 2   People smoke for many reasons; therefore, it is important for smokers to identify the reasons why they smoke. Analyzing the origin of the habit is the first positive step toward kicking the habit. For most people, smoking is a learned behavior; consequently, smokers tend to come from families where one or more of their parents were smokers. The majority of them are anxious people who started smoking because it seemed to provide a temporary release from current or future distress and uncertainties. Some tobacco users started smoking to be cool and to fit in with the crowd; moreover, others started smoking because they enjoyed the taste of tobacco upon trying it out. While others did not necessarily enjoy the act of smoking, they felt addicted to the nicotine and needed to continue to satisfy their cravings. Now, with the origin of the habit exposed, the smoker is empowered with the knowledge of why he or she smokes and can seek out healthier alternatives to satisfy needs.

Topic Sentence → 3   Developing a plan with a method for cessation of smoking is the next important step. There are many products on the market today, available with or without prescription, which can be helpful to the smoker trying to quit. Smokers need to decide which method would be most effective for them; some methods are more costly than others although not necessarily more effective. Nicotine patches, gum, and tablets are some of the many aids available to the smoker. Therefore, discussing these aids with the smoker's physician, friends, family, and co-workers can be helpful in stopping the habit because many of them have knowledge, either directly or indirectly, about these products and how they have worked for themselves and/or friends and loved ones. Alternative methods such as hypnotism and sleep-induced behavior modification have been viewed with skepticism by the medical community and should be approached with caution and research by the smoker. Once smokers choose a method they believe will work best for them, it is important to make the commitment to stay with it. Additionally, smokers must realize there will be times when they will feel the method is not working. There will be times when they will fall off the quit-smoking-wagon and will need to climb back on again. If they expect this and have a plan to handle the climb back up, they can reach their goal.

Topic Sentence → 4   Receiving support from friends, family, and co-workers in the effort to quit smoking can be one of the deciding factors in whether or not a smoker will stop smoking and remain smoke free. Letting those closest to the smoker know that the smoker's intention is to quit smoking gives the smoker a support system. Finding someone who would also like to quit can be effective because the two can support each other by calling on one another when they feel weak in their effort to give up. Family members, friends, and co-workers should be sensitive to the ups and downs the smoker will experience by smoking only in designated areas until such time as the smoker feels strong enough to be around other smokers without joining them. Engaging the support of a former smoker can be helpful in getting smokers trying to quit over the rough spots.

5   On every package of cigarettes there is a warning by the Surgeon General: "Smoking Causes Lung Cancer, Heart Disease, Emphysema, and May Complicate Pregnancy." Health related illnesses are the number one reason most people would like to quit smoking. Beyond that, it is a smelly, messy, and expensive addiction. Sadly, it is one of the hardest addictions to break. However, with determination and support, quitting smoking can be done, and succeeding greatly increases the chance for continued good health.

Process Technique Questions

1. Although the essay is informational, how many steps does the writer focus on in the process?

   Three: "exploring the reasons for smoking," "developing a plan for stop-

   ping smoking," and "obtaining support from family and friends."

2. The writer does not use many transitional expressions as illustrated in this chapter. Point out some places in the essay where transitional expressions could be used. How would they make the essay more effective?

   Answers will vary.

3. Why does the writer focus on smokers' motivations for smoking? Would-n't it be better to write a directional process essay so smokers could follow steps that would stop them from smoking? Explain.

Possible answer: Quitting smoking is very difficult. It requires commitment,

planning, and support from others. Before any step-by-step process can

be followed, these other psychological and intellectual aspects of the

process must be taken into consideration.

Sample Professional Essay: YOU SURE YOU WANT TO DO THIS?

Maneka Gandhi

In this essay, first published in the *Baltimore Sun* newspaper, Maneka Gandhi, a professional writer and columnist for the *Illustrated Weekly* of India, unveils the process of how lipstick is manufactured and how its unhealthy ingredients create the beautiful results that men and women find so appealing. Along the way, Gandhi promotes vegetarianism and animal rights in a tone that suggests we may be finding out more than we want to know about a beauty enhancement that we assume to be an innocent and safe product. Pay particular attention to how her description of the process both amuses and horrifies the reader simultaneously.

Vocabulary
Meaning comes primarily from words. Before you begin to read, use a dictionary to look up the definitions of the following words that appear in the essay.

bulk	bunged	castor oil	congealed	equivalent
extent	hydrogenated	iridescent	metamorphoses	molten
rancid	rigid	smear	suggestive	

You Sure You Want to Do This?

1   Are you one of those women who feel that lipstick is one of the essentials of life? That to be seen without it is the equivalent of facial nudity? Then you might like to know what goes into that attractive color tube that you smear on your lips.

2   At the center of the modern lipstick is acid. Nothing else will burn a coloring sufficiently deeply into the lips. The acid starts out orange, then sizzles into the living skin cells and metamorphoses into deep red. Everything else in the lipstick is there just to get the acid into place.

3   First lipstick has to spread. Softened food shortening, such as hydrogenated vegetable oil, spreads very well, and accordingly is one of the substances found in almost all lipsticks. Soap smears well, too, and so some of that is added as

well. Unfortunately, neither soap nor shortening is good at actually taking up the acid that's needed to do the dyeing. Only one smearable substance will do this to any extent: castor oil.

4   Good cheap castor oil, used in varnishes and laxative, is one of the largest ingredients by bulk in every lipstick. The acid soaks into the castor oil, the castor oil spreads on the lips with the soap and shortening till the acid is carried where it needs to go.

5   If lipstick could be sold in castor oil bottles there would be no need for the next major ingredient. But the mix has to be transformed into a rigid, streamlined stick, and for that nothing is better than heavy petroleum-based wax. It's what provides the "stick" in lipstick.

6   Of course, certain precautions have to be taken in combining all these substances. If the user ever got a sniff of what was in there, there might be problems of consumer acceptance. So a perfume is poured in at the manufacturing stage before all the oils have cooled—when it is still a molten lipstick mass.

7   At the same time, food preservatives are poured into the mass, because apart from smelling rather strongly the oil in there would go rancid without some protection. (Have you smelled an old lipstick? That dreadful smell is castor oil gone bad.)

8   All that's lacking now is shine. When the preservatives and the perfume are being poured in, something shiny, colorful, almost iridescent—and, happily enough, not even too expensive—is added. That something is fish scales. It's easily available from the leftovers of commercial fish-packing stations. The scales are soaked in ammonia, then bunged in with everything else.

9   Fish scales, by the way, mean that lipstick is not a vegetarian product. Every time you paint your lips you eat fish scales. So lipsticks without them actually are marked "vegetarian lipstick."

10   Is that it, then? Shortening, soap, castor oil, petroleum wax, perfume, food preservatives and fish scales? Not entirely. There is still one thing missing: color.

11   The orange acid that burns into the lips only turns red on contact. So that what you see in the tube looks like lip color and not congealed orange juice, another dye has to be added to the lipstick. This masterpiece of chemistry and art will be a soothing and suggestive and kissable red.

12   But it has very little to do with what actually goes on your face. That, as we said, is—but by now you already know more than you wanted to.

Process Technique Questions

1. What process is being explained in the essay?

Answers will vary. The obvious answer is the process of what goes into

making makeup. However, a subtle process being explained is deciding,

based on what you learn, whether or not to wear makeup.

2. Is the essay intended to be directional or informational?

Informational.

3. How many steps are explained?

Six: castor oil is added to make the makeup spreadable, petroleum-based

wax is added to make the mixture rigid, perfume is added to make the

mixture smell good, food preservatives are added to prevent the product

from becoming rancid, fish scales are added to provide a shine, and

orange acid that turns red on contact with the skin is added to provide

color.

4. Identify any transitional expressions that are used. Do they help organize the information chronologically? Explain.

Transitional expressions do not play a prominent role in the essay. "Then"

is used three time, "when" once, and "next" once. Because the essay is

informational, not directional, most likely the author did not feel that the

correct chronology was important.

5. Would other transitional expressions be more effective? Which ones would you add, and where would you place them?

Answers will vary.

Critical Thinking Writing Opportunities

1. In her directional process essay "A Step-by-Step Guide to Photography," Stephanie Weidemann relies on *personal experience* to provide important information about photography. She understands from her close involvement with photography that processes done correctly, not expensive equipment, provide the photographer with the best opportunity to create successful prints. Write a directional process essay that outlines the steps in a hobby or activity you are involved with. Using your personal experience, provide the reader with important information that will make their efforts successful. Before you begin, make a list of the steps in the hobby or activity and put them in chronological order. Be certain your essay includes appropriate transitional expressions.

2. In her informational process essay "How to Be Successful at Kicking the Smoking Habit," Stephany K. Higgs uses *concepts and ideas* to help smokers understand why they should quit smoking. The author mixes tangible activities with the psychological motivations that must be understood to make the process of quitting smoking effective. Write an informational process essay about how you or someone you know broke a habit or addiction. In the essay, you should use concepts and ideas to make the process clear for the reader. Remember, your intent is to have the reader understand the process, not duplicate it. As in the essay about smoking, there is no way to guarantee that a smoker will quit smoking even if they understand the process.

3. In her process essay "You Sure You Want to Do This?" writer Maneka Gandhi focuses on *implications and consequences* as she unveils how the lipstick manufacturing process uses ingredients (fish scales, acid, ammonia, and dyes) that would make putting makeup on your face an unsavory practice. Look in your medicine cabinet or on a pharmacy shelf, and find a product that is applied to the body. Make a list of the ingredients, and then find out what some of the chemicals are used for other than in the product you have found. Write an essay focusing on the implications and consequences of applying such chemicals to the body and how knowing this information beforehand might affect our initial decision to buy and use the product in the first place.

Topics for a Process Essay

Here are some possible topics for directional and informational essay writing assignments. Remember, your process essay should have a clearly defined purpose.

1. How to repair an appliance (for example: lamp, toaster, radio).
2. How to act on a first date in order to guarantee a second date.
3. How to preserve a food (for example: pickles, peaches, tomatoes).
4. How a camera works.
5. How stars form (and/or die).
6. How a cure for a disease was discovered.
7. How legislation becomes a bill.

8. How to install computer hardware (for example: sound card, modem, zip drive).

9. How to start a home-based business.

10. How to propose marriage.

Chapter Review

■ A process essay explains how something happened, how to do or make something, or how something works. Directional process essays explain how to do something or make something, and their purpose is to enable the reader to duplicate the process. Informational process essays explain how something was done or made, and their purpose is to have the reader understand the process but not duplicate it.

■ In a process paragraph, the steps of the process are usually organized chronologically, and transitional expressions help keep the step in sequence.

■ In a process essay, the introductory paragraph introduces the process, outlines the main steps, and explains the importance of the process. The body paragraphs develop the main steps in sequence. In the concluding paragraph, an evaluation of the process is a possible approach.

Visit *The Write Start* Online!

For additional practice with the materials found in this chapter, visit our Website at

http://www.ablongman.com/checkett

The Website also features additional readings, quizzes, writing activities, and Internet links, as well as a bulletin board and interactive chat.

CHAPTER

12

The Comparison or Contrast Essay

$\mathbf{A}$s your writing opportunities increase, often you will need to discuss an object, person, idea, event, or item not only in terms of its own features, but also in terms of how it relates to another object, person, idea, event, or item. This type of writing can be challenging because it forces you to think about each item independently of the other and then to think about how the items relate to each other. Are they alike? Are they different? How? Why? Developing a topic in this fashion is called comparison or contrast.

Identifying Your Purpose

When using **comparison-contrast** to organize a paragraph or essay, you are looking for similarities and differences. When *comparing*, you are looking for similarities. When *contrasting*, you are looking for differences. For example, consider two computers. In comparing them, you might notice that the monitor screens both measure 14 inches, the housings are made of a high-impact plastic, the keyboards have all the same function keys, and the hard drives have the same information storage capacity. In contrasting them, however, you might notice that one has a black housing and the other has a blue one, one has a combination battery and CD-ROM port and the other does not, and one has a monitor and a CPU that stand separate from the keyboard while the other system has the monitor, CPU, and keyboard self-contained in one housing. By comparing and contrasting, then, you know that both units are computers, but that one is a traditional desktop model while the other is a new laptop version. Comparison and contrast, therefore, helps you understand one person, place, feeling, idea, event, or object in relation to another. Look at the following two examples.

Example Comparison Paragraph

The occupations of cosmetologist and nurse may seem very different, but they share many common attributes. For instance, the cosmetologist makes the client's appearance better by using the proper grooming techniques. The nurse uses the latest medical procedures when treating a patient. A cosmetologist's client often feels depressed or anxious about his or her appearance. By using the coloring products appropriate to the client's complexion and age, the cosmetologist can change her appearance dramatically, making the client feel good about herself once again. The nurse makes the patient feel better by administering the proper medications or exercise appropriate for the patient's problem and age group. Both the cosmetologist and the nurse make people in their care feel better about themselves.

Even though the occupations of cosmetologist and nurse do not seem very similar on the surface, points of comparison can be found. Of course, there must be a purpose to the comparison and, in the comparison above, the fact that both the cosmetologist and the nurse make their patients feel better is the important consideration.

Example Contrast Paragraph

In the novel *Runaway Jury*, by John Grisham, the character development is superb because the writer alludes to certain aspects of the characters' personalities throughout the development of the plot. One of the strong points of this novel is that the reader is being fed only enough information about the characters at crucial times; therefore, a desire is created within the reader to know each character more intimately and to know how they will relate to the rest of the story. In contrast, *The Testament*, also by John Grisham, has a glaring lack of character development from the very beginning of the story. There is some confusion in the first few chapters as to who the main characters are. Instead of revealing the nature of each personality throughout the book, the author gives bland, generic, and brief descriptions of them. There also is an overabundance of characters who truly are not necessary to the development and enrichment of the plot, so the desire to know the characters better and to see how the plot relates to them is not achieved.

Although both novels are written by the same author, and both novels involve lawyers and the law (John Grisham trademarks), the contrasts clearly are definable and important on several levels. First, if you are going to shell out $24.95 for a novel, you certainly want its characters to be well developed and interesting. Secondly, on a technical level, you want to know that a writer you are considering investing time and money in is an accomplished artist who can bring his characters to life in an interesting and compelling way that will hold your interest.

You might, at times, be called on to compare and contrast many people, places, events, or items. But most of the time you will be comparing or contrasting two items and, for the sake of simplicity, that is what you will learn how to do in this chapter.

Answers will vary.

Look at the following pairs of topics. Indicate whether it would be better to compare or contrast each pair by putting a check mark in the space provided.

	Compare	Contrast
1. Fire and ice	_____	_____
2. Alaska and Arizona	_____	_____
3. Capitalism and communism	_____	_____
4. Men and women	_____	_____
5. Soccer and rugby	_____	_____
6. Email and snail mail	_____	_____
7. Swimming in a river or lake	_____	_____
8. Canoeing and kayaking	_____	_____
9. Thin and deep-pan pizza	_____	_____
10. Being married and being single	_____	_____

Writing a Comparison or Contrast Paragraph

When you write a paragraph about two items, your first task is to decide whether to compare or contrast them. Once that is done, you can select the appropriate supporting details, write an appropriate topic sentence, and decide how to organize the points in your paragraph.

Deciding to Compare or to Contrast and Selecting Supporting Detail

Sometimes, it will be obvious to you whether to compare or contrast two items. At other times, the similarities and differences may not jump out at you. After you have chosen your pair of topics to develop, what is the best method to use to help you decide if you should compare or contrast the two items? How will you know if there are enough elements between the two items to make comparing or contrasting them worthwhile? Creating a diagram like the one in the following example is an easy method that helps you make such decisions.

Compare and Contrast Diagram

Two items:

Humungous University   TinyTown College

Similarities:

Great humanities departments   Exceptional fine arts

Faculty 90% PhDs	Faculty 85% PhDs
Computer friendly campus	Each student receives laptop
In-state campus near home	Out of state but only 100 miles away

Differences:

All traditional sports teams	"Club" sports and intramurals
Federal & state financial aid	Private and government aid
50,000 students	5,000 students
Student/faculty ratio 30:1	Student/faculty ratio 11:1
Many graduate degrees	M.A. & M.F.A. degrees only

Once you have filled in the similarities and differences of the two items, it should become obvious which approach will result in the better paragraph. You will also be able to use the items in your list as supporting details as you develop the paragraph. So, using the diagram can make developing your paragraph much easier.

PRACTICE 2

Answers will vary.

Choose one of the topics from Practice 1 and complete a compare and contrast diagram for it.

Compare and Contrast Diagram

Two items:

_____   _____

Similarities:

_____   _____

_____   _____

_____   _____

Differences:

_____   _____

_____   _____

_____   _____

The Topic Sentence in a Comparison or Contrast Paragraph

The topic sentence in a comparison or contrast paragraph clearly states the two items being developed and why comparing or contrasting them is important. The following is an example of a topic sentence for a comparison or contrast paragraph.

> When you choose between ice hockey and roller hockey for your child's participation, cost is usually the deciding factor.

This topic sentence clearly states the two items for comparison: ice hockey and roller hockey. The important reason for discussing the topic is the cost factor, which also indicates that contrast, not comparison, will be the method of development.

PRACTICE 3

Write a topic sentence for the subject you chose in Practice 1 and for which you completed a comparison and contrast diagram in Practice 2.

Organizing a Comparison or Contrast Paragraph

Once you know whether you are comparing or contrasting and the supporting details you will use, you need to organize your thoughts and decide how to present them. There are two commonly used organizational plans for comparison and contrast paragraphs: block and point-by-point. The *block method* presents all the information about one item first, then uses this information for comparison or contrast when presenting information about the second item. The *point-by-point method* presents the information about both items together, creating an ongoing series of comparisons and contrasts.

In the following paragraph about ice hockey and roller hockey, the block method is used.

Block Method Example

When you choose between ice hockey and roller hockey for your child's participation, cost is usually the deciding factor. Playing roller hockey in small in-house leagues costs on average seventy-five dollars. If children show talent, they may play for a "select" tournament team, and the average cost will skyrocket to three hundred dollars. Equipment for roller hockey, although expensive, is necessary for protection against injury. Well-padded, durable skates can cost an average of two hundred dollars; helmets, on average, cost fifty dollars; and kneepads, girdle, and pants can cost one hundred and fifty dollars. This brings the total average cost of roller hockey to four hundred seventy-five dollars for an in-house league and seven hundred fifty dollars for a select tournament team. Ice hockey is considerably more expensive than roller hockey because more equipment is required. Playing ice hockey in an in-house league costs an average of three hundred fifty dollars, and playing for a select tournament team can cost six hundred dollars. As with roller hockey equipment, ice hockey equipment is expensive. In addition, ice hockey requires shoulder pads while roller hockey does not. The pads can cost upwards of seventy-five dollars. Also, ice hockey requires a thicker, heavier stick that can cost ninety to one hundred dollars. Ice hockey skates have an average cost of three hundred dollars, which is one hundred dollars more than roller hockey skates. Helmets, kneepads, girdle, and pants can cost two hundred to three hundred fifty dollars. The total average cost for playing ice hockey in an in-house league is nine hundred to twelve hundred dollars.

Notice that the cost elements of roller hockey are discussed in the first half of the paragraph (without mention of ice hockey). Then the same elements in regard to ice hockey are discussed in the second half of the paragraph. But this time as each ice hockey item is mentioned, reference is made to the corresponding roller hockey item as well. In this way, the comparison between the elements is continually made. If this were not done, then the two halves of the paragraph would seem disconnected, and the contrast would not exist.

The block method can be diagrammed in this manner:

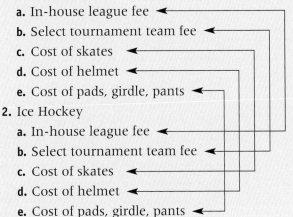

Block Method Diagram

Topic sentence: When you choose between ice hockey and roller hockey for your child's participation, cost is usually the deciding factor.

1. Roller Hockey
    a. In-house league fee
    b. Select tournament team fee
    c. Cost of skates
    d. Cost of helmet
    e. Cost of pads, girdle, pants
2. Ice Hockey
    a. In-house league fee
    b. Select tournament team fee
    c. Cost of skates
    d. Cost of helmet
    e. Cost of pads, girdle, pants

Remember, when using the block method, you discuss all the factors in the first item of comparison or contrast in the first part of the paragraph without mentioning the second item being compared or contrasted. Then, in the second half of the paragraph, you discuss each point regarding the second item in the comparison or contrast, remembering to make reference to each item that was mentioned in the first half of the paragraph. This will connect the two items so that the paragraph will not seem to be about two items that have nothing to do with one another.

In the point-by-point method, the similar point in regard to the second item in the comparison or contrast follows each point concerning the first item. The point-by-point method is diagrammed in this manner:

Point-by-Point Method Diagram

Topic sentence: When you decide on ice hockey or roller hockey for your child's participation, cost is usually the deciding factor.

First Point: **a.** Roller hockey in-league fee
               b. Ice hockey in-league fee

Second Point: **a.** Roller hockey Select Tournament Team
               b. Ice hockey Select Tournament Team

Third Point: **a.** Roller hockey skates
               b. Ice hockey skates

Fourth Point: **a.** Roller hockey helmets
               b. Ice hockey helmets

Fifth Point: **a.** Roller hockey pads, girdle, pants
               b. Ice hockey pads, girdle, pants

For the point-by-point method, the paragraph contrasting ice hockey and roller hockey might be rewritten like this:

Point-by-Point Method Example

When you choose between ice hockey and roller hockey for your child's participation, cost is usually the deciding factor. When playing roller hockey in small in-house leagues, the average cost is seventy-five dollars. On the other hand, playing ice hockey in an in-house league costs an average of three hundred fifty dollars. If children show talent, they may play for a "select" tournament team, and the average roller hockey team cost will skyrocket to three hundred dollars. Whereas, on a select ice hockey tournament team, the costs can soar to six hundred dollars. Equipment for roller hockey, although expensive, is necessary for protection against injury. Well-padded, durable roller hockey skates can cost an average of two hundred dollars, while ice hockey skates have an average cost of three hundred dollars and up. In roller hockey, helmets, on average, cost fifty dollars. Similarly, ice hockey helmets cost about fifty to sixty dollars. Knee pads, girdle, and pants for roller hockey can cost one hundred fifty dollars. However, ice hockey knee pads, girdle, and pants can cost two hundred to three hundred fifty dollars. In addition, ice hockey requires shoulder pads while roller hockey does not. The pads can cost upwards of seventy-five dollars. Also, ice hockey requires a thicker, heavier stick than does roller hockey, and the stick can cost ninety to one hundred dollars. In conclusion, the average cost for playing in a roller hockey in-house league is four hundred seventy-five dollars and nine hundred to twelve hundred dollars for playing in an ice hockey in-house league. While the cost for playing for a roller hockey select tournament team can rise to seven hundred fifty dollars, playing for an ice hockey select team can be as much as fourteen hundred dollars.

PRACTICE 4

Using the topic sentence you wrote in Practice 3, write a comparison or contrast block method paragraph for the topic you have chosen. Then rewrite the paragraph using the point-by-point method.

Using Transitional Expressions to Connect Comparisons or Contrasts

Transitional expressions are important because they stress either comparison or contrast, depending on the type of paragraph you are writing. They also help keep the reader on track, because as we have seen, the organization of points in a comparison or contrast paragraph can be complex.

Transitional Expressions Showing Comparison

and	in addition
again	in the same way
also	like
as well as	likewise
both	neither
each	similarly
equally	similar to
furthermore	so
just as	the same
just like	too

Transitional Expressions Showing Contrast

although	on the contrary
but	on the other hand
despite	otherwise
different from	nevertheless
even though	still
except for	though
however	whereas
in contrast	while
instead	yet

PRACTICE 5

Add appropriate transitional expressions to one of the paragraphs you wrote for Practice 4. When you have finished, compare the two paragraphs. The paragraph with the transitional expressions should connect related ideas more effectively as well as add rhythm to the writing.

Moving from Paragraph to Essay

Now that you have studied and practiced the techniques to create effective comparison or contrast paragraphs, it is time to expand your ideas to a larger writing unit: the comparison or contrast essay. Using the techniques you learned in Part 1 regarding developing the essay paragraphs and the comparison or contrast techniques you have just learned enables you to write the comparison or contrast essay. This might be a good time to return to Part 1 and review the techniques for developing the full essay.

Creating the Introductory Paragraph

A comparison or contrast essay needs a clearly defined organization and a thesis statement to announce to the reader just how the subject will be developed. The thesis sentence of the introductory paragraph should state the items to be compared or contrasted, the writer's controlling idea or attitude toward the subject, and the organizational structure. By using an appropriate lead-in technique, the thesis should blend naturally into the rest of the introductory paragraph.

By using a variation of the compare and contrast diagram you have already practiced to produce a comparison or contrast paragraph, you can extend and develop the ideas expressed in the diagram to help you create the thesis sentence for a comparison and contrast essay.

Comparison and Contrast Essay Diagram
Two items:

1. _____   2. _____

Controlling idea or attitude:

1. _____ in relation to **2.** _____

Comparison and contrast points:

1. _____   _____

2. _____   _____

3. _____   _____

4. _____   _____

5. _____   _____

6. _____   _____

Thesis sentence:

_____

_____

_____

Once you have chosen your two items and have listed elements that are similar and different, choose whether you are going to compare or contrast the two topics. Next, decide what your controlling idea or attitude is toward the subject.

Then, choose the *three comparison or contrast points* from your list that you want to use in your essay. These will be the three subtopics for the essay map in your thesis sentence.

Finally, write the thesis sentence by following the elements you have listed in your diagram.

Example

Two items:

Sequoia Medical School   Oceana Medical School

Controlling idea or attitude:

Sequoia Medical School *is better than* Oceana Medical School

Contrast points:

1. Faculty to student ratio

2. Tuition costs

3. Medical facilities

Thesis sentence:

Sequoia Medical School *is better than* Oceana Medical School because of

its faculty to student ratio, tuition costs, and medical facilities.

Creating the Body Paragraphs

For an essay contrasting two medical schools, the focus of the body paragraphs will be the paragraph topics listed in the thesis sentence's essay map. The first body paragraph's topic will be "faculty to student ratio"; the second body paragraph's topic will be "tuition costs"; the third body paragraph's topic will be "medical facilities." Remember, as you write about each of these topics, your focus should be that these are the reason *Sequoia Medical School is better than Oceana Medical School.* You can develop each of the body paragraphs using either the block method or the point-by-point method, but be consistent in the method you use within a single essay.

Creating the Concluding Paragraph

The approach of the concluding paragraph should flow naturally from the essay's main topic. Because the essay's focus is that the characteristics of one medical school makes it preferable to another, an *evaluation* of the main points seems appropriate. You might talk briefly about how the school's programs and features will help you gain acceptance to an area of medicine you want to specialize in, or how these elements will help you grow both as a person and as a professional. You might even mention if the school has professional connections to private companies that might offer employment possibilities in research. (Refer to Chapter 5 for other approaches for concluding paragraphs.)

Create a compare or contrast essay diagram for the topic you chose in Practice 4. After you have completed the diagram, write your essay.

Sample Comparison Student Essay: COMMERCIAL VS. RESIDENTIAL REAL ESTATE SALES

Nancy Smith

> Real estate sales is a popular and expanding job category. It may appear on the surface that selling commercial buildings and residential homes would be quite dissimilar. But in this essay, "Commercial vs. Residential Real Estate Sales," student writer and real estate agent Nancy Smith dispels the myth that commercial real estate sales is the more lucrative side of the business. While the essay is comparison, the writer does clarify an important difference. But by doing so, she in no way compromises the integrity of the essay's focus.

Vocabulary

Meaning comes primarily from words. Before you begin reading, use a dictionary to look up the definitions of the following words that appear in the essay.

applicant	aspect	commission
dwelling	flexible	flyers
lack	solicit	striking

Commercial vs. Residential Real Estate Sales

1   Thinking about a career in real estate? With the proper training and hard work, you can make real estate a rewarding profession. Whether you choose commercial or residential sales, the decision can be easy when all the facts are known to the applicant. **Commercial and residential real estate are very similar in the areas of marketing, client development, and income potential.**

Thesis Sentence ⟶
Topic Sentence ⟶   2   **The marketing costs for commercial real estate are paid for by the real estate company; similarly, in residential real estate, costs are usually picked up by the real estate company as well.** Like residential real estate agents, commercial real estate agents send out thousands of flyers that advertise property for lease or sale. For example, both commercial and residential agents announce available properties by mailing advertising brochures to area residents and to other agents. Both commercial and residential agents can act alone or share commissions with other agents when a property is sold, rented, or leased.

Topic Sentence ⟶   3   **Residential sales requires a lot of work to build up a good client base; likewise, commercial agents rely on repeat customers for fifty percent of their business.** Commercial as well as residential agents also have to solicit business by "cold-calling" potential customers who may or may not be in the process of wanting to relocate. You might be surprised to find out that while businesses are looking for real estate for working space, many residential agents must provide the same characteristics for family dwellings. In families in which both parents work, "in home" office space is increasingly necessary

Topic Sentence ⟶ 4   While there are many similarities between the two sales positions, there are some striking differences. The commercial agent usually has to make fewer sales to achieve the same commissions as does the residential agent. However, because more families relocate at any given time than do businesses, the residential agent can make up in volume what the average residential commission lacks in amount.

5   With a healthy economy and more people becoming skilled in the areas employers desire, the job market for both commercial and residential real estate agents is booming. And one should not overlook the "people skills" aspect of both sales environments. Selling real estate, whether commercial or residential, is as much art as it is science. With the addition of flexible work scheduling and improved benefits, most agents are finding the world of real estate a profitable, rewarding, and fun career.

Comparison Technique Questions

1. How many points of similarity does the author use? Identify them. Is the amount enough to be convincing? Explain.

   Three: marketing, client development, and income potential. (The remaining answers will vary.)

2. The real estate company does quite a bit to help each agent. But what personal attributes or "people skills" might an agent have to have to be successful?

   Answers will vary.

3. Although this is a comparison essay, the writer identifies a contrasting point in the last body paragraph. Why does the author provide the apparent difference?

   Most people probably think that commercial sales is more lucrative, but the author wants to clarify that while residential sales commissions are usually smaller, the greater sales volume makes up the difference.

4. What organizational pattern does the writer use, point-by-point or block?

   Point-by-point.

Sample Contrast Student Essay: TWO DIFFERENT NEIGHBORS

Tayde Cruz

The United States and Mexico have been neighbors for over two centuries, both countries are democratic in their political makeup, and they share some economic fortunes with the North American Free Trade Agreement (NAFTA). Yet, in this essay, "Two Different Neighbors," student writer Tayde Cruz states that the two countries are not very similar at all. Born and raised in Mexico, Cruz moved to the United States with her family right after graduating from high school. She develops the essay around subtopics that are of interest to persons her age. Cruz believes that the United States is a better place for a long-term stay rather than a short-term visit.

Vocabulary

Meaning comes primarily from words. Before beginning to read, use a dictionary to look up the following words that appear in the essay.

economically	festive	millennium
optimistic	pyramid	salsa dancing

Two Different Neighbors

1   Living in the United States means living in a country where there can be a good future for just about anybody; however, the United States is not the best place to vacation if you are looking for a place with activities going on all day long, each day of the year. Mexico, on the other hand, doesn't necessarily have all the advantages of the United States when planning a future, but it has many advantages when it comes to planning a short-term vacation. In Mexico, one can be active from the moment when one awakes. For instance, there are breakfast places beside the hotel pool, so the visitor can combine swimming and pool activities with the first meal of the day. What a wake-up call! Mexico is a better vacation destination than the United States because of its historical sites, festive atmosphere, and low drinking age.

Thesis Sentence →
Topic Sentence →

2   The United States has many historical sites but, in contrast to Mexico, these places are very young. For example, the Statue of Liberty is not even a century old. Another place to visit in the United States is Philadelphia. Philadelphia is an important city to visit because of its connection to the colonies winning independence from England two hundred years ago. On the other hand, in Mexico, the pyramids found at Tenochtitlan are at least a millennium old, predating the Liberty Bell by over eight hundred years. Despite its current modern architecture, Mexico City's political importance goes back to the early 16th century when the Aztec Empire fell and colonial rule was instituted by the Spanish conquerors.

Topic Sentence →

3   Festivals occur in the United States, mostly on specific weekends several times during the year. New Year's Eve happens on one night. While the evening is long and full of excitement, it is over rather quickly for such a momentous event. Mardi Gras is another popular festive event. Although it lasts for four or five days, the party is localized to one city, New Orleans. And,

in the United States, fireworks are reserved for one night only, the Fourth of July. In Mexico, there's no need for a specific reason to celebrate. If one goes to Mexico, festive atmospheres are found all year long in almost any location, particularly on the coast. Puerto Vallarto has become known worldwide for its year round partying. Fireworks are exploded all year in Mexico to celebrate, well . . . anything!

Topic Sentence ⟶ 4   In most states in America, the legal drinking age is 21 years of age. Young people can die for their country in the armed forces or vote for president, but they have to wait three years to have an alcoholic drink. All summer long and during spring break on college campuses throughout the United States, young people flock to Mexico because the legal drinking age is eighteen years of age. Cancun, Mazatlan, Tiajuana, and Acapulco are just a few of the cities young Americans visit to drink without worry of arrest while they celebrate graduations, a break from schoolwork, and any other rite of passage they can think of.

5   Mexico, in general, might not be the greatest place to live. It has severe financial problems, and its government is not always reliable in taking care of its citizens; whereas, it is a wonderful place to visit if only for a weekend. Mexico is a great place to get away to and forget about work, school, or the ordinary world that we all have to put up with. Still, no matter how poor Mexico's economy might be, it always has a festive and optimistic outlook on life. That is the true beauty of Mexico—its people!

Contrast Technique Questions

1. What is the writer contrasting in the essay?

   The United States and Mexico as a vacation destination.

2. What organizational pattern does the writer use, point-by-point or block?

   Point-by-point.

3. Which transitional expressions does the writer use to move you smoothly from idea to idea?

   Paragraph 1: "however," "on the other hand," "For instance"; paragraph

   2: "in contrast," "For example," and "on the other hand"; paragraph 3:

   "While," "Although"; paragraph 4: "In most" and "but"; paragraph 5: "in

   general," "whereas," and "Still."

4. Does the writer use enough specific examples to develop and clarify the contrast? Explain.

   Yes. In paragraph 2, the writer uses examples such as the Statue of Liberty

   and Philadelphia, the pyramids at Tenochtitlan, the Liberty Bell, and the

Aztec Empire. In paragraph 3, the examples are festivals: New Year's Eve,

Mardi Gras, and the Fourth of July. In paragraph 4, the writer uses exam-

ples of Mexican cities and resorts where the drinking age is only eighteen:

Cancun, Mazatlan, Tiajuana, and Acapulco.

Sample Professional Essay: LIGHT SKIN VERSUS DARK

Charisse Jones

The following essay, "Light Skin versus Dark," by Pulitzer Prize–winning *New York Times* journalist Charisse Jones, first appeared in *Glamour* magazine. In it, the author recounts a time during her high school years when she was first confronted with "colorism," a type of racism that she considers even more injurious because it comes from those of her own race. It is an unusual issue for whites because they are not confronted with this type of bias within their own race. In this regard, as you read the essay, try to decide what audience Jones is writing for, whites or blacks.

Vocabulary

Meaning comes primarily from words. Before you start reading, use a dictionary to look up the definitions of the following words that appear in the essay.

eradicate	foil	lexicon
litany	mantra	notorious
nuance	revel	smirking
spectrum	subtext	synonymous

Light Skin versus Dark

1   I'll never forget the day I was supposed to meet him. We had only spoken on the phone. But we got along so well, we couldn't wait to meet face-to-face. I took the bus from my high school to his for our blind date. While I nervously waited for him outside the school, one of his buddies came along, looked me over, and remarked that I was going to be a problem, because his friend didn't like dating anybody darker than himself.

2   When my mystery man—who was not especially good-looking—finally saw me, he took one look, uttered a hurried hello, then disappeared with his smirking friends. I had apparently been pronounced ugly on arrival and dismissed.

3   That happened nearly fifteen years ago. I'm thirty now, and the hurt and humiliation have long since faded. But the memory still lingers, reinforced in later years by other situations in which my skin color was judged by other African Americans—for example, at a cocktail party or a nightclub where light-skinned black women got all the attention.

4   A racist encounter hurts badly. But it does not equal the pain of "colorism"—being rejected by your own people because your skin is colored cocoa

and not cream, ebony and not olive. On our scale of beauty, it is often the high yellows—in the lexicon of black America, those with light skin—whose looks reap the most attention. Traditionally, if someone was described that way, there was no need to say that person was good-looking. It was a given that light was lovely. It was those of us with plain brown eyes and darker skin hues who had to prove ourselves.

5 I was twelve, and in my first year of junior high school in San Francisco, when I discovered dark brown was not supposed to be beautiful. At that age, boys suddenly became important, and so did your looks. But by that time—the late 1970s—black kids no longer believed in that sixties mantra, "Black is beautiful." Light skin, green eyes, and long, wavy hair were once again synonymous with beauty.

6 Colorism—and its subtext of self-hatred—began during slavery on plantations where white masters often favored the lighter-skinned blacks, many of whom were their own children. But though it began with whites, black people have kept colorism alive. In the past, many black sororities, fraternities, and other social organizations have been notorious for accepting only light-skinned members. Yes, some blacks have criticized their lighter-skinned peers. But most often in our history, a light complexion had been a passport to special treatment by both whites *and* blacks.

7 Some social circles are still defined by hue. Some African Americans, dark and light, prefer light-skinned mates so they can have a "pretty baby." And skin-lightening creams still sell, though they are now advertised as good for making blemishes fade rather than for lightening whole complexions.

8 In my family, color was never discussed, even though our spectrum was broad—my brother was very light; my sister and I, much darker. But in junior high, I learned in a matter of weeks what had apparently been drummed into the heads of my black peers for most of their lives.

9 Realizing how crazy it all was, I became defiant, challenging friends when they made silly remarks. Still, there was no escaping the distinctions of color.

10 In my life, I have received a litany of twisted compliments from fellow blacks. "You're the prettiest dark-skinned girl I have ever seen" is one; "you're pretty for a dark girl" is another.

11 A light-complexioned girlfriend once remarked to me that dark-skinned people often don't take the time to groom themselves. As a journalist, I once interviewed a prominent black lawmaker who was light-skinned. He drew me into the shade of a tree while we talked because, he said, "I'm sure you don't want to get any darker."

12 Though some black people—like film-maker Spike Lee in his movie *School Daze*—have tried to provoke debate about colorism, it remains a painful topic many blacks would rather not confront. Yet there has been progress. In this age of Afrocentrism, many blacks revel in the nuances of the African American rainbow. Natural hairstyles and dreadlocks are in, and Theresa Randle, star of the hit film *Bad Boys*, is only one of several darker-skinned actresses noted for their beauty.

13 That gives me hope. People have told me that color biases among blacks run too deep ever to be eradicated. But I tell them that is the kind of attitude that allows colorism to persist. Meanwhile, I do what I can. When I notice that a friend dates only light-skinned women, I comment on it. If I hear that a movie follows the tired old scenario in which a light-skinned beauty is the love interest while a darker-skinned woman is the comic foil, the butt of "ugly" jokes, I don't go see it. Others can do the same.

14 There is only so much blacks can do about racism, because we need the cooperation of others to make it go away. But healing ourselves is within our control.

15   At least we can try. As a people we face enough pain without inflicting our own wounds. I believe any people that could survive slavery, that could disprove the lies than pronounced them less than human, can also teach its children that black is beautiful in all of its shades.

16   Loving ourselves should be an easy thing to do.

Comparison and Contrast
Technique Questions

1. Is there a thesis sentence that clearly states the topic to be discussed? If so, identify it. If not, state what you think is the thesis of the essay.

Answers will vary. Students usually identify the second sentence of para-

graph 3, the last sentence in paragraph 6, the second sentence in para-

graph 9, and the last sentence in paragraph 15.

2. How does the author distinguish between "colorism" and "racism"?

"Racism" occurs when people from another race treat you in a negative

manner based on your ethnicity; "colorism" occurs when those of your

own race treat you negatively based on your "skin tone."

3. The author believes that "colorism" is more harmful than "racism." Do you agree with her assessment? Explain.

Answers will vary.

4. What examples in the essay point to the author writing for a black audience? What examples point to her writing for a white audience?

Answers will vary. The examples students point to will depend largely on

how much they assume whites and blacks know about the difference

between "racism" and "colorism"—if anything. It would be interesting to

have your students define these two terms prior to reading the essay to

see if they can differentiate between them.

5. The title suggests the pair of items being contrasted. What other subtopics are contrasted or compared in the essay?

"beauty and ugliness," "immediate acceptance versus proving oneself,"

"tradition and change," and "self-hatred and self-pride."

Critical Thinking Writing Opportunities

1. In her essay "Commercial vs. Residential Real Estate Sales," Nancy Smith attempts to dispel the myth that sales representatives make more money in commercial real estate sales than do those selling in the residential market. Her evidence is mostly *information* in the form of *facts* as she compares the two sides of selling real estate. Write an essay comparing or contrasting two jobs or two aspects of a job you have had or in which you are currently employed. Use facts to correct a misconception that most people might have about some aspect of the job.

2. In her essay "Two Different Neighbors," Tayde Cruz uses a mixture of information in the form of *facts* and *personal observation/experience* to come to a conclusion: Mexico is better than the United States for a short vacation, but the United States is a better place to live over the long term. Write an essay comparing or contrasting two countries, states, or regions you have visited. Use facts and personal observation/experience as the basis for your conclusion.

3. In her essay "Light Skin versus Dark," journalist Charisse Jones uses information in the form of *personal observation/experience* and *definition* to make her audience aware of "colorism," a form of racism that is particularly harmful because it is used by some African Americans against others of their own race. Have you ever been hurt or embarrassed by being treated differently because of some physical characteristic, such as skin color, freckles vs. clear skin, blonde vs. black or brunette hair color, a prominent nose or pug nose vs. a small or straight nose, thin vs. heavy, or tall vs. short? In many cultures, some of these features are looked upon in a positive way, while in other cultures, they are not. Write an essay comparing or contrasting two cultural attitudes about some physical characteristic you have and its negative effects on you. Use information in the form of *personal observation/experience* and *definition* (if others think you are a "geek," for instance, you should provide an explanation of this label) to support your ideas.

Topics for a Comparison or Contrast Essay

Here are some possible topics for both comparison or contrast essay writing assignments. Remember, your comparison or contrast essay should have a clearly defined purpose.

Frederic Leighton, *Study of a Lady*   Pablo Picasso, *Head of a Woman*, 1939

1. Two pieces of art.
2. A famous person's public image versus his or her private image.

3. Two colleges.

4. Two bosses or co-workers.

5. Past attitudes about AIDS, lesbianism, or male homosexuality when it first became an issue and attitudes today.

6. A falsely held belief or myth and the factual reality.

7. How a friend of yours acts in private and how he or she acts in public.

8. A former attitude you had about a political issue and how you feel about it now.

9. How your life is today and how you thought it was going to be years ago.

10. Two places you have lived in or visited.

Chapter Review

■ When you compare two or more items, you are looking for similarities. When you contrast them, you are looking for differences.

■ When you write a comparison or contrast paragraph, you must first decide whether to compare or contrast the two items. In a compare and contrast diagram, you can list similarities and differences and so choose whether to compare or to contrast based on the strength of the details. The topic sentence of a compare or contrast paragraph clearly states the items to be compared or contrasted and the controlling idea or attitude.

■ There are two basic methods for organizing a comparison or contrast paragraph. In the block method, you present all the information about one item first, then use this information when you present information about the second item. In the point-by-point method, you present information about both items together, creating a series of comparisons or contrasts. Transitional expressions help make the organization of comparison and contrast paragraphs clear to the reader.

■ In the introductory paragraph of a comparison or contrast essay, the thesis sentence states the two items to be compared or contrasted, the controlling idea or attitude, and the subtopics that will be compared or contrasted. In the body paragraphs, either the block method or point-by-point method can be used to develop the subtopics. Finally, evaluation is a good approach to the concluding paragraph of a comparison or contrast essay because it allows you to express a judgment about the items you've been comparing or contrasting.

Visit *The Write Start* Online!

For additional practice with the materials found in this chapter, visit our Website at

http://www.ablongman.com/checkett

The Website also features additional readings, quizzes, writing activities, and Internet links, as well as a bulletin board and interactive chat.

CHAPTER 13

The Definition Essay

As you write, you may use concepts, terms, and words that you think your reader may not understand. You might use a term such as *black hole* or *macroeconomics*. Concepts such as *domino theory* or *Jungian psychology* may be foreign to your reader, so you may need to explain them so your reader fully understands what you are trying to communicate. Read the following short paragraph.

> "Purple cows are purple cows because they are colored purple." The tautological reasoning embedded in the statement makes its truthful wording obvious and unnecessary.

What is the paragraph trying to tell you? Is the meaning clear? Unless you know what *tautological* means, you probably will not understand the meaning the writer is trying to get you to understand. A better paragraph might look like this:

> "Purple cows are purple because they are colored purple." The statement contains all logical possibilities and, therefore, is always true. The statement, then, is a tautology, a needless repetition of the same, obvious concepts.

Defining the concept of *tautology* helps the reader understand why the statement regarding the purple cow is unnecessarily obvious and repetitive. The statement does not adequately explain why the cow is purple, just that it is—which is already obvious just by looking at it. A tautology, then, is considered circular reasoning.

Identifying Your Purpose

When we clearly explain the meaning of words, terms, and concepts, we are using **definition** as a method of communicating to the reader. There are two types of definition, simple and extended.

145

Simple Definition

Simple definitions are brief explanations such as those you might find in a dictionary. There are three types of simple definitions:

■ **Synonym definition** defines a word by supplying another simpler word that means the same thing. For example, *conundrum* means *riddle* or *puzzle*, while *cacophony* means *noise*.

■ **Class definition** defines a word by placing it in a broad class of similar things that readers will readily understand, and then provides a specific detail that makes the original term or word different from the others in the class. For example, a *convertible* is a *car* with *a top that goes up and down*. In this definition, *convertible* is the term being defined. It is put into *a class of similar things (cars)*, and then it is made different from other cars, such as sedans and coupes, because *it has a top that goes up and down*.

■ **Definition by negation** begins by saying what a given word or term *is not* before saying what the word or term *actually is*. For example, a *bagel* just *isn't* a doughnut-shaped piece of bread that's deep-fried. A bagel is much more than that. It's actually *a unique type of bread that's boiled before it's baked*.

Definition is important because clear communication depends upon clear understanding. Precise language is essential if you are to understand what someone else means. One word can have multiple meanings, so it is essential that you define terms for your reader.

PRACTICE 1

Answers will vary.

Write a synonym, class, and negation definition for one of the following words: freedom, rustic, malevolent, prude, shark, tomato, symbol, topography, simplicity.

_____

_____

_____

_____

_____

_____

_____

_____

Extended Definition

At times, terms such as *black hole, macroeconomics, domino theory,* and *Jungian psychology* cannot be adequately defined using a simple definition. Instead, you may need to use a few sentences or an entire paragraph to define such terms so that they are understood clearly. This longer type of definition is called an **extended definition.** Extended definition can be accomplished by means of any one mode of development or any combination of the modes of development: description, narration, example, classification, process, comparison and contrast, and cause and effect.

Therefore, to help you define your term, you might

- describe some of its characteristics
- incorporate it into a story
- give some examples
- place it into a category
- explain its process (how it works)
- compare or contrast it to other things
- explain its causes or its effects

PRACTICE 2

Answers will vary.

Write an extended definition for the word you chose in Practice 1.

_____

_____

_____

_____

_____

_____

_____

Writing an Extended Definition Paragraph

In an extended definition paragraph, you may use just one of the modes listed above to develop your definition, or you may use as many modes in your paragraph as you find necessary. For example, if you were writing a simple definition for the term *soul music,* it might read as follows: music relating to or characteristic of African American culture. This definition, while informative, does not give the reader the full flavor of just how soul music represents a part of the American culture. An extended definition might expand on this idea:

Example

Soul music is a merging of gospel and blues, two African American musical styles. While blues praised the worldly desires of the flesh, gospel extolled the virtues of spirituality. This opposition of themes was melded into a wide-ranging and extremely diverse style, full of passions, pride, and optimism mixed with the historical emotion of pain and discrimination.

Developing a term or concept more fully allows readers to appreciate a broader set of ideas. It gives them a clearer understanding of the purpose and importance of the term or concept.

Using one or more of the modes of development you have studied (description, example, compare or contrast, etc.), write an extended definition paragraph for a term from Practice 1 that you have not yet defined.

The Topic Sentence of an Extended Definition Paragraph

The topic sentence of an extended definition paragraph clearly states the term being defined, indicates the mode of development that will be used to define the term, and explains why defining the term is important. There are many reasons for supplying a reader with a definition and many types of terms you might need to define in your writing. Therefore, your topic sentence must clarify why you are defining a given term. For example, you may be defining

■ a specialized term that is unfamiliar to most people, such as *quantum theory* or *eyelet cell transplant*

■ an abstract term that can have a variety of meanings, such as *independence* or *responsibility*

■ a concept that is often misunderstood, such as *free speech* or *Generation X*

■ a new slang or cultural term, such as *extreme sports* or *anime*

Here is an example of a topic sentence for a definition paragraph about anabolic steroids:

> Anabolic steroids offer help in suppressing autoimmune diseases.

This topic sentence clearly states the term to be defined, "anabolic steroids," and why it is important to define the term (because they offer help in fighting disease). It indicates the mode of development for defining the term, through examples of the types of diseases (autoimmune) they help to fight. The entire paragraph might read as follows:

> Anabolic steroids offer help in suppressing autoimmune diseases. Fortunately, modified steroids aid in Addison's disease by regulating fat, carbohydrate, and protein metabolism. To help overcome severe allergies and arthritis, adrenocorticotropic hormone is used as an anti-inflammatory to alleviate the symptoms. By taking prescription steroids, patients may enjoy life without having uncontrollable pains in joints as well as constant fatigue.

Using Transitional Expressions in Definition Paragraphs

Definition writing uses any and all modes of development: description, narration, example, classification, process, compare and contrast, and cause and effect. Therefore, you must decide how you are developing your definition as you write, and then you must use the appropriate transitional expressions to help connect related ideas and to add rhythm to your writing.

For example, the paragraph above regarding the use of anabolic steroids is defined primarily through example. If the writer used appropriate example transitional expressions, the paragraph might look like this:

> Anabolic steroids offer help in suppressing autoimmune diseases. **For example,** modified steroids aid in Addison's disease by **specifically** regulating fat, carbohydrate, and protein metabolism. To help overcome severe allergies and arthritis, **for instance,** adrenocorticotropic hormone is used as an anti-inflammatory to alleviate the symptoms. By taking prescription steroids, **as a case in point,** patients may enjoy life without having uncontrollable pains in joints as well as constant fatigue.

When the two paragraphs are compared, it is obvious that the one with the transitional expressions is easier to understand and easier to read because the examples are announced and the sentence variety adds rhythm to the writing.

After you have decided which mode of development to use for your definition essay, refer to the appropriate chapter in this textbook to find the list of transitional expressions for the mode you are using.

PRACTICE 4

Rewrite the paragraph you created for Practice 3. First, find the chapter dealing with the mode of development that you used in the paragraph. Second, select and add the appropriate transitional expressions to connect related ideas and to add rhythm to the paragraph. Finally, compare the two paragraphs when you have finished. The paragraph with the transitional expressions should be easier to understand and to read.

Moving from Paragraph to Essay

Now that you have studied and practiced the techniques to create effective definition paragraphs, it is time to expand your ideas to a larger writing unit: the definition essay. Using the techniques you learned in Part 1 regarding developing the essay paragraphs and the definition techniques you have just learned enables you to write the definition essay. This might be a good time to return to Part 1 and review the techniques for developing the full essay.

Creating the Introductory Paragraph

Like all essays, the definition essay needs a clearly defined organization at the beginning to announce to the reader just how the subject will be developed. The thesis sentence should state the item to be defined, the writer's controlling idea or attitude toward the subject, and the organizational structure. By using an appropriate lead-in technique, the thesis sentence should blend naturally into the introductory paragraph.

For example, read the following introductory paragraph that would introduce the body paragraph regarding anabolic steroids you read earlier. The thesis sentence is underlined for identification purposes.

> Many believe anabolic steroids were developed to create the perfect superhuman. Searching for the perfect body eventually spawned a new breed of athlete; these athletes found steroids gave them more muscles and bulk, allowing them to enhance their performances. As time passed, athletes, in an effort to become even bigger and stronger, abused steroids. Because of this abuse, steroids have a bad reputation with the general public. However, steroids, when used properly for the right reasons, provide excellent health benefits. The medical use of steroids is beneficial because they help fight autoimmune diseases, facilitate muscular development in patients with arm and leg immobility, and aid in the regeneration of dysfunctional organs.

Creating the Body Paragraphs

Notice that the first item in the essay map above speaks to steroids helping to fight autoimmune diseases. As has been mentioned already, this essay would use example as its mode, or method, of developing the topic in the body paragraphs. The first body paragraph's topic would be how steroids "help fight autoimmune diseases"; the second body paragraph's topic would be how steroids "facilitate muscular development in patients with arm and leg immobility"; the third body paragraph's topic would be how steroids "aid in the regeneration of dysfunctional organs." Remember, as you write about each of these topics, your focus should be that steroid use *is beneficial*. Your focus should not be on the *harmful effects of steroid abuse,* or on the *illegality* or the *cost* of steroids. Keep your focus on the *beneficial* aspects of steroid use.

However, the essay about steroids could just as easily be written as a process essay that specifies how steroids work effectively to aid in the fight against disease, limb, and organ disabilities. The writer has the responsibility to choose the mode that he or she thinks will best develop the topic.

For example, in the following paragraph regarding the definition of a "perfect store," the writer could have chosen to develop the topic through example, by giving examples of characteristics that define a perfect store, such as friendly employees, fast service, and fair pricing. But the writer chose to use process to define the perfect store.

> While shopping in a perfect store, customers are generally sold products at an inexpensive price. Shoppers are typically offered items that are clearly marked with price tags on each separate package. This allows customers to choose rapidly and easily the product that gives them the best buy. There aren't any reasons to look for the price on the store shelf and then have to worry about whether or not the item matches the price tag. A perfect store does not only honor its own sales coupons, but it also accepts other department store advertised prices and coupons. This gives the customers the convenience of shopping at one store instead of having to go to two or three. No matter what store shoppers patronize, these pricing policies offer them the opportunity to receive the best possible price.

Before deciding on which mode of development to use in the body paragraphs, you might try planning a paragraph using two or more modes. This technique can help you choose the mode that works best for the paragraph's topic. In other words, you might find that developing the topic *choosing a career* is clearer and more effective if you write it as an *example paragraph* rather than as a *compare or contrast paragraph*. In many definition essays, including the two sample student essays that follow, the writer uses a different mode (and sometimes combines modes) for each body paragraph.

PRACTICE 5

Rewrite the paragraph you wrote in Practice 4 using a different mode of development. Don't forget to use the transitional expressions appropriate to your new mode of development choice.

Creating the Concluding Paragraph

The approach of the concluding paragraph should flow naturally from the essay's main topic. Because our essay's focus is the beneficial use of steroids, a *warning* would seem an appropriate choice. Since the lead-in mentioned how some athletes abuse steroids in their search for more power and strength, you might mention some of the adverse effects that misusing steroids can have, such as brain tumors, cancer, and loss of bone mass. (Refer to Chapter 5 for other approaches for concluding paragraphs.)

Sample Definition Student Essay: "WHO" IS OUT THERE?

Martin Brink

In his essay "'Who' Is Out There?" student writer Martin Brink defines *Doctor Who*, a long-running BBC television series, as a successful science fiction television show because of elements that appeal to a wide-ranging audience throughout the world. The author's deep insights are supported by many well-chosen words that support his attitude toward the series.

Vocabulary

Meaning comes primarily from words. Before you start reading, use a dictionary to look up the definitions of the following words appearing in the essay.

contemplating	diverse	eccentric	evolve	genre
incessant	irresistible	mode	mutual	narrative
oligarchic	patronize	regeneration	renegade	resolve
saga	sentient	treachery	unique	

"Who" Is Out There?

1   When contemplating a favorite science fiction television series, *who* comes to mind? How about the "Doctor"? *Doctor Who,* that is—an eccentric, renegade time lord dedicated to saving the universe from the incessant, evil

treachery of alien beings out to conquer the universe. The science fiction saga first aired on November 16, 1963, and is still in production at the BBC in London. *Doctor Who* is an internationally successful science fiction series because of a unique story line, theoretical concepts, and an appeal to a diverse television audience.   ← **Thesis Sentence with Essay Map**

Topic Sentence →   2   Time Lords, such as the Doctor, are the oligarchic rulers of the planet Gallifrey, on which lives one of the most sentient and advanced races to have evolved in the universe. The Doctor travels the universe in a time machine with companions who accompany him on his adventures. He believes in interfering with the affairs of the universe in a positive way—to put things right wherever his travels take him. When the Doctor is killed (there have been at least seven or eight different stars of the show), his body goes through regeneration, giving him a new body and personality, but retaining his memories of previous selves and bits of past personalities.

Topic Sentence →   3   The story line is a showcase of scientific, theoretical concepts used to create an action-oriented adventure. Traveling the universe in a TARDIS (Time and Relative Dimensions in Space) machine that looks like a red, British phone booth is just one of the many humorous and inventive concepts used to support a fantastic and creative story. With a wide range of cultural issues dealt with, each show explores what might happen when earth and alien beings come together to resolve a mutual problem—always with the Doctor's help, of course. With a mix of writing styles and story-line genres, *Doctor Who* is an irresistible fantasy that provides a look at society no matter what planet he might be visiting.

Topic Sentence →   4   The classic theme of good battling evil in outer space has attracted audiences crossing all genders, ages, classes, and nationalities. People as young as two years of age to senior citizens in their seventies in as many as forty countries around the world have tuned into *Doctor Who* for over thirty years. The program was originally intended for children; the Doctor quickly became popular with adults. It is one of a few television programs that doesn't patronize or insult the intelligence of children; therefore, the show is adult enough to appeal to the bigger children in all us grown-ups.

5   Over the years, cliffhangers, action-filled dramas, and new "Doctors" from time to time have made *Doctor Who* a favorite for all audiences. This science fiction program is unique for experimenting with new ideas and narrative styles. Complex themes and a variety of aliens and story lines during each episode make the show more interesting and successful than *Star Trek*. Because of worldwide appeal, *Doctor Who* has become the longest-running science fiction series in television history. "Long live 'The Doctor'!"

Definition Technique Questions

1. While the show *Doctor Who* is being defined, does the writer define anything else?

    He defines the Doctor Who character, what a Time Lord is, the TARDIS (a

    time machine), and the *Doctor Who* audience (young and old).

2. What lead-in technique does the writer use to introduce the thesis sentence?
    The "series of questions" technique.

3. What modes of development are used in the essay?

Paragraph 2 uses mostly process, describing what Time Lords do and how the Doctor is regenerated each time he is killed. Paragraph 3 uses both example and description as the writer describes the TARDIS as a red, British phone booth. Examples of the story lines are also offered, showcasing scientific and theoretical concepts, and the cultural problems on a variety of alien planets. Paragraph 4 is predominantly compare and contrast. The writer talks about the show's classic theme of good versus evil, and he contrasts the huge variety of age groups that make up the show's audience.

4. Does the writer use transitional expressions to connect related ideas and add rhythm? Point them out. If not, could you suggest some that might be appropriate? Where would you put them?

Mostly at the beginning of sentences: "When" in both paragraph 1 and 2; "With" twice in paragraph 3; "Over the years," and "Because" in paragraph 5; an adverbial conjunction, "therefore," is used in paragraph 4.

(Other answers will vary.)

Sample Definition Student Essay: A SHRIMPER'S LIFE

Donna Morris

In this essay, "A Shrimper's Life," student writer Donna Morris defines a job that most people are not familiar with. Most people love to eat shrimp, but there is little doubt that most people have little or no idea about how shrimp are caught and what the people are like who do the catching. Originally from Louisiana, the author plans to live in Florida, where she would like to start her own shrimping business on the Caribbean coast.

Vocabulary

Meaning comes primarily from words. Before you begin reading, use a dictionary to look up the definitions of the following words that appear in the essay.

approximately	dwellers	equity	lurking
marine	pelagic	octopi	tasks

A Shrimper's Life

1　Everyone knows what a shrimp is (at least they think they do), but few know what life is like for those taking on the task of bringing the shrimp from the ocean to the table. Shrimp come in a variety of sizes, ranging from those no bigger than an insect to monsters over eight inches long. While most shrimp inhabit shallow coastal waters, there are shrimp that live their lives swimming in the open ocean. Shrimp come in both freshwater and saltwater varieties. While the most common commercially harvested shrimp is the white shrimp, other varieties include the brown-grooved and pink-grooved shrimp. Except for the pelagic shrimp, all others are bottom dwellers feeding on smaller animals and plants; therefore, catching them involves quite a lot of work. Since demand for the small shellfish is high during a booming economy, the profits for successful shrimpers are equally high. Shrimping is a rewarding occupation because of the relatively short work season, low equity risk, and the fascinating marine life.　←── **Thesis Sentence with Essay Map**

Topic Sentence ──→ 2　Before leaving shore, the boats fuel up and take on board plenty of ice to keep the shrimp frozen. The workers take a trip to the grocery store and buy enough supplies for the two-week trip. Although two weeks sounds like a long time, shrimpers only work a few of these excursions each year. Ninety percent of their time is spent on shore planning for the next trip, tending to their shrimp nets, and making sure the shrimp boat is in tip-top shape. Even the shrimper's daytime hours are spent eating, sleeping, and getting ready for the harvesting. Shrimp boats travel during the day and fish at night because shrimp sleep during the day and hunt for food by moonlight. Yes, shrimpers are definitely night-owls.

Topic Sentence ──→ 3　Expenses for shrimpers are relatively low compared to other fishermen. Commercial tuna and cod fishermen, for instance, have heavy expenses. Not only do they have to have larger boats to handle their loads, their nets have to be heavier and larger, they have to stay at sea for longer periods of time, and their crews have to be larger in number, meaning more money and bonuses have to be paid out after the harvesting profit is realized. Because of the high profit with shrimp, one catch usually pays for the year's fuel, groceries, and crew's salaries. Because of the smaller shrimp boat, shrimpers do not have high fuel bills, and maintenance is not high either.

Topic Sentence ──→ 4　The best aspect of being a shrimper is the exotic marine life you discover in the shrimp nets. Because the shrimp nets are sent to the bottom of the ocean as they are dragged to harvest the shrimp, all residents lurking on the bottom are gathered into the nets as well. Sea cucumbers, hermit crabs, dogfish, and sea anemones are just a few of the unusual marine life that are pulled up in the shrimp nets. The shrimp are then picked out and buried in the ice to keep them as fresh as possible. Crabs, octopi, and stingrays, along with the other captives, are returned to their ocean home to live another day. A marine biologist would do well to work on a shrimp boat once in awhile.

5　As with any job, shrimping is not all fun and games. Sometimes the ocean can get pretty rough, and sometimes the catch can be pretty small. Couples with small children will have to make some sacrifices if someone is to stay home with the kids. And those wanting the rigid schedule of a nine-to-five job would never get used to the odd hours that the shrimper must get used to. However, if you don't mind some danger and excitement every so often, as well as some awesome sunsets at sea, then maybe the shrimper's life is for you.

Definition Technique Questions

1. What are the modes of development used in the essay?

   Paragraph 2 uses process. The writer defines a shrimper's life by explain-

   ing the steps taken before the fishing trip actually begins. Paragraph 3 is

   compare and contrast as the writer contrasts the differences between

   shrimpers and other types of fishermen. Paragraph 4 is mostly example.

   The writer identifies the various types of marine life that are caught in the

   shrimp nets.

2. Point out an example of defining by negation.

   In paragraph 3, the writer defines shrimpers by explaining what equipment

   and salary expenses cod fishermen have that shrimpers *do not* have.

3. Identify an instance where comparison is used to define.

   In paragraph 3, shrimpers are compared to cod fishermen.

4. How is "shrimp" defined in the introductory paragraph?

   By size (insects to eight-inch monsters), what environment they live in

   (shallows or deep ocean; freshwater or saltwater; top or bottom dwellers),

   varieties (by color: white, brown, or pink), and by what they feed on (smaller

   animals and plants).

Sample Definition Professional Essay: A JERK

Sydney J. Harris

This essay, "A Jerk," by the late Sydney J. Harris, a syndicated columnist for the *Chicago Daily News* and the *Chicago Sun-Times*, appeared in his book *Last Things First*. Harris was famous for writing about every aspect of contemporary American life. His musings appeared daily in his column, "Strictly Personal." While this may not look like the type of essay you have been writing in college, it is an extended definition that also uses a variety of definition formats, such as class definition and simple definition.

Vocabulary

Meaning comes primarily from words. Before you begin reading, use a dictionary to look up the definitions of the following words that appear in the essay.

apt	aroma	coined	cum laude	egotist
emanating	extent	fluffed	inane	insight
persuasive	shuddering	subtle	tactless	utterly

A Jerk

1   I don't know whether history repeats itself, but biography certainly does. The other day, Michael came in and asked me what a "jerk" was—the same question Carolyn put to me a dozen years ago.

2   At that time, I fluffed her off with some inane answer, such as "A jerk isn't a very nice person," but both of us knew it was an unsatisfactory reply. When she went to bed, I began trying to work up a suitable definition.

3   It is a marvelously apt word, of course. Until it was coined, not more than 25 years ago, there was really no single word in English to describe the kind of person who is a jerk—"boob" and "simp" were too old hat, and besides they really didn't fit, for they could be lovable, and a jerk never is.

4   Thinking it over, I decided that a jerk is basically a person without insight. He is not necessarily a fool or a dope, because some extremely clever persons can be jerks. In fact, it has little to do with intelligence as we commonly think of it; it is, rather, a kind of subtle but persuasive aroma emanating from the inner part of the personality.

5   I know a college president who can be described only as a jerk. He is not an unintelligent man, nor unlearned, nor even unschooled in the social amenities. Yet he is a jerk *cum laude*, because of a fatal flaw in his nature—he is totally incapable of looking into the mirror of his soul and shuddering at what he sees there.

6   A jerk, then, is a man (or woman) who is utterly unable to see himself as he appears to others. He has no grace, he is tactless without meaning to be, he is a bore even to his best friends, he is an egotist without charm. All of us are egotists to some extent, but most of us—unlike the jerk—are perfectly and horribly aware of it when we make asses of ourselves. The jerk never knows.

Definition Technique Questions

1. Identify the similar terms that Harris puts in the same class as "jerk." How does he define "jerk" differently than the other terms in the class?

He places "boob" and "simp" into the same class, but he says that they

can be lovable, and a jerk cannot. He states that a "fool" or a "dope" is

not clever, and that a jerk is sometimes very clever.

2. Harris begins the essay by relating a brief story about his daughter and son asking him to define "jerk." How does this anecdote help introduce the topic?

It shows that generations often have to define the same terms, and it

makes us reevaluate our thinking: we often take for granted that we have

a good understanding of something when we actually don't.

3. Where in the essay does Harris give a simple definition for the term "jerk"?

The first sentence of the last paragraph.

4. Identify some examples where Harris defines "jerk" by negation.

In paragraphs 3 and 4: Harris defines a jerk by commenting that a jerk is

not like a boob, a simp, a fool, a dope, and that being defined as a jerk

has little to do with intelligence.

Critical Thinking Writing Opportunities

1. In his essay "'Who' Is Out There?" Martin Brink defines a long-running British television show by focusing on the elements of the show that appeal to all ages of an international audience. Brink uses *concepts and ideas* such as time travel (a theoretical concept), a futuristic machine called a TARDIS (Time and Relative Dimension in Space), and the classic theme of good vs. evil, to develop his definition of the show and explain why it has achieved such worldwide success. Pretend you are a television writer in Hollywood, and you have an idea for a new television show that you want to sell to one of the major studios. Using concepts and ideas, write an essay defining the show for the studio producer who will decide whether or not to buy your idea.

2. In her essay "A Shrimper's Life," Donna Morris defines a job that is unfamiliar to most audiences. She uses *information* in the form of *personal observation and experience* to define the shrimper's life. Even though the shrimper's life is not one most people know much about, the author's firsthand knowledge and insights make her definition easier to understand. Write an essay defining an occupation that you think your audience will not know much about. Although you will use one mode of development predominantly, don't be afraid to use one or more of the other modes as you develop the essay. Use information (data, facts, observation, and personal experience) to define the occupation.

3. In his essay "A Jerk," professional writer Sydney J. Harris writes about a particular element of contemporary society—the jerk. Harris uses *concepts and ideas,* particularly a variety of *definitions,* to define what a jerk is and to distinguish that type of person from other similar but less obnoxious categories. Write an essay defining your generation's term for "jerk." Harris states that his generation uses "boob" and "simp." "Geek" and "nerd" are recent slang terms. You might include other similar terms in the class, and then clarify how your generation's term is different from the others. You also might try defining your generation's term by negation—defining by stating what the term does not mean.

Topics for a Definition Essay

Here are some possible topics for extended definition essay writing assignments. Remember, your definition essay should have a clearly defined purpose.

1. Reality television programs
2. Pornography
3. Democracy
4. Heroism or cowardice
5. Talk show
6. Success or failure
7. A fanatic

8. Stand-up comedian

9. A new term from an extreme sport

10. The perfect sandwich (or pizza, dessert, barbecue, etc.)

Chapter Review

■ A definition clearly explains the meaning of words, terms, and concepts. Definitions can be simple, as a dictionary definition, or extended, in which a term is described at length.

■ An extended definition paragraph uses one or more of the modes of development to describe its topic. The topic sentence states the term and explains why it is important and it is being defined. Transitional expressions help the reader follow as the topic is developed.

■ In a definition essay, the thesis sentence states the topic to be defined, the controlling idea or attitude toward the topic, and the main points that are going to be made. The thesis sentence should suggest the mode or modes that will be used in the body paragraphs. In a definition essay, the body paragraphs often vary in mode, and sometimes modes are blended within a single body paragraph. The concluding paragraph's approach should flow from the content of the previous paragraphs.

Visit *The Write Start* Online!

For additional practice with the materials found in this chapter, visit our Website at

http://www.ablongman.com/checkett

The Website also features additional readings, quizzes, writing activities, and Internet links, as well as a bulletin board and interactive chat.

CHAPTER 14

The Cause or Effect Essay

When attempting to persuade others about a belief or point of view you hold, often you try to convince them by pointing out special relationships that different things or events share. By doing this, you are using a powerful tool that focuses on a strong logical method of developing a topic: cause or effect. This mode of development analyzes **causal relationships,** the connection between cause and effect.

Identifying Your Purpose

Cause or effect development explains the reasons associated with some thing or event: *cause* analysis develops *why* something happens, and *effect* analysis explains *the results and consequences* stemming from causes. Causal relationships help us understand why things happen in the world around us, and the possible consequences that may result from actions or events.

For example, a writer might ask the question, "Why did President Clinton lie to the American public about the Monica Lewinsky affair?" as a way of finding out the possible causes of his action. (*Possible causes:* he didn't define his actions with Monica Lewinsky as "having sex"; he didn't want the First Lady, Hillary Rodham Clinton, to find out about his relationship with Lewinsky; he did not want to be embarrassed publicly in the press; he didn't want history to focus on this aspect of his presidency.) The writer also might ask, "What might happen because President Clinton lied to the American public?" as a way of figuring out the events that might occur in the future as a result of the lying. (*Possible effects:* he might have been impeached for "high crimes and misdemeanors"; history books might focus on this aspect of his presidency rather than his successes with domestic and foreign affairs; the Democratic Party might find it harder to get legislation passed through Congress; Democratic candidates might find it difficult to get elected or re-elected to office.)

Writing a Cause or Effect Paragraph

Obviously, the search for cause or effect answers can be a complex undertaking. More than one explanation usually can be found, and often many of the answers are possible. This complexity can be helpful in achieving thorough development of an issue. Thoroughly developing your point of view can help you persuade your reader that your view of an issue has been both logically and reasonably stated. Look at the following two examples of paragraphs focusing on cause and effect.

Example Cause Paragraph

Obtaining money and managing money are common causes of stress, especially for those who have little. For students, and those hoping to attend college, securing funds becomes a top priority. Of course, there are grants, loans, and scholarships, but sometimes those resources are not enough. Getting a job or obtaining a loan doesn't ease any of the tension and, more likely, will cause even more stress. Once you have money, you must know how to manage it. A poor expenditure plan can leave you without the needed funds to complete your education or to pay your bills. If you get in debt, not only will you need money to pay your bills, but you will need extra money to pay penalties and interest. Money isn't the root of all evil—poor planning is!

In the paragraph above, *obtaining money* and *money management* are the twin *causes* of stress. The link between the two causes is that once you do get the money, you must manage the funds properly or more troubles can occur.

Example Effect Paragraph

The possibility of health risks is extremely high for a prescription drug addict. Every medication that is taken has side effects, such as headache, nausea, and sleep problems. Constipation results from many potent prescription drugs. A high emotional and physical feeling followed by a corresponding low emotional and physical state are effects that often occur when prescription drugs are abused. The addict usually takes different types of drugs to counteract this emotional roller coaster. The effect of this new addiction is potential heart problems. Other effects stemming from prescription drug abuse are dental problems and poor immunity against diseases because prescribed drugs can remove essential vitamins and minerals from the body.

In the paragraph above, health risks, such as *headache, nausea, sleep deprivation, emotional highs and lows,* and *potential heart problems* are the effects of prescription drug abuse. The link between the effects is that new drugs to counteract one set of effects can lead to other negative effects.

Causal Chains

Whether you are focusing on cause or effect, it is helpful, before you begin writing, to develop a **causal chain.** A causal chain demonstrates the series of events that can develop and can help clarify the relationships that exist between events.

Cause and Effect Diagram 1

Causes		Effects
Too many unpaid bills	can lead to	increased physical tension.
Increased physical tension	can lead to	severe headaches.
Severe headaches	can lead to	nausea and loss of appetite.
Nausea and loss of appetite	can lead to	physical and mental fatigue.
Physical and mental fatigue	can lead to	health problems.

In the example above, notice how an effect can become a cause for the next effect. Things and events do not exist in a vacuum isolated from the other things and events around them. Yes, you can focus on cause, and you can focus on effect, but to be most persuasive, you should share with readers the special insights you have learned from the causal chain.

Another method for identifying causes and effects is to use the following diagram:

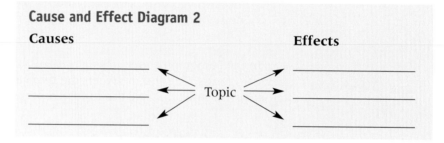

Cause and Effect Diagram 2

By filling in the spaces under Causes and Effects, you can separate the links in the causal chain. By doing so, you can decide which elements you want to be the focus of your essay.

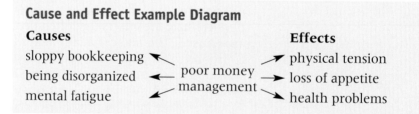

Cause and Effect Example Diagram

Once readers know *why* something has happened (causes) and the consequences that might stem from the causes (effects), they are much more likely to be receptive to your conclusions about the topic. In other words, they understand your view of a topic, and understanding an issue is often half the battle to accepting the writer's ideas concerning the issue.

PRACTICE 1

Create a causal chain for each of the following topics. While you can make the chain as long as you want, try to have at least three causes and effects in the chain. Use both techniques illustrated in Diagram 1 and Diagram 2 to develop your chain and then to separate the causes from the effects.

- road rage
- overbuilding houses
- ozone depletion

Problems to Avoid

When using cause and effect reasoning, do not confuse **chronological order** and **coincidence** with true cause and effect relationships. Do not assume that, because one event follows another in time, the first event causes the second to occur. No true causal relationship exists between two events just because one follows the other.

> ### Example
>
> Every time a black cat crosses my path, something bad happens to me.

Bad things indeed may happen to you, but the proverbial black cat as a cause of bad luck is a superstition that has no basis in reality. Your bad luck is probably due to your not being properly prepared for the events in your life or possibly just being at the wrong place at the wrong time—coincidence. Do not assume that, because two or more events occur around the same time, one causes the other and that a cause and effect relationship exists between them.

> ### Example
>
> After I attended a movie, several days later I came down with a cold. Someone in the theater must have been ill, and I must have caught it from them. Therefore, my going to the movies caused me to catch a cold.

Many people that you come in contact with each day may have colds. You could catch a cold from any one of them. Cause and effect is posited in the example, but there is no proof of a link. In this case, coincidence is just as likely a possibility.

PRACTICE 2

Explain why the following events do not have a causal relationship, either because of *chronological order* or *coincidence*.

1. The successful field goal, passing through the uprights just as the final gun sounded, won the game by a score of 17 to 14.

   The problem is one of *chronological order*. All 17 points were necessary

   to win the game, as well as the outstanding defensive plays, the coaching

   strategy, the other team's mistakes, and perhaps luck. Just because one

   event occurs (kicking the field goal) close to another event (the final gun

   sounding to end the game) does not establish a true causal relationship,

   nor does it accurately reflect *why* the game was won.

2. I always get sick the day after Thanksgiving. I need to stop eating so much, and I guess I'll have to stop going on those brisk, long walks that my family always takes after dinner.

   The problem is one of *coincidence*. The problem may have nothing to do

with overeating or being exposed to cold weather on a walk. It would be

unusual for the person never to have overeaten on other holidays. Did

the person become sick then? Most likely the person is exposed to cold

weather during the winter months on other occasions, such as playing in

the snow with family or friends, waiting for a bus, or walking the dog. Did

illness occur after these events? If the answer is no, then the cause lies

elsewhere. A good candidate would be an allergy to a specific food such

as turkey, cranberries, or pumpkin pie, foods that are commonly eaten

on holidays.

The Topic Sentence in a Cause or Effect Paragraph

The topic sentence in a cause or effect paragraph clearly states the topic and why the topic's causes or effects are being developed. After choosing your subject, create your causal chain to identify the causes and effects stemming from the topic. When this step is completed, it is time for you to decide whether you are going to focus on causes or effects. The topic sentence will announce your purpose to the reader, and it will clarify the paragraph's development.

> **Examples**
>
> *Focus on Causes*
> Proper nutrition can lead to a long, healthful life. (This paragraph will develop *proper nutrition* as a cause of a *long, healthful life*.)
>
> *Focus on Effects*
> A long, healthful life can increase earnings potential. (This paragraph will develop *earnings potential* as an effect or result of a *long, healthful life*.)

PRACTICE 3

Answers will vary.   This practice will help you develop a paragraph that focuses on causes.

1. Pick one of the following topics.
   a phobia (an unreasonable fear, such as fear of heights, spiders, open spaces, flying)
   looking for a new job
   a good relationship

2. List as many causes of your topic choice as you can think of.

   a. _____

   b. _____

   c. _____

d. _____

e. _____

3. If any of the causes in your list are merely chronological or coincidental, draw a line through them.

4. Write a topic sentence that focuses on causes.

_____

_____

_____

_____

5. Write a sentence for each of the causes in your list that is not merely chronological or coincidental.

_____

_____

_____

_____

_____

_____

_____

6. On a separate sheet of paper, rewrite your sentences into paragraph form.

PRACTICE 4

Answers will vary.

This practice will help you develop a paragraph that focuses on effects.

1. Pick one of the following topics.
having a child out of wedlock
children watching too much television violence
using a cell phone while driving

2. List as many effects of your topic choice as you can think of.

a. _____

b. _____

c. _____

d. _____

e. _____

3. If any of the effects in your list are merely chronological or coincidental, draw a line through them.

4. Write a topic sentence that focuses on effects.

_____

_____

_____

_____

5. Write a sentence for each of the effects in your list that is not merely chronological or coincidental.

_____

_____

_____

_____

_____

_____

_____

6. On a separate sheet of paper, rewrite your sentences into paragraph form.

Using Transitional Expressions in Cause and Effect Writing

There are several transitional expressions you will find useful when writing about causes or effects.

Cause	Effect
because	as a consequence of
causes, caused by	as a result (of)
the reason	consequently
since	then
therefore	resulting in

PRACTICE 5

Add appropriate transitional expressions to the cause paragraph you created for Practice 3 and the effect paragraph you created for Practice 4. When you have finished, compare the paragraphs pairs. The paragraphs containing the transitional expressions should be easier to read and understand.

Moving from Paragraph to Essay

Now that you have studied and practiced the techniques to create effective cause and effect paragraphs, it is time to expand your ideas to a larger writing unit: the cause or effect essay. Using the techniques you learned in Part 1 regarding developing the essay paragraphs and the cause or effect techniques you have just learned, you can create the cause or effect essay. This might be a good time to return to Part 1 and review the techniques for developing the full essay.

Creating the Introductory Paragraph

A cause or effect essay needs a clearly defined organization in the introductory paragraph to announce to the reader just how the subject will be developed. The thesis sentence should state whether the essay will focus on cause or effect, the writer's controlling idea or attitude toward the topic, and the organizational structure. By using an appropriate lead-in technique, the thesis should blend naturally into the rest of the introductory paragraph.

Using one of the causal chain techniques you have studied can help you identify causes and effects. You then can extend and develop the ideas expressed in the diagrams to create the thesis sentence for a cause or effect essay.

> ### Example Cause Thesis Sentence
> Sloppy bookkeeping, lack of organization, and mental fatigue can lead to poor money management.
>
> ### Example Effect Thesis Sentence
> Poor money management can lead to physical tension, loss of appetite, and health problems.

Although both essays are concerned with poor money management, the focus of each essay is different: The first essay will focus on causes of poor money management, while the second essay will focus on the effects of poor money management.

Creating the Body Paragraphs

For an essay on the causes of poor money management, the focus of the body paragraphs will be the paragraph topics listed in the thesis sentence's essay map. The first body paragraph's topic will be "sloppy bookkeeping," the second body paragraph's topic will be "lack of organization," and the third body paragraph's topic will be "mental fatigue." Remember, as you write about each of the topics, your focus should be that these are the *causes for poor money management*. Your focus should not be on how reading the *Wall Street Journal* can help you be more successful in picking stocks or how reading *GQ* magazine can help you dress more like a businessperson. Keep your focus on the controlling idea or attitude: the three causes can lead to poor money management.

For an essay on the effects of poor money management, the focus of the body paragraphs will be the paragraph topics listed in the thesis sentence's essay map. The first body paragraph's topic will be "physical tension," the second body paragraph's topic will be "loss of appetite," and the third body paragraph's topic will be "health problems." Remember, as you write about these topics, your focus should be that these are the negative effects caused by poor money management. Your focus should not be how poor money management can reduce the value of your stock portfolio or how it can cause your company's plans for expansion to be put on hold. Keep your focus on the controlling idea: that poor money management can lead to health-related problems.

Creating the Concluding Paragraph

The approach of the concluding paragraph should flow naturally from the essay's main topic. Because the first essay's focus is the causes leading to poor money management, a *call to action* would seem an appropriate choice. You might suggest some actions business people can take to help correct sloppy bookkeeping practices. You might even suggest that they survey some bookkeeping services that will handle their accounts for a reasonable fee. You might suggest that they take a workshop on enhancing organization skills, or that they enroll in a yoga or tai chi class to get rid of unwanted, destructive tension.

Because the second essay's focus is the effects caused by poor money management, a *warning* would seem an appropriate choice. You might warn the reader that there are other negative consequences that might come from poor money management: negative credit reports, relationship problems (with spouses, business partners, and friends), and short- or long-term business plans. Remember to keep the focus connected to the essay's idea of importance or attitude: the negative effects caused by poor money management. (Refer to Chapter 5 for other approaches for concluding paragraphs.)

Sample Cause Student Essay: PROBLEMS IN PARENTING

Mark Collom

> Raising a family is a challenging endeavor no matter what the age or socio-economic status of the parents. Literally thousands of books and articles have been written about parenting. In this essay, "Problems in Parenting," student writer Mark Collom, speaking from his own experiences as a student-parent, focuses on the rewarding but difficult aspects of raising children.

Vocabulary

Meaning comes primarily from words. Before you begin reading, use a dictionary to look up the definitions of the following words that appear in the essay.

abstract	baton	bestow	commendable
conversely	depict	endeavor	enterprise
extravagance	intrinsic	precedence	pungent

Problems in Parenting

1   Can you think for a moment or two and recall the name of some commendable young man or woman? If the background of the admirable person were known, more often than not, they would be considered the product of a

good mother and father. Conversely, all quickly can point to some delinquent character and assess that poor parenting was the cause of that person's problems. Good parenting might appear to be an easy skill, perhaps, even an art. But good parents are made, not born. Being a proper Mom and Dad is one of life's most challenging enterprises and one of its most rewarding, as well. The abstract mixture of love, discipline, and sacrifice make good parenting a difficult task. ⟵ **Thesis Sentence with Essay Map**

Topic Sentence ⟶ 2   When the first newborn is proudly brought home from the hospital, life makes an almost complete change for the parents. The new child, with helpless innocence, is the focus of all the love the parents can bestow. "Precious Moments" figurines are likely to depict parental love as a baby being cradled in the arms of the mother; however, the parent's love is also represented in many other not so pleasant events. Volumes of stained, pungent diapers in need of attention, equally offensive vomit upon Mother's newest blouse, and months of "yo-yo" nights of interrupted sleep are all taken in stride. Countless adversities are magically reduced by love into mere inconveniences.

Topic Sentence ⟶ 3   Good parenting relies upon the conscience of the adults making decisions for the welfare of the youngsters. Although limitations upon the children are easy to point out, usually such judgments also result in restrictions on the mother and father. With the children sprawled about the family-room floor, Mom and Dad opt for *Sabrina the Teen-age Witch* and *Boy Meets World* because the movie on another station carries the "R" rating. Even though both grown-ups would prefer to watch the "other" movie, good parenting dictates the more suitable program. The weather may be stormy, and the bed warm and comfortable, but Mom and Dad will rise to get the kids ready so the family can make it to church on Sunday. Parental obligations confront the adults at every turn.

Topic Sentence ⟶ 4   Yes, Mom does deserve the Caribbean cruise she's always wanted. No, Dad's aged sedan is not a classic, yet he's not shopping for a new car. The Caribbean will wait; the old Buick can make another winter or two, for children inhabit a home, and extravagances are not high on the parental agenda. Decisions are made with offspring in mind, for the parents realize years pass quickly and the young will soon be grown and gone. New bicycles on birthdays, hockey trips with the team, and Christmas trees buried in a mound of Santa's gifts all take precedence in the eyes of Mom and Dad. Soon enough, the two will cruise the southern seas.

5   Parenting is a swirl of all the emotions. It is pride in seeing your own name on the little pitcher's uniform as he strikes out an opponent, yet sorrow when the boy cannot find the strike zone any longer, and the midget hurler walks in the winning run. It is a delight when a little girl joyfully speeds to Daddy's arms after she makes her first successful twirl on her new skates; however, a sadness overcomes the father when, years later, the teenager runs out the door to be with her boyfriend without even saying goodbye. With all the intrinsic difficulties, being a good parent is the most challenging of all endeavors. The role is also the most fulfilling; therefore, every generation will continue to accept the passing of the baton.

Cause Technique Questions

1. What causes does the writer focus on that make parenting difficult?

The overwhelming *love* parents have for their newborn infant, the *discipline*

involved in good decision making, and the financial *sacrifices* in providing

for the needs of the children versus the needs of the parents.

2. Does the writer use many transitional expressions? If not, which ones would be appropriate, and where would you place them?
   Answers will vary.

3. Identify some of the specific sacrifices that parents often have to make.
   Cleaning diapers and stained clothing due to baby's vomiting; watching

   "G" rated programs because the children are home, and getting the family

   ready for church even if the weather is horrible; not taking a well-earned

   vacation or doing without a new car so bicycles, hockey trips, and Christ-

   mas gifts can be paid for.

4. What does the writer mean by "yo-yo" nights of interrupted sleep?
   Answers will vary but should include the concept of getting up and down

   several times a night like a yo-yo.

Sample Effect Student Essay: GIVING OUT

Yvonne Olsen

Most people would think that a person applying for a volunteer position would be doing so only because the effects of helping others would bring the charitable person a great measure of satisfaction and personal growth. In this essay, "Giving Out," just the opposite happens. Student writer Yvonne Olsen relates how a friend took a position for a somewhat selfish reason, but that some unforeseen, beneficial effects became a part of the total equation.

Vocabulary
Meaning comes primarily from words. Before you begin to read, use a dictionary to look up the definitions to the following words that appear in the essay.

diverse	eager	devices	gourmet	energetic
interact	miraculous	mumbled	tragic	volunteer

Giving Out

1   Cindy left the interview feeling undecided about the job she had just gotten. She did not interview for a paying job; rather, she had sought a volunteer position at a local hospital. Cindy wanted to volunteer at the hospital because she wanted to see what the medical profession was all about. She was a good science student, so she thought going to medical school might be an option. She wasn't all that excited about getting up at 5:30 in the morning each day, and the thought of having to do a lot of work without pay wasn't high on her list, either. She thought it was going to be a long summer. Instead, the volunteer position turned out to be very rewarding mentally, socially, and educationally. ⟵ **Thesis Sentence with Essay Map**

Topic Sentence ⟶ 2   The first day at the hospital was a mental shock. Cindy was working on the full admit floor where the patients were very ill. Most of them had spent weeks in the hospital. Most were elderly, depressed, or bored. Some of them looked lifeless, for all hope of leaving the hospital had been delayed when a physician scheduled them for another set of tests or for another surgery. When Cindy saw that most of the patients were hooked to oxygen, she learned to appreciate her own good health. The first few times at the hospital were depressing for her, as well, but soon she began to focus on some positive aspects. A feeling of happiness ran through her mind when she got to take discharged patients out of the hospital to meet their families. These patients, seemingly in the depths of despair only days earlier, now were all smiles because they knew that soon they would be home. The patients were eager to see their families, and they would tell her about what they were going to do once they left the hospital. Of course, not all of the discharged patients were going home; some would be going to nursing homes or to other extended care facilities. Positive feelings rose in her chest when she was helping nurses run specimens to the lab, picking up prescriptions from the pharmacy, and serving patients their breakfast. When patients wanted a newspaper or fresh gourmet coffee, she would go to the lobby and return to smiling faces and outstretched hands. They often were grateful for such small things while people on the outside of the hospital were often discourteous or accepted such favors without thanks. Cindy's self-esteem began to rise.

Topic Sentence ⟶ 3   Besides all of the mental benefits, there were also social benefits that she hadn't anticipated. Cindy had always been a bit shy, but being with so many patients and co-workers helped her to become more talkative. She talked to elderly patients about their families and illnesses. She listened to endless love stories of when they were her age. They liked the fact that there was someone to listen to their stories. Of course, not all of the patients were easy to talk to. The younger patients would not want to speak to anyone because they were angry at being stuck in a hospital away from friends and video games. Cindy could not understand all of her patients, particularly those who were heavily sedated and could only mumble. She learned that even if she could not understand the patient, she could pretend to just to make them feel important. At times, she would assure nervous patients that the tests or the surgeries were not as serious as they seemed. As it became easier to relate to the patients, it became easier to interact with her co-workers. Questions became easier to ask, and thoughts became easier to express. As the weeks went by, Cindy lost most of her shyness.

Topic Sentence ⟶ 4   Volunteering also turned out to be a great educational experience. After all, the hospital does have many nursing and medical students. She learned the structure of the hospital from the maintenance crew to the kitchen personnel to the neurosurgeons. She learned about the different medical tools that were used in the various departments. Cindy heard of many medical conditions that she never knew existed. Speaking to doctors and nurses helped her to see what their professions were like. Nurses worked hard to make the patients comfortable and assist the doctors in curing the patients. Volunteering taught her about good, energetic life and about weak, dying life. These educational experiences helped Cindy decide that a career in medicine was going to be her life's calling.

5   The volunteer position helped Cindy in many ways. Being around people less fortunate than her taught her to be grateful that her family and friends were healthy, which she used to take for granted. After her volunteer experience, she realized that illness could strike at any time. But most of all, she got a sense of how she wanted to direct her life. Cindy decided to go to medical school because she saw how a good physician could help a patient recover miraculously. Even though she was not paid for her services, Cindy felt that volunteering in the hospital earned her more than she could ever calculate.

Effect Technique Questions

1. What effects does the writer focus on that finally made Cindy's experience worthwhile?

The *mental or psychological* rewards from seeing patients leave the hospital and being reunited with their families, *overcoming her basic shyness* while having to interact with many patients, and the *educational experiences*, such as learning how the hospital is organized, what medical equipment is used for, and about specific medical conditions.

2. How did Cindy's expectations differ from the reality she found at the hospital?

Her expectations were low. She didn't like the prospect of getting up early, of working as a volunteer instead of a paying job; she thought it was going to be a *long* summer. In actuality, she found the position challenging and rewarding: mentally, socially, and educationally.

3. Did the writer use many transitional expressions? If not, which ones would be appropriate, and where would you place them?

Answers will vary.

_____

_____

_____

_____

4. How does the title "Giving Out" provide additional meaning now that you have read the essay?

Answers will vary.

_____

_____

_____

_____

Sample Professional Essay: WHY ENGLISH-ONLY LAWS ARE USELESS

Rosa Rivera

There has been much written about making English the official language of the United States. Legislation has been introduced (but so far not passed) in Congress. Much of the debate for such a law is a reaction to the numbers of minority communities in the United States where languages other than English are commonly spoken. This essay, "Why English-Only Laws Are Useless," was written for the University of Rochester's *Campus Times* by Rosa Rivera when she was a senior. Rivera is a former president of the university's Spanish and Latin Students' Association.

Vocabulary

Meaning comes primarily from words. Before you begin reading, use a dictionary to look up the definitions of the following words that appear in the essay.

access	crucial	electoral	integral	invalidation
mandate	medium	repercussion	resurgence	unified

Why English-Only Laws Are Useless

1   The newest move to bash immigrants in the United States has arrived with the resurgence of the "English-only" movement. The type of legislation called for by this movement is sure to have negative repercussions for American society at large.

2   In 1996, the Supreme Court agreed to review a lower court's invalidation of Arizona's 1988 constitutional amendment making English the official language of that state. This law mandates that voting ballots be in English only and that English be the official language of all government functions and actions, including government documents. Government officials and employees are to conduct business in English only. Additionally, schools are not allowed to teach in any other language unless the class is specifically geared toward teaching a foreign language.

3   Legislation that would make English the official language of the United States would affect institutions that are crucial to all Americans: elections, government, and education. Citizens who cannot understand the English language would not be able to understand voter registration forms. They would not be able to vote in local or national elections, even though they have a constitutional right to participate in electoral politics. Government documents that are currently printed in several languages in addition to English would only be printed in English. That would mean that non-English-speaking people applying for housing, health care, welfare and other social services would no longer have access to these services. In addition, students who do not speak English would not be able to learn—their access to education would be cut off. Should government officials want to help the affected individuals by explaining application procedures or school policies, they would not be able to; according to the law, official business must be conducted in English. Should the proposed legislation be passed, government employees probably would not have the necessary language skills to assist people. There would probably be no hiring preferences given to those with knowledge of a foreign language and, therefore, no motivation to learn one.

4   Aside from my concern about the consequences that this proposed legislation might have on a large group, the whole issue strikes me as un-American. This country was founded by immigrants and now it is trying desperately to turn its back on them. Immigrants have it hard enough in this country without being forced to abandon their native language. Language is an integral part of culture; it is the medium through which the culture is passed on from generation to generation. The "English-only" movement (and others like it) is trying to create something in the United States that our rich history prevents: one unified culture.

5   Presidential candidate Bob Dole and others argue that making English the official language of the United States would unify the country. I disagree. Ethnic divisions and racism go a lot deeper than language.

Cause and Effect Technique Questions

Answers will vary.

1. Does this essay focus primarily on cause or effect? Identify some of the causes or effects depending upon which one you choose.

_____

_____

_____

_____

2. Why does Rivera list such specific services as housing, health care, welfare, and education? Why doesn't she simply say "English-only" laws would deny non-English-speaking individuals access to government?

_____

_____

_____

_____

3. What does Rivera think an "English-only" law will create in the United States?

_____

_____

_____

_____

4. Give some examples of why Rivera titles her essay "Why English-Only Laws Are Useless."

_____

_____

_____

_____

Critical Thinking Writing Opportunities

1. In his essay "Problems in Parenting," Mark Collom writes about the difficulties that parents confront during their years of parenting. Primarily, the essay is a _definition_ of a "good parent." The author arrives at this definition by focusing on the things parents do for their children as the causes for their being defined as "good parents." Write an essay defining your "good parenting" experiences or about your parents and the causes that make you think of them as good parents. Or talk with some students from other countries. Find out what they think are the causes for American parents being defined as either good or poor, generally speaking. Write an essay about their definition based on the causes they have related to you.

2. In her essay "Giving Out," Yvonne Olsen tells a story about a friend who took a job as a hospital volunteer to learn about the medical profession, even though she did not like many of the job's characteristics. Olsen's main approach for developing the essay is to focus on her friend's original _purpose_ for taking the job and to show how the effects of the job shed new light on new purposes arising from her experience that made the job more appealing. Write an essay about an experience you had that taught you things about yourself that you never anticipated. Focus on the initial or original purpose of the experience or event and how that eventually changed.

3. In her essay "Why English-Only Laws Are Useless," Rosa Rivera focuses on a particular *question at issue*—whether or not English should be, by law, established as the official language of the United States. In the concluding paragraph, she gives the reader her answer to the question: no. Write an essay examining why you think a law declaring English the only official language of the United States should or should not be passed. Choose one position or the other, not both.

Topics for a Cause or Effect Essay

Here are some possible topics for cause or effect essays. Remember, cause or effect writing must have a purpose, so don't forget to create a thesis sentence. Use the essay map to organize the topics for your body paragraphs.

Causes
1. The causes of drug abuse
2. The causes of the increasing high school dropout rate
3. The causes of test anxiety
4. The causes of high taxation
5. The causes of road rage or for being relaxed behind the wheel
6. The causes of divorce or for a long-lasting, happy marriage
7. The causes of spousal abuse or for diffusing tension in a relationship
8. The causes of a high teen pregnancy rate
9. The causes of low unemployment
10. The causes of high prison populations

Effects

1. The effects of a large corporation leaving a small town
2. The effects of pollution
3. The effects of a week's vacation
4. The effects of over-prescribing antibiotics
5. The effects of high speed limits
6. The effects of owning a pet
7. The effects of international trade agreements
8. The effects of reading a popular book or seeing a movie
9. The effects of a tornado
10. The effects of prejudice

Chapter Review

- ■ A cause or effect essay explains the reasons associated with some thing or event: cause analysis develops *why* something happens, and effect analysis explains *the results and consequences* stemming from the causes.

- ■ Developing a causal chain is a prewriting activity that can help you focus on important causes and effects.

- ■ While developing cause or effect writing, avoid seeing a causal relationship when either coincidence or simple chronology is at work.

- ■ In a cause or effect paragraph, the topic sentence announces the topic and indicates whether causes or effects will be discussed. Transitional expressions help show cause and effect relationships.

- ■ In a cause or effect essay, the thesis sentence in the introductory paragraph indicates the topic, controlling idea, and the causes or effects that will be discussed in the remainder of the essay.

Visit *The Write Start* Online!

For additional practice with the materials found in this chapter, visit our Website at

http://www.ablongman.com/checkett

The Website also features additional readings, quizzes, writing activities, and Internet links, as well as a bulletin board and interactive chat.

CHAPTER 15

The Persuasive Essay

When writers try to convince someone else that their point of view or belief is correct, they are using **persuasion.** Persuasion is one of the most common types of writing in college. Persuasive writing attempts to convince the reader that a particular point of view is justifiable because of the evidence used to explain and support the topic. For your point of view to be persuasive, your writing must have a clearly stated position and specific support to make your opinion believable.

Identifying Your Purpose

Persuasive writing can be informal, formal, or semiformal. Think of informal persuasion as when you and your friends or family try to convince one another about the rightness of your opinions on issues ranging from which college basketball team should be number one to which fast food restaurant has the best pizza. Commercials on radio and television also are types of informal persuasion. So are public service ads for nonprofit organizations and most political advertisements.

Formal persuasion is usually called **argumentation.** This type of persuasion requires not only that you argue for your own beliefs but also that you argue directly against someone else's beliefs. Argumentation uses evidence from primary and secondary sources (information often found in the library) that are cited using a formal documentation process (Modern Language Association or American Psychological Association, for example). Research papers, analytical essays, and certain business reports fall into this category. You will be introduced to the argument research essay in Chapter 16.

However, in this chapter, we are interested in semiformal persuasion—a type of persuasion that falls somewhere between the two mentioned above. Semiformal persuasion requires a bit more logical thought and organization than is needed around the kitchen table in informal arguing but not quite the rigid structure that is made necessary by the quotations and accompanying documentation of formal argumentation.

Writing a Persuasive Paragraph

Students are required to argue for and against ideas in quizzes, papers, and exams. Therefore, learning the fundamentals of persuasive writing is one of the most important skills a student writer can learn. The following is a persuasive paragraph that tries to convince the reader that the author has a well-thought-out point of view.

**Exhibit 15.1
The Persuasion
Paragraph**

> Mandatory drug testing will help eliminate poor job performance. Workers will do quality work to meet the standards of the company. The company will be more successful because of the quality of the product the workers will produce. Additionally, the workers' job performance will increase because of a better attitude. Mandatory drug testing also will reduce the number of job-related accidents; that, in turn, will enhance performance. A safe work environment promotes better performances as employees will feel safer and more secure as they perform their jobs. Workers having more confidence in the employer, fellow employees, and the workplace will complete tasks more confidently and successfully.

In the paragraph above, the writer's conclusion, that "mandatory drug testing will help eliminate poor job performance," is supported by statements that suggest that mandatory drug testing will create a safer workplace and a safer employee. A safer atmosphere creates a better attitude on the part of the worker who, in turn, will perform better on the job. The ideas that support the conclusion are not outlandish or overblown; rather, they are reasonably expressed and developed in a convincing manner.

The Topic Sentence in a Persuasive Paragraph

In a persuasive paragraph, the topic sentence states the writer's conclusion or point of view about a particular topic. The writer's conclusion either can be for or against (pro or con) the idea concerning the topic. Therefore, the topic sentence is the key to a successful persuasive paragraph. The verbs used in a persuasive topic sentence are usually *should/should not* or *must/must not*.

Examples

The pending legislation on the right of citizens to carry concealed handguns should be defeated.

This paragraph will argue against (con) citizens having the right to carry concealed handguns.

Employers should provide day care for their employees.

This paragraph will argue for (pro) companies providing day care for the children of their employees.

> *Euthanasia should be legalized because of our constitutional rights of personal freedom.*
>
> This paragraph will argue for (pro) physician-assisted suicide.
>
> *Athletics should not receive more funding than academics.*
>
> This paragraph will argue against (con) sports receiving more money than academics.

PRACTICE 1

Answers will vary, but sample responses are provided.

For the ten topics listed below, write either a pro (for) topic sentence or a con (against) topic sentence. Try to write five pro sentences and five con sentences.

1. Topic: Selling cigarettes to teens under eighteen years of age

   Pro: Selling cigarettes to teens under eighteen years of age should be legalized.

   Con: Teens under eighteen years of age should not be permitted to buy cigarettes.

2. Topic: Regulation of sexually explicit material on the Internet

   Pro: Sexually explicit material should be freely available on the Internet to all adults.

   Con: Sexually explicit material should be banned on the Internet

3. Topic: Organized prayer in public schools.

   Pro: Organized prayer should be permitted in public schools to promote morality.

   Con: To ensure the separation of church and state, organized prayer should not be allowed in public schools.

4. Topic: Lower speed limits on federal highways

   Pro: To save lives, the speed limit on federal highways should be decreased.

   Con: The speed limit on federal highways should not be decreased because doing so would interfere with commerce.

5. Topic: Military draft for eighteen-year-old males and females

   Pro: All eighteen-year-olds should be drafted into the armed services.

   Con: Eighteen-year-olds should not be drafted into military service.

6. Topic: Adoption of children by gay and lesbian couples

Pro: Gay and lesbian couples must be allowed to adopt children.

Con: Gay and lesbian couples must not be allowed to adopt children.

7. Topic: Safety inspections for automobiles

Pro: The government should require periodic safety inspections for automobiles.

Con: The government should not require periodic safety inspections for automobiles.

8. Topic: Elimination of athletic scholarships

Pro: All athletic scholarships should be eliminated.

Con: Athletic scholarships should not be eliminated.

9. Topic: Increasing the income tax

Pro: The income tax must be increased.

Con: The income tax must not be increased.

10. Topic: Legalization of marijuana

Pro: Marijuana should be legalized.

Con: Marijuana should not be legalized.

The Pro and Con List

Once you have decided on a topic, it is vital that you know the major argument points on both sides of the issue, whether or not you know which side you are going to take. First, list as many points for each side that you can think of in a pro and con list.

**Exhibit 15.2
The Pro and
Con List**

Pro and Con List

Topic: Nuclear Energy

Pro (For) List	*Con (Against) List*
Cheaper fuel costs	Radioactive waste
Less dependence on foreign oil	Unemployment in fossil-fuel industries
Creates high tech jobs	Environmental pollution
Saves natural resources	Nuclear power plant accidents
Insures strong nuclear arsenal	Nuclear weapons proliferation

Once you have listed as many points as you can think of, consider the points on both sides of the argument, and choose the side you wish to argue for. Decide which points you will use in your paragraph to support your topic.

PRACTICE 2

Answers will vary.

Create a pro and con list for each of the following topics. Think of as many items for each list as you can.

1. Topic: Teaching sex education in mixed-gender classes

Pro	Con
_____	_____
_____	_____
_____	_____
_____	_____
_____	_____

2. Topic: Gays serving in the military

Pro	Con
_____	_____
_____	_____
_____	_____
_____	_____
_____	_____

3. Topic: Smoking in public places

Pro	Con
_____	_____
_____	_____
_____	_____
_____	_____
_____	_____

4. Topic: Foreign language requirements in high school and college

Pro	Con
_____	_____
_____	_____
_____	_____
_____	_____
_____	_____

5. Topic: Affirmative action in employment

Pro	Con
_____	_____
_____	_____
_____	_____
_____	_____
_____	_____

Techniques to Support the Argument

To persuade the reader that a particular position is convincing, writers use a variety of support techniques in the persuasive paragraph: answering the opposition, referring to an authority, predicting consequences, stating facts, and providing examples. While you probably will never use all of them in one paragraph, you will use them when you write persuasively.

Answering the Opposition

At times, the best way to persuade your reader is to respond directly to an opponent's point. This also shows your reader that you are aware of your opponent's side of the issue, not just your own.

Referring to an Authority

An authority is a person or a group that is considered an expert on the subject under discussion and will give an unbiased but knowledgeable opinion.

Predicting Consequences

Predicting consequences can strengthen an argument and persuade your reader to agree with your point of view and disagree with your opponent's.

Stating Facts

Facts are those things that actually exist or have existed, such as people, places, things, and events. A *fact* differs from an *opinion* in a quite significant way. An opinion is how we think about, or interpret, facts. For instance, it is a *fact* that in 1978 the U.S. Congress removed our currency from the gold standard (the dollar amount of paper money and coins in circulation could not exceed the dollar amount of gold stored at Fort Knox in Kentucky). That fact cannot be argued. However, whether or not you think it was a good idea to remove the gold standard is your *opinion*, and that can be argued. Whether your *opinion* or your opponent's *opinion* is the more persuasive, the *fact* remains that the gold standard was removed in 1978.

Providing Examples

Good examples can develop an idea quickly and clearly and help convince your reader of your point of view. Examples also are used to clarify, illustrate, or make concrete a general idea about the subject. Therefore, be certain that your examples support your position or convincingly argue against your opponent's.

PRACTICE 3

Select one of the pro and con lists you created in Practice 2. Write a sentence for each of the pro items you listed, and write a sentence for each of the con items you listed. Next, write a topic sentence for the group of pro sentences, and write a topic sentence for the group of con sentences. Finally, rewrite your sentences into standard paragraph form. These are your rough drafts for your persuasive paragraphs on both sides of an issue.

False Logic

When choosing the supportive evidence that proves your point, keep in mind that some ideas will sound good at first but might reveal flaws on closer inspection. Some support information might be irrelevant, misleading, oversimplified, unfair, or lead to erroneous conclusions. These proofs actually prove nothing, and they can destroy an otherwise good argument.

It is very important that you recognize statements that exhibit false logic. These statements are known as *logical fallacies*. If readers catch you using logical fallacies as proof, they will think you are a poor arguer, or that you are an unethical arguer because you are purposely trying to be deceptive.

Although there are many logical fallacies, a few of the more common ones are listed below.

■ **Ad hominem** (Latin: "to the man") arguments attack the person's character rather than the person's ideas. Example (politics): *My opponent is an avowed atheist; therefore, he cannot lead this country out of the economic disaster we find ourselves in.* While many voters may not like the fact that a particular candidate does not believe in God, such a spiritual position probably has little if anything to do with the candidate's ability to handle economic problems. The ad hominem argument shifts the focus away from the argument and to the person.

■ **Bandwagon** arguments suggest that because everyone else is doing something, so should you. Example (advertising): *Millions of people are using ampheta-cal to lose weight. So what are you waiting for?* Even if the claim were true, an amphetamine-based product that overstimulates the central nervous system may be medically dangerous. The bandwagon argument tries to persuade you to be like everyone else.

■ **Either-or** arguments state that there are only two ways of dealing with a problem. Example (law): *Abortions should either be permitted in all situations or be illegal under any circumstances.* This argument does not allow for alternative choices, such as allowing abortions when the mother's life is in danger or the pregnancy is due to rape, or disallowing abortions when one of the parents is willing to raise the child or adoptive parents are available. The either-or argument does not allow for compromise.

■ **Hasty generalization** arguments jump to conclusions using too little evidence. Example (education): *All inner-city students don't do well on standardized tests because they don't study enough.* Inner city students may study as much as students in the suburbs or rural locales. Standardized tests often are biased against inner-city students because of the language and examples used in developing questions. Also, how is "inner-city" being defined? What population must a city have to qualify for the study? Do the inner-city students come from various ethnic groups or a particular ethnic group? What are the boundaries of the "inner city" as opposed to the "outer city"? Has such a distinction been made, and if so, what is the rationale for making the distinction? The hasty generalization argument often jumps to a conclusion based on too few examples or unfairly designed definitions.

■ **Non sequitur** (Latin: "it does not follow") arguments have a conclusion that does not follow from the evidence. Example (business): *Women should not own businesses because they don't play golf as well as men.* While it may be true that some business is conducted on golf courses, the vast majority of successful business transactions have nothing whatsoever to do with the game of golf. In fact, most businessmen and businesswomen don't play golf at all. The non sequitur argument is not an argument at all. In fact, the evidence does not provide for a logical, reasonable conclusion.

■ **Red herring** arguments create false issues that lead the reader away from the real argument. (The term "red herring" comes from the practice of English dog trainers dragging a sack of dead herring across the scent of a fox in an attempt to distract the dogs.) Example (sports): *Our football team is not playing well because the owners never come to the games.* The real reason for the team not playing well probably has little to do with owners attending or not attending games. Poor coaching, play calling, player selection, and conditioning are more likely to be the reasons for the team's poor play. The red herring argument makes use of misleading information to misguide the reader's attention from the real issue.

PRACTICE 4

Write the name of the logical fallacy in the space provided after each of the argument statements listed below.

1. It's not safe to swim in the ocean because there have been several shark attacks over the past few years in Australia and South Africa.

   Hasty generalization

2. Are we going to increase the number of mounted police in the park, or are we going to abandon it to the homeless, to the drug dealers, and to robbers and rapists?

   Either-or

3. I'm sure Raoul's parents are wealthy because he drives a new car to school.

Non sequitur

4. Mom, I need a Palm Pilot because all the kids at school have them.

Bandwagon

5. She would not make a good governor because her husband has never been involved in politics, his business takes him out of town a lot, and he wasn't even born in this country.

Red herring

6. My opponent doesn't support handgun legislation because he is a coward interested more in his own safety than the well being of defenseless women and children.

Ad hominem

Organization Patterns

Once you have made your pro and con list and have chosen the types of evidence you want to use to support your topic, you will need to organize your paragraph for an effective presentation. There is no defined pattern that a writer has to use when writing persuasively. However, there are several patterns that will logically organize your points into a convincing persuasive paragraph.

Pattern 1: Arguing Only Your Own Points

In the first organizational pattern, you use only support points that argue for your point of view. Therefore you use only pro list items if you are arguing for a point of view, or you use only con list items if you are arguing against a point of view.

> **Example: Arguing Only Your Own Points**
>
> Nuclear energy should not be more widely used because of radioactive waste disposal problems and the possibility of a nuclear reactor accident. One of the problems with nuclear energy is waste management. Radioactive waste can remain dangerous for thousands of years; therefore, disposal sites must meet rigid safety standards to keep the public safe. Sites must be deep in the ground to shield the public from possible radiation exposure, and they must be immune to earthquake damage. Such sites are hard to find and expensive to maintain. In addition to the waste disposal problem, nuclear accidents pose a real danger to people living near nuclear reactors. In 1986, in the Ukrainian town of Chernobyl, a nuclear reactor accident put thousands at risk of radioactive poisoning. A radiation cloud spread over northern Europe and Great Britain. Thirty-one Soviet citizens died, and over 100,000 had to be evacuated from surrounding areas. The risks involved in the long-term control and management of such a volatile substance as radioactive materials makes it a very risky proposition. Until more trustworthy safeguards can be developed in both the use and disposal of radioactive substances, we should not increase our use of nuclear energy.

Pattern 2: Arguing Against Your Opposition's Points

Another way to organize a persuasive paragraph is to state only your opposition's support points (either pro or con) and then argue against them.

Example: Arguing Against the Opposition

Despite the possible benefits to society, nuclear energy should not be more widely used as a fuel source. Many scientists and researchers claim nuclear energy is desirable as an energy source because it creates enormous amounts of power from small resources. While this may be true, other costs outweigh the purely monetary. In 1986, in the Ukrainian town of Chernobyl, a nuclear reactor accident killed 31 Soviet citizens and caused 100,000 people to be evacuated. A radioactive cloud covered much of northern Europe and Great Britain. Military leaders in Washington, D.C., state that a nuclear energy industry will also insure a continuous source of radioactive material necessary to maintain our nuclear weapons arsenal for the defense of the nation. However, every year there are reports of nuclear byproducts missing from government inventories. Enemies of the United States could use this material to build nuclear weapons with which to threaten us. Also, unfriendly nations could steal the technology for nuclear reactors that could be used to produce materials for making nuclear weapons. The potential for disaster far outweighs the potential benefits coming from the nuclear energy industry. Nuclear energy is not a safe or practical energy source.

Pattern 3: Alternating Your Points with Arguing Against the Opposition

The third pattern of organization is alternating use of support points for your side of the argument and listing your opponent's points and arguing against them. Note that this is a hybrid or mixing of patterns 1 and 2.

Example: Alternating Your Points with Arguing Against the Opposition

Despite the possible benefits to society, nuclear energy should not be more widely used as a fuel source. One of the problems with nuclear energy is waste management. Radioactive waste can remain dangerous for thousands of years; therefore, safe deposit sites must meet rigid safety standards to keep the public safe. Sites must be deep in the ground to shield the public from possible radiation exposure, and the sites must be immune to earthquake damage. Many scientists and researchers claim nuclear energy is desirable as an energy source because it creates enormous amounts of power from small resources. While this may be true, other costs outweigh the purely monetary. In 1986, in the Ukrainian town of Chernobyl, a nuclear reactor accident killed 31 Soviet citizens and caused 100,000 people to be evacuated. A radioactive cloud covered much of northern Europe and Great Britain. Nuclear weapons proliferation is another problem if nuclear energy production is increased. Every year there are reports of nuclear byproducts missing from government inventories. Enemies of the United States could use this material to build nuclear weapons with which to threaten our security. Economists like to say that increasing the nuclear energy industry will create more high-tech jobs, but the same industry will cause widespread unemployment in traditional fossil-fuel industries like coal, oil, and gas. The potential for both disaster and a negative impact on the economy should convince lawmakers to not increase our use of nuclear energy as a fuel source.

Once you have chosen an organization pattern for your paragraph, select several points from the appropriate list or lists and write sentences for each. Arrange the sentences according to the organization pattern you have chosen.

PRACTICE 5

Using the rough draft persuasive paragraph you created in Practice 3, rewrite the paragraph three times, using the three organizational patterns you have just studied.

Using Transitional Expressions in the Persuasive Paragraph

Transitional expressions are useful for connecting related ideas and adding rhythm to a paragraph so that it reads more smoothly. Although transitional expressions can be used anywhere they are appropriate, writers often use them to signal the types of evidence they are using in persuasive paragraphs.

Example: Alternating Your Points with Arguing Against the Opposition

Despite the possible benefits to society, nuclear energy should not be more widely used as a fuel source. One of the problems with nuclear energy is waste management. Radioactive waste can remain dangerous for thousands of years; therefore, safe deposit sites must meet rigid safety standards to keep the public safe. Sites must be deep in the ground to shield the public from possible radiation exposure, and the sites must be immune to earthquake damage. Many scientists and researchers claim nuclear energy is desirable as an energy source because it creates enormous amounts of power from small resources. While this may be true, other costs outweigh the purely monetary. In 1986, in the Ukrainian town of Chernobyl, a nuclear reactor accident killed 31 Soviet citizens and caused 100,000 people to be evacuated. A radioactive cloud covered much of northern Europe and Great Britain. Nuclear weapons proliferation is another problem if nuclear energy production is increased. Every year there are reports of nuclear byproducts missing from government inventories. Enemies of the United States could use this material to build nuclear weapons with which to threaten our security. Economists like to say that increasing the nuclear energy industry will create more high-tech jobs, but the same industry will cause widespread unemployment in traditional fossil-fuel industries like coal, oil, and gas. The potential for both disaster and a negative impact on the economy should convince lawmakers to not increase our use of nuclear energy as a fuel source.

Transitional Expressions for Persuasive Writing

Answering the Opposition and Referring to Authority	Predicting Consequences and Stating Conclusions	Facts and Examples
according to	consequently	another, next
although	in conclusion	because, since
nevertheless	therefore	finally, last
of course	thus	first, second
on the other hand		for
others may say		

Go back and read the paragraph example in Exhibit 15.1. Then, read that same paragraph as illustrated below with transitional expressions included. The transitional expressions are in boldface for identification purposes.

> Mandatory drug testing will help eliminate poor job performance. **Consequently,** workers will do quality work to meet the standards of the company. The company, **therefore,** will be more successful because of the quality of the product the workers will produce. **Next,** the workers' job performance will increase **because** of a better attitude. Mandatory drug testing also will reduce the number of job-related accidents; that, **of course,** will enhance performance. **Thus,** a safe work environment promotes better performances as employees will feel safer and more secure as they perform their jobs. **Lastly,** workers having more confidence in the employer, fellow employees, and the workplace will complete tasks more confidently and successfully.

PRACTICE 6

Using appropriate transitional expressions, rewrite the three persuasive paragraphs you wrote for Practice 5. After you have finished, compare the two sets of paragraphs. The ones exhibiting the transitional expressions should be easier to understand and easier to read.

Moving from Paragraph to Essay

Now that you have studied and practiced the techniques to create effective persuasion paragraphs, it is time to expand your ideas to a larger writing unit: the persuasive essay. Using the techniques you learned in Part 1 regarding developing the essay paragraphs and the persuasion techniques you have just learned, you can write a persuasive essay. This might be a good time to return to Part 1 and review the techniques for developing the full essay.

Creating the Introductory Paragraph

Like all essays, the persuasive essay needs a clearly defined organization and a thesis statement to announce to the reader just how the subject will be developed. The thesis sentence should state the topic, the writer's attitude toward the topic, and the organizational structure. By using an appropriate lead-in technique, the thesis sentence should blend naturally into the rest of the introductory paragraph.

Using the Pro and Con Lists to Create the Thesis Sentence for a Pro Essay

Before writing an essay about students working while in college (reprinted below), one student created pro and con lists. After examining both lists, he chose the pro position and constructed a thesis sentence with an essay map consisting of three of the five items on the pro side of the list. Notice that the pro and con lists, when used as the basis for the essay map, act both as an organizational tool and a working outline. The pro and con lists and thesis are illustrated below.

Topic: Working While in College

Pro	Con
1. Compels the students to pursue education more seriously.	1. Working would have a negative impact on the students' grade point average.
2. Working teaches the students responsibility.	2. Parents created the students, so parents ought to pay for college.
3. Working removes the financial burden from parents.	3. Going to college teaches the students to be responsible.
4. Working causes the students to appreciate college.	4. Working takes away from study time.
5. Working gives the student extra money for living expenses and extra-curricular activities.	5. Working would make the student tire easily at college.

Using the numbers 1, 2, and 3 in the Pro list, the writer constructed the following thesis sentence.

Thesis Sentence: Students should work their way through college because doing so compels the students to pursue education more seriously, teaches the students responsibility, and removes the financial burden from parents.

The topic of the essay is "students working while attending college," and the writer's idea of importance toward the subject is that "students should work while attending college" (pro) as opposed to a paper that might argue "students should not work while attending college" (con). Notice that the essay map in this thesis sentence comes as a series at the end of the sentence. The three items in the series will be the topics of the first, second, and third body paragraphs, respectively.

Creating the Body Paragraphs

In the sample student essay on working while in college, the three items in the essay map form the basis of the three body paragraphs: students will pursue education more seriously, learn responsibility, and ease the parents' financial burden. In writing the body paragraphs, you can use only one of the organization patterns for a persuasive paragraph, or you can mix them as appropriate.

Creating the Concluding Paragraph

As in all types of essays, the concluding paragraph should grow out of the introductory and body paragraphs. All of the approaches to the concluding paragraph work well in persuasive essays. For example, *evaluation* is a good approach, especially if you have chosen the pattern in which you answer the opposition or use a mix of arguing your own points and answering the opposition. With evaluation, you can emphasize the strength of your position and the weakness of the opposition's position. If you have chosen simply to argue for your own position, you might take the *prediction* approach to the concluding paragraph, indicating the future benefits if your point of view prevails. If you have chosen to argue primarily against the opposition, *warning* would be a good technique to use. You can indicate the dire consequences that may come to pass if your opposition's point of view prevails. Finally, a *call to action* in the concluding paragraph works well to persuade the reader to join you in working to see that your point of view is adopted.

Sample Student Essay: WORKING PAYS OFF

Randy Raterman

> In this essay, "Working Pays Off," student writer Randy Raterman favors students working while in college. Notice how well the author develops each topic in the body paragraphs. His attention to detail makes the reader feel that he has thought about the issues very thoroughly, and that he probably worked during his college career.

Vocabulary

Meaning comes primarily from words. Before you begin reading, use a dictionary to look up the following words that appear in the essay.

altered	compels	convey	diligently
excel	excursions	fathom	imposes
paraphernalia	proclaim	shebang	tedious

Working Pays Off

1   Many students have argumentative perspectives toward working their way through college. Some students feel working would have a negative impact on the grade point average. As far as being responsible, numerous students believe going to lectures every day, taking notes, and cramming for exams imposes enough responsibility in itself; additionally, others feel the parents ought to pay for college because it was Mom and Dad who created them. Somehow, the attitude of students not working needs to be altered so that the students better appreciate college education. Students should work their way through college because doing so compels the students to pursue education

more seriously, teaches the students responsibility, and removes the financial burden from parents. ←— **Thesis Sentence with Essay Map**

Topic Sentence —→ 2   Many working class students experience firsthand what it's like to have backbreaking, monotonous jobs with no particular ladder to climb. The main goals of these individuals are to do everything humanly possible to excel in college, graduate, and quit their dead-end, tedious, everyday jobs. Consequently, several students argue grade points averages would be substantially lower if they had to work. Being concerned about a lower G.P.A. is a good point, but one having no leg to stand on. True, the extra load of working along with going to school robs time from social activities and family excursions; however, working students labor diligently on scholastics knowing failure leads nowhere and climbs no ladders. Unemployed students never experience the level of gratification gained by employed students with high G.P.A.'s. Yes, employment may consume a little of the students' study time; although time can be regained by reevaluating priorities, numerous students will continue searching for excuses not to work. While nobody will ever proclaim working their way through college was easy, the experience is truly rewarding and compels the student to be responsible.

Topic Sentence —→ 3   Being a responsible adult is another admirable trait hard work leaves ingrained in your personality. Numerous unemployed students lack perseverance and have carefree attitudes originating from parents paying the bills for tuition, books, and other paraphernalia. A majority of the jobless who are enrolled for classes only fear being kicked off of their parents' insurance or losing various funds provided by Uncle Sam if they flunk out. Nevertheless, employed students convey to others, after having finished the process, that paying for college teaches responsibility. True, nonworking students attending classes and achieving good grades show signs of a responsible nature, but the high magnitude of responsibility is much more prevalent in working students. Many employed students maintain a high G.P.A. along with raising a family. Children add an enormous amount of additional responsibility to a student's daily grind. Yes, working can make you tire easily, but the hard work, long hours, and high level of responsibility are extremely gratifying when college is completed and the students can quit their dead-end, fatiguing, tedious jobs.

Topic Sentence —→ 4   The employed students also can be proud of keeping their financial burden off their parents, or at least of keeping monetary setback to a minimum. Many loving parents go to their wits end trying to support their offspring though college. While mortgaging the family residence, working two and three jobs, and depleting life savings, parents become overwhelmed by the cost of education. Stress, due to insufficient funds for the children's education, can sometimes cause major difficulties between the parents. There have even been divorces caused by such financial problems. The responsible, working students pay their own way through school or at least pay a significant portion of the tuition, easing the stress and monetary problems of the parents. Proud parents of children working their way through college will have enough funds to help out and enough to help with their own retirement. In the future, this can be a blessing to both parents and children. Unfortunately, a few students believe that since their parents brought them into the world, the parents owe them everything. After all, they didn't ask to be born! Such attitudes may stem from a lack of responsibility during the development stage when they were young. Although it is true that the parents did bring the children into the world, they should not pay for the whole shebang; no, such thinking on the part of the children is not socially or morally acceptable.

5   Many working students simultaneously envy and despise the nonworking student. Although most students wish they were born with a silver spoon in their mouths, few ever are; as a result, many college goers are employed and do work their way through college. Working also provides students with money for living expenses and extracurricular activities, so going to a movie theater is not a financial dilemma. Nevertheless, students working their way through college can be proud of scholastic accomplishments while carrying high levels of responsibility from day to day. The enormous level of gratification and satisfaction students experience while working their way through college is one which nonworking students will never fathom.

Persuasion Technique Questions

1. What organization pattern does the writer use?

Pattern 3: alternating use of support points and listing the opposition's

points and arguing against them. He starts off each body paragraph with

a pro point, and then he shifts back and forth between pro and con points.

2. Does the writer use mostly opinion, or does he use mostly facts? Point out sentences that support your answer.

All opinion. There are no facts featured in the essay. Students can choose

almost any of the pro sentences as evidence.

3. How convincing is the support evidence? Does the writer make any claims that seem too extreme or opinionated? Point out examples.

Answers will vary depending on the reader's personal experience.

Creating the Introductory Paragraph and Thesis Sentence for a Con Essay

Before writing an essay about mixed-gender training in the military (reprinted below), one student created pro and con lists. After examining both lists, he chose the con position and constructed a thesis sentence with an essay map consisting of three of the four items in his con list. Notice that the pro and con lists, when used as the basis for the essay map, act both as an organizational tool and a working outline. The pro and con lists and thesis are illustrated below.

Topic: Men and Women Training Together in the Military

Pro	*Con*
1. Men and women have to work together at some point, so let them train together.	**1.** There would be more sexual harassment cases.
2. If you separate by sex, then why not by race and religion. It's the same concept.	**2.** It would increase complaints of favoritism.
3. Good manners and behavior are a part of military custom whether women are around or not.	**3.** Men would be concentrating on whether they might say or do something offensive to women rather than concentrating on duties.
4. There would still be complaints of being separate but not equal.	**4.** Mixed-sex units would cause less unit cohesion.

Using numbers 1, 2, and 4 in the Con list, the writer constructed the following thesis sentence.

Thesis Sentence: Training men and women in same-sex units would lead to a breakdown in unit cohesion, more complaints of sexual harassment, and increased complaints of favoritism.

The first, second, and third body paragraphs, then, will develop the topics of a breakdown in unit cohesion, more sexual harassment complaints, and increased favoritism.

Sample Student Essay: GUYS AND GALS

Bryan Kemper

In his essay "Guys and Gals," student writer Bryan Kemper, a military veteran, explains why he is against men and women training together in the same military units. Kemper is neither against women being in the military, nor is he against women receiving equal training. His conclusion is that, if they were trained separately, both men and women would be better trained and therefore the military's effectiveness would be increased.

Vocabulary

Meaning comes primarily from words. Before you begin reading, use a dictionary to look up the following words that appear in the essay.

cohesion	comply	consumptive
designated	harassment	integration
preferential	reprimanded	stereotypes

Guys and Gals

1   The integration of women and men has become an increasing problem in the American military. There are concerns about women being sexually harassed in the workplace, and concerns about men receiving preferential treatment. Other issues include women having easier standards to comply with, and men having to attend time-consuming sensitivity training. Both men and women should receive the same opportunities and fair treatment. Training men and women in same-sex units would lead to more complaints of sexual harassment, a breakdown in unit cohesion, and increased complaints of favoritism.   ←— **Thesis Sentence with Essay Map**

Topic Sentence ⟶ 2   Sexual harassment is a problem that will not go away, and the problem will not get any better as long as men and women are being trained together. Some advocates of same-sex training units believe that men and women will have to work together at some point in their military careers. Because the military is about discipline and teamwork, men and women should be trained together so they will learn to get along with each other. However, when there are men and women working together, there is the potential for sexual harassment to occur. Training in two separate units can insure that men and women are given equal amounts of quality training. Separate male and female units would also afford women the opportunity to prove their abilities to perform the same duties as any male unit in the military after the proper amount of training, without the added pressure of performing in front of their male counterparts before they are ready.

Topic Sentence ⟶ 3   Under the current system, women are not allowed the same opportunities for duty assignments as men. The different job assignments allowed for women, especially in combat units, are very limited. Separation of male and female units would not lessen the opportunity of duty assignments for women; separate units would increase women's opportunity for different duty positions made available. Female training units should be specially designated for the performance of certain combat duty assignments; moreover, units should be set aside to perform exactly the same duties as a male unit. Women should be given the same training as men, using the same standards. Because of equal opportunity for separate male and female units, there would be no complaints of favoritism or preferential treatment. Separate units would be more beneficial for women and men alike; in the end, each unit would be more cohesive, and the military, as a whole, would become more effective in succeeding in its missions.

Topic Sentence ⟶ 4   Women and men are not judged by the same standard in today's military; consequently, there are complaints that women receive preferential treatment. Often men are reprimanded for incidents involving sexual harassment or misconduct; the man's side of the story often is not taken into consideration. Men are given more opportunity for job promotion or advancement than women, and there are more men in leadership positions. Because of gender stereotypes, women are excused from performing required duties. Favoritism can be argued for either side. If trained separately, men and women would be evaluated among their peers based solely on merit and job performance. If evaluated with peers of the same sex, neither men nor women would receive favoritism according to their gender.

5   Men and women are still going to have to work together in the military. Not all units and job assignments should be separate, but there are many combat units where they should be segregated. If there are separate units for men and women, they still should be trained to work together; however, the units should be kept separate as much as possible. Perhaps a block of training hours could be set aside every week for just such a purpose. But, for the most part, men and women should be trained in separate units for real equal opportunity employment conditions to exist.

Persuasion Technique Questions

1. What organizational pattern does the writer use?

A variation of Pattern 3. In paragraphs 2 and 4, the writer begins with his con points before shifting to the opposition's points and then shifting back to his points; in paragraph 3, however, he begins with his opposition's points before concluding the paragraph with points in his favor.

2. Does the writer use mostly opinion or mostly facts? Point out sentences that support your answer.

He states many of his opinions as if they were facts, but they are still opinions. In particular, the topic sentences in all the body paragraphs are stated as if they were true and not open to debate.

3. How convincing is the support evidence? Does Kemper make any claims that seem too extreme or opinionated? Point out examples.

Answers will vary.

Sample Professional Essay: LAST RITES FOR THE INDIAN DEAD

Suzan Shown Harjo

> This essay, "Last Rites for the Indian Dead," was written by Suzan Shown Harjo, a Native American of Cheyenne descent, and it first appeared in the *Los Angeles Times*. In her essay, Harjo identifies a problem that affects Native Americans, but she also argues that the issue poses an ethical conflict for all Americans.

Vocabulary

Meaning comes primarily from words. Before you begin reading, use a dictionary to look up the definitions for the following words that appear in the essay.

abhorrent	archaeological	cranial	curation
decapitated	desecrated	exhumed	funerary
macabre	mastodons	pseudo-	relic
rummaging	strewn		

Last Rites for the Indian Dead

1   What if museums, universities, and government agencies could put your dead relatives on display or keep them in boxes to be cut up and otherwise studied? What if you believed that the spirits of the dead could not rest until their human remains were placed in a sacred area?

2   The ordinary American would say there ought to be a law—and there is, for ordinary Americans. The problem for American Indians is that there are too many laws of the kind that make us the archaeological property of the United States and too few of the kind that protect us from such insults.

3   Some of my own Cheyenne relatives' skulls are in the Smithsonian Institution today, along with those of at least 4,500 other Indian people who were violated in the 1800s by the U.S. Army for an "Indian Cranial Study." It wasn't enough that these unarmed Cheyenne people were mowed down by the cavalry at the infamous Sand Creek massacre; many were decapitated and their heads shipped to Washington as freight. (The Army Medical Museum's collection is now in the Smithsonian.) Some had been exhumed only hours after being buried. Imagine their grieving families' reaction on finding their loved ones disinterred and headless.

4   Some targets of the Army's study were killed in noncombat situations and beheaded immediately. The officer's account of the decapitation of the Apache chief Mangas Coloradas in 1863 shows the pseudoscientific nature of the exercise. "I weighed the brain and measured the skull," the good doctor wrote, "and found that while the skull was smaller, the brain was larger than that of Daniel Webster."

5   These journal accounts exist in excruciating detail, yet missing are any records of overall comparisons, conclusions, or final reports of the Army study. Since it is unlike the Army not to leave a paper trail, one must wonder about the motive for its collection.

6   The total Indian body count in the Smithsonian collection is more than 19,000, and it is not the largest in the country. It is not inconceivable that the 1.5 million of us living today are outnumbered by our dead stored in museums, educational institutions, federal agencies, state historical societies, and private collections. The Indian people are further dehumanized by being exhibited alongside the mastodons and dinosaurs and other extinct creatures.

7   Where we have buried our dead in peace, more often than not the sites have been desecrated. For more than 200 years, relic hunting has been a popular pursuit. Lately, the market in Indian artifacts has brought this abhorrent activity to a fever pitch in some areas. And when scavengers come upon Indian burial sites, everything found becomes fair game, including sacred burial offerings, teeth, and skeletal remains.

8   One unusually well-publicized example of Indian grave desecration occurred two years ago in a western Kentucky field known as Slack Farm, the site of an Indian village five centuries ago. Ten men—one with a business card stating "Have Shovel, Will Travel"—paid the landowner $10,000 to lease digging rights between planting seasons. They dug extensively on the 40-acre farm, rummaging through an estimated 650 graves, collecting burial tools, tools, and ceremonial items. Skeletons were strewn about like litter.

9   What motivates people to do something like this? Financial gain is the first answer. Indian relic-collecting has become a multimillion-dollar industry. The price tag on a bead necklace can easily top $1,000; rare pieces fetch tens of thousands.

10   And it is not just collectors of the macabre who pay for skeletal remains. Scientists say that these deceased Indians are needed for research that someday could benefit the health and welfare of living Indians. But just how many dead Indians must they examine? Nineteen thousand?

11   There is doubt as to whether permanent curation of our dead really benefits Indians. Dr. Emery A. Johnson, former assistant surgeon general, recently observed, "I am not aware of any current medical diagnostic or treatment procedure that has been derived from research on such skeletal remains. Nor am I aware of any during the 34 years that I have been involved in American Indian…health care."

12   Indian remains are still being collected for racial biological studies. While the intentions may be honorable, the ethics of using human remains this way without the full consent of relatives must be questioned.

13   Some relief for Indian people has come on the state level. Almost half of the states, including California, have passed laws protecting Indian burial sites and restricting the sale of Indian bones, burial offerings, and other sacred items. Representative Charles E. Bennett (D–Fla.) and Sen. John McCain (R–Ariz.) have introduced bills that are a good start in invoking the federal government's protections. However, no legislation has attacked the problem head-on by imposing stiff penalties at the marketplace, or by changing laws that make dead Indians the nation's property.

14   Some universities—notably Stanford, Nebraska, Minnesota, and Seattle—have returned, or agreed to return, Indian human remains; it is fitting that institutions of higher education should lead the way.

15   Congress is now deciding what to do with the government's extensive collections of Indian human remains and associated funerary objects. The secretary of the Smithsonian, Robert McAdams, has been valiantly attempting to apply modern ethics to yesterday's excesses. This week, he announced that the Smithsonian would conduct an inventory and return all Indian skeletal remains that could be identified with specific tribes or living kin.

16   But there remains a reluctance generally among collectors of Indian remains to take action of a scope that would have a quantitative impact and a healing quality. If they will not act on their own—and it is highly unlikely that they will—then Congress must act.

17   The country must recognize that the bodies of dead American Indian people are not artifacts to be bought and sold as collectors' items. It is not appropriate to store tens of thousands of our ancestors for possible future research. They are our family. They deserve to be returned to their sacred burial grounds and given a chance to rest.

18   The plunder of our people's graves has gone on too long. Let us rebury our dead and remove this shameful past from America's future.

Persuasion Technique Questions

1. What kind of conclusion does Harjo use to end the essay? Why is this an effective choice?

> The essay concludes with the last two paragraphs. The writer evaluates
>
> the topic's importance to the Indian culture—that the Indian dead are not
>
> artifacts to be bought and sold as commerce. They are members of a fam-
>
> ily. She also gives a call to action. Because the Indian dead are members
>
> of a family, they should be returned to their families. By doing this, Amer-
>
> ica will begin to remove itself from a shameful past.

2. Does Harjo use mostly opinion or mostly facts in the essay? Point out some examples.

> She uses many facts in almost every paragraph. For example, she gives
>
> the number of skulls in the Smithsonian Institution, gathered for a govern-
>
> ment "Indian Cranial Study" during the 1800s, and she mentions the Sand
>
> Creek massacre (¶ 3); she uses a quote from the official account of the
>
> beheading of the Indian Chief Mangas Coloradas in 1863 (¶ 4) and the
>
> fact that some universities have returned skulls already (¶ 14); she states
>
> the fact that Congress is considering legislation on the issue and that
>
> the secretary of the Smithsonian has stated that the Smithsonian would
>
> be doing an inventory of all skulls with the outcome being their return to
>
> identifiable tribes and families (¶ 15).

3. Is the evidence that Harjo uses effective in convincing you that her ideas should be taken seriously by Congress and by average Americans? Explain.

Answers will vary.

_____

_____

_____

_____

4. Harjo clearly points out that desecrating Indian graves is a problem. But what is the ethical issue she raises that confronts the entire nation?

Answers will vary. In paragraph 2, she states that there are national laws

that allow the government to define human remains as property. In para-

graph 9, she writes that financial gain is often the reason abuse and

unethical behavior occur. In paragraph 10, she states that scientific

research is often cited as a reason to allow the desecration of human

remains. In paragraph 18, she explains that government sanction is an

historic reminder of how America treated a group of people barbarically,

and it further legitimizes such governmentally sanctioned actions.

Critical Thinking Writing Opportunities

1. In his essay "Working Pays Off," Randy Raterman indicates that students should work while they are in school to take the financial burden off of their parents. His _point of view_ or _frame of reference_ is evident throughout the essay in the conclusions he comes to about working and nonworking students. Write an essay for or against parents supporting their children who want to come back home to live, perhaps because of divorce or sudden unemployment. Or write an essay for or against children supporting their parents during retirement or a debilitating illness. Before writing your essay, make a pro and con list that exemplifies the point of view or frame of reference of both parents and children.

2. In his essay "Guys and Gals," Bryan Kemper explains why he is against men and women training together in the same military units. He uses _inference_ and _assumption_ to form many of his conclusions and solutions about what would happen if the sexes trained together. Write an essay either for or against women participating with men in traditionally all-male sports, such as wrestling, baseball, football, ice hockey, or basketball. Or write an essay about a behavior that in the past was considered unacceptable for women but today is considered permissible, such as women asking men out on a date, women working as mechanics or racecar drivers, or single women adopting children to raise on their own. Before writing your essay, make a pro and con list that reflects the inferences or assumptions that lead to conclusions and solutions by people on either side of the issue.

3. In her essay "Last Rites for the Indian Dead," Suzan Shown Harjo identifies a problem that affects Native Americans specifically, but she also argues that the issue poses an ethical problem for all Americans. She uses *information* in the form of *facts* to make her case contemporary, relevant, and compelling. Write an essay for or against the United States government making reparation payments to the families of Japanese Americans whose homes, possessions, and businesses were confiscated and who were interred in American concentration camps during World War II. Or write an essay for or against the United States government making reparation payments to the families of African Americans who were held as slaves up until the end of the Civil War. Before writing your essay, make a pro and con list of facts to support your opinion. To complete the assignment, you may have to consult an encyclopedia or do some research at the library or on the Internet.

Topics for a Persuasive Essay

Here are possible topics for persuasive essay writing assignments. Remember, your essay should have a clearly defined purpose. Pick either a pro or a con position for your essay.

1. Organized prayer in public schools should (not) be allowed.
2. Parents on welfare should (not) be required to work.
3. Controversial organizations (Communist Party, Ku Klux Klan) should (not) be allowed to advertise in campus publications.
4. Two years of studying a foreign language should (not) be required in high school.
5. Parents should (not) be held legally responsible for their minor children's actions.
6. Affirmative action should (not) be implemented for college enrollment.
7. The legal drinking age should (not) be 18 years of age.
8. Marijuana should (not) be legalized for medical purposes.
9. English should (not) be legally designated as the official language of the United States.
10. Single adults should (not) be allowed to adopt children.

Chapter Review

■ A persuasive essay attempts to convince the reader that a particular point of view is correct. Persuasive writing can be informal, semiformal, or formal (also called argumentation).

■ In a persuasive paragraph, the topic sentence states the writer's point of view about a topic—pro or con. In developing such a paragraph, it's useful first to list the pros and cons about the topic. The pro and con list can help you adopt a position and choose supporting points for the paragraph.

■ Techniques to support an argument include answering the opposition, referring to an authority, predicting consequences, using facts, and using examples. Transitional expressions help signal which technique is being used.

■ A persuasive paragraph has three basic patterns of organization: arguing only your own points, arguing against your opposition's points, and alternating arguing your own points and arguing against the opposition.

■ When you write a persuasive essay, you can use the pro and con list to develop your controlling attitude (pro or con) and to select the items for the essay map, and consequently, the body paragraphs.

■ The four approaches to the concluding paragraph—evaluation, warning, prediction, and call to action—can all be used effectively in a persuasive essay.

Visit *The Write Start* Online!

For additional practice with the materials found in this chapter, visit our Website at

http://www.ablongman.com/checkett

The Website also features additional readings, quizzes, writing activities, and Internet links, as well as a bulletin board and interactive chat.

PART 3

Special Writing Situations

As you progress in your academic life, you will encounter three special writing situations on numerous occasions: **the research paper, timed in-class writing, and literary analysis.** Although all writing relies on the principles and skills you have developed in your basic writing classes, these three special writing situations call for additional approaches and techniques if you are to complete them successfully.

The Research Paper

You will be required to write research papers in many of your classes. Research papers give you the opportunity to dig deeply into a topic. You will find information about the topic through many sources in the library and on the Internet. In your essay, you will document your sources. More times than not, you will argue against a point of view that you have discovered by offering your own conclusions on the subject. You will use the source material you have found to support your conclusions.

Timed In-Class Writing

One of the most common types of writing you will encounter in college is the in-class essay exam. Because you will have a limited amount of time to answer, there is an added dimension to this type of writing experience: time pressure. To be successful, you must have a method to organize your thoughts quickly in order to effectively construct a developed essay in a short amount of time.

Literary Analysis

Many classes, not just English, will require you to interpret and analyze literature: novels, short stories, drama, and poetry. Sociology, political science, history, and many other courses use literature to study various cultures, events, and famous people. Literary analysis often takes a persuasive approach, meaning you will have to take a position about some aspect of the work and defend it by using your interpretation of what certain aspects of the work mean to you.

In the following three chapters, you will be introduced to the elements and techniques that will enable you to write successfully in these three areas of your college work.

chapter 16

The Research Paper

The research paper is an extended essay. Because you will be using documented sources to support, clarify, and exemplify your observations and conclusions, the research paper is generally from eight to 20 pages long. The work involved in writing a research paper is considerable, so you should allow yourself as much time as you need—usually a month or more—to research, write, and proofread the paper.

The research paper writing process can be divided into distinct steps:

1. Select a topic that you know you can find information about in the library or on the Internet.
2. Limit the topic by stating the paper's purpose.
3. Research the topic and take notes.
4. Outline your paper.
5. Select the quotations and citations you have on your note cards and print-outs that you will use to support your stated purpose.
6. Arrange the quotations and citations in the order in which they will be used in your paper.
7. Write the paper.
8. Document the paper using the appropriate format.
9. Proofread the paper for grammatical, spelling, and documentation format errors.
10. Prepare the paper for submission by making the necessary changes you found while proofreading.

Following these basic steps can save you a lot of time and energy as you make your way through the research process. For a thorough understanding of the research writing process, you should read the detailed explanations that follow.

Select a Topic

It is of vital importance that the subject you choose to write about can be researched. Generally speaking, this means that the subject must have books, articles, and critical essays written about it. If it does not, then you will not be able to find sources written by others that agree with your point of view to use as support for your conclusions.

A lack of source material is not usually a problem when you are doing research about famous people, places, and events of the past. However, when writing about current people, places, and events, you must be careful that there is enough information from which to draw your support material.

Before you do anything else, go to the library and make certain that there are enough books, articles, and critical essays about your topic to make continuing the process worthwhile. If you can find a minimum of ten to 20 books, articles, and critical essays about your topic, you should be able to find enough material to support your views. If you cannot, you should probably select another topic.

Limit the Topic

Research papers, like all writing, must have a clearly defined purpose. Use the techniques you studied in Chapter 3 regarding constructing a thesis sentence to clearly define the parameters of your paper's approach.

The thesis sentence with essay map will automatically limit your paper to the stated subtopics, and it will clearly define the paper's organization and your idea of importance and attitude toward the topic. Using the thesis sentence with essay map also will help you bring into focus those specific areas (the essay map subtopics) for which you will collect your support material. This will save you a lot of time and effort because you only will use 5 to 10 percent of all the material you find. The more focused the research, the less time you will waste.

Before finalizing your thesis sentence, however, you might want to do some research and reading to gain a clear perspective on your final subtopics.

Research the Topic and Take Notes

To find information in a library regarding your topic, you can use the following sources to focus your research: the general catalog, *The Reader's Guide to Periodical Literature, The Bibliographic Index,* and the specific indexes for such disciplines as the humanities and the social sciences. Your library, in all probability, uses *NewsBank,* which you can use to access over a thousand newspapers for information, or it may subscribe to other computerized databases of periodicals and journals. Most libraries also have source information on microfilm, microfiche, and CD-ROM.

You also can use a variety of encyclopedias to find information regarding your topic. Many instructors will not allow you to use information from encyclopedias in your formal research paper, but they are good sources in which to find general background information that can lead you to other sources and ideas.

You can search for information on the Internet by doing a simple *word search.* Ask the reference librarian for assistance if you are not familiar with this process.

As you gather information related to your stated purpose, you need to save citations and quotations to use in your paper. You can use index cards or computer printouts for keeping such information. It is best to use a separate index card for each citation or quotation.

Outline the Paper

Follow whatever outlining method you are comfortable with or that your instructor has required. Some instructors require you to submit an outline, and some do not. There are *essay map outlines, sentence outlines, paragraph outlines,* and *topic outlines.* Your instructor will explain which one he or she wants you to use. Whichever outline you use, begin fleshing out your ideas in the order that your outline suggests, and incorporate your support materials where appropriate.

Select the Researched Support Material

Before you use any support material in your paper, you must decide whether or not it will actually support your points and conclusions. To do this, ask a series of questions about the material:

- Does the material support the main topic and the idea of importance and attitude as stated in the thesis sentence?

- How current is the information? This may not be important if you are dealing with a historical subject, such as the Spanish Inquisition or World War II. However, if you are writing about a new medical procedure such as Lasik eye surgery or a new photographic technique such as a CCD (Charged Coupled Device), information that is only a few years old may be out of date.

- Does the information come from an objective or biased source? The best sources for gathering information are those that are not published or written by people having a particular political, social, or monetary reason for publishing the information. In other words, if they have a lot to gain personally by persuading people with the information, then the material might be too biased to be convincing. On the other hand, if you use material from persons or groups who do not stand to gain personally by convincing others to support their position, then the information is usually more objective. Using support material that is objective usually is considered more convincing.

- What kind of material should you look for to support your ideas and conclusions? The most convincing evidence to support your claims are appeals to reason, not emotion. To persuade the reader that a particular position is convincing, use the following support evidence: *answering the opposition, referring to an authority, predicting consequences, stating facts,* and *providing examples.* See Chapter 15 for information regarding these types of evidence.

Arrange the Quotations

With the outline completed, you should arrange your index cards and computer printouts in the order in which you will use them in the paper. You can identify their placement in the paper by marking them with numbers or letters corresponding to those of your outline sections.

Write the Paper

Remember to include your thesis sentence in the introductory paragraph, and develop your subtopics in the body paragraphs. The research paper, because of its length, has more body paragraphs than the short essay model you have been studying in this textbook. In addition, the thesis sentence with essay map may be too short for this type of paper. You can use several sentences or short paragraphs to introduce the paper's overall topic and the topics of the body paragraphs.

Finish the essay by using one of the techniques you have studied for concluding paragraphs. See Chapters 3, 4, and 5 to review the basic elements of the introductory, body, and concluding paragraphs.

As you write your paper, try to use transitional expressions you have studied in this textbook to connect related ideas, add sentence variety, and create rhythm within the paper.

Document the Paper

When using the work of others in your paper, you must tell the reader from what source you quoted or cited the material. The borrowed information must be cited within the text of the paper and at the end of the paper in the Works Cited section.

Use the Appropriate Format

Different disciplines use different documentation formats. For example, in the humanities (English, speech communication, theater, foreign language, and art), the Modern Language Association (MLA) is commonly used; whereas in the sciences (biology, botany, psychology, nursing, and chemistry), the American Psychological Association (APA) documentation format is commonly used.

Because this is a textbook for an English course, the MLA documentation format will be explained later in this chapter. You will also see examples of documentation in a student-written research paper, as well as a research paper written by a professional writer.

Avoid Plagiarism

Beware of plagiarism. It can cause your paper to receive a failing grade, and it can cause you other academic problems, such as suspension or expulsion from school. **Plagiarism** occurs when you use someone else's ideas as if they were your own and do not give the other person credit. Plagiarism also includes buying a paper or letting someone else substantially write or edit your work for you.

Plagiarism can arise because of poor note taking. Misquoting or inaccurately summarizing or paraphrasing can also cast suspicion on the integrity of your writing. When you take notes for a quotation or citation, be certain you copy the information carefully. If you put someone else's idea into your own words by summarizing or paraphrasing, you are still required to document the information. Failure to do so is considered plagiarism.

Plagiarism is the worst kind of academic dishonesty because it degrades our ability to trust that others are writing honestly and with integrity about their own thoughts and ideas and about the thoughts and observations of others.

Proofread the Paper

Submitting a paper that is substantially free of errors will create a positive impression in your instructor's mind. A paper free of misspelled words, grammatical errors, and documentation errors tells the reader that the writer cares about the writing and the reader's experience in reading it.

Conversely, a paper full of errors reflects poorly on the writer and the assignment. Errors reduce the pleasure of the reading experience, sidetrack the reader's attention from the paper's purpose, and create the impression that the writer is either careless, uneducated, or both.

Proofreading is the process of eliminating mechanical and content errors. *Mechanical errors* encompass misspelled words (including typos), punctuation, capitalization, and spacing. *Content errors* include incorrect facts or inaccurate or misleading information that makes the expressed ideas difficult or confusing to understand. It is the writer's responsibility, with minor assistance from others, such as tutors and writing lab staff, to find and correct both types of errors. Generally, proofreading is more effective if you do it at least twice: once for content errors and again for mechanical errors.

Prepare the Paper for Submission

Instructors often have their own preferences, but there are some standard guidelines for preparing research papers for submission. Needless to say, a research paper should not be handwritten. It should be prepared on a computer or word processor using the following guidelines.

- Use bright, white, unlined computer paper. Do not use gray or colored paper.
- Use 25-lb. paper. This paper weight is substantial enough to resist creases and tears.
- Use black ink.
- Set margins at 1 to 1½ inches.
- Double space. Your instructor has to read many papers, and double spacing makes them easier to read. In addition, the double spacing leaves room for the instructor's comments.
- Anchor the pages with a staple in the upper left corner of the paper.
- Look through the paper. If it is not professional in appearance, make the necessary changes before submitting the paper to your instructor.
- Hand the paper in flat, not folded.

The Modern Language Association (MLA) Documentation Format

This section illustrates just a few of the many entry examples for documenting citations from sources such as books, periodicals, and electronic media. You can find complete guides to documenting in a variety of formats in any bookstore, library, or on the Internet.

When documenting sources from which you have used information, you must cite the material in two places in your research paper, within the narrative of the paper and at the end in the Works Cited section.

Citing within the Paper

MLA uses a parenthetical documentation method to cite sources when they are quoted or paraphrased. When citing a source, the borrowed material is followed by parentheses ( ) containing the last name of the author, a space, and then the page number where the information can be found. If the quotation is introduced with a statement containing the author's name, the name is not repeated in the parentheses. Two examples follow.

> "There is no truth to the rumor that the chemical formula tested by the company did not answer the problem that had surfaced," stated Dr. Angela Washington (28).

> A prominent chemist stated, "There is no truth to the rumor that the chemical formula tested by the company did not answer the problem that had surfaced" (Washington 28).

Some points to remember regarding citations in the text:

- Use only the last name of the author in the parentheses. If you quote from two different people having the same last name, include the initial of the first name to distinguish between the two authors.
- Do not use a comma to separate the author's name from the page number.
- Place the parentheses immediately after the quotation. If it is at the end of a sentence, place it before the period.
- Parentheses usually do not follow citations taken from the Internet because these sources rarely have page numbers, and MLA suggests mentioning the author's name in the text, or frame (frames will be discussed later in this chapter). If you do not place the author's name in the frame, or a page number is available, then you do place this information in parentheses. Do not place the URL (online address) after the quotation. MLA considers URLs too long and cumbersome for inclusion in the text. They appear only in entries in the Work Cited section.
- If a quotation is taken from an article that appears only on one page of a magazine or journal, it is not necessary to duplicate the page number in the parentheses following the quotation.

In-text and Block Citations

If your quotation is short, no more than three or four typed lines, provide an **in-text citation.** An in-text citation incorporates the material into the text. Place quotation marks around the quoted material. Be certain that your finished sentence is grammatically correct.

> **In-text Citation**
>
> According to a well-documented theory, "the most likely reason the dinosaurs became extinct was a large meteor struck the earth throwing up enough dust to block out sunlight for months" (Smith 74). The theory has been supported by evidence from around the world. A thin layer of iridium has been found at the K-T boundary in Europe, North and South America, Asia, and Africa.

If your quotation is five or more typed lines, separate it from the text by using a **block citation.** Indent the entire quotation ten spaces from the left margin. Leave the right margin alone. Do not put quotation marks at the beginning and end of the quoted material as you do for an in-text quotation. Be certain to follow the quotation with the parenthetical citation.

Block Method Citation

A child's performance in school has a lot to with his home environment. According to Dr. Gerald Gaines, an expert in elementary education issues,

> However well-meaning advocates of testing and standards are, the current plan does not factor in the changing composition of American families and how these changes have affected a child attending school today. Children coming through the schoolhouse doors may have just left a home that would have been largely unrecognizable thirty years ago. The phenomenal increase in single-parent families, poverty level income families, and families in which child abuse occurs on a regular basis has changed how these children face their day in school. (143)

The government needs to take a closer look at how welfare money and services are interfacing with the educational models that have been poor predictors as to how children will fare in their formative educational years.

Framing the Quotation

You should never put a quotation into your writing without introducing it to the reader. You can introduce the quotation by stating the name of the person you are quoting, their title, or their expertise. You can even offer a brief comment on the quotation's content. This information is called a **frame**, and it can be placed before the quotation, after the quotation, or in the middle of the quotation.

In a *front frame,* the punctuation (a comma or colon) is placed after the final word of the frame but always before the opening quotation mark.

The Front Frame

Company spokesperson Ashonti Mekela said, "Marketing expertise can guarantee good sales over a short period of time even though the product has no real perceived value to the consumer" (12).

In the *end frame,* the punctuation (comma) is placed after the final word of the quotation and is always *before* the closing quotation mark.

> **The End Frame**
>
> "Marketing expertise can guarantee good sales over a short period of time even though the product has no real perceived value to the consumer," said company spokesperson Ashonti Mekela (12).

In the *middle frame,* the first punctuation (comma) is placed after the last word in the first part of the quotation but always *before* the first closing quotation mark, while the second punctuation (comma) is placed after the last word of the frame but always *before* the second opening quotation mark.

> **Middle Frame**
>
> "Marketing expertise," according to company spokesperson Ashonti Mekela, "can guarantee good sales over a short period of time even though the product has no real perceived value for the consumer" (12).

Try not to use the same framing style repeatedly. Like all other characteristics of good writing, variety shows maturity of content and style.

Citing at the End of the Paper— The Works Cited Section

As stated earlier, when you use someone else's information, you must cite the information in two places in your paper. You have just studied the first place, in the text of the paper using a parenthetical citation. The second place you must cite the borrowed information is at the end of the paper in the **Works Cited** section. The parenthetical citation in the text of your paper indicates to the reader where in the Works Cited section the full citation information can be found.

The Works Cited section lists only those works that you cited in your paper. Do not list any sources that you did not quote from or paraphrase. When constructing your Works Cited list, adhere to the following criteria:

■ Entries in the list appear alphabetically according to the author's last name.

■ Entries are not numbered.

■ Entries without an author appear alphabetically by the first word in the title.

■ The first line of an entry extends to the left margin. Subsequent lines of the entry are indented five spaces.

■ Double-space the entries.

See the Works Cited pages of the student and professional research papers at the end of this chapter for examples of how this section should be set up.

Examples of Works Cited Entries

Use the following models to guide you as you construct your Works Cited section.

Books

Book by One Author

Rodriquez, Mario. <u>The Middle Child</u>. New York: Century, 1999.

The author's last name is placed first, followed by the first name. Titles of books are underlined. The city where the publishing company is located comes next, followed by a full colon and then the name of the publishing company. A comma follows the name of the publisher, and the publication date follows the comma.

Book by Two or More Authors

Han, Yichuan, and Mel Simons. <u>The Black Hole: Galaxy-Eater</u>.

London: Yorkshire, 2000.

The first author's name appears as it did for the Book by One Author entry, but all subsequent authors' names appear first name first, followed by the last name.

Book by Unknown Author

<u>Growing Flowers in an Apartment</u>. Phoenix: Piaget, 1998.

If the author is not known, the title of the book comes first.

Periodicals

Periodicals are publications that come out on a regular basis: daily, weekly, monthly, quarterly, semiannually, and annually. They include journals, magazines, and newspapers. Journal, magazine, and newspaper article entries use the following order:

1. Author(s)
2. Article's title
3. Name of the periodical
4. Series number, if available
5. Volume number (usually for journals)
6. Issue number, if available
7. Publication date
8. Page numbers of the entire article

Article with One Author

Washington, Pervis. "The Black Experience." <u>Personal Life Digest</u> 16

(1999): 31–47.

Titles of articles are enclosed by quotation marks. The publication in which they appear is underlined. The series or volume number is followed by the publication date in parentheses to separate it from the series or volume number (to avoid confusion). Use a full colon after the date of publication, followed by the page numbers for the entire article.

Article with Unknown Author

"Computers and You." <u>Computer Journal</u> 4 (Winter 2000): 118–24.

If the author is not known, the title of the article comes first.

Article in a Weekly Magazine

Bigtree, Watasha. "Climate for Change in the Industrial Regions in the United States." <u>Social Issues</u> 10 Sept. 2000: 13–36.

"10 Sept." is the indicator that this is a weekly periodical.

Article in a Monthly Magazine

Miller, Judy. "Attention to Detail in the Boardroom: Planning for an Effective Meeting." <u>Female Executive</u> Jan. 1999: 57–62.

"Jan." is the indicator that this is a monthly periodical.

Article in a Newspaper with Numbered Sections

Edwards, Connie. "Parenting in the Millennium." <u>Globe-Sentinel</u> 8 Aug. 2000, sec. 7: 3.

The first number after "sec." is the section, followed by the specific page number.

Article in a Newspaper with Lettered Sections

Achiba, Kwazi. "Using Filers in Astrophotography." <u>Daily Gazette</u> 3 May 1999: C2.

"C" is the section heading, followed by the specific page number—in this entry, "2."

Electronic Sources: Internet and CD-ROM

Entries for Internet sources look just like entries for periodicals with one major exception: the Universal Resource Locator (URL—the online address). The URL always follows the information in the entry. MLA style is to enclose URLs in angle brackets, as shown in the examples that follow. The URL should not be underlined, nor should it be a different color from the rest of the text. However, when you type a URL using a computer, most programs automatically change the address to a hyperlink. If your printer has a color cartridge, the address will print in blue and will be underlined. If your printer has a black ink cartridge, the URL will print in black and will be underlined. Most instructors are used to seeing these URLs in student papers. Unless your instructor tells you to do otherwise, leave it alone. Or you can ask what format your instructor prefers.

Online Journal Article

Bahamma, Rahal. "Some New Thoughts about Pi." <u>Math-Mavin</u> 3 (2000). 4 Sept. 2000 <http://www.mathmavin.org/journals.html>.

Online Magazine Article

Sahad, Ahmad. "Genetic Mutations in Genome Sequences." <u>Genome</u>

Feb. 1999. 15 Mar. 1999 <http://www.genseqpro.com/1999/html>.

When there are two dates in the source, the first date indicates when the information was placed online. It is followed by a period. The second date indicates when you accessed the information. It is not followed by a period.

Article on CD-ROM

Mirinakov, Mikail. "Political Reformation in Former Russian Satellite

Countries." <u>Soviet Daily Citizen</u> 21 Oct. 2000: 7. <u>Soviet Daily</u>

<u>Citizen Ondisc</u>. CD-ROM. Infoquest. Dec. 2000.

CD-ROMs, like other electronic sources, do not always have complete publication information. In such cases, provide the information that is available.

Sample Student Research Paper with Documentation: SHANGHAIED ON TRADE

Julia Murphy

This research paper, "Shanghaied on Trade," by student writer Julia Murphy, argues against legislation that would guarantee China permanent normal trade relations with the United States. Murphy uses material from a variety of secondary sources to support her conclusions, and she documents it using the MLA format. Although paragraph numbers appear in the margins of the student research papers that follow, these are provided for reference purposes within this text only and are not a standard element in the MLA format

Julia Murphy

English 102.01

Professor Checkett

May 12, 2001

Shanghaied on Trade

1   Congress has the opportunity to significantly alter trade relations with China through passing into a law a negotiated deal that will confirm permanent normal trade relations (PNTR) with the

United States. Many in Congress believe it is necessary to establish PNTR in order to stay competitive in a rapidly expanding world market fed by developing countries. They believe equally important to the economic gains and progression of both countries is the outward appearance of China's inclusion onto the world stage. With China currently basking in a more favorable light, those in favor of offering China PNTR are determining that the risks would be well worth the effort when weighed against Beijing reprisals.

2   In exchange for an approved PNTR with China, advocates hang their hats on the belief the United States will receive more open markets and reduced tariffs by as much as seventy-five percent. This is a naïve outlook based on legislative representatives' refusal to take their heads out of the stock exchange index listings long enough to review the recent history as well as the long-term mistreatment of ongoing Sino-American agreements. Bernstein and Munro remind us that

> [...] the United States trade report for 1996 [...] pointed out how agreements on ending protectionist tariffs made between China and the United States in 1992 were undermined when Chinese authorities introduced new protectionist measures that negated parts of the original understanding. So too did newly introduced nontariff [sic] barriers make a mockery of many of the tariff cuts [...]. (206)

Continually extending fiscal opportunities to China when there is a proven track record of noncompliance with negotiated deals made in good faith and honored on our part leaves the United States in a weakened position. The incentive for China to abide by any equilateral economic accord is nonexistent by virtue of the conventional American response that includes empty threats of sanctions whispered into deaf ears.

3   Liberals predict that Chinese goods would not displace domestic production and vow to protect them from import surges and unfair pricing. American labor unions as well as citizen watchdog organizations construct a much different position based partly on historical data gathered following similar shell-game legislation. In Washington, D.C., working-class constituents from

across the nation gathered in an appeal to their democratic voices. They stated that "800,000 jobs will be lost as American companies set up manufacturing plants in China, not just to serve Chinese consumers, but also as a base of low-wage operations to serve customers all over the world" (Meyers). By passage of PNTR the United States forfeits the leverage of an annual congressional review designed primarily as an economic enforcement tool for Beijing as well as annual humanitarian evaluation. Continually taking the same actions (predicting and believing China will sustain her covenant) while expecting different results (<u>this</u> time China will not betray the United States) should greatly sound an alarm in the White House and the legislative halls as it already rings across the mountains, valleys, and plains of this great nation. Without any basis to hold trade partners to the same standard the United States is unafraid to maintain, the inequity of the relationship can begin to harbor resentments in the fertile field of homegrown repercussions felt at the ballot box.

4   The United States lawmakers have duped the American public before while lining their own pockets; entrenched upon the backs of hard-working citizens is an army of legislators marching to the drumbeat of "capitol" gains. The North American Free Trade Agreement (NAFTA) implemented January 1, 1994, was presented to the American public as a solution for generating new U.S. jobs created from the as yet unseen increased demand of U.S. consumer goods exported to Mexico. Theoretically, those products were to be purchased by newly trained Mexican employees working in American manufacturing plants established south of the border in part as an effort to turn around the United States trade surplus. Following a five-year waiting period, Global Trade Watch, an arm of Public Citizen, a watchdog group that does not accept corporate or government support, conducted a detailed study of the results in a number of the critical areas of chief concern. In the field of job creation, Public Citizen concluded, "Using trade flow data to calculate job loss under NAFTA (incorporating exactly the formula used by NAFTA's backers to predict 200,000 per year NAFTA job creation) yields net job destruction numbers in the hundreds of

thousands" ("Talking Points"). Much of the same rhetoric used in coercing the American public that NAFTA was a good course of action has been repeated across the heartland to convince well-intentioned citizens of the alleged necessity of one trade program or another, including PNTR. Repeatedly our government offers foreign countries unparalleled access to U.S. talent, skills, and ingenuity in the name of progress while failing to strike a balance on return (in the guise of well-paying American jobs), save for the golden parachutes the politicians ensure for themselves, big corporate America, and their lobbyists.

5   The White House frequently fails to mention a significant area of concern involving the Geneva-based World Trade Organization (WTO) and the rulings that affect trade between China and the United States. Beijing is quite anxious for Washington, D.C., to legislate PNTR in order to pave the way for China's inclusion into the WTO, for that would greatly benefit China; leftist lawmakers in Congress have neatly wrapped domestic propaganda around the disingenuous position that passage of this bill would be a requirement for continued trade opportunities. Lori Wallach, director of Public Citizen's Global Trade Watch, stated in a Senate Commerce Committee meeting, "Thus, even if Congress opposes China PNTR, US [sic] exporters would obtain the potential benefits China must provide other nations if it enters the WTO while retaining the effective U.S. trade enforcement mechanisms forbidden under the WTO, such as Section 301" ("Testimony"). Section 301 is a part of the Factual Aspects part of the 1974 Jackson-Vanik trade agreement bill. Its contents list the rights, benefits, and authorized actions the U.S. may engage in when there is evidence of mistreatment of labor or unfair labor practices.

6   Long-term documentation of compliance with the WTO could stand as evidence of a precursor to real change in the People's Republic of China since actions carry the weight of evidence. By sustaining PNTR the United States stands to lose its ability to have a meaningful enforcement policy (annual review) that is swift in nature and directly involved with across the board compliance. Wallach continued, "As we have seen with assorted US-EU fights,

WTO dispute resolution takes at least two years and ultimately relies on something entirely missing in China: commitment to the rule of law. The ability to make forward progress is hobbled by the relentless mistrust of substantial trade partners resulting from a history of deceit, double speak, and bureaucratic red tape. Negotiated agreements currently in place will prove to be the best position Americans can maintain in a "watch and wait" atmosphere.

7   While proponents of permanent normal trade relations would have the American public believe Chinese reformers are soon to be governed less by ideology and more by market principles, we have no indication this will materialize. In June 1989, following two months of peaceful demonstration by Chinese citizens, including artisans, students, and professors, the communist dictatorship crushed the longing of its people: the opportunity to breathe the sweet air of liberty which was their "soul" aspiration. Richard Gephardt, a Democratic politician from Missouri stated, "It is our birthright as Americans to keep the flame of freedom glowing for everyone, not just ourselves. That's what this debate is really about, and that is why I will cast a vote to show the world that the spirit of liberty burns strong and bright in this new millennium" (Eilperin). Despite Gephardt's position as minority leader of the House of Representatives, a partisan relationship with the White House, and his home district's cradle as a headquarters for many international corporations, he possesses the integrity to see through the smoke and mirrors.

8   Endorsers use inflated rhetoric to influence taxpayers of the absolute necessity to fling wide open the doors to permanent trade with China lest the United States be shut out of the opportunity to trade in this growing Asian market. The very same politicians have long held their sights on passage of this legislation since many are elected through generous donations of corporate dollars. William J. Holstein reported in April 1997, "Major American companies are part of the investment wave and see their presence in China as vital to their global strategy. Their interests have played a much more decisive role in administration policy than has any suspected Chinese political contribution." Forfeiture of any mechanism currently in

place that provides fiscal intervention in the name of humanity should never be on the auction block. There is no benefit to the mistreatment of an entire populace, but sanctioned injustice by the United States through the unwillingness to put principle before profit is shamefully egregious.

9   The United States Congress must be willing to put aside their own hidden agendas to take a real, educated look at the sacrifices to be made on both sides of the trading portal. "Washington is hoping to use the WTO to bind China into a system of international trading norms. China wants to join to obtain permanently favorable tariff rates for its exports but resists being bound by regulations that will create too much economic pain," reported Holstein. Over and over again Beijing continues to signal its uncooperative nature when asked to honor the most basic principles outlined in the negotiated agreement already in place between China and the United States. Using the WTO as an end-run to American products, the Chinese have once more demonstrated total disregard for *any* rules outside their own dictatorship. Ralph Nader, citizen advocate, proclaims, "Real patriotism is caring enough about your country to roll up your sleeves and do something to make it more humane, moral, and caring" (Bollier). There is very little evidence China is entertaining the possibilities of sacrifice on behalf of themselves and their posterity, nor is there movement from the official government towards even the willingness to pull together as a nation in need of righteousness. Seemingly they would not have to when financial coercion from special interest groups encourages the United States Congress to embellish another welfare cash drawer open to the East.

10   Alternative solutions exist for the many questions swirling inside and outside the beltway concerning the most humane yet fiscally advantageous pathway to broader, less restrictive access to the trade markets. A long-term graduated implementation trade commitment leading to permanent normal trade relations could be constructed in such a way that all parties committed enough to stay the course would be satisfied. With continued success at the one-year anniversary in all areas of concern that are currently being revived,

China may well advance to the next level with a three-year mandatory evaluation. Over time, insofar as there was continued compliance and meaningful domestic civil liberty progress, assessments could be extended to a series of examinations every fifth year. Depriving ourselves of the capability to analyze the circumstances and respond in a legitimate and timely manner leaves the United States vulnerable against "the world's sixth-largest and fastest growing market" (Zuckerman). With all the earnestness the leadership of the People's Republic of China can collect, an agreement can be woven which will allow the participants to save face and leave the table with confidence and standing tall. However, should Congress pass this bill, the American citizenry has the obligation to stay informed and vocal unless we are prepared to continually elect representatives unashamed to collect the wealth left on the nightstand.

11   There is little basis to warrant passage of PNTR in its current form. The disadvantages to the majority citizenry of both countries are cause enough to drive each negotiating team back to the conference table with more willingness for success. All persons, great and small, are encouraged to stay committed to legitimate, lasting, and mutually profitable trade evolution.

Works Cited

Bernstein, Richard, and Ross H. Munro. The Coming Conflict with China. New York: Knopf, 1997.

Bollier, David. Citizen Action and Other Big Ideas: A History of Ralph Nader and the Modern Consumer Movement. Center for Study of Responsive Law: June 1991 the Nader Page Feb. 2000: Chapter 1. Essential Information 19 July 2000 <http://www.nader.org/history/bollier_chapter_1. html>.

Eilperin, Juliet. "Gephardt Wants to Maintain Leverage on China; Arguing for Annual Reviews, Democratic House Leader Will Oppose Permanent Trade Status." Washington Post 20 Apr. 2000. 24 July 2000 Infotrac, Gale Group. <http://web4.infotrac.galegroup.com...5!ar_fmt&bkm_5_2?sw_aep=sccld_win>.

Holstein, William J., et al. "The Year of the Hawk?" <u>U.S. News & World Report</u> 7 Apr. 1997. 23 July 2000 <http://www.usnews.com/ usnews/issue/ 970407?7chw.htm>.

Meyers, Lisa. "Labor Confronts a Wavering Congress." <u>NBC News</u>. 22 May 2000. MSNBC. 19 July 2000 <http://www.msnbc.com/news/ 411002.asp>.

"Report of the Panel on United States—Sections 301–310." <u>Trade Act of 1974</u>. Organization of American States: 22 Dec. 1999. <u>World Trade Organization</u>: II. SICE 19 July 2000 <http://www.sice.oas.org/DISPUTE/ wto/trac01.asp>.

"Talking Points." <u>Global Trade Watch</u> 24 May 2000. Public Citizen. 19 July 2000 <http://www.citizen.org/prtrade/china/talkingpts.htm>.

"Testimony of Lori Wallach, Public Citizen's Global Trade Watch." <u>Senate Commerce Committee</u>. 11 Apr. 2000. 19 July 2000 <http://www.senate.gov/ ~commerce/hearings/0411wal.pdf>.

Zuckerman, Mortimer B. "A Truly Fruity Idea." <u>U.S. News & World Report</u> 15 May 2000: 64.

Research Paper Technique Questions

1. Identify the thesis sentence.

"There is little basis to warrant passage of PNTR in its current form." (The first sentence in the last paragraph of the essay is the best candidate.)

2. At the time this paper was written, Congress had already passed legislation making China a favored trading partner. Why do you think the writer bothered writing the paper?

The status of the legislation does not negate the author's right to hold a differing position. Also, legislation is always susceptible to change, so the writer has a chance to change opinion about the current legislative position of Congress.

3. In the essay's second paragraph, there is a block quotation containing [...] markings. What does this indicate has happened to the original quotation?

The markings are "ellipses," and they indicate that material in the original

quotation has been omitted, but the meaning of the quotation was not

altered by omitting part of the quotation.

4. In paragraph 10, the writer did not include a page number in the parenthetical reference marker at the end of the quotation "the world's sixth-largest and fastest growing market" (Zuckerman). Is this proper MLA formatting?

Yes. The entire article in the 15 May 2000 *U.S. News & World Report* **is con-**

tained on one page—64. In MLA documentation, if a quotation is made

from a source appearing on one page, the page number does not have

to be placed in the parentheses.

Sample Professional Research Paper with Documentation: THE ECSTASY OF WAR

Barbara Ehrenreich

This research paper, "The Ecstasy of War," by professional writer, social critic, and lecturer Barbara Ehrenreich was taken from her book *Blood Rites: Origins and History of the Passions of War* (1997). In the paper, she analyzes the psychology of war and argues that the "aggressive instinct" is prominent in men. She further concludes that it generates a mental zone during war in which "men enter an alternative realm of human experience, as far removed from daily life as those things which we call 'sacred.'"

The Ecstasy of War

So elemental is the human need to endow the shedding of blood with some great and even sublime significance that it renders the intellect almost entirely helpless. (Van Creveld 166).

—Van Creveld

1   Different wars have led to different theories of why men fight them. The Napoleonic Wars, which bore along with them the rationalist spirit of the French Revolution, inspired the Prussian officer Carl von Clausewitz to propose that war itself is an entirely rational undertaking, unsullied by human emotion. War, in his famous aphorism, is merely a "continuation of policy … by other means," with policy itself supposedly resulting from the same kind of clearheaded deliberation one might apply to a game of chess. Nation-states were the leading actors on the stage of history, and war was simply one of the many ways they advanced their interests against those of other nation-states. If you could accept the existence of this new superperson, the nation, a battle was no more disturbing and irrational than, say, a difficult trade negotiation—except perhaps to those who lay dying on the battlefield.

2   World War I, coming a century after Napoleon's sweep through Europe and northern Africa, led to an opposite assessment of the human impulse of war. World War I was hard to construe as in any way "rational," especially to that generation of European intellectuals, including Sigmund Freud, who survived to ponder the unprecedented harvest of dead bodies. History textbooks tell us that the "Great War" grew out of the conflict between "competing imperialist states," but this Clausewitzian interpretation has little to do with the actual series of accidents, blunders, and miscommunications that impelled the nations of Europe to war in the summer of 1914.[1] At first swept up in the excitement of the war, unable for weeks to work or think of anything else, Freud was eventually led to conclude that there is some dark flaw in the human psyche, a perverse desire to destroy, countering Eros and the will to live (Stromberg 82).

3   So these are, in crude summary, the theories of war which modern wars have left us with: That war is a means, however risky, by which men seek to advance their collective interests and improve their lives. Or, alternatively, that war stems from subrational drives not unlike those that lead individuals to commit violent crimes. In our own time, most people seem to hold both views at once, avowing that war is a gainful enterprise, intended to meet the material needs of the groups engaged in it, and, at the same time, that it fulfills deep and "irrational" psychological needs. There is no question about the first part of this proposition—that wars are designed, at least ostensibly, to secure necessaries like land or oil or "geopolitical advantage." The mystery lies in the peculiar psychological grip war exerts on us.

4   In the 1960s and '70s, the debate on the psychology of war centered on the notion of an "aggressive instinct," peculiar to all humans or only to human males. This is not the place to summarize that debate, with its endless examples of animal behavior and clashes over their applicability to human affairs. Here I would simply point out that, whether or not there is an aggressive instinct, there are reasons to reject it as the major wellspring of war.

5   Although it is true that aggressive impulses, up to and including murderous rage, can easily take over in the heat of actual battle, even this statement must be qualified to take account of different weaponry and modes of fighting. Hand-to-hand combat may indeed call forth and even require the emotions of rage and aggression, if only to mobilize the body for bursts of muscular activity. In the case of action-at-a-distance weapons, however, like guns and bows and arrows, emotionality of any sort can be a distinct disadvantage. Coolness, and the ability to keep aiming and firing steadfastly in the face of enemy fire, prevails. Hence, according to the distinguished American military historian Robert L. O'Connell, the change in the ideal warrior personality wrought by the advent of guns in the fifteenth and sixteenth centuries, from "ferocious aggressiveness" to "passive disdain" (119). So there is no personality type—"hot-tempered," "macho," or whatever—consistently and universally associated with warfare.

6   Furthermore, fighting itself is only one component of the enterprise we know as war. Wars are not barroom brawls writ large, or domestic violence that has been somehow extended to strangers. In war, fighting takes place within battles—along with much anxious waiting, of course—but wars do not begin with battles and are often not decided by them either. Most of war consists of *preparation* for battle—training, the organization of supplies, marching and other forms of transport—activities which are hard to account for by innate promptings of any kind. There is no plausible instinct, for example, that impels a man to leave his home, cut his hair short, and drill for hours in tight formation. As anthropologists Clifton B. Kroeber and Bernard L. Fontana point out, "it is a large step from what may be biologically innate leanings toward individual aggression to ritualized, socially sanctioned, institutionalized group warfare" (166).

7   War, in other words, is too complex and collective an activity to be accounted for by a single warlike instinct lurking within the individual

psyche. Instinct may, or may not, inspire a man to bayonet the first enemy he encounters in battle. But instinct does not mobilize supply lines, manufacture rifles, issue uniforms, or move an army of thousands from point A on the map to B. These are "complicated, orchestrated, highly organized" activities, as social theorist Robin Fox writes, undertaken not by individuals but by entities on the scale of nations and dynasties (15). "The hypothesis of a killer instinct," according to a commentator summarizing a recent conference on the anthropology of war, is "not so much wrong as irrelevant" (McCauley 2).

8   In fact, throughout history, individual men have gone to near-suicidal lengths to avoid participating in wars—a fact that proponents of a warlike instinct tend to slight. Men have fled their homelands, served lengthy prison terms, hacked off limbs, shot off feet or index fingers, feigned illness or insanity, or, if they could afford to, paid surrogates to fight in their stead. "Some draw their teeth, some blind themselves, and others maim themselves, on their way to us" (Mitchell 42), the governor of Egypt complained of his peasant recruits in the early nineteenth century. So unreliable was the rank and file of the eighteenth-century Prussian army that military manuals forbade camping near a woods or forest: The troops would simply melt away into the trees (Delbrück 303).

9   Proponents of a warlike instinct must also reckon with the fact that even when men have been assembled, willingly or unwillingly, for the purpose of war, fighting is not something that seems to come "naturally" to them. In fact, surprisingly, even in the thick of battle, few men can bring themselves to shoot directly at individual enemies.[2] The difference between an ordinary man or boy and a reliable killer, as any drill sergeant could attest, is profound. A transformation is required: The man or boy leaves his former self behind and becomes something entirely different, perhaps even taking a new name. In small-scale, traditional societies, the change was usually accomplished through ritual drumming, dancing, fasting, and sexual abstinence—all of which serve to lift a man out of his mundane existence and into a new, warriorlike mode of being, denoted by special body paint, masks, and head-dresses.

10   As if to emphasize the discontinuity between the warrior and the ordinary human being, many cultures require the would-be fighting man to leave his human-nests behind and assume a new form as an animal.[3] The

young Scandinavian had to become a bear before he could become an elite warrior, going "berserk" (the word means, "dressed in a bear hide"), biting and chasing people. The Irish hero Cuchulain transformed himself into a monster in preparation for battle: "He became horrible, many-shaped, strange and unrecognizable," with one eye sucked into his skull and the other popping out of the side of the face (Davidson 84). Apparently this transformation was a familiar and meaningful one, because similarly distorted faces turn up frequently in Celtic art.

11   Often the transformation is helped along with drugs or social pressure of various kinds. Tahitian warriors were browbeaten into fighting by functionaries called Rauti, or "exhorters," who ran around the battlefield urging their comrades to mimic "the devouring wild dog" (Keeley 146). The ancient Greek hoplites drank enough wine, apparently, to be quite tipsy when they went into battle (Hanson 126); Aztecs drank pulque; Chinese troops at the time of Sun Tzu got into the mood by drinking wine and watching "gyrating sword dancers" perform (Griffith in Sun Tzu 37). Almost any drug or intoxicant has served, in one setting or, another, to facilitate the transformation of man into warrior. Yanomamo Indians of the Amazon ingest a hallucinogen before battle; the ancient Scythians smoked hemp, while a neighboring tribe drank something called "hauma," which is believed to have induced a frenzy of aggression (Rolle 94–95). So if there is a destructive instinct that impels man to war, it is a weak one, and often requires a great deal of help.

12   In seventeenth-century Europe, the transformation of man into soldier took on a new form, more concerted and disciplined, and far less pleasant, than wine. New recruits and even seasoned veterans were endlessly drilled, hour after hour, until each man began to feel himself part of a single, giant fighting machine. The drill was only partially inspired by the technology of firearms. It's easy enough to teach a man to shoot a gun; the problem is to make him willing to get into situations where guns are being shot and to remain there long enough to do some shooting of his own. So modern military training aims at a transformation parallel to that achieved by "primitives" with war drums and paint: In the fanatical routines of boot camp, a man leaves behind his former identity and is reborn as a creature of the military—an automaton and also, ideally, a willing killer of other men.

13   This is not to suggest that killing is foreign to human nature or, more narrowly, to the male personality. Men (and women) have again and again proved themselves capable of killing impulsively and with gusto. But there is a huge difference between a war and an ordinary fight. War not only departs from the normal; it inverts all that is moral and right: In war one <u>should</u> kill, <u>should</u> steal, <u>should</u> burn cities and farms, should perhaps even rape matrons and little girls. Whether or not such activities are "natural" or at some level instinctual, most men undertake them only by entering what appears to be an "altered state"—induced by drugs or lengthy drilling, and denoted by face paint or khakis.

14   The point of such transformative rituals is not only to put men "in the mood." Returning warriors may go through equally challenging rituals before they can celebrate victory or reenter the community—covering their heads in apparent shame, for example; vomiting repeatedly; abstaining from sex (Keeley 144). Among the Maori, returning warriors could not participate in the victory celebration until they had gone through a whaka-hoa ritual, designed to make them "common" again: The hearts of slain enemies were roasted, after which offerings were made to the war god Tu, and the rest was eaten by priests, who shouted spells to remove "the blood curse" and enable warriors to reenter their ordinary lives (Sagan 18). Among the Taulipang Indians of South America, victorious warriors "sat on ants, flogged one another with whips, and passed a cord covered with poisonous ants, through their mouth and nose" (Métraux 397). Such painful and shocking postwar rites impress on the warrior that war is much more than a "continuation of policy … by other means." In war men enter an alternative realm of human experience, as far removed from daily life as those things which we call "sacred."

Works Cited

Davidson, Hilda Ellis. *Myths and Symbols in Pagan Europe: Early Scandinavian and Celtic Religions*. Syracuse, NY: Syracuse UP, 1988.

Delbrück, Hans. *History of the Art of War, vol. 4. The Dawn of Modern Warfare*. Lincoln: U of Nebraska P, 1985.

Dumézil, Georges. *Destiny of the Warrior*. Chicago: U of Chicago P, 1969.

Fox, Robin. "Fatal Attraction: War and Human Nature." *The National Interest* (Winter 1992/93): 11–20.

Grossman, Lt. Col. Dave. *On Killing: The Psychological Cost of Learning to Kill in War and Society*. Boston: Little, Brown, 1995.

Hanson, Victor Davis. *The Western Way of War: Infantry Battle in Classical Greece*. New York: Knopf, 1989.

Keeley, Lawrence H. *War Before Civilization: The Myth of the Peaceful Savage*. New York: Oxford UP, 1996.

Kroeber, Clifton B., and Bernard L. Fontana. *Massacre on the Gila: An Account of the Last Major Battle Between American Indians, with Reflections on the Origin of War*. Tucson: U of Arizona P, 1986.

McCauley, Clark. "Conference Overview." *The Anthropology of War*. Ed. Jonathan Haas. Cambridge: Cambridge UP, 1990. 1–25.

Métraux, Alfred. "Warfare, Cannibalism, and Human Trophies." *Handbook of South American Indians*, vol. 5. Ed. Julian H. Steward. New York: Cooper Square, 1963. 383–409.

Mitchell, Timothy. *Colonizing Egypt*. Berkeley: U of California P, 1991.

O'Connell, Robert L. *Of Arms and Men: A History of War, Weapons, and Aggression*. New York: Oxford UP, 1989.

Rolle, Renate. *The World of the Scythians*. Berkeley: U of California P, 1989.

Sagan, Eli. *Cannibalism: Human Aggression and Cultural Form*. New York: Harper and Row, 1974.

Stoessinger, John G. *Why Nations Go to War*. New York: St. Martin's, 1993.

Stromberg, Roland. *Redemption by War: The Intellectuals and 1914*. Lawrence: U of Kansas P, 1982.

Sun Tzu. *The Art of War*. Trans. Samuel B. Griffith. London: Oxford UP, 1971.

Van Creveld, Martin. *The Transformation of War*. New York: Free Press, 1991.

Notes

[1] See, for example, Stoessinger, *Why Nations Go to War*, 14–20.

[2] See Grossman, *On Killing*.

[3] In the mythologies of the Indo-European tradition, Dumézil relates, thanks "either to a gift of metamorphosis, or to a monstrous heredity, the eminent warrior possesses a veritable animal nature" (140).

Research Paper Technique Questions

1. What do you think is Ehrenreich's purpose in writing the essay? Point out a passage in the essay that supports your answer.

   Answers will vary, but Ehrenreich's essay makes the point that male

   aggression is normal, but war is not. Paragraph 13 best expresses this

   point of view: "War not only departs from the normal; it inverts all that is

   moral and right" and "most men undertake [war] only be entering what

   appears to be an 'altered state'—induced by drugs or lengthy drilling, and

   denoted by face paint or khakis."

2. What other information in the essay caused you to take the position you did in Question 1?

   Answers will vary.

3. In the parenthetical reference marker following the quotation in paragraph 5, the author's name is not included along with the page number. Is this proper MLA formatting?

   Yes. Because Robert L. O'Connell's name is included in the front frame,

   it does not have to be repeated in the parenthetical reference marker fol-

   lowing the quotation.

4. In paragraph 1, Ehrenreich quotes the famous Prussian military officer Clausewitz's conclusion that wars are brought about in a rational, nonemotional way. Explain why you agree or disagree with Clausewitz's statement.

   Answers will vary.

Chapter Review

■ A research paper is an extended essay that uses documented sources to support, clarify, and exemplify your observations and conclusions.

■ There are ten steps in writing a research paper: (1) Select a topic that you know you can find information about in the library or on the Internet. (2) Limit the topic by stating the paper's purpose. (3) Research the topic and take notes. (4) Outline your paper. (5) Select the quotations and citations that you will use to support your stated purpose. (6) Arrange the quotations and citations in the order they will be used. (7) Write the paper. (8) Document the citations using the appropriate format. (9) Proofread the paper for grammatical, spelling, and documentation format errors. (10) Prepare the paper for submission by making the necessary changes you found while proofreading.

■ The documentation format used in a research paper depends on the subject area of the paper. Two frequently used formats are the Modern Language Association format and the American Psychological Association format.

Visit *The Write Start* Online!

For additional practice with the materials found in this chapter, visit our Website at

http://www.ablongman.com/checkett

The Website also features additional readings, quizzes, writing activities, and Internet links, as well as a bulletin board and interactive chat.

CHAPTER 17

The Essay Exam

It's one thing to write an essay when you have time to plan your approach and organization, do research, write a rough draft, and seek the advice and counsel of teachers and tutors. It is quite another when you have to write an in-class essay, most often without benefit of notes but with the added pressure of a very short time in which to accomplish the task.

Time and Grade

How you prepare quickly to answer a prompt for an essay exam rests largely on three elements: (1) the exam's time frame; (2) whether the exam is comprised of one essay question, multiple short-answer essay questions, or a mix of essay and other types of questions; (3) how much grading weight has been given to the various parts of the exam.

A one-hour exam might include true-or-false questions, fill-in-the-blank questions, one or more short essay questions, or one long essay question. It is important to know how much the test is worth as part of the semester grade, and it is also important to know how much each part of the test is worth. How much time and effort you spend on any one part of an exam ultimately depends on the value of each section of the test.

For instance, suppose the exam period is one hour. The exam consists of a single essay prompt and some true or false questions, and the essay is worth 75 points out of 100 for the entire exam. You should certainly spend 30–45 minutes out of the hour on it, with 10–15 minutes given to the other questions. Or, if you have 90 minutes to answer three short-answer essay questions, then you would want to give 30 minutes to each question because they surely will be given equal weight when graded by the instructor.

It goes without saying that you should always try to do your best on any exam. But you should take into account time frames and weight of grade when you allot the time necessary to finish an essay exam or the essay portion of an exam with a variety of questions.

Key Terms in Essay Questions

Essay questions are *prompts*. The prompt either identifies one topic or a list from which you can choose one or more topics to write about. After receiving the prompt, never begin writing immediately. Take a few minutes to make a plan.

Before making a plan, however, you need to be certain what the prompt is asking you to do. Understanding the key terms of the prompt will go a long way in helping you figure out how to respond. Study the following steps.

1. Read the prompt several times to identify the key terms in the prompt. These key terms will often tell you the approach (the kind of response) the instructor is looking for.
   - ■ *analyze/explain*: explain how a process works and why the process is important.
   - ■ *argue/discuss*: take a stand or have a definite point of view supported by evidence (such as facts, statistics, examples, and quotations from experts).
   - ■ *cause/effect*: if cause, identify the reasons for something occurring; if effect, identify the results of something occurring. Some questions will want you to explain both the causes and effects.
   - ■ *classify*: divide the topic idea into categories and relate why the categories are important.
   - ■ *compare/contrast*: if comparison, discuss how two or more items are similar; if contrast, discuss how two or more items are different from one another.
   - ■ *define*: write an extended definition in which you choose examples to illustrate the concept's meaning.
   - ■ *evaluate*: discuss the pros and cons of an issue, and make a judgment.
   - ■ *illustrate:* give specific examples of a general topic.
   - ■ *narrate:* describe something that happened.
   - ■ *summarize*: briefly present the main ideas from a list of many ideas, some major and some minor.

2. Once you have the topic and the approach identified, select those specific ideas that will support your thesis concerning the topic. Because you have studied the thesis sentence with essay map in this book, we suggest using it to organize your response. The essay map is a multiple item series that identifies the subtopics you will use to explain your response to the overall topic. The essay map allows you to state your conclusion and organizational approach to a topic quickly and clearly. It is an outline in sentence form.

3. Use each of your essay map items (we suggest two or three) as the topic of each corresponding body paragraph in which you will develop your ideas concerning the overall topic.

4. Try to save a few minutes to check your essay for sentence fragments (incomplete ideas) and spelling errors. Neatly write in corrections.

Prompts with Thesis Sentence and Essay Map Examples

Following are examples of prompts that could be asked in a variety of college courses. Also provided are possible thesis sentences that are mini-outlines for the essay to be written.

Sociology	
Prompt:	Explain the meaning of "class stratification" in relation to education and employment.
Key term: meaning.	The approach is to define the term by showing how it relates to two aspects of society.
Possible thesis:	Class stratification negatively affects poor people by making it more difficult for them to go to college and to get meaningful employment.

History

Prompt:	Analyze the reasons for the rise of Germany's militarism prior to World War II.
Key term: analyze.	The approach will be to explain how the events after World War I led to the rise of Hitler and his military forces.
Possible thesis:	The stringent terms placed on Germany by the Treaty of Versailles, coupled with the worldwide economic depression, led to the rise of Hitler's military machine prior to World War II.

Business

Prompt:	Discuss the causes of the 1982 economic stagnation in the United States.
Key term: causes.	The approach will be to identify and discuss those economic policies and events that led to the economic downturn.
Possible thesis:	High interest rates, soaring fuel costs, and high unemployment led to the 1982 economic crisis in America.

Art

Prompt:	Summarize the history of Modern Art from the mid-19th century until the present using three specific "schools" as your reference points.
Key term: summarize.	The approach will be to divide Modern Art into three parts and briefly explain why each of three "schools" represents modern artistic evolution.
Possible thesis:	The history of modern art can be traced to the elements of three schools of painting: Impressionism, Surrealism, and Cubism.

Criminology

Prompt:	Defend the position that the insanity defense should be abolished.
Key term: defend (argue).	The approach will be to use evidence to support the idea that the insanity defense should be eliminated.
Possible thesis:	The insanity defense should be abolished because "insanity" is a legal term not a psychological one, incarceration in a mental institution is not punishment, and parole boards do not have control over when the "prisoner/patient" is released.

Literature

Prompt:	Compare two symbols in Frost's poems "Stopping by Woods on a Snowy Evening" and "Desert Places."
Key term: compare.	The approach is to choose two symbols in each poem and discuss their similarities.
Possible thesis:	The snow and the woods in Frost's poems "Stopping by Woods on a Snowy Evening" and "Desert Places" represent loneliness.

Remember, before you can write about a topic, you must understand the question's focus regarding the topic. Identify the key term in the prompt, and then write your thesis.

Your skill and confidence in taking essay exams will increase the more you practice timed essay writing. Over the next few weeks, practice by writing essays for the following prompts. Be certain to use only the amount of time stated in each prompt.

1. *The prompt:* In any discussion, the participants must define terms to avoid misunderstanding and confusion. Pick one of the following terms and write an essay clarifying what you mean when you use it in a specific context: freedom, conservative, maturity, intelligence, liberal, beauty, success, independent, wealth.

   Time: 15 minutes.

   Grade value: 25% of exam.

   Key term: _____**define**_____

2. *The prompt:* Scientists have been cloning sheep, mice, and other animals for a number of years. Now, however, scientists are exploring cloning a human. Write an essay in which you evaluate the pros and cons of cloning a human.

   Time: 30 minutes.

   Grade value: 50% of exam.

   Key term: _____**evaluate**_____

3. *The prompt:* Although a few young people from poor backgrounds find success in movies such as *Good Will Hunting* and *Finding Forester*, poor economic environments cause many young people to fail in school and in their personal lives. Write an essay about poverty's devastating effects on young people.

   Time: 60 minutes

   Grade value: 100% of exam.

   Key term: _____**effects**_____

4. *The prompt:* Imagine you live next to a small, beautiful park. The park consists of a pond, a walking trail, a gazebo, and stands of shade trees and flowering shrubs. You find out that there is a plan being put before the city council to build a mega-store and parking lot where the park is located. The mega-store will mean 200 full- and part-time jobs and tens of thousands of tax dollars for the community. Write an essay in which you contrast the value of the new mega-store versus that of the park for the people of the community.

   Time: 2 hours

   Grade value: 25% of total semester grade.

   Key term: _____**contrast**_____

Introductory and Concluding Techniques

While you may not be able to quote statistics or famous people in the introduction or conclusion of your exam essay (unless the exam is open-book or one for which you can bring prepared notes), you can construct a good introduction and conclusion. Refer to Chapter 3, The Introductory Paragraph, and Chapter 5, The Concluding Paragraph, to review the techniques for effectively introducing your thesis and for giving your essay a sense of completeness. Try to memorize the various types of techniques; often, the prompt will suggest an idea that will help you create a few interesting lead-in sentences in the introductory paragraph and a relevant concluding remark.

Chapter Review

■ Writing an essay exam always involves the added pressure of limited time, and usually involves the added challenge of relying on your memory for ideas and facts. It's a good idea to pace yourself on an essay exam, allowing time in proportion to the essay question's value in the exam or semester grade.

■ Essay questions are prompts, and they contain key terms that indicate the approach that you should take in your answer.

■ Use an essay map to plan your essay before writing it.

Visit *The Write Start* Online!

For additional practice with the materials found in this chapter, visit our Website at

http://www.ablongman.com/checkett

The Website also features additional readings, quizzes, writing activities, and Internet links, as well as a bulletin board and interactive chat.

CHAPTER 18

Literary Criticism

Criticism has various meanings. In academic work, it refers to the act of making judgments, evaluations, or interpretations of original creations in the world of art, music, literature, philosophy, or the various social sciences. Such judgments may be favorable, unfavorable, or neutral. A critical essay or term paper contains the student's evaluation or interpretation of some aspect of another person's work.

But what of the audience that will read your critical papers? You may be asking yourself, what can my interpretations of an artistic or literary work do for other people? We can approach this question by pursuing another question: What do *you* look for when you read a review of a movie, play, or book? Do you want to know why a certain character behaved in a certain way? Did the plot puzzle you? Do you want to confirm your own ideas about a work by seeking the knowledgeable opinion of someone else? These are all reasons we read movie reviews and other criticism. As a writer of criticism, you should approach these very same questions when you critique another's work.

What are the demands placed upon a critical writer? First, the writer must have firsthand knowledge of the work. Also, the writer must be perceptive, sensitive, and analytical. The writer must also support his or her opinions by directly referring to specific passages or characteristics of the work to support the points made in the criticism.

In college, much of the criticism you write is literary criticism. When you write literary criticism, you should try to satisfy the demands that you as a reader make on other critics. The first step in the process is a careful reading of the poem, story, novel, play, or essay. But how do you go about this? What is it that you should look for in a literary work that will lead you to conclusions about the work itself?

The Elements of Literary Analysis

When reporters construct a story, they answer six questions about the events: who, what, where, when, why, and how. When analyzing literature, the critical writer takes the same approach. Only in literature, different labels are used when you analyze the events of the poem, short story, novel, or play: character (who), plot (what), setting (where), time (when), theme (why), and technique (how).

The Questions	The Areas	The Issues
Who?	Character	The function, traits, and credibility of the people in the work.
What?	Plot	The series of related actions involving a problem that builds to a crisis and is resolved.
Where?	Setting	The physical location and general environs, including social, political, and other conditions affecting the characters.
When?	Time	The time structure of the work and the period it is set in.
Why?	Theme	The central or controlling idea that is conveyed mainly through the characters and plot.
How?	Technique	The author's use of language devices to make an effect.

By asking these questions of a literary work and by searching for satisfying answers, you should be better able to analyze and understand it. You should then be better able to communicate your judgments about the work to your reader.

Character: Who?

How Do Writers Develop a Character?

There are two basic ways that writers develop their characters:

■ In the *expository method,* the narrator tells us about the characters.

■ In the *dramatic method,* the characters reveal themselves through their own words, thoughts, and actions.

What Is the Result of the Characterization?

The characters can be thought of in terms of the way they are characterized:

■ **Static characters** remain essentially unchanged throughout the work.

■ **Developing characters** undergo some significant change or changes.

■ **Round characters** are presented as complicated, multidimensional individuals.

■ **Flat characters** are portrayed as representative, incomplete, or not complex—as types rather than individuals.

What Is the Character's Function?

Characters usually function in one of three ways:

■ **Central characters** have a great impact on the story, and the story revolves around these characters. For example, in Herman Melville's classic novel about whaling and personal obsession, *Moby Dick,* central character Captain Ahab is obsessed with hunting down and killing the great white whale that bit off his leg in a previous encounter, even to the point where he endangers the ship and crew. Another central character is Ishmael, a naïve sailor and the narrator of the story, who is the spiritual opposite of Ahab.

- **Supporting characters** add to the overall understanding of the story. As Ahab's first officer, Starbuck must continually balance his loyalty to his captain and his loyalty to the crew and to the ship's owners. He must explain Ahab's actions to the crew to keep them from mutiny, and he must remind Ahab that the ship's owners expect their whaling contract to be fulfilled, and that the ship and its crew are not there to help Ahab seek revenge against Moby Dick.

- **Background characters** add to the overall description and reality of the story. The seamen, as they go about their ship's chores, represent the delights and fears and the knowledge and ignorance of all people who are at the mercy of an unfair and maniacal authority. The crew, because of their dress, activities, language, and interactions with each other, help flesh out the story and give it authenticity.

Does the Character Change?

Most central characters in a literary work change as a result of their experiences. For example, in Stephan Crane's novel *The Red Badge of Courage,* set during the Civil War, Henry Fleming goes off to war as a young man full of bravado, commits an act of cowardice, and then, by facing his fears, redeems himself through discovering his own courage.

But some central characters do not change. In stark contrast to Henry Fleming, Captain Ahab, in *Moby Dick,* does not change at all from the first time we meet him until the last we see him as he disappears beneath the sea, lashed to the great white whale's body by the rope of his own harpoon.

Look for a change, determine whether and how and why it takes place—or does not—and you will gain more insight into the character.

What Is Your Overall Impression of the Character?

After you have answered the questions above, you are ready to run a tally. What does it all add up to? Is the character admirable or not? Or, more crudely put, is the character a good guy or a bad guy? Sometimes the answer is simple. For example, Fagin in *Oliver Twist* is a villain because he trains young boys to steal and rob, while Antony in *Julius Caesar* is a hero because his actions are motivated by his desire to have Rome governed by moral and responsible leadership.

More often than not, central characters are somewhere in between, not pictured as all good or all evil. Trying to arrive at some conclusion about them, therefore, forces you to analyze them in some depth.

How Credible Is the Character?

When you evaluate whether a character is credible or believable, look at the following:

- *Motivation.* Does the character have believable motives for his or her actions?
- *Consistency.* Are the characters consistent? Generally, we should be able to anticipate how a character will respond in certain situations based on previous actions. Jim, in Joseph Conrad's *Lord Jim,* dreams of being a hero, yet he fails to act heroically time after time when presented with situations in which bravery is called for.
- *Individuality.* A character must be handled reasonably. Although consistency is important, if a character behaves too consistently, he or she may lack the complexity necessary for growth. Individual idiosyncrasies must be allowed for if the characters are to represent mankind with all its frailties and

aberrations. There is a need in most central characters for a certain complexity for depth of meaning and reader interest. Therefore, the inept Willie Loman, in Arthur Miller's *Death of a Salesman,* can be both a loving husband and father, and a womanizer and poor role model for his sons.

Plot: What?

The plot consists of a series of related actions. The events build to a climax, and then the problems developed as the plot unfolds come to a resolution. The events of the plot can occur in the following manner:

- The events in **chronological plots** are portrayed in natural time sequence.

- In **inverted plots**, the events are portrayed out of sequence.

- In some plots, a **flashback** is used to interrupt the chronological sequence so that a past event can be introduced.

The Basic Elements of the Plot

A plot has several basic elements: exposition, complication, rising action, climax, falling action, and resolution. Usually they occur in that order.

- **Exposition** introduces you to the universe of the work and to the characters and their interrelationships. It allows you to discover where you are, who the people are, and what kind of social, physical, and cultural surroundings they live in. It also informs you about the narrator's point of view.

- **Complication** closely follows the exposition because readers require some problem or conflict to stimulate interest.

- **Rising action** occurs because of the conflicts arising from the complication. Increased emotional effect is created when additional events or ramifications happen.

- **Climax** is the point at which the protagonists learn a truth that forever changes them. In Sophocles' play *Oedipus,* the married King and Queen of Thebes, Oedipus and Jocasta, learn that they are mother and son and that Oedipus killed Jocasta's first husband, Laius (Oedipus' father).

- **Falling action** are those events that happen after the climax. Normally, there is a lessening of tension, and the actions are less dramatic.

- **Resolution** (often called *denouement*) occurs when the complications are resolved, but not necessarily in a satisfactory way when compared to the traditional legal, ethical, or moral values of society.

When evaluating a plot or piece of a plot you should also consider foreshadowing, reliance on chance, unity, and the plausibility of the ending.

- **Foreshadowing** is a device to prepare readers for what is to follow. It may take the form of a strange remark ("Beware the Ides of March" in *Julius Caesar*), a prophecy, or some other foreboding image.

- **Reliance on chance** occurs when the lives of the characters are manipulated by chance occurrences or by probable happenings. Generally, chance is fine in the exposition to make things more complicated, but you should be wary of chance in the resolution of a work because the author may be using it to create an easy way out of a complicated plot.

- **Unity** is achieved when all the events in the plot contribute to the development of the plot. Are they necessary? For example, are the sex scenes in much of today's popular literature really necessary for plot development, or are they thrown in to titillate the reader? Is it soul or sale that the author is interested in?

■ **Plausibility of the ending** is achieved when the resolution is both logical, growing naturally out of the plot, and satisfying, concluding logically from the issues raised in the work. You should be particularly wary of happy endings created by chance or by sudden character transformations (for example, a hardened criminal suddenly wants to become a priest).

Setting: Where?

Setting consists of both spatial (house, community, region, country) and cultural qualities (social, moral, economic, political, psychological). The setting can create an atmosphere, playing on our feelings about certain locations. Poe's settings in "The Fall of the House of Usher" and "The Cask of Amontillado" greatly add to the suspense and to the mood of gloom, melancholy, and apprehension in those stories.

The setting can also serve as a force in conflict with human desires and endeavors. In James Dickey's *Deliverance,* the central characters battle the river as much as they battle human antagonists. In Ernest Hemingway's *The Old Man and the Sea,* Santiago fights nature's creatures (sharks) as well as himself.

Setting also includes the human environment apart from the physical. We are shaped by the religious, social, moral, and political worlds in which we live. We must consider these aspects of life when we critique how characters act and respond to their world.

Time: When?

In what period of time does the work take place? What is the significance of its being set at that time? What difference would it make if the work were set in another time?

How does the author handle the passage of time in the work? Does the plot follow a natural, chronological time sequence, or does the author use flashbacks or inverted plot elements? For example, Kurt Vonnegut Jr. uses flashbacks in *Slaughterhouse Five*. What are the advantages or disadvantages of each method?

Theme: Why?

The question "Why?" as it applies to literary analysis of theme commits you to examine the ideas, particularly the central idea, in a work to determine what statement it makes about life in general or about a specific facet of life. Every work, no matter how slight, contains some basic observation about the nature of people, the freedom of the individual, the opportunity for happiness, the role of society, the importance of love, the discovery of self, the existence of evil, or some other important subject.

The theme grows out of the ending or, more specifically, out of how the complications are resolved. Often, at this point, either the action exemplifies the central idea, or a favorably presented character expresses it. But there are other ways to support and express opinions about a theme. Almost everything in a work, all those elements we have talked about so far, should point to and contribute to the theme.

Questions to Determine Theme

In some works, thematic ideas are not stated by characters or suggested in titles. Here are some questions you should ask of the work to determine theme.

■ What happens to the central character or characters? Why?

■ Was what happened the characters' own fault or due to forces beyond their control? If the action was a character's own fault, what weakness did it reveal?

■ If the character overcame a difficulty, what new realization or trait did the resolution require?

■ Did the other characters have similar problems? What do their actions reveal?

■ If the central character's problem cannot be attributed to human weakness, what was it caused by?

■ Can this problem be overcome? If so, how? If not, how can human beings cope with it?

■ Are people or things (animals, etc.) portrayed as good or evil or indifferent?

■ Do the characters find happiness? If not, why not? If so, why? How?

■ Is nature favorable or unfavorable, hospitable or inhospitable? Why?

■ Does the work make any statement about ethical, religious, economic, social, or political matters?

■ Does the work provide any insight into psychological problems about sex, love, death, guilt, alienation, chance happenings, or other issues?

Generally, a theme should not be a moral, a commandment, or a directive about how to live or what to do. Rather, it is a statement about life and people—an observation, a pronouncement, a verdict.

Of all the elements in a literary work, the theme is the most difficult to perceive. The difficulty in uncovering the theme stems from the work's presentation of specifics: certain characters in certain places at certain times engaged in certain actions. On the other hand, the theme is an abstraction, a generalization. Consequently, you need to consider all the elements in a work to arrive at the theme. Once you have established the theme after considering all the elements, you can then discuss the theme in relation to each element independent of the other elements.

Problems to Avoid

When discussing theme, you should avoid two problems:

1. Unless it is a specific instruction in the assignment, do not discuss how the work affected you personally. Although it is natural to identify with characters and situations, you should detach yourself when writing critically. Suppress your personal grievances and preferences and respond to the work on its own merits, objectively and intellectually. Focus on the work, not on your own emotional reaction to it.

2. Do not assume that you know what the author intended the work to mean—even if you have read his or her comments about it. You should not ignore an author's comments, but you should realize that the comments are not the only possibilities. For instance, the author could be untruthful, might not remember all the thematic values, or might not realize some of the unconscious networks of ideas connected in the work. Criticize the work based on the elements of literary analysis you are studying in this chapter.

Technique: How?

No work can be adequately discussed without an analysis of how the writer crafted it. In literary analysis this usually involves *point of view, language devices,* and *word selection.*

Point of View

Point of view refers to the type of narrator. Who tells the story?

■ A *first-person observer* is a narrator involved in the story from the sidelines who speaks as "I." This first-person narrator tells the story from his or her perspective. The information you get is limited by what the narrator can know or surmise. Therefore, it is not necessarily true or accurate.

■ A *first-person participant* is a narrator involved in the action who speaks as "I." This narrator relates the story as if it is just occurring, although flash-backs can be used to give new information or perspectives to episodes of the plot. This narrator is also one of the characters in the story. The events of the story, therefore, are filtered through the eyes of the narrator and are, consequently, open to inaccuracies and misperceptions.

■ A *third-person narrator* relates the story in the third person and does not speak as "I" or appear as a character. Sometimes the third-person narrator comments on the thoughts of the characters and passes judgment. Sometimes this narrator simply records the action without commentary. The information from this narrator is considered accurate and truthful.

Language Devices

Writers often attempt to clarify and explain ideas through the use of special language devices. These language constructions also make the story, its characters, and its themes more interesting and compelling. For example, writers frequently make use of symbols. A **symbol** is an object that has taken on abstract meaning and value. The most effective symbols are a natural part of the story. In *The Old Man and the Sea*, for instance, the sharks are both natural inhabitants of the setting and representatives of the natural forces around us with which we must cope.

Concepts can also be symbols. The "Catch-22" rule in the novel of the same name is a rule that comes to represent the stupid workings of bureaucracy and the frustration of trying to cope logically and reasonably with entities that have top-heavy administrations, such as those found in the military and the corporate world. A writer can use a symbol to communicate the theme or central idea of the work.

Another language device is **metaphor,** a statement in which one thing is used to explain another. In a metaphor, a description is offered in the form of an equation as if one thing *is* another, even though we know it actually is not. "Smith is a lion among men." Metaphors state an imaginary identity. They claim that fictions are, in a symbolic way, unusual truths. We know Smith is not a lion, but the metaphor suggests that he shares many lion-like qualities: he is powerful, loud, aggressive like a predator, and he is king of the jungle.

A **simile,** like a metaphor, creates a relationship between two entities. With a simile, however, the relationship is not as forceful. Whereas the metaphor infers that one thing *is* another, the simile states that one thing is "like" or "as" another thing. For example, a simile would state that "Smith is *like* a lion among men." Or "Smith is gentle *as* a lamb."

In **personification,** animals, objects, or even ideas are given human emotions or characteristics. For example, "The hyenas *cheated* the vultures out of a meal," or "The sled *rested* in the basement after a long day on the snowy hill," or "Love *danced* in their eyes."

A **paradox** is a statement that appears self-contradictory on first reading, but after a closer reading, the statement actually makes sense. For instance, a parent, just before spanking a child, might say, "This is going to hurt me worse than it will you." The parent means that punishing the child will cause the parent emotional pain.

An **oxymoron** is a form of paradox. An oxymoron occurs when two words are used side by side to create a startling or unusual effect. "Jumbo shrimp," "deafening silence," and "sweet sorrow" are examples of oxymorons.

Word Selection

The words that writers choose and how those words are put together influence the reader's perception of the meaning that the writer is trying to portray. Words and combinations of words can have *denotative* and *connotative* meaning.

Denotative language is the use of words in their accepted, dictionary-defined sense. For example, the heart is an organ in the body that acts as a pump in circulating blood throughout the body. On the other hand, **connotative** language is the use of words which have (or develop) associations and implications apart from their explicit sense. Thus, the heart represents love ("She has given her heart to her partner"), empathy ("He has a lot of heart"), or courage ("She has the heart of a lion"—this is also a metaphor).

Abstract language is the use of words that refer to ideas or concepts that cannot be perceived through the senses: "He wears his heart on his sleeve" (*heart* is used to indicate an emotional state).

Concrete language is the use of specific words to portray the unique complex nature of the real world: "The hot asphalt sent waves of volcanic steam into the teeming, sweating crowd jostling shoulder to shoulder under the sweltering heat of the noonday sun" (a passage to support the idea that the city can be a difficult place in which to live).

Irony can be either *verbal* or *situational*. It creates a reality the opposite from what appears true. *Verbal irony* occurs when someone says something but means the opposite, such as when someone does something less than intelligently and is told, "Way to go, Einstein!" *Situational irony* occurs when something that happens creates a reality that is the opposite of what is expected. For example, Oedipus kills Laius, but Oedipus does not know that Laius is his father. In killing him, Oedipus unknowingly fulfills a prophecy that he would someday kill his father.

The Thesis Sentence in Literary Analysis

When called upon to write a literary analysis, you will need a central idea that focuses on a topic and states your opinion about some aspect of the topic. The thesis sentence will focus your thoughts about the topic.

The thesis sentence should exhibit five properties:

1. Author
2. Genre
3. Title
4. Topic
5. Evaluation of topic

Examples

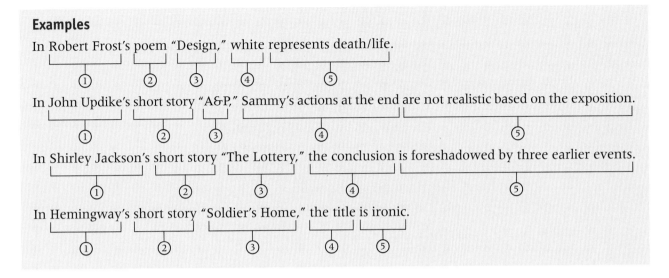

In Robert Frost's poem "Design," white represents death/life.
① ② ③ ④ ⑤

In John Updike's short story "A&P," Sammy's actions at the end are not realistic based on the exposition.
① ② ③ ④ ⑤

In Shirley Jackson's short story "The Lottery," the conclusion is foreshadowed by three earlier events.
① ② ③ ④ ⑤

In Hemingway's short story "Soldier's Home," the title is ironic.
① ② ③ ④ ⑤

Your thesis can also display a sixth element, the essay map that you have studied elsewhere in this text (some texts also call this a *forecasting thesis*), because the elements of the thesis sentence are the body paragraph topics that support and explain the overall topic.

If an essay map were included in each of the thesis sentences above, each would become a forecasting thesis and might be rewritten as follows.

Examples

In Robert Frost's poem "Design," the **white spider, moth, and flower** represent a cycle of life/death.

In John Updike's short story "A&P," Sammy's actions at the end of the story are not realistic based on his **character, the setting, and the atmosphere** as offered in the exposition.

In Shirley Jackson's short story "The Lottery," the conclusion is foreshadowed by the condition of the **lottery items and rituals, the crowd's nervousness, and the boys' actions.**

In Ernest Hemingway's short story "Soldier's Home," Harold's relationships with his **parents, other soldiers, and females** causes the title to be ironic.

Sample Literary Analysis of a Poem: "AFTER APPLE-PICKING"

The following is an analysis of the Robert Frost poem "After Apple-Picking," from his book of poems *North of Boston* (1914). The paper focuses on the central metaphor of the poem (apple-picking) that the poet has created to carry the theme. The paper also cites from outside sources and uses the MLA documentation format (see Chapter 16).

After Apple-Picking
Robert Frost

My long two-pointed ladder's sticking through a tree
Toward heaven still,
And there's a barrel that I didn't fill
Beside it, and there may be two or three
Apples I didn't pick upon some bough.   5
But I am done with apple-picking now.
Essence of winter sleep is on the night,
The scent of apples: I am drowsing off.
I cannot rub the strangeness from my sight
I got from looking through a pane of glass   10
I skimmed this morning from the drinking trough
And held against the world of hoary grass.
It melted, and I let it fall and break.
But I was well
Upon my way to sleep before it fell,   15
And I could tell
What form my dreaming was about to take.
Magnified apples appear and disappear,
Stem end and blossom end,
And every fleck of russet showing clear.   20
My instep arch not only keeps the ache
It keeps the pressure of a ladder-round.
I feel the ladder sway as the boughs bend.
And I keep hearing from the cellar bin
The rumbling sound   25
Of load on load of apples coming in.
For I have had too much
Of apple-picking: I am overtired
Of the great harvest I myself desired.
There were ten thousand thousand fruit to touch,   30
Cherish in hand, lift down, and not let fall.
For all
That struck the earth,
No matter if not bruised or spiked with stubble,
Went surely to the cider-apple heap   35
As of no worth.
One can see what will trouble
This sleep of mine, whatever sleep it is.
Were he not gone,
The woodchuck could say whether it's like his   40
Long sleep, as I describe its coming on,
Or just some human sleep.

John Smith

Literature 302

Professor Jones

June 1, 2001

To Pick or Not To Pick—That Is the Question

1   In Robert Frost's poem "After Apple-Picking," the analogy

between a person's life and the seasons is well paralleled. The metaphor is quite simply stated: as apple-picking takes place in late fall, when the harvest of life is over and the prospect that awaits is winter, is the season of snow and ice a coming of death or merely a temporary dormancy?

2   Apple-picking becomes, then, the central metaphor of a particular activity within the larger construct of life. The problem proffered is whether to attach to the "After" of the title a finality (death) or a shorter cessation that has at its core a continuation. That latter thesis seems to have more support within the conventions of the poem.

3   On the surface, the poem's description of the activity is told in a straightforward fashion. A farmer has just finished harvesting the crop of apples in his orchard, and the toughness of the job has made him enormously tired. One can empathize with the farmer because he has obviously taken great care to tend the trees through the spring and summer and has worked very long hours in harvesting the crop. But his excitement is tempered by the aching in his arches from standing long hours on the ladder picking the apples and from the realization that he won't be able to harvest all of the apples. Many of them lay bruised and battered on the ground and are destined for the "cider-apple heap" (35). On the surface of it, this might be interpreted as human endeavors often end up negatively.

4   But, on further inquiry, the loss of some apples should be expected. To make too much of this scene is to bring to it too much of the ideal and not enough of the real. Frost's realism would be undermined if one expected no loss during the process. Even the tiredness of the farmer should be expected. After all, according to Alvan Ryan,

> Few of Frost's protagonists are passive victims, nor do they escape into a romantic dream-world; we see them at a moment of crisis confronting the existential situation in all its ironic reality. And they have the integrity that comes with the awareness, however dim, that more than circumstances is involved in their trials. Somehow they have chosen, and would not have it otherwise. (136)

All around the farmer autumn is setting in and making ready for the long winter. The woodchuck is hibernating in its burrow, and the leaves are falling off the trees as they go dormant. Even the farmer lies on his bed wearied from his toil. It would seem obvious, then, that winter, commingled with these other details, becomes death. However, other interpretations come to the fore upon closer examination.

5   In the first two lines, the "two-pointed ladder's sticking through a tree / Toward heaven still" (1–2) could readily be seen as an affirmation of something joyously attained after hard work is finished. Heaven, after all, has an aspect of death necessary for its attainment, but it also is a symbol of rebirth because of the infinitely wonderful life bestowed on its entrants. Additionally, the woodchuck is only hibernating—he will awaken from his "death" in the spring to resume life. Both the ladder pointing skyward and the woodchuck represent the potential for a reawakening to occur in the spring. The cycle is not at all interrupted; rather, it is a process that unfolds naturally, albeit haltingly, on an annual basis.

6   The farmer, to be sure, is apprehensive, frustrated, and somewhat overwhelmed. But considering the Puritan work ethic endemic in the eastern United States (and one Frost was particularly aware of and did not altogether share), this should not be unexpected. As Lawrance Thompson observes,

> Most of the Puritans were more bold than talented in their attempts to prove that art is concerned with directing the individual to apprehension; that art is therefore a means to knowledge and truth [...]. Robert Frost's poetic theory, quite at odds with Puritan aesthetics, is nevertheless colored by his Yankee heritage of Puritan teaching. His own belief in poetry as "a clarification of life" seems to have close relation to the Puritan ideal "provided they could be inspired with flexible vitality." (32)

7   The frustration and weariness sets in because of the emotional let-down occurring when the farmer realizes that the original goal of picking the "ten thousand thousand fruit" (30) was not possible—that no matter how good and noble our intentions, the

fruit of our life's work will often be bruised and apportioned to the apple-cider pile (34–5). With this realization comes a certain resignation that, coupled with weariness, the daily toil seems not worth all the effort. This, again, is a quite natural feeling produced by circumstance.

8   But the farmer says "I am done with apple-picking now" (6). It is important to note that the line ends with the word "now," not "forever." Again, there is the hint, the suggestion, that the farmer's mental and spiritual predicament is only a temporary state. The resolution comes to the farmer in the form of an evolutionary triumvirate of thought: to rest from the work, to judge his performance, and to eventually accept his conclusion.

9   Thankfully, Frost does not lead us to a prettily wrapped conclusion. His observations of humans and their world are depicted in terms that solidify humanity's cyclical relationship with nature in both positive and negative terms. Each symbol works, making the metaphorical insights move toward a rendering that both pleases and disturbs in its tenuous fragility.

Works Cited

Ryan, Alvan S. "Frost and Emerson: Voice and Vision." <u>Critical Essays on Robert Frost</u>. Ed. Phillip Gerber. Boston: G. K. Hall, 1982. 124–37.

Thompson, Lawrance. "Robert Frost's Theory of Poetry." <u>Robert Frost: A Collection of Critical Essays</u>. Ed. James Cox. Englewood Cliffs: Prentice-Hall, 1962. 16–35.

Sample Literary Analysis of a Novel: *SULA* BY TONI MORRISON

The following is an analysis of Nobel Laureate Toni Morrison's 1973 novel *Sula*. The essay focuses on the difficulties that young black women have in transitioning into adulthood, considering that their chance is slim of meeting a black man who is ready and able to establish and carry on a mature relationship.

Black Woman's Burden

1   Toni Morrison's novel <u>Sula</u> (1973) concerns the lifelong relationship between two black women, Sula and Nel. Growing up in a poor, black neighborhood, Sula and Nel develop a relationship of shared dreams and secret desires. But their beautiful bond suffers when Sula leaves to conquer the unknown cities of America while Nel settles down as wife and mother. When Sula returns, she has changed to the extent that she is a virtual stranger, repelling everyone, including Nel.

2   A brief sketch of the males presented in the novel is necessary to indicate the overwhelmingly negative effect that males have on the evolution of black females in Toni Morrison's world.

<u>Shadrack</u>: A World War I soldier who went to fight for his country and returned insane. He symbolizes, through the town's establishment of a National Suicide Day, the eventual destruction of community, as portrayed by Shadrack leading townspeople to a tunnel that collapses, killing them.

<u>Plum</u>: A junkie. He is not only a negative role model representative of the lack of potential husbands for black women, but he is killed by his mother so that he won't destroy her life. In this instance, the male is shown to be a negative force through his own choices (drugs) and through the destruction of the black male by the female (out of self-preservation). The irony is as obvious as it is terrible. Throughout the novel, Morrison lets the reader know that this emasculation is as complex for the male as the maturation process is for the female.

<u>Chicken Little</u>: The male child who symbolizes the male potential. He dies "accidentally" at the hand of Sula as Nel watches, as a silent co-conspirator of sorts. Considering Sula's promiscuity in later life and Nel's unfulfilled married life later on, this event is fraught with self-destructive overtones.

<u>White, Irish boys</u>: They torment the black children on the way home from school. Sula attempts to overcome their brutishness, but she only ends up cutting off the tip of her finger in a futile gesture of defiance.

<u>Wiley</u>: Nel's father, a cook on a ship. His absence sets up a matriarchal family situation.

<u>Jude</u>: Nel's husband, who has an adulterous affair with Sula. This is double commentary on the role of black men and the capriciousness of female relationships without acceptable and complementary relationships with black men.

<u>Ajax</u>: Sula's husband, who leaves her because he feels that she is becoming too possessive.

3   It becomes obvious that the absence of black role models in reference to the possibility of future stable relationships between black women and black men (i.e. marriages) is accidental, self-induced, and both societal and self-imposed by black males. This is, then, a very complex situation that black females find themselves in, and it is understandably difficult for them to complete the initiation process into complete, mature, defined adulthood. As Jane Bakerman comments, "Both the Peace and Wright families are essentially fatherless; thus, the girls learn their most important lessons from their mothers, and in each case, the mother fails her daughter" (549). The problem, then, becomes the quintessential "vicious circle." The mother, unable to form a good, long-lasting union with a mature male, hasn't the ability to be a comprehensive role model for her daughters. Bakerman continues, "Though the initiations of Sula Peace and Nel Wright also fail [...] it is still made clear that Sula and Nel are undervalued and that their families legislate toward the initiation failure, [sic] both girls make specific decisions and choices which also contribute" (548). But it must be remembered that Sula and Nel have mothers and grandmothers whose actions are based predominantly on a lack of support by males. They are forced to do what black females, left economically disadvantaged in a hostile society, can only do given their meager environment.

4   The main thrust of the novel falls on Sula and Nel. Their friendship is ultimately destroyed because of their inability to become "whole" women, just as this eluded their mothers and grandmothers. Their initiation left them incomplete. As this drew them together, it eventually tore them apart. Toni Morrison comments, "that there was a little bit of both in each of those two women, and that if they had been one person, I suppose they would have been a rather marvelous person. But each one lacked something the other one had" (Stepto 476). Sula represents "freedom," and Nel represents "constraint." But neither fulfills these designations. Morrison continues, "[Sula] is a

woman who's an adventurer, who breaks rules [...]. Not a law-abiding woman. Nel knows and believes in all the laws of that community [...]. But there's a fatal flaw in all of that, you know, in both of those things. Nel does not make that "leap"—she doesn't know about herself" (476). But, ultimately, neither does Sula.

5   Sula is as incomplete as Nel. She not only loses Ajax, but because of her seduction of Nel's husband, she loses Nel as well. Their symbiotic relationship is never consummated later in life as it should be for old friends. As Carolyn Jones observes,

> During their childhood and adolescence, Nel provides Sula with restraint, and Sula offers Nel courage [the freedom and constraint paradigm]. More important, they offer each other a kind of security that neither finds in her own family [...]. Sula is cut off from the only relationship that gives her life meaning [...] [and] Nel too is rendered incomplete when her friendship with Sula dissolves. (621)

Of course, their adult relationship really never had a chance because the adolescent one was never wholly formed. This is shown starkly by Sula's affair with Nel's husband and Sula and Nel's failure to accept responsibility in the death of Chicken Little. Sula feels guilt, but that is not necessarily the same thing. The bitter irony is evident from the start in the foreshadowing elicited by their last names. Sula never achieves "peace," and Nel cannot find the "wright" relationship with either a man or her community that will take the place of the part of her that never developed.

6   Sula and Nel are inexorably linked like Siamese twins—destined never to be whole—whether together or apart.

Works Cited

Bakerman, Jane. "Failure of Love: Female Initiation in the Novels of Toni Morrison." <u>American Literature</u> 52 (1981): 541–63.

Jones, Carolyn. "Toni Morrison's Narratives of Community." <u>African American Review</u> 27 (1993): 615–26.

Stepto, Robert. "Intimate Things in Place: An Interview with Toni Morrison." <u>Massachusetts Review</u> 18 (1977): 473–89.

PRACTICE 1

Write an essay about the following poem in which you analyze these symbols and how they relate to the theme: the red wheelbarrow, rainwater, white chickens.

The Red Wheelbarrow
William Carlos Williams

so much depends
upon

a red wheel
barrow

glazed with rain   5
water

beside the white
chickens.

PRACTICE 2

Write an essay explaining how the birth and death images in the following story, "Love," by Jesse Stuart, support a specific theme.

Vocabulary
Meaning comes primarily from words. Before you begin reading, look up the definitions for the following words that appear in the story.

incubate	limber	loamy	mattock
poised	riddled	spud	stubble
wilted	windlass		

Love

1   Yesterday when the bright sun blazed down on the wilted corn my father and I walked around the edge of the new ground to plan a fence. The cows kept coming through the chestnut oaks on the cliff and running over the young corn. They bit off the tips of the corn and trampled down the stubble.

2   My father walked in the cornbalk. Bob, our Collie, walked in front of my father. We heard a ground squirrel whistle down over the bluff among the dead treetops at the clearing's edge. "Whoop, take him, Bob," said my father. He lifted up a young stalk of corn, with wilted dried roots, where the ground squirrel had dug it up for the sweet

grain of corn left on its tender roots. This has been a dry spring and the corn has kept well in the earth where the grain has sprouted. The ground squirrels love this corn. They dig up rows of it and eat the sweet grains. The young corn stalks are killed and we have to replant the corn.

3   I could see my father keep sicking Bob after the ground squirrel. He jumped over the corn rows. He started to run toward the ground squirrel. I, too, started running toward the clearing's edge where Bob was jumping and barking. The dust flew in tiny swirls behind our feet. There was a big cloud of dust behind us.

4   "It's a big bull blacksnake," said my father. "Kill him, Bob! Kill him, Bob!"

5   Bob was jumping and snapping at the snake so as to make it strike and throw itself off guard. Bob has killed twenty-eight copperheads this spring. He knows how to kill a snake. He doesn't rush to do it. He takes his time and does the job well.

6   "Let's don't kill the snake," I said. "A blacksnake is a harmless snake. It kills poison snakes. It kills the copperhead. It catches more mice from the fields than a cat."

7   I could see the snake didn't want to fight the dog. The snake wanted to get away. Bob wouldn't let it. I wondered why it was crawling toward a heap of black loamy earth at the bench of the hill. I wondered why it had come from the chestnut oak sprouts and the matted greenbriars on the cliff. I looked as the snake lifted its pretty head in response to one of Bob's jumps. "It's not a bull blacksnake," I said. "It's a she-snake. Look at the white on her throat."

8   "A snake is an enemy to me," my father snapped. "I hate a snake. Kill it, Bob. Go in there and get that snake and quit playing with it!"

9   Bob obeyed my father. I hated to see him take this snake by the throat. She was so beautifully poised in the sunlight. Bob grabbed the white patch on her throat. He cracked her long body like an ox whip in the wind. He cracked it against the wind only. The blood spurted from her fine-curved throat. Something hit against my legs like pellets. Bob threw the snake down. I looked to see what had struck my legs. It was snake eggs. Bob had slung them from her body. She was going to the sand heap to lay her eggs, where the sun is the setting hen that warms them and hatches them.

10   Bob grabbed her body there on the earth where the red blood was running down on the gray-piled loam. Her body was still writhing in pain. She acted like a green-weed held over a new-ground fire. Bob slung her viciously many times. He cracked her limp body against the wind. She was now limber as a shoestring in the wind. Bob threw her riddled body back on the sand. She quivered like a leaf in the lazy wind, then her riddled body lay perfectly still. The blood covered the loamy earth around the snake.

11   "Look at the eggs, won't you?" said my father. We counted thirty-seven eggs. I picked an egg up and held it in my hand. Only a minute ago there was life in it. It was an immature seed. It would not hatch. Mother sun could not incubate it on the warm earth. The egg I held in my hand was almost the size of a quail's egg. The shell on it was thin and tough and the egg appeared under the surface to be a watery egg.

12   "Well, Bob, I guess you see now why this snake couldn't fight," I said. "It is life. Stronger devour the weaker even among human beings. Dog kills snake. Snake kills birds. Birds kill the butterflies. Man conquers all. Man, too, kills for sport."

13   Bob was panting. He walked ahead of us back to the house. His tongue was out of his mouth. He was tired. He was hot under his shaggy coat of hair. His tongue nearly touched the dry dirt and white flecks of foam dripped from it. We walked toward the house. Neither my father nor I spoke. I still thought of the dead snake. The sun was going down over the chestnut ridge. A lark was singing. It was late for a lark to sing. The red evening clouds floated above the pine trees on our pasture hill. My father stood beside the path. His black hair was moved by the wind. His face was red in the blue wind of day. His eyes looked toward the sinking sun.

14   "And my father hates a snake," I thought.

15   I thought about the agony women know of giving birth. I thought about how they will fight to save their children. Then, I thought of the snake. I thought it was silly of me to think such thoughts.

16   This morning my father and I got up with the chickens. He says one has to get up with the chickens to do a day's work. We got the posthole digger, ax, spud, measuring pole and the mattock. We started for the clearing's edge. Bob didn't go along.

17   The dew was on the corn. My father walked behind with the posthole digger across his shoulder. I walked in front. The wind was blowing. It was a good morning wind to breathe and a wind that makes one feel like he can get under the edge of a hill and heave the whole hill upside down.

18   I walked out the corn row where we had come yesterday afternoon. I looked in front of me. I saw something. I saw it move. It was moving like a huge black rope winds around a windlass. "Steady," I says to my father. "Here is the bull blacksnake." He took one step up beside me and stood. His eyes grew wide apart.

19   "What do you know about this," he said.

20   "You have seen the bull blacksnake now," I said. "Take a good look at him! He is lying beside his dead mate. He has come to her. He, perhaps, was on her trail yesterday."

21   The male snake had trailed her to her doom. He had come in the night, under the roof of stars, as the moon shed rays of light on the quivering clouds of green. He had found his lover dead. He was coiled beside her, and she was dead.

22   The bull blacksnake lifted his head and followed us as we walked around the dead snake. He would have fought us to his death. He would have fought Bob to his death. "Take a stick," said my father, "and throw him over the hill so Bob won't find him. Did you ever see anything to beat that? I've heard they'd do that. But this is my first time to see it." I took a stick and threw him over the bank into the dewy sprouts on the cliff.

Chapter Review

- A work of criticism involves interpreting and evaluating someone else's work. Literary criticism involves analyzing a poem, story, novel, play, or essay.
- When analyzing a work of literature, you must consider the characters (who), plot (what), setting (where), time (when), theme (why), and technique (how).
- The thesis sentence of a literary analysis essay should include the author, genre, title, topic, and evaluation of topic.

A Final Word

We hope your experiences using this text have convinced you that it is essential for you to develop the skills necessary to construct a claim and support it through evidence from both primary and secondary sources. Expository writing, in all its various modes as demonstrated in this text, is an essential form of communication in many areas of your life. Whether you are presenting a report to your boss at work or a literary analysis to your professor at college, clear and concise communication is important. In the end, the clarity and coherence of your written communications will bear directly on how others think of you. We hope you will always remember that learning is a lifelong endeavor, and that learning, to be truly useful, requires a dialogue.

Visit *The Write Start* Online!

For additional practice with the materials found in this chapter, visit our Website at

http://www.ablongman.com/checkett

The Website also features additional readings, quizzes, writing activities, and Internet links, as well as a bulletin board and interactive chat.

The Writer's Resources

PARTS OF SPEECH

Nouns

Nouns are words that stand for people, places, or things. They can be *singular* or *plural*.

Nouns	Singular	Plural
Person	man	men
	woman	women
	child	children
Place	cave	caves
	beach	beaches
	forest	forests
	yard	yards
	mountain	mountains
Thing	ring	rings
	computer	computers
	discussion	discussions
	truth	truths
	sport	sports
	idea	ideas
	vacation	vacations
	conversation	conversations

To form the plural of most nouns, you simply add an *–s* or *–es* to the end of the word. However, there are some exceptions:

1. Nouns ending in *–f* or *–ve* form the plural by adding *–ves*:

half	halves
shelf	shelves

2. Hyphenated nouns (nouns that are formed by joining several short words with hyphens) form plurals by adding *–s* or *–es* to the main word in the phrase:

mother-in-law	mothers-in-law
sergeant-at-arms	sergeants-at-arms

3. Some nouns form plurals in other ways, such as by changing the spelling of the plural form. These are sometimes called irregular forms of plural nouns:

foot	feet
child	children
criterion	criteria

woman	women
man	men

4. Other nouns do not change at all when forming the plural. These exceptions must simply be memorized:

fish	fish
deer	deer
shrimp	shrimp

Nouns can also be classified as *proper* or *common. Proper nouns* are the specific names or titles of people, places, or things, and they are capitalized. *Common nouns* are general terms for people, places, or things, and they are not capitalized.

Common Nouns	Proper Nouns
singer	Sheryl Crow
beach	Corona Del Mar
magazine	*Time*
student	Julianne

PRACTICE: FINDING NOUNS

Underline the nouns in the following sentences. (*Note:* Sentences for the Writer's Resources exercises are based on the professional essays used in the text.)

Example: The <u>family</u> travels to the <u>mountains</u> every <u>weekend</u>.

1. I was twelve, and in my first <u>year</u> of junior <u>high school</u>.

2. I discovered <u>black</u> was not supposed to be beautiful.

3. At that <u>age</u>, <u>boys</u> suddenly became important.

4. But by that <u>time</u>, black <u>kids</u> no longer believed in that sixties <u>mantra</u>, "<u>Black</u> is beautiful."

5. Light <u>skin</u>, green <u>eyes</u>, and long, wavy <u>hair</u> were once again synonymous with <u>beauty</u>. (Jones, "Light Skin Versus Dark")

READ all about it

To read the full essay from which this paragraph is excerpted, see page 140.

Pronouns

A **pronoun** is a word that takes the place of, or refers to, a noun. The noun that the pronoun refers to is known as the antecedent of the pronoun.

> **Example**
> <u>Fariba</u> said that <u>she</u> did not understand the question. (The pronoun is *she,* and *Fariba* is its antecedent.)

Pronouns can be divided into several categories. The most common categories are *personal pronouns, relative pronouns, demonstrative pronouns, indefinite pronouns,* and *reflexive pronouns.*

Personal Pronouns

Personal pronouns refer to a specific person or thing *(I/me, you, he/him, she/her, it, we/us, they/them)*. Personal pronouns are divided into three forms, depending on how they are used in a sentence. These forms are **subjective** (pronoun used as a subject), **objective** (pronoun used as an object), or **possessive** (pronoun used to indicates possession/ownership).

Subjective Pronouns

	Singular	**Plural**
1st person	I	we
2nd person	you	you
3rd person	he, she, it	they

Objective Pronouns

	Singular	**Plural**
1st person	me	us
2nd person	you	you
3rd person	him, her, it	them

Possessive Pronouns

	Singular	**Plural**
1st person	my (mine)	our (ours)
2nd person	your (yours)	your (yours)
3rd person	his (his)	their (theirs) its
	her (hers)	
	its (its)	

The following examples demonstrate the uses of these three types of personal pronouns:

I frequently listen to music when I drive. (Subjective pronoun; the pronoun is used as a subject)

They enjoy decorating their home. (Subjective pronoun)

Dave is starting to annoy you. (Objective pronoun; the pronoun is the object of the sentence)

He gave the same gift to him. (Objective pronoun)

That is my sweater. (Possessive pronoun; the pronoun shows ownership or possession)

He borrowed her keys. (Possessive pronoun)

PRACTICE: PERSONAL PRONOUNS

In the following paragraph, underline subjective pronouns once, objective pronouns twice, and possessive pronouns three times. Some sentences may contain more than one type.

READ all about it

To read the full essay from which this paragraph is excerpted, see page 140.

A racist encounter hurts badly. But it does not equal the pain of "colorism"—being rejected by your own people because your skin is colored cocoa and not cream, ebony and not olive. On our scale of beauty, it is often the high yellows—in the lexicon of black America, those with light skin—whose looks reap the most attention. Traditionally, if someone was described that way, there was no need to say that person was good-looking. It was a given that light was lovely. It was those of us with plain brown eyes and darker skin hues who had to prove ourselves. (Jones, "Light Skin Versus Dark")

Relative Pronouns

Relative pronouns introduce a qualifying or explanatory clause.

Relative Pronouns	
who	Used as a subject in reference to people
whom	Used as an object in reference to people
which	Used as a subject in reference to things
that	Used as a subject in reference to things
whoever	Used as a subject in reference to an uncertain number of people
whichever	Used as a subject in reference to an uncertain number of things

The following examples illustrate the use of relative pronouns:

Who made the phone call? (*Who* is used as the subject)

The phone call was made by whom? (*Whom* is used as the object)

Which movie shall we watch tonight? (*Which* is used as a subject referring to things)

I don't like that! (*That* is used as the object referring to a thing)

Demonstrative Pronouns

Demonstrative pronouns point out or specify certain people, places, or things.

Demonstrative Pronouns	
Singular	**Plural**
this	these
that	those

Indefinite Pronouns

Indefinite pronouns refer to general or indeterminate people, places, or things.

Indefinite Pronouns

These pronouns do not refer to specific people, places, or things.

Singular

each	another	anybody	neither
everybody	somebody	anyone	nobody
everyone	someone	anything	no one
everything	something	either	nothing

Singular or plural

all	more	none
any	most	some

Plural

both	few	many	several

Reflexive Pronouns

Reflexive pronouns are formed by adding –*self* or –*selves* to certain pronouns. They are used to indicate action performed to or on the antecedent.

Reflexive Pronouns

	Singular	**Plural**
1st person	myself	ourselves
2nd person	yourself	yourselves
3rd person	himself	themselves
	herself	
	itself	

The following sentences illustrate the use of the reflexive pronoun:

We gave *ourselves* a party to celebrate the end of the school year.
Vinh found *himself* in an impossible situation.

The reflexive pronoun form can also be used to intensify meaning. This is called an *intensifier*.

> The instructor *herself* found the concepts confusing.
> Raoul *himself* had made the engine.

Pronoun-Antecedent Agreement

It is important that pronouns agree with their antecedents. For example, the singular antecedent *everyone* must be used with the singular pronouns *he* or *she*.

The following sentences illustrate sentences in which pronouns agree with the antecedent:

> If *someone* works late at night, *he* or *she* may not be able to concentrate in class the next morning.
>
> When Adam works late at night, *he* is not able to concentrate in class the next morning.
>
> *Each ticket holder* stood in line waiting for *his* or *her* refund.
>
> *Many* were angry that *their* efforts had not been rewarded.

PRACTICE: PRONOUN-ANTECEDENT AGREEMENT

Fill in the blanks with the correct pronouns. Underline the antecedent of each pronoun.

Example: All students must do _____**their**_____ assigned reading before class.

1. Dr. Brenda Izen washed _____**her**_____ car on a rainy afternoon.

2. Janet and Wayne are remodeling _____**their**_____ basement.

3. The bankers and the insurance agents met today; _____**they**_____ discussed many problems facing the elderly.

4. The highway looks slick because _____**it**_____ is covered with a layer of black ice.

5. Everyone should be responsible for _____**his or her**_____ behavior.

6. Anyone failing the test today must do well on _____**his or her**_____ test at mid term.

7. Each lawyer presented _____**his or her**_____ argument.

8. Have Ramona and Luis paid for _____**their**_____ concert tickets?

9. Most of the <u>exercises</u> in this book have _____**their**_____ specific objectives.

10. Each <u>child</u> left _____**his or her**_____ home early for school.

PRACTICE: PRONOUN USE

Correct the following paragraph for pronoun use. The first pronoun has been done for you; the correct answer is in parentheses. Some sentences are correct.

READ all about it

To read the full essay from which this paragraph is excerpted, see page 380.

> **myself**
> I didn't disappoint ~~himself~~. I reveled in killing, maiming, bloodletting, and
> **I**
> gutting. Never did ~~you~~ have the slightest thought regarding carrying capac-
> ity, overbrowsing, population dynamics, or any other game-management con-
> **my, their**
> cept. The arguments that hunters advanced in defense of ~~his~~ sport were alien
> **I**
> to me. I hunted in order to kill: ~~you~~ did not kill in order to have "the hunt-
> ing experience." (Ruggeri, "Why I Don't Hunt")

PRACTICE: PRONOUN USE

Edit the following paragraph for pronoun usage. The first pronoun has been done for you. Some may be correct.

READ all about it

To read the full essay from which this paragraph is excerpted, see page 380.

> **I**
> Why don't I hunt? ~~He~~ could allude to the fruits of exhaustive research into
> the ecological and biological consequences of hunting, and to the collective
> insight of biologists, ecologists, and naturalists which challenge the prevail-
> ing wildlife-management dogma. Yet, fundamentally, the answer can be
> expressed in simple moral terms: Hunting is wrong, and should be acknowl-
> **those who**
> edged to be so not only by ~~these that~~ espouse the strict precepts of the ani-
> mal-rights credo, but by those who hold a common sense of decency, respect,
> **they**
> and justice. When ~~he~~ have exposed the specious reasoning of the hunters'
> **their**
> apologists and stripped ~~its~~ sport of its counterfeit legitimacy, the naked bru-
> tality of hunting defines itself: killing for the fun of it. (Ruggeri, "Why I
> Don't Hunt")

Verbs [ESL]

A **verb** is a word indicating action, feeling, or being. Verbs can be divided into three classes: **action verbs, linking verbs,** and **helping verbs.** Additionally, the form of the verbs can indicate the time of the action: **present, past,** or **future** (also known as **tense**). Each of these tenses has many forms which we use every day. The most commonly used tenses are *simple present* and *simple past*.

Present Tense

Verbs in the Simple Present Tense
Sample verb: dance

	Singular	Plural
1st person	(I) dance	(we) dance
2nd person	(you) dance	(you) dance
3rd person	(he, she, it) dances	(they) dance

Use an *–s* or *–es* ending on the verb when the subject is *he, she,* or *it,* or the equivalent.

Past Tenses for Regular Verbs

Regular verbs are those verbs which form the past tense by adding *–ed* or *–d.* The simple past tense is used to refer to an action that began and ended at one time period in the past.

Simple Past Tense of Regular Verbs
Sample verb: dance

	Singular	Plural
1st person	(I) danced	(we) danced
2nd person	(you) danced	(you) danced
3rd person	(he, she, it) danced	(they) danced

Past Tenses for Irregular Verbs

Many irregular verbs (more than 100 in English) do not form the past tense by adding *–ed* or *–d.* Some verbs do not change forms at all. Some verbs form the past tense by changing the spelling of the entire word (these are called *stem-changing verbs*). The following is a list of the most commonly used irregular verbs.

An Alphabetical List of Irregular Verbs

Simple Form	Simple Past	Past Participle
arise	arose	arisen
be	was, were	been
bear	bore	borne/born
beat	beat	beaten/beat
become	became	become

(Continued)

Simple Form	Simple Past	Past Participle
begin	began	begun
bend	bent	bent
bet	bet	bet
bid	bid	bid
bind	bound	bound
bite	bit	bitten
bleed	bled	bled
blow	blew	blown
break	broke	broken
breed	bred	bred
bring	brought	brought
broadcast	broadcast	broadcast
build	built	built
burst	burst	burst
buy	bought	bought
cast	cast	cast
catch	caught	caught
choose	chose	chosen
cling	clung	clung
come	came	come
cost	cost	cost
creep	crept	crept
cut	cut	cut
deal	dealt	dealt
dig	dug	dug
do	did	done
draw	drew	drawn
eat	ate	eaten
fall	fell	fallen
feed	fed	fed
feel	felt	felt
fight	fought	fought
find	found	found
fit	fit	fit
flee	fled	fled
fling	flung	flung
fly	flew	flown
forbid	forbade	forbidden
forecast	forecast	forecast
forget	forgot	forgotten
forgive	forgave	forgiven
forsake	forsook	forsaken

Simple Form	Simple Past	Past Participle
freeze	froze	frozen
get	got	gotten
give	gave	given
go	went	gone
grind	ground	ground
grow	grew	grown
hang	hung	hung
have	had	had
hear	heard	heard
hide	hid	hidden
hit	hit	hit
hold	held	held
hurt	hurt	hurt
keep	kept	kept
know	knew	known
lay	laid	laid
lead	led	led
leave	left	left
lend	lent	lent
let	let	let
lie	lay	lain
light	lit/lighted	lit/lighted
lose	lost	lost
make	made	made
mean	meant	meant
meet	met	met
mislay	mislaid	mislaid
mistake	mistook	mistaken
pay	paid	paid
put	put	put
quit	quit	quit
read	read	read
rid	rid	rid
ride	rode	ridden
ring	rang	rung
rise	rose	risen
run	ran	run
say	said	said
see	saw	seen
seek	sought	sought
sell	sold	sold
send	sent	sent

(Continued)

Simple Form	Simple Past	Past Participle
set	set	set
shake	shook	shaken
shed	shed	shed
shine	shone/shined	shone/shined
shoot	shot	shot
show	showed	shown/showed
shrink	shrank/shrunk	shrunk
shut	shut	shut
sing	sang	sung
sit	sat	sat
sleep	slept	slept
slide	slid	slid
slit	slit	slit
speak	spoke	spoken
speed	sped/speeded	sped/speeded
spend	spent	spent
spin	spun	spun
spit	spit/spat	spit/spat
split	split	split
spread	spread	spread
spring	sprang/sprung	sprung
stand	stood	stood
steal	stole	stolen
stick	stuck	stuck
sting	stung	stung
stink	stank/stunk	stunk
strive	strove	striven
strike	struck	struck/stricken
string	strung	strung
swear	swore	sworn
sweep	swept	swept
swim	swam	swum
swing	swung	swung
take	took	taken
teach	taught	taught
tear	tore	torn
tell	told	told
think	thought	thought
throw	threw	thrown
thrust	thrust	thrust

Simple Form	Simple Past	Past Participle
understand	understood	understood
undertake	undertook	undertaken
upset	upset	upset
wake	woke/waked	woken/waked
wear	wore	worn
weave	wove	woven
weep	wept	wept
win	won	won
wind	wound	wound
withdraw	withdrew	withdrawn
wring	wrung	wrung
write	wrote	written

The following are some differences in verb forms between American English and British English.

American	British
bet-bet-bet	*bet-bet-bet* or *bet-betted-betted*
fit-fit-fit	*fit-fitted-fitted*
get-got-gotten	*get-got-got*
quit-quit-quit	*quit-quitted-quitted*

American: *burn, dream, kneel, lean, leap, learn, smell, spell, spill, spoil* are usually regular: *burned, dreamed, kneeled, leaned, leaped,* etc.

British: simple past and past participle forms of these verbs can be regular but more commonly end with *–t: burnt, dreamt, knelt, leant, leapt, learnt, smelt, spelt, spilt, spoilt.*

Source: Betty S. Azar, *Understanding and Using English Grammar,* 2nd ed. (Englewood Cliffs, NJ: Prentice Hall Regents), 18–19. Used with permission.

Some irregular verbs do not follow the stem changing pattern.

Irregular Verbs That Do Not Change Their Form
(All end in *–t* or *–d.*)

Present Form	Past Form	Past Participle
bet	bet	bet
cost	cost	cost
cut	cut	cut
fit	fit	fit
hit	hit	hit
hurt	hurt	hurt
quit	quit	quit
spread	spread	spread

The Verb *Be*

Because the verb *be* is used so often as a helping verb, as a linking verb, and to form verb tenses, it is useful to see how irregular the form is.

To be (infinitive form)

	Present Tense		**Past Tense**	
	Singular	*Plural*	*Singular*	*Plural*
1st person	I am	we are	I was	we were
2nd person	you are	you are	you were	you were
3rd person	he, she, it is	they are	he, she, it was	they were

Progressive Tenses and the Present Participle

The verb *be* is used to form the progressive tenses. To form the present progressive, past progressive, and future progressive tenses, combine the appropriate form of *be* + a verb + –*ing*.

Present Progressive	**Past Progressive**	**Future Progressive**
I am talking	I was talking	I will be talking
They are dancing	They were dancing	They will be dancing

The verb form ending in –*ing* is called the **present participle** (*talking, dancing*).

PRACTICE: CHOOSING THE CORRECT VERB FORM

Supply the missing past tense or present participle in the following sentences.

Example: (sing) For her recital, the soprano _____ **sang** _____ a variety of arias.

1. (date) I once _____ **dated** _____ a boy who called me a hillbilly because my family has lived in the Ozarks in southern Missouri for several generations.

2. (realize) I took offense, not _____ **realizing** _____ that as a foreigner to the United States he was unaware of the insult.

3. (mean) He had _____ **meant** _____ it as a term of endearment.

4. (start) I _____ **started** _____ thinking about the implications of the term to me, my family, and my community.

5. (grow) While _____ **growing** _____ up I was often surprised at the way television belittled "country" people.

6. (offend) We weren't _____**offended**_____ by the self-effacing humor of *The Andy Griffith Show* and *The Beverly Hillbillies*.

7. (learn) (wonder) As I _____**learned**_____ about tolerance and discrimination in school, I _____**wondered**_____ why stereotypes of our lifestyle went unexamined.

8. (be) Actors playing "country" people on TV _____**were**_____ usually comic foils or objects of ridicule.

9. (seem) Every sitcom _____**seemed**_____ to have an episode where country cousins, wearing high-water britches and carrying patched suitcases, visited their city friends.

10. (know) Li'l Abner and the folks on *Hee Haw* were amusing, but we on the farm _____**knew**_____ that our work did not lend itself to bare feet, gingham bras, and revealing cutoff jeans. (Kirkendall, "Who's a Hillbilly?")

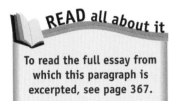

READ all about it

To read the full essay from which this paragraph is excerpted, see page 367.

Complex Verb Forms

In addition to simple forms, there are more complex verb forms. The following chart illustrates the most commonly used verb tenses. Each tense expresses a specific time or duration. Students for whom English is a foreign language need to practice the use of each tense in spoken and written English.

Common Verb Tenses
Sample verb: talk

Tense	First Person Singular	Sample Sentence
present	I talk	I like to talk in a group.
present progressive	I am talking	I am talking on the phone now!
present perfect	I have talked	I have talked about this often.
present perfect progressive	I have been talking	I have been talking since dawn!
past	I talked	I talked to him last night.
past progressive	I was talking	I was talking about my car.
past perfect	I had talked	I had talked before I decided.
past perfect progressive	I had been talking	I had been talking before they sang.
future	I will talk	I will talk to you tomorrow.
future progressive	I will be talking	I will be talking all morning tomorrow.
future perfect	I will have talked	I will have talked enough by then.
future perfect progressive	I will have been talking	I will have been talking for three hours by the time the meeting is over.

Present Perfect and Past Perfect Tenses

The present perfect and past perfect tenses are formed by combining the appropriate form of the verb *have* with the **past participle** form of a verb. The past participle form of a verb usually ends with *–d, –ed,* or *–en.*

Present Perfect Tense

has or *have* + past participle of the main verb

Singular	**Plural**
He has talked	They have talked

Past Perfect Tense

had + past participle of the main verb

Singular	**Plural**
He had talked	They had talked

The **present perfect tense** is used to describe an action that started in the past and continues to the present time. It can also be used to describe an action that has recently taken place or an action for which the exact past time is indefinite.

Julia *has played* with the symphony for five years.

This sentence means that Julia began playing with the orchestra five years ago and is still playing with the symphony today.

Asim *has traveled* to Pakistan several times recently.

This sentence indicates no specific time for the travel mentioned. If a specific time is mentioned, the simple past would be used.

Asim *traveled* to Pakistan last December.

The **past perfect tense** is used to describe an action that occurred in the past before another point in time in the past or before another past activity.

Julia *had played* with the symphony for five years before she retired.

This sentence means that Julia played in the symphony for five years, and then she retired. All of this activity took place in the past.

PRACTICE: PRESENT PERFECT AND PAST PERFECT TENSES

READ all about it

To read the full essay from which this paragraph is excerpted, see page 360.

Change the verb tenses from present to past, changing perfect tenses as needed. The first sentence has been done for you.

A volatile inner-city drama ~~is taking~~ **took** place in New York where blacks ~~have been~~ **had been** boycotting Korean groceries for four months. The recent attack on three Vietnamese men by a group of blacks who mistook them for Koreans ~~has brought~~ **had brought** this long-simmering tension between two minority groups to the world's attention. Korean newspapers from San Francisco to Seoul ~~have been~~ **had been** running front-page stories. Non-Asian commentators around the country, whose knowledge of Korea may not be much more than images from the Korean war and the ridiculous television series *M.A.S.H.*, ~~are making~~ **were making** all sorts of comments. (Kang, "A Battle of Cultures")

Passive Voice

Most writing is done in the **active voice** for direct, concise expression. The **passive voice** is chosen when the actor of the sentence is not important or when the writer wishes to avoid naming the subject.

In the passive voice, the object of an active verb becomes the subject of a passive verb. The form of the verb becomes *be + past participle*.

	S V O
Active:	Carol tells the story.
	S V O
Passive:	The story was told by Carol.

The Active Voice Compared to the Passive Voice

In the *active voice*, the subject of the sentence does the acting (action verb/transitive verb).

In the *passive voice*, the subject is acted upon.

The students finished the project. (subject = *students*; active verb = *finished*)

The project was finished by the students. (subject = *project* [acted upon by students]; passive verb = *was finished*)

The following list shows the conversion of the active to the passive voice for the important verb tenses:

	Active	Passive
Present	Carol tells the story.	The story is told by Carol.
Present progressive	Carol is telling the story.	The story is being told by Carol.
Present perfect	Carol has told the story.	The story has been told by Carol.
Past	Carol told the story.	The story was told by Carol.
Past progressive	Carol was telling the story.	The story was being told by Carol.
Past perfect	Carol had told the story.	The story had been told by Carol.
Future	Carol will tell the story.	The story will be told by Carol.
Future progressive	Carol will be telling the story.	The story is going to be told by Carol. (*going to* is often used instead of *will*)
Future perfect	Carol will have told the story.	The story will have been told by Carol.

PRACTICE: ACTIVE VOICE

The following sentences are written in passive voice. Rewrite each in active voice.

1. The house was destroyed by the earthquake.

The earthquake destroyed the house.

2. The garden was planted by my mother.

My mother planted the garden.

3. Creative recipes were developed by the chefs.

The chefs developed creative recipes.

4. Our mortgage payment was increased by the bank.

The bank increased our mortgage payment.

5. The cake was devoured by the children.

The children devoured the cake.

PRACTICE: PASSIVE VOICE

The following sentences are written in active voice. Rewrite each in passive voice.

1. The fire almost destroyed Yellowstone National Park.

Yellowstone National Park was almost destroyed by fire.

2. The insurance company did not raise their rates.

The rates were not raised by the insurance company.

3. Tiger Woods broke the tournament record.

The tournament record was broken by Tiger Woods.

4. The thief mugged his grandfather in the park.

His grandfather was mugged in the park by the thief.

5. The new skiers finally mastered the bunny slope.

The bunny slope was finally mastered by the new skiers.

PRACTICE: CORRECT VERB FORM AND TENSE

Change the verb tense in the following paragraph from present to past. Next, underline all the verbs in the paragraph. The first one is done for you.

READ all about it

To read the full essay from which this paragraph is excerpted, see page 334.

On December 8, 1941, the day after the Japanese attack on Pearl Harbor in
barricaded
Hawaii, my grandfather barricades himself with his family—my grandmother,

my teenage mother, her two sisters and two brothers—inside of his home in
was
La'ie, a sugar plantation village on Oahu's North Shore. This is my maternal
called
grandfather, a man most villagers call by his last name, Kubota. It
could have meant
could mean either "Wayside Field" or else "Broken Dreams," depending on
used **ran**
which ideograms he uses. Kubota runs La'ie's general store, and one night,
cam **pounde**
after a long day of bad news on the radio, some locals come by, pound on
made **was** **have brandished** **were**
the front door, and make threats. One is said to brandish a machete. They are
was
angry and shocked, as the whole nation is in the aftermath of the surprise
was
attack. Kubota is one of the few Japanese Americans in the village and pres-
had become
ident of the local Japanese language school. He has become a target for their

rage and suspicion. (Hongo, "Kubota")

In the following paragraph, supply the correct form or tense of the verbs in the spaces provided. The first sentence has been done for you. Be careful to use the perfect tenses when appropriate.

READ all about it

To read the full essay from which this paragraph is excerpted, see page 334.

He was a *kibei,* a Japanese American born in Hawaii (a U.S. territory then, so he _____**was**_____ (be) thus a citizen) but who was subsequently _____**sent**_____ (send) back by his father for formal education in Hiroshima, Japan, their home province. *Kibei* is _____**written**_____ (write) with two ideograms in Japanese: one is the word for "return" and the other is the word for "rice." Poetically, it _____**means**_____ (mean) one who returns from America, _____**known**_____ (know) as the Land of Rice in Japanese (by contrast, Chinese immigrants _____**called**_____ (call) their new home Mountain of Gold).

Kubota _____**was graduated**_____ (be, graduate) from a Japanese high school and then _____**came**_____ (come) back to Hawaii as a teenager. He _____**spoke**_____ (speak) English—and a Hawaiian creole version of it at that—with a Japanese accent. But he _____**was**_____ (be) well liked and good at numbers, scrupulous and hard working like so many immigrants and children of immigrants. (Hongo, "Kubota")

Subject-Verb Agreement

Subjects and verbs should agree in number. Thus, singular subjects require verbs with singular endings, and plural subjects require verbs with plural endings. The following sentences illustrate correct subject-verb agreement.

> The *woman* (singular subject) *takes* (singular verb form) a cab.
> The *men* (plural subject) *take* (plural verb form) a cab.

In the following sentences, choose the correct form of the verb in the parentheses.

First, underline the subject and decide whether it is singular or plural.

Next, underline the verb form that correctly agrees with the subject. The tense must also be accurate.

Example: <u>He</u> always (carry, <u>carries</u>) a credit card in his wallet.

READ all about it

To read the full essay from which this paragraph is excerpted, see page 367.

1. Every summer weekend in Missouri, the <u>freeways</u> leading out of our cities (is, <u>are</u>) clogged with vacationers.

2. <u>Minivans and RVs</u> (edge, edges) toward a clear river with a campground and canoe rental, a quiet lake resort, or craft show in a remote Ozark town.

3. Along these popular vacation routes, the rural <u>hosts</u> of convenience stores, gift shops, and corner cafes (<u>accept</u>, accepts) condescension along with personal checks and credit cards.

4. On a canoeing trip not long ago, <u>I</u> (<u>recall</u>, recalls) sitting on the transport bus and listening, heartbroken, as a group of tourists ridiculed our bus driver.

5. <u>They</u> (yells, <u>yelled</u>) "Hey, plowboy, ain't ya got no terbacker fer us?" <u>They</u> (point, <u>pointed</u>) at the young man's sweat-stained overalls as <u>he</u>, seemingly unaffected by their insults, singlehandedly (carries, <u>carried</u>) their heavy aluminum canoes to the water's edge.

6. That <u>"plowboy"</u> (<u>was</u>, were) one of my high-school classmates. He greeted the tourists with a smile and tolerated their derision because he knew tourism brings dollars and jobs. (Kirkendall, "Who's a Hillbilly?")

Compound Subject-Verb Agreement

Some sentences contain a compound subject. A **compound subject** is formed by two or more simple subjects joined with a coordinating conjunction. The verb form *must agree in number with the subject.* If the coordinating conjunction is *and,* the verb is usually plural.

> Fredric and Elise *are* working together on the project.

However, if the compound subject is thought of as a unit, a singular verb is used.

> Macaroni and cheese *is* a favorite dish for children.

If the compound subject is preceded by a singular term such as *each* or *every,* the verb is singular.

> After the storm, *every* person, plant, and animal *was* drenched.

If the compound subject is connected with the correlative conjunctions *either/or, neither/nor, not only/but also,* the verb must agree with the following rules: If both subjects are singular, the verb is singular.

> Either Fredric or Elise *is* going to turn in the project to the boss.

If both subjects are plural, the verb is plural.

> Neither the violins nor the cellos *need* to rehearse their parts with the conductor.

If one subject is singular and the other is plural, the verb agrees with the subject closest to the verb.

> Either my sisters or my friend *is* going to help plan the reception.

PRACTICE: SUBJECT-VERB AGREEMENT WITH COMPOUND SUBJECTS

In each sentence, underline the verb that agrees with the compound subject.

Example: During the summer, parents and children (look, looks) forward to vacations.

1. The top of the slalom course and the bottom (appear, appears) far apart.

2. Every mountain and ocean (is, are) indicated on the new map.

3. The sea lion and her cub (stands, stand) on the dock near Fisherman's Wharf.

4. Each gymnast and coach (congratulate, congratulates) the winner of the competition.

5. The costume on the mannequin and the one on my child (fit, fits) differently.

6. Each towel, sheet, and pillow case (turns, turn) pale in the bleach-filled water.

7. Members of the anniversary party or the guests (is, are) in the pictures in the album.

8. Either exhaustion or procrastination (delay, delays) my progress.

9. Neither a calculator nor a dictionary (was, were) available in the bookstore.

10. My sisters or my mother (are, is) going to join me for a vacation.

PRACTICE: SUBJECT-VERB AGREEMENT

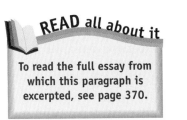

To read the full essay from which this paragraph is excerpted, see page 370.

Edit the following paragraph for subject-verb agreement. The first sentence has been done for you. Some sentences may be correct.

          know   **are**

We ~~knows~~ we have friends; at least I know my friends ~~is~~ with me, if not

                                               need

always, at least most of the time. And most of the time I ~~needs~~ them, and

               reach

they me. We ~~reaches~~ over the phone lines for that word of comfort, the

                need   **has**

encouragement we ~~needs~~ to go on when our own store of willpower ~~have~~

become depleted. (Franco, "A Magic Circle of Friends")

PRACTICE: SUBJECT-VERB AGREEMENT

To read the full essay from which this paragraph is excerpted, see page 370.

Edit the following paragraph for subject-verb agreement. The first verb has been done for you.

                                                         have

We will do it instead at a slower pace, because, along the way, we ~~has~~

                                                   is

learned lessons both small and big: for example, that the world ~~are~~ in no

                                      have

hurry to be changed and that we will ~~has~~ a better shot at it after a good night's

sleep. We may not complete our plans by tomorrow, or even by the end of the

                                                     interfere

week, because the details of our lives may ~~interferes~~, such as a child home

from college, or a neighbor's emergency. (Franco, "A Magic Circle of Friends")

PRACTICE: SUBJECT-VERB AGREEMENT

To read the full essay from which this paragraph is excerpted, see page 370.

Edit the following passage for subject-verb agreement. The first sentence has been done for you.

          call   **are**

They ~~calls~~ us "late bloomers," they call us "returnees." We ~~is~~ sought by

schools, thanks to the sheer numbers we represent, not to mention the life

experience and the common sense that even the least bright among us ~~bring~~ **brings**
to the classroom. We ~~feels~~ **feel** flattered and surprised, and our ego is bolstered
by the realization that we ~~is~~ **are** indeed quite capable....

    We may just be beginning to feel a few arthritic pangs in our toes and
fingers, but with our hair neatly streaked and some expensive dental work,
we ~~knows~~ **know** we still look good. We know we are still strong, smart, vital and,
most especially, ready to work. This time around we will ~~makes~~ **make** a big difference. We ~~knows~~ **know**, because for sure, we already ~~was~~ **were** different. (Franco, "A Magic
Circle of Friends")

Adjectives ESL

An **adjective** is a word that modifies (or describes) a noun or pronoun.
Although adjectives usually come before the nouns they describe, they can also
follow the noun (in the predicate of the sentence).

> The *glistening* ocean sparkled in the sunset.
> The coffee tasted *hot*.

Adjectives can be *objective* (describing nouns with sensory details) or *subjective* (describing concepts, feelings, or ideas in more general terms that are
open to personal interpretation). Both are useful in good writing and enhance
meaning, especially in combination.

Objective Adjectives	Subjective Adjectives
glowing	beautiful
crashing	harsh
stabbing	painful
twisted	ugly
strident	persistent
tender	loving

Adverbs ESL

An **adverb** is a word that modifies (describes) a verb, an adjective, or another
adverb. Often adverbs end in *–ly*. Another test to identify an adverb is if it
answers one of the questions *where, how,* or *when*. Adverbs describe the action

of a passage; in some cases they refer to other adverbs to intensify meaning. As with adjectives, the careful use of effective adverbs can improve the style.

Lisa stormed *angrily* up the stairs. (modifies the verb)
He was *very* cold. (modifies the adjective)
The guests were *too* early to dinner. (modifies the adverb)

Commonly Used Adverbs

happily	harshly	quietly	sadly	rudely
softly	perfectly	poorly	politely	slowly
sadly	loudly	quickly	carefully	very

PRACTICE: ADJECTIVES AND ADVERBS:

Answers will vary.

In the blanks provided, write an appropriate adjective or adverb from the lists of adjectives and adverbs above.

1. It was a _____ night. The _____ colors of the sunset burned in the west as the sun set _____ .

2. The _____ limbs of the _____ tree grew up harshly into the winter sky.

3. The _____ wound was very _____ to the touch.

4. The _____ bellow of the car's horn blared _____ in front of the house.

5. _____ demands of course work often interfere with _____ made plans.

PRACTICE: ADJECTIVES AND ADVERBS

Construct a descriptive paragraph of 5 to 8 sentences, using at least one adjective and one adverb in each sentence.

Answers will vary.

_____

_____

_____

_____

_____

_____

_____

_____

_____

_____

Clauses and Phrases

Independent and Dependent Clauses

A **clause** is a group of related words containing both a subject and a verb. Clauses can be *independent* or *dependent*. An **independent clause** can stand alone as a complete sentence. A **dependent clause** (or subordinate clause) begins with a subordinating conjunction or relative pronoun and cannot stand alone as a sentence.

> We went shopping during the holidays. *independent clause*
>   (subject = *we*; verb = *went*)
>
> although we went shopping during the holidays. *dependent clause*
>   (subordinate conjunction = *although*; subject = *we*; verb = *went*)
>
> Carl and Louisa were often late to class. *independent clause*
>   (subject = *Carl and Louisa*; verb = *were*)
>
> because Carl and Louisa were often late to class. *dependent clause*
>   (subordinate conjunction = *because*; subject = *Carl and Louisa*; verb = *were*)

Restrictive and Nonrestrictive Clauses

Some clauses can be *restrictive* or *nonrestrictive*. **Restrictive clauses** are essential to identify nouns or to complete the meaning. These clauses simply follow the nouns or ideas they are modifying. No commas are used to offset restrictive clauses.

> In the line, the young woman *who was wearing a red bandana and hoop earrings* needed a ticket. (This relative clause is essential to identify which woman needed a ticket.)

Most clauses beginning with *that* are restrictive clauses and are not set off with commas.

> Where is the report *that he left on the desk this morning?*

Nonrestrictive clauses are not essential to complete the meaning of the sentence. You can remove them from the sentence, and the basic meaning of the sentence will remain clear. Because they are nonessential, these clauses are always offset by commas.

> Linda and Burt, *who just returned from Alaska,* would go on another vacation tomorrow. (This relative clause is not essential because it just adds interesting details to the sentence; without it, the meaning of the sentence is still clear.)
>
> The cockatiels, *which were chirping loudly to the music of the nearby television,* should live for up to twenty years. (This clause is nonessential, supplying interesting details but not essential information.)

Combining Clauses

Often, clauses are combined using conjunctions. Independent clauses are combined using a comma and the following coordinating conjunctions.

Coordinating Conjunctions

for	and	nor	but
or	yet	so	

Example

The parents speak, *but* the children refuse to listen.

Independent clauses may also be joined with a semicolon (*The parents speak; the children refuse to listen*) or with a semicolon and an **adverbial conjunction.** These conjunctions may also serve as transition words.

Common Adverbial Conjunctions

accordingly	hence	nonetheless
additionally	however	now
also	incidentally	otherwise
anyway	indeed	similarly
besides	likewise	still
certainly	meanwhile	then
consequently	moreover	thereafter
finally	nevertheless	thus
furthermore	next	undoubtedly

Example

The team practiced in the morning; *furthermore,* they practiced again in the evening.

Dependent clauses are joined to independent clauses with the addition of a **subordinate conjunction.**

Common Subordinate Conjunctions

after	even though	when
although	if (as if)	whenever
as	since	wherever
because	though	whether
before	unless	while
during	until	

Example
The ship returned to port *because its propeller was broken.*

When a dependent clause precedes an independent clause, a comma follows the dependent clause.

Because its propeller was broken, the ship returned to port.

Common Punctuation Errors for Clauses

Fragments, comma splices, and run-on sentences are the most common errors when students practice combining independent and dependent clauses.

Fragments

Fragments are dependent clauses or phrases punctuated as if they are complete sentences.

Because the propeller was broken.
Running up the stairs.

To correct a fragment, attach the dependent clause to an independent clause or add a subject or verb to the phrase.

Because the propeller was broken, the ship returned to port.
She tripped as she was running up the stairs.

Comma Splices

A **comma splice** occurs when a comma is used instead of a semicolon to combine independent clauses.

Comma Splice
Brian studies the cello, David studies the piano.

> **Corrected Versions**
> Brian studies the cello, and David studies the piano.
> Brian studies the cello; David studies the piano.

Run-on Sentences

A **run-on sentence** (or fused sentence) occurs when a sentence contains two or more independent clauses with nothing joining them together.

> **Run-on Sentence**
> Brian plays the cello David plays the piano.

> **Corrected Versions**
> Brian plays the cello; David plays the piano.
> Brian plays the cello, and David plays the piano.

Phrases

A **phrase** is a group of related words without a subject, verb, or both subject and verb. Phrases are used in sentences to complete thoughts or add descriptive detail. To avoid problems with ambiguous meaning or errors in punctuation, phrases must be placed near the noun, verb, or other part of speech to which the phrase refers.

Several types of phrases are used as modifiers in sentences: **appositives, prepositional phrases, participial phrases, gerund phrases, infinitive phrases,** and **absolute phrases.**

Appositives

Appositives are words or phrases that rename the preceding words or phrases. Appositives are often identified as *noun phrases*.

> My friend *Mary* loves to cook with chocolate. (appositive as single word)
> Mary, *a chocolate lover,* shops carefully for the best chocolate in town. (appositive as a phrase)
> The novel *The Grapes of Wrath* is often studied in college English classes.

The punctuation of appositive words and phrases follows the rules for restrictive and nonrestrictive clauses.

Prepositional Phrases

A **prepositional phrase** contains a **preposition** (for example, *in, on, over, before, after*) and its object.

> He waited *for the train.*
> The cat prefers to stay *in the house.*
> They enjoy going out *for pizza after the football games.*

Participial Phrases

A **participial phrase** is a group of words consisting of a **participle** and its completing words. All verbs have present participle and past participle forms.

> *Staring at the blank computer screen,* Martin found himself unable to finish his essay. (present participle form)
>
> *Interrupted by the demands of his hungry two-year-old,* he could not finish reading the paper. (past participle form)
>
> *Walking down the hall,* she was hit by the door as it flew open at the end of class.
>
> *Bewildered by the question,* the student could not finish the test.

Gerund Phrases

A **gerund** is the *–ing* form of a verb that functions as a noun in a sentence. A **gerund phrase** includes a gerund and its completing words.

> *Dancing* is her favorite activity. (*Dancing* functions as the subject of the sentence.)
>
> *Writing a collection of poems* remains Sophia's secret hobby. (The gerund phrase functions as the subject of the sentence.)
>
> Employees will not be paid without *completing the weekly projects.* (The gerund phrase functions as the object of the preposition *without.*)

In some cases, the possessive form of a noun or pronoun precedes a gerund.

> The parents were not thrilled with their *son's tattooing a snake on his arm.*
>
> *Her dancing in the moonlight* amazed the children.

Infinitive Phrases

An **infinitive phrase** is a group of words consisting of *to* plus a verb and its completing words. An infinitive phrase can function as a noun, adjective, or adverb.

> *To read* is the best way to study grammar. (The infinitive phrase functions as a noun, the subject of the sentence.)
>
> Disneyland is one of the best places *to visit while on vacation.* (The infinitive phrase functions as an adjective and modifies the noun *places*).
>
> Her daughter was too nervous *to play the piano in front of an audience.* (The infinitive phrase functions as an adverb, modifying the adjective *nervous.*)

Absolute Phrases

An **absolute phrase** consists of a noun or pronoun and a **participle** plus any other completing words. Absolute phrases modify the entire sentence and cannot be punctuated as a complete sentence.

> *Their project nearly completed,* the painters began to clean their equipment. (The past participle *completed* is used in the phrase.)
>
> The violinist, *her arms and shoulders aching with pain,* practiced long hours every night. (The present participle *aching* is used in this verb phrase.)

PRACTICE: IDENTIFYING CLAUSES AND PHRASES

In the blank to the side of each group of words, write *IC* if the group of words is an independent clause, *DC* if the group of words is a dependent clause, and *P* if the group of words is a phrase. If the group of words is a phrase, identify the type of phrase.

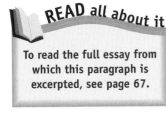

To read the full essay from which this paragraph is excerpted, see page 67.

Example: _____P (prepositional)_____ Under the floor

1. _____P (prepositional)_____ From the center of downtown Tucson

2. _____P (absolute)_____ the ground sloping gently away to Main Street

3. _____IC_____ Here lies the section of the city

4. _____P (participial)_____ known as El Hoyo

5. _____IC_____ In no sense it is a hole

6. _____DC_____ as its name would imply

7. _____IC_____ Its inhabitants are Chicanos

8. _____DC_____ who raise hell on Saturday night

9. _____P (participial)_____ listening to Padre Estanislao

10. _____P (prepositional)_____ on Sunday morning. (Suarez, "El Hoyo")

Misplaced and Dangling Modifiers

Misplaced modifying phrases modify the wrong word in a sentence or are placed so that it is not clear which word is being described.

> Incorrect: The courier delivered the material to the vice president *in the red envelope.*
>
> Correct: The courier delivered the material *in the red envelope* to the vice president.

Dangling modifiers do not seem to modify anything in the sentence, or they may appear to describe a word in a way that makes no logical sense. Dangling modifiers usually occur at the beginning of a sentence. To correct the sentence, add the correct subject or verb to the phrase, or restructure the sentence for accurate meaning.

> Incorrect: *After painting the house,* the furniture was rearranged.
> Correct: After painting the house, we rearranged the furniture.

PRACTICE: MISPLACED OR DANGLING MODIFIERS

The sentences below have misplaced or dangling modifying phrases. Underline the misplaced or dangling phrase in each sentence and rewrite the sentence so that the meaning is clear and accurate.

Example: David fed the birds in his robe and slippers.

In his robe and slippers, David fed the birds.

1. The storekeeper did not sell the book to the customer with the cover missing .

   The storekeeper did not sell the book with the cover missing to the customer.

2. Walking down the hall, the VCR cart nearly pushed her into the wall.

   Walking down the hall, she was nearly pushed into the wall by the VCR cart.

3. The mail carrier delivered the package to the woman wrapped in holiday wrapping paper.

   The mail carrier delivered the package wrapped in holiday wrapping paper to the woman.

4. To lift the exercise equipment up the stairs, a great deal of strength is required.

To lift the exercise equipment up the stairs requires a great deal of strength.

5. After losing her job, her parents encouraged her to move back home with them.

After she lost her job, her parents encouraged her to move back home with them.

6. Singing in the basement, the dog began to whine, and the cat dashed up the stairs.

As the man was singing in the basement, the dog began to whine, and the cat dashed up the stairs.

7. The teacher gave the class a lecture with only five students.

The teacher gave the class, with only five students, a lecture.

8. The salesman answered the angry customer's accusations smiling.

Smiling, the salesman answered the angry customer's accusations.

9. Driving past the house, the signs of a forbidden party were suddenly obvious.

Driving past the house, they noticed the obvious signs of a forbidden party.

10. Testing the samples, the lab suddenly filled with smoke.

As they tested the samples, the lab suddenly filled with smoke.

Prepositions ESL

A **preposition** connects a noun or pronoun to the rest of the sentence, often showing location or time.

Common Prepositions				
about	before	despite	of	to
above	behind	down	off	toward(s)
across	below	during	on	under
after	beneath	for	out	until
against	beside	from	over	up
along	besides	in	since	upon
among	between	into	through	with
around	beyond	like	throughout	within
at	by	near	till	without

                S   **V**

(a) The student studies *in the library*.
                            PREP O of PREP
                                (NOUN)

     S   **V**

(b) We enjoyed the party *at your house*.
                          PREP O of PREP
                              (NOUN)

(c) We went **to the zoo in the afternoon**.
             (place)   (time)

(d) **In the afternoon,** we went to the zoo.

An important element of English sentences is the prepositional phrase. It consists of a preposition **(PREP)** and its object **(O of PREP)**. The object of a preposition is a noun or pronoun.

In (a): *in the library* is a prepositional phrase.

In (c): In most English sentences, place comes before time.

In (d): Sometimes a prepositional phrase comes at the beginning of a sentence.

PRACTICE: PREPOSITIONS

Find the subjects (S), verbs (V), objects (O), and prepositional phrases (PP) in the following sentences.

                    S   **V**   **O**   **PP**

Example: Jack put the letter in the mailbox.

                    S   **V**   **PP**

1. The children walked to school.

        S   V   O

2. Beethoven wrote nine symphonies.

        S   V   O   PP

3. Mary did her homework at the library.

        S   V   PP

4. Bells originated in Asia.

             S   V   O   PP

5. Chinese printers created the first paper money in the world.

Preposition Combinations ᴱˢᴸ

The following list of preposition combinations is important for ESL students to study and practice, because these phrases can be unusual and idiomatic.

Prepositional Combinations with Adjectives and Verbs

A *be* absent from
accuse of
be accustomed to
be acquainted with
be addicted to
be afraid of
agree with
be angry at, with
be annoyed with
apologize for
apply to, for
approve of
argue with, about
arrive in, at
be associated with
be aware of

B believe in
blame for
be blessed with
be bored with

C *be* capable of
care about, for
be cluttered with
be committed to
compare to, with
complain about
be composed of

be concerned about
be connected to
consist of
be content with
contribute to
be convinced of
be coordinated with
count (up)on
cover with
be crowded with

D decide (up)on
be dedicated to
depend (up)on
be devoted to
be disappointed in, with
be discriminated against
distinguish from
be divorced from
be done with
dream of, about
be dressed in

E *be* engaged to
be envious of
be equipped with
escape from
excel in
be excited about

(Continued)

Prepositional Combinations with Adjectives and Verbs

excuse for

be exposed to

F *be* faithful to

be familiar with

feel like

fight for

be filled with

be finished with

be fond of

forget about

forgive for

be friendly to, with

be furnished with

G *be* grateful to, for

be guilty of

H hide from

hope for

I *be* innocent of

insist (up)on

be interested in

be involved in

J *be* jealous of

K *be* known for

L *be* limited to

look forward to

M *be* made of, from

be married to

O object to

be opposed to

P participate in

be patient with

be polite to

pray for

be prepared for

prevent from

prohibit from

protect from

be proud of

provide with

be provided with

R recover from

be related to

be relevant to

rely (up)on

be remembered for

rescue from

respond to

be responsible for

S *be* satisfied with

be scared of

stare at

stop from

subscribe to

substitute for

succeed in

T take advantage of

take care of

be terrified of

thank for

be tired of, from

U *be* upset with

be used to

V vote for

W *be* worried about

Articles ESL

An **article** is a type of word that introduces a noun and indicates whether it is specific or countable. The most frequently used articles are *a, an,* and *the.*

Using Articles: Generic Nouns

Ø means no article is used.

| **Singular Count Noun** | (a) **A** *banana* is yellow.* |

A speaker uses generic nouns to make generalizations. A generic noun represents a whole class of things; it is not a specific, real, concrete thing but rather a symbol of a whole group.

| **Plural Count Noun** | (b) Ø *Bananas* are yellow. |

In (a) and (b): The speaker is talking about any banana, all bananas, bananas in general. In (c): The speaker is talking about any and all fruit, fruit in general.

| **Noncount Noun** | (c) Ø *Fruit* is good for you. |

Notice that no article (Ø) is used to make generalizations with plural count nouns and noncount nouns, as in (b) and (c).

Using *A* or *Some:* Indefinite Nouns

| **Singular Count Noun** | (d) I ate *a banana*. |

Indefinite nouns are actual things (not symbols), but they are not specifically identified.

| **Plural Count Noun** | (e) I ate *some* bananas. |

In (d): The speaker is not referring to "this banana" or "that banana" or "the banana you gave me." The speaker is simply saying that she or he ate one banana. The listener does not know nor need to know which specific banana was eaten; it was simply one banana out of that whole group of things in this world called bananas.

| **Noncount Noun** | (f) I ate *some* fruit. |

In (e) and (f): *Some* is often used with indefinite plural count nouns and indefinite noncount nouns. In addition to *some,* a speaker might use *two, a few, several, a lot of* with plural count nouns, or *a little, a lot of* with noncount nouns.

*Usually *a* or *an* is used with a *singular generic count noun:*
> *A window* is made of glass.
> *A doctor* heals sick people.
> Parents must give *a child* love.
> *A box* has six sides.
> *An apple* can be red, green, or yellow.

The is sometimes used with a singular generic count noun (not a plural generic count noun, not a generic noncount noun). Generic ***the*** is commonly used with, in particular:

1. Species of animals
   > *The whale* is the largest mammal on earth.
   > *The elephant* is the largest land mammal

2. Inventions
   > Who invented *the telephone? the wheel? the refrigerator? the airplane?*
   > *The computer* will play an increasingly large role in all our lives.

3. Musical instruments
   > I'd like to learn to play *the piano.*
   > Do you play *the guitar?*

Using *The:* Definite Nouns

Singular Count Noun   (g) Thank you for *the* banana.

A noun is definite when both the speaker and the listener are thinking about the same specific thing.

Plural Count Noun   (h) Thank you for *the* bananas.

In (g): The speaker uses *the* because the listener knows which specific banana the speaker is talking about, i.e., that particular banana which the listener gave to the speaker.

Noncount Noun   (i) Thank you for *the* fruit.

Notice that *the* is used with both singular and plural count nouns and with noncount nouns.

General Guidelines for Article Usage

(a) *The* sun is bright today.
   Please hand this book to *the* teacher.
   Please open *the* door.
   Jack is in *the* kitchen.

GUIDELINE: Use *the* when you know or assume that your listener is familiar with and thinking about the same specific thing or person you are talking about.

(b) Yesterday I saw *some dogs*.
   The dogs were chasing *a cat*.
   The cat was chasing *a mouse*.
   The mouse ran into *a hole*.
   The hole was very small.

GUIDELINE: Use *the* for the second mention of an indefinite noun.*
In (b): First mention = *some dogs, a cat, a mouse, a hole*. Second mention = *the dogs, the cat, the mouse, the hole*.

(c) Incorrect: *The apples* are my favorite fruit.
   Correct: *Apples* are my favorite fruit.

GUIDELINE: Do not use *the* with a plural count noun (e.g., apples) or a noncount noun (e.g., gold) when you are making a generalization.

(d) Incorrect: *The gold* is a metal.
   Correct: *Gold* is a metal.

(e) Incorrect: I drove *car*.
   Correct: I drove *a car*.
   I drove *the car*.
   I drove *that car*.
   I drove *his car*.

GUIDELINE: Do not use a singular count noun (e.g., *car*) without:
   1. an article (*a/an* or *the*); or
   2. *this/that*; or
   3. a possessive pronoun.

*_The_ is not used for the second mention of a generic noun. Compare:
   1. What color is *a banana* (generic noun)? *A banana* (generic noun) is yellow.
   2. Tom offered me *a banana* (indefinite noun) or an apple. I chose *the banana* (definite noun).

Source: The material on prepositions and articles was adapted from Betty S. Azar, *Understanding and Using English Grammar* (Englewood Cliffs, NJ: Prentice Hall Regents). Used with permission.

PRACTICE: ARTICLES

In the following dialogues, try to decide whether the speakers would probably use *a/an* or *the*.

1. A: I have _____an_____ idea. Let's go on _____a_____ picnic Saturday.

B: Okay.

2. A: Did you have fun at _____the_____ picnic yesterday?

B: Sure did. And you?

3. A: You'd better have _____a_____ good reason for being late!

B: I do.

4. A: Did you think _____the_____ reason Jack gave for being late was believable?

B: Not really.

5. A: Where's my blue shirt?

B: It's in _____the_____ washing machine. You'll have to wear _____a_____ different shirt.

6. A: I wish we had _____a_____ washing machine.

B: So do I. It would make it a lot easier to do our laundry.

7. A: What happened to your bicycle? _____The_____ front wheel is bent.

B: I ran into _____a_____ parked car when I swerved to avoid _____the_____ big pothole in the street.

A: Did you damage _____the_____ car?

B: A little.

A: What did you do?

B: I left _____a_____ note for _____the_____ owner of _____the_____ car.

A: What did you write on _____the_____ note?

B: My name and address. I also wrote _____an_____ apology.

8. A: Can you repair my car for me?

B: What's wrong with it?

A: _____The_____ radiator has _____a_____ leak, and one of _____the_____ windshield wipers doesn't work.

B: Can you show me where _____the_____ leak is?

9. A: Have you seen my boots?

B: They're in _____the_____ closet in _____the_____ front hallway.

PRACTICE: ARTICLES

Complete the sentences with **a/an, the,** or **Ø** (**Ø** means no article).

1. _____Ø_____ beef is a kind of _____Ø_____ meat.

2. _____The_____ beef we had for dinner last night was excellent.

3. Jack is wearing _____a_____ straw hat today.

4. Jack likes to wear _____Ø_____ hats.

5. _____A_____ hat is _____an_____ article of clothing.

6. _____Ø_____ hats are _____Ø_____ articles of clothing.

7. _____The_____ brown hat on that hook over there belongs to Mark.

8. Everyone has _____Ø_____ problems in _____Ø_____ life.

9. My grandfather had _____a_____ long life.

10. That book is about _____the_____ life of Helen Keller.

11. Tommy wants to be _____an_____ engineer when he grows up.

12. The Brooklyn Bridge was designed by _____an_____ engineer.

13. John Roebling is _____the_____ name of _____the_____ engineer who designed the Brooklyn Bridge. He died in 1869 from _____an_____ infection. He died before _____the_____ bridge was completed.

14. _____Ø_____ people wear _____Ø_____ jewelry to make themselves more attractive.

15. _____The_____ jewelry Diana is wearing today is beautiful.

16. Mary is wearing _____a_____ beautiful ring today. It is made of _____Ø_____ gold and _____Ø_____ rubies. _____The_____ gold in her ring was mined in Canada. _____The_____ rubies came from Burma.

17. One of the first things you need to do when you move to _____a_____ new city is to find _____a_____ place to live. Most _____Ø_____ newspapers carry _____Ø_____ advertisements (called "want ads") for _____the_____ apartments that are for rent. If you find an ad for a furnished apartment, _____the_____ apartment will probably contain _____a_____ stove and _____a_____ refrigerator. It will also probably have _____Ø_____ furniture such as _____Ø_____ beds, _____Ø_____ tables, _____Ø_____ chairs, and maybe _____a_____ sofa.

18. My wife and I have recently moved to this city. Since we're going to be here for only _____**a**_____ short time, we're renting _____**a**_____ furnished apartment. We decided that we didn't want to bring our own furniture with us. _____**The**_____ apartment is in _____**a**_____ good location, but that's about the only good thing I can say about it. Only one burner on _____**the**_____ stove works. _____**The**_____ refrigerator is noisy, and _____**the**_____ refrigerator door won't stay closed unless we tape it shut. _____**The**_____ bed sags in the middle and creaks. All of the rest of _____**the**_____ furniture is old and decrepit too. Nevertheless, we're still enjoying living in this city. We may have to look for _____**Ø**_____ another apartment, however.

Fill in the blanks in the following paragraph with the appropriate article or Ø.

Fisherman's Wharf offers the visitor _____**a**_____ wide array of fascinating attractions. _____**The**_____ fishing fleet docks along _____**the**_____ Jefferson Street promenade. _____**An**_____ early morning stroll along "Fish Alley" will allow you to see fishermen at work. Jefferson Street has _____**a**_____ host of _____**Ø**_____ specialty shops and _____**Ø**_____ entertainment for _____**the**_____ entire family. _____**The**_____ Wharf has its share of museums, but they are _____**a**_____ bit out of _____**the**_____ ordinary. There's _____**a**_____ wax museum, _____**Ø**_____ Ripley's Believe It or Not! Museum, and _____**a**_____ museum in _____**the**_____ guise of _____**a**_____ medieval dungeon. If you're not too claustrophobic, you can visit _____**Ø**_____ Pier 45 and tour _____**the**_____ USS *Pampanito*, _____**a**_____ retired WWII submarine. Also, you might want to visit Ghirardelli Square and pick _____**a**_____ souvenir or two from _____**the**_____ many specialty shops located there. Finally, before you leave _____**the**_____ Wharf, make certain you take with you _____**a**_____ loaf or two of San Francisco's famous sourdough bread. You'll probably want to visit Fisherman's Wharf several times before your vacation is over. (from "San Fransisco or Bust!", Ch. 3)

PUNCTUATION AND OTHER RULES OF STYLE

Capitalization

1. Capitalize proper nouns: for example, the names of specific people, places, and products. Capitalize proper adjectives (formed from proper nouns).

> Fredric Chopin
> Sacramento, California
> Fords
> German class

2. Capitalize the days of the week, names of months, and the titles of holidays.

> Saturday, August 28
> Friday the 13th
> Christmas holiday

3. Capitalize the first word of every sentence.

> The dog, cat, and birds all began to bark, growl, and chirp at once.

Numbers

1. Numbers (instead of words) should be used for dates, street addresses, page numbers, and time stated in terms of a.m. and p.m. (but words are used with the phrase "o'clock").

> August 29, 1998
> 321 Walnut St.
> page 34
> 12:00 a.m. (twelve o'clock)

2. Use numbers for figures above 100 (although some authorities tell us to spell out numbers that can be expressed in one or two words).

> 1,000 pages to be completed
> twenty-four hours
> $15.99 per ticket
> $20,000 (or twenty thousand dollars)

3. Use numbers in a short passage in which several numbers are used.

> On the initial placement test, Julia scored 75, Celia scored 60, and Luis scored 85.

4. Never begin a sentence with a number.

> 25 students filled the course. (Incorrect)
> Twenty-five students filled the course. (Correct)

Apostrophes

The **apostrophe** is used to indicate contractions or possession/ownership.

1. Some words can be combined, usually in informal writing, by using an apostrophe. This is a contraction.

> *Isn't* this strange? (is + not)
> We *couldn't* drive any farther. (could + not)

2. Add an apostrophe plus "*s*" to a noun to indicate possession.

> *Anna's* papers were left in the office.

3. To a plural noun ending in "*s*," add only an apostrophe to indicate possession.

> *Parents'* advice often is ignored.

4. For some words, an apostrophe plus "*s*" should be added to a singular word ending in *s*. This is most often true for a proper name.

> *Tom Billings's* recipe book

5. An apostrophe plus "*s*" can be used to form the plurals of figures, letters, and words being treated as words in isolation. (It is also acceptable to leave out this apostrophe.)

> Many students are not satisfied with *C's*.
> He scored *98's* on both tests.
> Don't use so many *"okay's"* when you speak.

Quotation Marks

1. Use quotation marks to set apart words that are quoted or the spoken words in dialogue.

> My mother wrote, "We will be travelling in our mobile home."
>
> Jung said, "I need to change my grammar text."

2. Periods and commas are placed inside the quotation marks, whereas semi-colons and colons are placed outside the quotation marks. If the quoted material is a question, place the question mark inside the quotation marks. However, if the quoted material is part of a longer sentence that asks a question, put the question mark outside the quotation marks.

> "Do the bats fly at night?" he asked.
>
> Did I hear you say, "The bats fly at night"?
>
> He politely remarked, "I would like tea"; however, his wife asked for coffee.
>
> In the short story "Hills Like White Elephants," the male character makes several references to a "simple operation" as a solution to an inconvenient pregnancy.

3. Use quotation marks to set apart titles of essays, magazine articles, short stories, short poems, songs, and chapter headings that you refer to in your writing.

> The class discussed "The House on Mango Street" for two days.
>
> "Music of the Night" is her favorite song in *Phantom of the Opera*.
>
> The poem "Fire and Ice" by Frost illustrates two types of anger and destruction.
>
> "Letter from a Birmingham Jail" is an essay that effectively illustrates argumentation.

4. Quotation marks or italics can be used to set apart a word, phrase, or letter being discussed.

> Do not follow the conjunction *although* with a comma.
>
> Descriptive words such as "brilliant," "glowing," and "illuminating" support the dominant impression of "light."

5. Uncommon names or nicknames and words used in irony or sarcasm should be surrounded by quotation marks.

> James "Melon Ball" McCarthy prefers to shave his head.
>
> His crime of adultery almost made him "public enemy number one."

6. Single quotation marks should be used to indicate a quotation within a quotation.

> Tasha said, "My favorite song is 'Layla' performed by Eric Clapton."

Parentheses

1. Parentheses are used to set off specific details giving additional information, explanations, or qualifications of the main idea in a sentence. This would include words, dates, or statements.

> Many students name famous athletes as heroes (Sammy Sosa, Mark McGwire, and Maurice Green, for example).
> *Tom Sawyer* (1876) is one of Mark Twain's most enduring works.

2. The period for the sentence is placed outside the parenthesis when the enclosed information occurs at the end of the sentence and is not a complete sentence itself. If the enclosed information is a complete sentence, the period is placed inside the parenthesis.

> Many students name famous athletes as heroes (for example, Sammy Sosa).
> Many students name famous athletes as heroes. (One example is Sammy Sosa.)

Brackets

1. Brackets are used in quoted material to set apart editorial explanations.

> "The tenor sang 'Angel of Music' [original version sung by Michael Crawford] for his encore."

2. Brackets are also used to indicate editorial corrections to quoted material. The word "sic" (which means "thus") placed in brackets next to an error in quoted material means that the mistake appeared in the original text and that it is not the writer's error.

> The dean wrote, "All faculty must teach sumer [sic] school."

Dashes

1. The **dash** is used to set apart parenthetical information that needs more emphasis than would be indicated by parentheses.

> Irina's new teacher—a dynamic sociology teacher—helped her to understand American society.

2. Use a dash before a statement that expands on or summarizes the preceding statement (this could also include ironic or humorous comments).

> He studied for the exam for two days—then fell asleep before he finished!

Hyphens

1. Hyphens are used to form compound adjectives before a noun.

> a well-written play
> a forty-year-old woman

2. Do not use a hyphen after an adverb that ends in –ly.

> a quickly changed opinion
> a beautifully designed home

3. Check the dictionary for compound words that always require a hyphen.

> compound numbers (twenty-five, fifty-six)
> good-for-nothing
> father-in-law, mother-in-law
> president-elect

4. Some words with prefixes use a hyphen; check your dictionary if you are unsure.

> ex-husband
> non-English-speaking

5. Use a hyphen at the end of a line if you have to break a word into syllables. Do not divide a one-syllable word.

> Do not forget to review dependent clauses and subordinate conjunctions.

Underlining and Italics

1. The titles of books, magazines, journals, movies, works of art, television programs, CDs, plays, ships, airplanes, and trains should be either underlined or formatted in *italic* type. Underlining is equivalent to or a symbol for italics.

> The Sun Also Rises
>
> *Good Housekeeping*
>
> The New York Times
>
> *The Last Supper*
>
> Tapestry
>
> *Buffy the Vampire Slayer*
>
> H.M.S. Queen Mary

2. There are some exceptions to this rule. For example, the Bible, titles of legal documents (including the U.S. Constitution), and the title of your own essay on your title page would not be underlined or italicized.

PRACTICE: PUNCTUATION

Add the correct capitalization and punctuation, including correct comma usage and periods, to the following paragraphs. The first sentence has been done for you.

READ all about it

To read the full essay from which this paragraph is excerpted, see page 173.

           T   **U**   **S**
the newest move to bash immigrants in the united states has arrived with
                   E   **T**
the resurgence of the english-only movement. the type of legislation called
                                        A
for by this movement is sure to have negative repercussions for american society at large.

          1996   **S**   **C**   **court's**
    In ~~nineteen ninety six~~, the supreme court agreed to review a lower courts
      Arizona's   **1988**
invalidation of ~~arizonas nineteen eighty eight~~ constitutional amendment
    E   **T**
making english the official language of that state. this law mandates that
          E   **E**
voting ballots be in english only and that english be the official language of
all government functions and actions, including government documents.
G   **E**
government officials and employees are to conduct business in english only;
additionally, schools are not allowed to teach in any other language unless
the class is specifically geared toward teaching a foreign language. (Rivera,
"Why English-Only Laws Are Useless")

PRACTICE: PUNCTUATION

Add the correct capitalization and punctuation to the following paragraphs.

To read the full essay from which this paragraph is excerpted, see page 93.

B   **I**
blind from birth, i have never had the opportunity to see myself and have

I
been completely dependent on the image i create in the eye of the observer.

T
to date, it has not been narcissistic.

T
there are those who assume that since I can't see, I obviously cannot hear.

V
very often people will converse with me at the top of their lungs, enunciat-

ing each word very carefully; conversely, people will also often whisper,

assuming that since my eyes don't work, my ears don't either.

F
for example, when I go to the airport and ask the ticket agent for assis-

tance to the plane, he or she will invariably pick up the phone, call a ground

H J
hostess, and whisper,"hi, jane, we've got a seventy-six here." I have concluded

E
that the word"blind"is not used for one of two reasons: either they fear that

if the dread word is spoken the ticket agent's retina will immediately detach,

or they are reluctant to inform me of my condition, of which I may not have

been previously aware. (Krents, "Darkness at Noon)

Interrupters

Sentences may be interrupted by nonrestrictive clauses, phrases, or appositives that clarify or provide additional meaning. These clauses and phrases are usually set off with commas.

> Their dog, *which was barking all night,* annoyed the neighbors.
> The red Toyota, *by the way,* is mine.

PRACTICE: PUNCTUATING NONRESTRICTIVE MODIFIERS

Punctuate the phrases or clauses in the following sentences correctly, putting commas only around non-essential phrases and clauses. Some sentences are correct.

1. The football players, who looked impressive in their new uniforms, marched in the homecoming parade.

2. The technical building, which had been built in 1960, was now in need of renovation.

3. Emeralds that are artificially created appear brighter than natural emeralds.

4. The mortgage, which was a large part of their budget, was due to be paid off in one more year.

5. The committee that I have been requested to join meets twice a week.

6. The gift basket we received for Christmas included gifts for the entire family.

7. The snowstorm descending from the northern states threatened to cancel the first week of spring semester.

8. Professor Wilson gave the test to her new group of students, who refused to read homework assignments.

9. We avoided only the speakers who presented outdated information.

10. The investments that were successful the previous year were less successful in the new year.

WORDS AND MEANING ESL

Commonly Misspelled Words

The following is a list of words that are frequently spelled incorrectly.

across	grammar	possible
address	height	prefer
answer	illegal	prejudice
argument	immediately	privilege
athlete	important	probably
beginning	integration	psychology
behavior	intelligent	pursue
calendar	interest	reference
career	interfere	rhythm
conscience	jewelry	ridiculous
crowded	judgment	separate
definite	knowledge	similar
describe	maintain	since
desperate	mathematics	speech
different	meant	strength
disappoint	necessary	success
disapprove	nervous	surprise
doesn't	occasion	taught
eighth	opinion	temperature
environment	particular	thought
embarrass	optimist	thorough
exaggerate	perform	tired
familiar	perhaps	until
finally	personnel	weight
government	possess	written

Words That Sound Alike

Words	Definition	Example
aural/oral		
aural (adj.)	having to do with hearing	The doctor said that he needs testing for *aural* skills.
oral (adj.)	having to do with speech/the mouth	He had to give an *oral* presentation.

Words	Definition	Example
buy/by		
buy (verb)	to purchase	They *buy* shoes whenever there is a sale.
by (prep.)	past; near; not later than	The dog sits *by* the door.
capital/capitol		
capital (adj.)	fatal; major	The class debated *capital* punishment. The college is making *capital* improvements.
capital (noun)	money; seat of government	He invested his *capital* in the stock market. Sacramento is the *capital* of California.
capitol (noun)	a legislative building	The *capitol* building in Washington, D.C., is often visited by tourists.
complement/compliment		
complement (noun)	something that adds to or completes	The drapery is a *complement* to the furniture.
complement (verb)	to add to or complete	The drapery *complements* the furniture.
compliment (noun)	praise or admiration	He rarely gives *compliments*.
compliment (verb)	to express praise or admiration	He rarely *compliment*s anyone.
passed/past		
passed (verb)	moved ahead	The jeep *passed* the car on the highway.
past (noun)	time before present	The *past* haunted him.
past (prep.)	beyond	The boys ran *past* the graveyard.
past (adj.)	not current	The storms were dangerous this *past year.*
plain/plane		
plain (adj.)	clear; ordinary	The letter lay on the table in *plain* sight.
plain (noun)	flat land with few trees	Early settlers lived in sod homes on *plains*.

(Continued)

Words	Definition	Example
plane (noun)	flat/level surface; aircraft; degree of development	As part of her geometry assignment, she was told to plot a line through a *plane*. He was afraid of *planes*. They talk on different *planes*.
presence/presents		
presence (noun)	being present; a person's way of behavior	Her *presence* calmed the child. The president has a hypnotic *presence*.
presents (noun)	gifts	Tamiko received piles of *presents* on her birthday.
principal/principle		
principal (adj.)	main; most important	The *principal* idea is truth. The *principal* violinist led the orchestra.
principal (noun)	head administrator of a public school; amount of money	The *principal* is rarely popular. The *principal* earns interest in the account.
principle (noun)	a basic truth, assumption	The *principle* of truth is crucial.
rain/reign/rein		
rain (noun)	water falling to earth from clouds	The *rain* ended the drought.
rain (verb)	to rain	It *rained* all morning.
reign (noun)	time during which a royal person rules	The *reign* of Queen Elizabeth II of England has been controversial.
reign (verb)	to rule	The Queen *reigned* for many years.
rein (noun)	a strap attached to the bridle used by a rider to control a horse	The young rider grabbed the *reins* in fear.
rein (verb)	to pull on the reins	He *reined* in the horse forcefully.
sight/site/cite		
sight (noun)	ability to see; a view	Her *sight* was excellent. The pep assembly was a confusing *sight*.
site (noun)	a location	They visited the *site* of their new home.

Words	Definition	Example
cite (verb)	to quote as an expert in research	Always *cite* any outside sources used in your writing.
to/too/two		
to (prep.)	toward a given direction	The students ran *to* class.
too (adverb)	very; also	The sale was *too* tempting. My friend bought a dress and shoes, *too*.
two (adj.)	the number 2	He needs *two* cups of coffee in the morning.
waist/waste		
waist (noun)	the middle of the body and the part of clothing that covers this area	The *waist* of the suit fit too snugly.
waste (verb)	careless use	Don't *waste* your time in class.
waste (noun)	objects/concepts that are discarded	Often, *waste* can be recycled.
weather/whether		
weather (noun)	conditions of the atmosphere	The *weather* in the Midwest changes hourly.
whether (conj.)	if this were the case	He does not know *whether* or not he will pass.
whole/hole		
whole (adj.)	all; complete	She read the *whole* novel in one day.
hole (noun)	an opening	The mouse came through the *hole* in the wall.
write/right/rite		
write (verb)	to convey ideas using words	The students will *write* several essays.
right (adj.)	correct; conforming to morality, justice, or law	She enjoys being *right*! We all know the *right* thing to do.
right (noun)	the location on the right-hand side; conservative political position	The president's agenda is shifting to the *right*.
rite (noun)	ritual; repeated ceremonial action	Getting a driver's license at age sixteen is a *rite* of passage for teenagers in our society.

(Continued)

Contractions That Sound Like Other Words

Contraction	Definition	Example
it's/its		
it's	contraction: *it is*	*It's* going to rain.
its	belonging to it	*Its* wings were broken.
they're/their/there		
they're	contraction: *they are*	*They're* ready for any adventure.
their	belonging to them	*Their* pets run their home.
there	at that place	The library is over *there,* not here.
we're/were/where		
we're	contraction: *we are*	*We're* going to the beach for vacation.
were	past tense of *are*	We *were* ready for a week.
where	in which location	*Where* is the map?
who's/whose		
who's	contraction: *who is*	*Who's* going to the party?
whose	belonging to whom	*Whose* socks are on the sofa?
you're/your		
you're	contraction: *you are*	*You're* in the way.
your	belonging to you	*Your* gift is in the mail.

Words That Sound or Look Almost Alike

Words	Definition	Example
accept/except		
accept (verb)	to acknowledge as true; to receive	She *accepted* his explanation. They *accepted* the wedding gifts.
except (prep.)	other than	All of the assignments *except* one were easy.
advice/advise		
advice (noun)	suggestions about solutions to a problem	He never listens to *advice*.
advise (verb)	to make suggestions; to give advice	The counselor *advises* the confused freshmen.
affect/effect		
affect (verb)	to influence	The weather will *affect* your mood.
effect (noun)	end product; result	The *effect* of the accident was obvious for years.
breath/breathe		
breath (noun)	air inhaled or exhaled	The swimmer held his *breath*.
breathe (verb)	to exhale or inhale	The cat *breathes* silently.
choose/chose		
choose (verb)	to pick or select (present tense)	They could not *choose* a restaurant.
chose (verb)	picked or selected (past tense)	They *chose* to order pizza.
conscience/conscious		
conscience (noun)	thought process acknowledging right and wrong	He has no *conscience*.
conscious (adj.)	aware of existence; capable of thinking	The students were not *conscious* after lunch.

(Continued)

Words	Definition	Example
council/consul/counsel		
council (noun)	group that meets/plans/governs	The city *council* meets each month.
consul (noun)	government official in foreign service	The German *consul* met with the president.
counsel (verb)	to advise	The department chair *counseled* the frustrated student.
desert/dessert		
desert (noun)	dry, barren land	The sunsets on the *desert* are spectacular.
desert (verb)	to leave alone; abandon	His friends *deserted* him.
dessert (noun)	last dish of a meal, often sweet	They decided to avoid sweet, fattening *desserts*.
diner/dinner		
diner (noun)	a narrow type of restaurant with counters and booths; a person who is eating	At the *diner*, they have an old juke box. The *diners* enjoy listening to oldies from the juke box.
dinner (noun)	the large, important meal at mid-day or evening	The fried chicken is for *dinner*.
emigrate/immigrate		
emigrate (verb)	to leave a country	They *emigrated* from China.
immigrate (verb)	to enter a new country	Lila *immigrated* to the United Kingdom.
farther/further		
farther (adv.)	greater distance (physically)	The sprinter ran *farther* than he had to.
further (adv.)	greater distance (mentally)	Most arguments can be *further* developed.
further (verb)	to advance an ideal or goal	The protesters *further* the cause of equality.
loose/lose		
loose (adj.)	not tight	*Loose* fitting clothing has been in style recently.

Words	Definition	Example
lose (verb)	to misplace or be unable to find; to fail to win	I always *lose* my earrings. He *lost* the tennis match.

personal/personnel

personal (adj.)	pertaining to the individual	*Personal* information should remain confidential.
personnel (noun)	employees	*Personnel* should be aware of their benefits.

quiet/quit/quite

quiet (adj.)	without noise; peaceful	The class is too *quiet*.
quit (verb)	to stop; to give up	The employee *quit* suddenly.
quite (adv.)	definitely	You were *quite* right.

special/especially

special (adj.)	unique	Their anniversary was a *special* event.
especially (adv.)	even more; very	Final exams can be *especially* difficult.

than/then

than (conj.)	word to make comparison	Sale prices are better *than* original prices.
then (adv.)	at that time	First they studied; *then* they took the exam.

thorough/though/thought

thorough (adj.)	detailed, complete, accurate	Social attitudes changed after several *thorough* studies were made.
though (conj.)	despite	*Though* the trees are changing colors, the temperature is warm.

through/threw

through (prep.)	in one side and out the other	The ball crashed *through* the window.
threw (verb)	past tense of *throw*	The president *threw* the first pitch.

Fill in the blanks of the following sentences with the correct word.

1. He was not telling her the ___**whole**___ (hole, whole) story about the ___**hole**___ (hole, whole) in the bay window.

2. Please ___**write**___ (rite/write/right) the ___**right**___ (write/rite/right) information in the insurance report.

3. The doctor will ___**cite**___ (sight/cite/site) statistics to his patients about the necessity of protecting their ___**sight**___ (site/sight/cite).

4. The boys want ___**to**___ (to, too, two) see ___**two**___ (to, too, two) movies tonight and hope you want to see them ___**too**___ (to, too, two).

5. The school ___**principal**___ (principal, principle) would never ask a teacher to betray her most basic ___**principle**___ (principle, principal).

6. Do not ___**accept**___ (except, accept) excuses from the students, ___**except**___ (accept, except) for me!

7. During his ___**reign**___ (rain, reign, rein), the King would never appear in public in the ___**rain**___ (rain, reign, rein).

8. Do not ___**waste**___ (waist, waste) my time by boasting about the effect of the new equipment on the size of the model's ___**waist**___ (waist, waste).

9. ___**Whether**___ (weather, whether) or not we attend the party depends on the ___**weather**___ (whether, weather).

10. The swimmer cannot ___**breathe**___ (breath, breathe) under water; therefore, he takes several deep ___**breaths**___ (breaths, breathes) before he dives.

Edit the following paragraph for correct word choice. Circle the errors, then write the correct words in the spaces provided.

Buy the time they reached the state (capital,) the students were very restless

from the long bus ride. They jumped off of the bus quickly and formed a line

in front of the tour guide. The tour guide greeted the fifth graders and (complemented) them on (there) (exceptable) behavior. She quickly gulped down an aspirin as she guided her charges up the steps to the state senate chambers. The students whispered and shuffled their feet as they (past) the halls where the lawmakers were working. They admired the portraits of famous governors, and stared up into the domed ceilings. After the tour was over, they ran down the (plane) cement steps and gathered, laughing and shouting , in the park to eat lunch.

capitol	**acceptable**
complimented	**passed**
their	**plain**

Confusing Verbs That Sound Alike

The verbs *lie/lay, rise/raise,* and *sit/set* are often confused. In order to understand how to use them correctly, it is important to understand the difference between *reflexive verbs,* which *do not* take an object (the verb needs no noun to complete the meaning of the sentence), and *transitive verbs,* which *do* take an object. *Lie, rise,* and *sit* are reflexive; *lay, raise,* and *set* are transitive.

Reflexive Verbs: Lie, Rise, Sit				
	Present Tense	**Present Participle**	**Past Tense**	**Past Participle**
lie (to rest or recline)	lie	lying	lay	has/have lain
rise (to move upward)	rise	rising	rose	has/have risen
sit (to move body into sitting position)	sit	sitting	sat	has/have sat

The family dog loves *to lie* by the front door.

Let the bread dough *rise* on the warm kitchen counter.

She *sits* in front of a computer for eight hours every day.

Reflexive verbs are often followed by a prepositional phrase, not a stand-alone noun.

Transitive Verbs: Lay, Raise, Set

	Present Tense	Present Participle	Past Tense	Past Participle
lay (to put an object down)	lay	laying	laid	has/have laid
raise (to lift or move something up)	raise	raising	raised	has/have raised
set (to carefully place something)	set	setting	set	has/have set

She *lay* <u>the flowers</u> carefully on the table.

Please *raise* <u>the window shades</u>.

He *set* <u>the chair</u> by the window.

The object (underlined) is necessary to complete the meaning of these sentences.

PRACTICE: LIE/LAY, RISE/RAISE, SIT/SET

Answers will vary.

Write your own sentences using each of the verbs listed below.

1. Lie

_____

_____

_____

2. Lay

_____

_____

_____

3. Rise

_____

_____

_____

4. Raise

_____

_____

5. Sit

_____

_____

6. Set

_____

_____

_____

Two- and Three-Word Verb Phrases ⬛ESL

Two-word and three-word verb phrases are often difficult for non-native speakers of English. Many of them are idiomatic expressions, and they need to be studied or memorized.

Phrasal Verbs (Two-Word and Three-Word Verbs)

The term _phrasal verb_ refers to a verb and preposition which together have a special meaning. For example, **_put_ + _off_** means "postpone." Some phrasal verbs consist of three parts. For example, **_put_ + _up_ + _with_** means "tolerate." Phrasal verbs are also called _two-word verbs_ or _three-word verbs_.

A phrasal verb may be either _separable_ or _nonseparable_.

Separable Phrasal Verbs

(a) I **handed** _my paper_ **in** yesterday. (b) I **handed in** _my paper_ yesterday.	With a separable phrasal verb, a noun may come either between the verb and the preposition or after the preposition, as in (a) and (b).
(c) I **handed it in** yesterday. (Incorrect: I handed in it yesterday.)	A pronoun comes between the verb and the preposition if the phrasal verb is separable, as in (c).

Nonseparable Phrasal Verbs

(d) I **ran into** an old friend yesterday. (e) I **ran into** her yesterday. (Incorrect: I ran an old friend into.) (Incorrect: I ran her into yesterday.)	With a nonseparable phrasal verb, a noun or pronoun must follow the preposition, as in (d) and (e).

Phrasal verbs are especially common in informal English. Following is a list of common phrasal verbs and their usual meanings. The phrasal verbs marked with an asterisk (*) are nonseparable.

A ask out .... *ask someone to go on a date*

B bring about, bring on .... *cause*

bring up .... *(1) rear children; (2) mention or introduce a topic*

C call back .... *return a telephone call*

call in .... *ask to come to an official place for a specific purpose*

call off .... *cancel*

*call on .... *(1) ask to speak in class; (2) visit*

call up .... *call on the telephone*

*catch up (with) .... *reach the same position or level*

*check in, check into .... *register at a hotel*

*check into .... *investigate*

check out .... *(1) take a book from the library; (2) investigate*

*check out (of) .... *leave a hotel*

cheer up .... *make (someone) feel happier*

clean up .... *make clean and orderly*

*come across .... *meet by chance*

cross out .... *draw a line through*

cut out .... *stop an annoying activity*

D do over .... *do again*

*drop by, drop in (on) .... *visit informally*

drop off .... *leave something/someone at a place*

drop out (of) .... *stop going to school, to a class, to a club, etc.*

F figure out .... *find the answer by reasoning*

fill out .... *write the completions of a question-naire or official form*

find out .... *discover information*

G *get along (with) .... *exist satisfactorily*

get back (from) .... *(1) return from a place; (2) receive again*

*get in, get into .... *(1) enter a car; (2) arrive*

*get off .... *leave an airplane, a bus, a train, a subway, a bicycle*

*get on .... *enter an airplane, a bus, a train, a subway, a bicycle*

*get out of .... *(1) leave a car; (2) avoid work or an unpleasant activity*

*get over .... *recover from an illness*

*get through .... *finish*

---

*Indicates a nonseparable phrasal verb.

	*get up	arise from bed, a chair
	give back	return an item to someone
	give up	stop trying
	*go over	review or check carefully
	*grow up (in)	become an adult
H	hand in	submit an assignment
	hang up	(1) conclude a telephone conversation; (2) put clothes on a hanger or a hook
	have on	wear
K	keep out (of)	not enter
	*keep up (with)	stay at the same position or level
	kick out (of)	force (someone) to leave
L	*look after	take care of
	*look into	investigate
	*look out (for)	be careful
	look over	review or check carefully
	look up	look for information in a reference book
M	make up	(1) invent; (2) do past work
N	name after, name for	give a baby the name of someone else
P	*pass away	die
	pass out	(1) distribute; (2) lose consciousness
	pick out	select
	pick up	(1) go to get someone (e.g., in a car); (2) take in one's hand
	point out	call attention to
	put away	remove to a proper place
	put back	return to original place
	put off	postpone
	put on	put clothes on one's body
	put out	extinguish a cigarette or cigar
	*put up with	tolerate
R	*run into, *run across	meet by chance
	*run out (of)	finish a supply of something
S	*show up	appear, come
	shut off	stop a machine, light, faucet
T	*take after	resemble
	take off	(1) remove clothing; (2) leave on a trip

(Continued)

*Indicates a nonseparable phrasal verb.

take out	(1) *take someone on a date;* (2) *remove*
take over	*take control*
take up	*begin a new activity or topic*
tear down	*demolish; reduce to nothing*
tear up	*tear into many little pieces*
think over	*consider carefully*
throw away, throw out	*discard; get rid of*
throw up	*vomit; regurgitate food*
try on	*put on clothing to see if it fits*
turn down	*decrease volume or intensity*
turn in	(1) *submit an assignment;* (2) *go to bed*
turn off	*stop a machine, light, faucet*
turn on	*begin a machine, light, faucet*
turn out	*extinguish a light*
turn up	*increase volume or intensity; arrive*

Source: The material on verb phrases is from Betty S. Azar, *Understanding and Using English Grammar* (Englewood Cliffs, NJ: Prentice Hall Regents). Used with permission.

PRACTICE: PHRASAL VERBS

Select from the following list of phrasal verbs and complete the following sentences.

Call in	Figure out
pick out	put up (with)
Get back (from)	pick up
Look up	take after
Keep out (of)	turn in

1. Please _____**pick up**_____ the toys after you are finished playing.

2. ____**Get back from**____ the edge of the canyon!

3. The students will _____**turn in**_____ their assignments at the beginning of class.

4. The young man examined all of the flowers as he tried to _____**pick out**_____ a corsage for his date.

5. __**Keep out of**__ the poison ivy!

6. I cannot __**figure out**__ the answer to this problem!

7. The child __**takes after**__ his father in looks but after his mother in personality.

8. While you are on vacation, please try not to __**call in**__ to the office too often.

9. The teacher would no longer __**put up with**__ the rudeness of the students.

10. If you are unsure about your project, __**look up**__ your topic on the online database at the library.

Additional Readings

DESCRIPTION

HAVE YOU EVER MET AN ASIAN MAN YOU THOUGHT WAS SEXY?

Eric Kim

> In this essay, the writer talks about stereotypes, an oversimplified opinion or conception based on conventional characteristics (for example, Asians are good at math; blondes are dumb). Think of some stereotypes that you might hold. Keep them in mind as you read the essay.

Vocabulary

Before you begin reading, look up the definitions of the following words that appear in the essay. The numbers in parentheses after each word refers to the paragraph number of the essay.

affront (3)	asexual (2)	caricatures (7)
chauvinist (4)	diatribe (5)	nonentity (6)
retrospect (2)	shun (4)	spewing (7)
waylay (7)		

Have You Ever Met an Asian Man You Thought Was Sexy?

1   "Yo, Bruce Lee! Hey, whatzaah happening?" That's what a group of teenage guys shouted at me a couple of years ago as I walked down the street with a friend. They followed that up with a series of yelps and shrieks that I took to be their attempts at kung fu sounds. As I was about to turn and respond, my friend quickly pointed out that it would be better, and safer, to ignore these guys.

2   In retrospect, though, I wonder if rising above it was the best response. Sometimes I don't believe I can change people's stereotypes about Asians without confronting them. At least Bruce Lee, the late martial arts expert, is at the macho end of the spectrum, along with the stereotype of the greedy, wealthy businessmen who are invading America. At the other end of the spectrum, Asian men in America are seen as geeks—short, nerdy, passive, and somewhat asexual "Orientals."

3   As a six-foot, 180-pound, Korean American guy, I always hated that people would assume I was a wimpy bookworm who couldn't play sports. It pleased me to see how upset non-Asians would get after a few Asian friends and I whipped them in a game of full-court basketball. Before we hit the court, the other guys would snicker and assume we'd be easy to beat. Afterward, they'd act as if being outdone in sports by an Asian was an affront to their masculinity.

4   It's different for Asian women, who are usually stereotyped as exotic, passive, sensual, the ultimate chauvinist fantasy. The reality of these stereotypes is played out on the street: Look around and you'll see an Asian woman with a Caucasian man a lot sooner than you'll see a white woman with an Asian date. Even Asian women sometimes shun Asian men as being either too wimpy or too dominating. I was born and grew up in Seoul, South Korea, and went to an international high school there. The student body was about 80 percent Asian and 20 percent Caucasian. I think being in the majority gave me

a certain social confidence. I never thought twice about dating or flirting with non-Asian girls. If I felt nervous or awkward, it was because I was shy, not because I wasn't white.

5   When I started college in the United States, I promised myself that I'd meet people of all races, since most of my friends in Seoul had been Asian. Yet when I arrived here, for the first time in my life I felt like a minority. For the first time in my life, I was told to "go back home" and had to listen to strangers on the bus give me their diatribes on Vietnam and Korea. Feeling I was a minority affected how I approached other people.

6   Even though there were a lot of attractive non-Asian women at school, I hesitated to approach them, because I imagined that they were only interested in Caucasian guys. I assumed that non-Asian women bought the Asian stereotypes and saw me as a nonentity. It wasn't that I kept trying and getting shot down; I simply assumed they would never consider me. The frustrating mix of my own pride and the fear of getting rejected always managed to keep me from approaching a non-Asian woman I was attracted to.

7   My girlfriend now is Asian American. There are many things I love about her, and it strengthens our relationship that we have a cultural bond. Relationships are about trust, vulnerability, and a willingness to open up. That can be hard for an Asian man to achieve with a non-Asian woman; though he may find her attractive, his emotions may be blocked by fear, waylaid by the caricatures of Asian men as paranoid deli owners, Confucius-spewing detectives, or kung fu fighters with fists of fury.

8   These images say little about what it means to be a twenty-four-year-old Asian man. These images don't reflect our athleticism, our love of rap, or our possible addiction to ESPN. Because of these images, Asian men are rarely seen for what we are—and so we may look at a non-Asian woman with interest, then tuck that interest away.

9   It's not easy to confess that I know many women don't find me attractive. But for me, the very process of facing down Asian stereotypes makes them less meaningful. Most of all, I try to keep a sense of humor about it. After all, when my friends and I whip some unsuspecting non-Asians on the basketball court, *they* are the ones who are victims of the stereotypes, not us.

Descriptive Technique Questions

1. Identify paragraphs in which the writer uses objective description and those in which he uses subjective description.

Objective: paragraphs 3, 4; Subjective: paragraphs 2, 7, and 8.

2. What does the author mean in the last paragraph when he says "*they* [non-Asians] are the ones who are victims of the stereotypes, not us"?

Possible answer: Opponents who assume that Asians are nonathletic are

likely to get beat.

3. How does the writer describe the stereotypical Asian male?

In paragraphs 2 and 3 Kim describes the Asian male stereotype as run-

ning the spectrum from the greedy businessman invading America solely

for money, or the Bruce Lee martial arts expert, to the short, nerdy book-

worm who is nonathletic and passive.

Descriptive Writing Opportunities

1. At the beginning of the essay, Kim recounts something a group of teenagers shouted at him. Write an essay describing a variety of people by the stereotypical things they say or believe.

2. Inspect your own talents and shortcomings, your physical features, and your clothing. Write an essay about how someone who doesn't know you might describe you in stereotypical terms.

THE JOY LUCK CLUB

Amy Tan

The following is an excerpt from Amy Tan's novel *The Joy Luck Club*. In the excerpt, Tan describes how the club started, surrounded by the devastation and atrocities committed by the Japanese when they invaded Kweilin, China, in the 1930s.

Vocabulary
Before you begin reading, look up the definitions of the following words that appear in the essay. The numbers in parentheses after each word refers to the paragraph number of the essay.

ingots (13)	kinky (3)	meager (14)
prolong (19)	rickshaw (8)	scurried (9)
shabby (5)		

The Joy Luck Club

1   My mother started the San Francisco version of the Joy Luck Club in 1949, two years before I was born. This was the year my mother and father left China with one stiff leather trunk filled only with fancy silk dresses. There was no time to pack anything else, my mother had explained to my father after they

boarded the boat. Still his hands swam frantically between the slippery silks, looking for his cotton shirts and wool pants.

2   When they arrived in San Francisco, my father made her hide those shiny clothes. She wore the same brown-checked Chinese dress until the Refugee Welcome Society gave her two hand-me-down dresses, all too large in sizes for American women. The society was composed of a group of white-haired American missionary ladies from the First Chinese Baptist Church. And because of their gifts, my parents could not refuse their invitation to join the church. Nor could they ignore the old ladies' practical advice to improve their English through Bible study class on Wednesday nights and, later, through choir practice on Saturday mornings. This was how my parents met the Hsus, the Jongs, and the St. Clairs. My mother could sense that the women of these families also had unspeakable tragedies they had left behind in China and hopes they couldn't begin to express in their fragile English. Or at least, my mother recognized the numbness in these women's faces. And she saw how quickly their eyes moved when she told them her idea for the Joy Luck Club.

3   Joy Luck was an idea my mother remembered from the days of her first marriage in Kweilin, before the Japanese came. That's why I think of Joy Luck as her Kweilin story. It was the story she would always tell me when she was bored, when there was nothing to do, when every bowl had been washed and the Formica table had been wiped down twice, when my father sat reading the newspaper and smoking one Pall Mall cigarette after another, a warning not to disturb him. This is when my mother would take out a box of old ski sweaters sent to us by unseen relatives from Vancouver. She would snip the bottom of a sweater and pull out a kinky thread of yarn, anchoring it to a piece of cardboard. And as she began to roll with one sweeping rhythm, she would start her story. Over the years, she told me the same story, except for the ending, which grew darker, casting long shadows into her life, and eventually into mine.

4   "I dreamed about Kweilin before I ever saw it," my mother began, speaking Chinese. "I dreamed of jagged peaks lining a curving river, with magic moss greening the banks. At the tops of these peaks were white mists. And if you could float down this river and eat the moss for food, you would be strong enough to climb the peak. If you slipped, you would only fall into a bed of soft moss and laugh. And once you reached the top, you would be able to see everything and feel such happiness it would be enough to never have worries in your life again.

5   "In China, everybody dreamed about Kweilin. And when I arrived, I realized how shabby my dreams were, how poor my thoughts. When I saw the hills, I laughed and shuddered at the same time. The peaks looked like giant fried fish heads trying to jump out of a vat of oil. Behind each hill, I could see shadows of another fish, and then another and another. And then the clouds would move just a little and the hills would suddenly become monstrous elephants marching slowly toward me! Can you see this? And at the root of the hill were secret caves. Inside grew hanging rock gardens in the shapes and colors of cabbage, winter melons, turnips, and onions. These were things so strange and beautiful you can't ever imagine them.

6   "But I didn't come to Kweilin to see how beautiful it was. The man who was my husband brought me and our two babies to Kweilin because he thought we would be safe. He was an officer with the Kuomintang, and after he put us down in a small room in a two-story house, he went off to the northwest, to Chungking.

7   "We knew the Japanese were winning, even when the newspapers said they were not. Every day, every hour, thousands of people poured into the city, crowding the sidewalks, looking for places to live. They came from the East, West, North, and South. They were rich and poor, Shanghainese, Cantonese, northerners, and not just Chinese, but foreigners and missionaries of every religion. And there was, of course, the Kuomintang and their army officers who thought they were top level to everyone else.

8   "We were a city of leftovers mixed together. If it hadn't been for the Japanese, there would have been plenty of reason for fighting to break out among these different people. Can you see it? Shanghai people with north-water peasants, bankers with barbers, rickshaw pullers with Burma refugees. Everybody looked down on someone else. It didn't matter that everybody shared the same sidewalk to spit on and suffered the same fast-moving diarrhea. We all had the same stink, but everybody complained someone else smelled the worst. Me? Oh, I hated the American air force officers who said habba-habba sounds to make my face turn red. But the worst were the northern peasants who emptied their noses into their hands and pushed people around and gave everybody their dirty disease.

9   "So you can see how quickly Kweilin lost its beauty for me. I no longer climbed the peaks to say, How lovely are these hills! I only wondered which hills the Japanese had reached. I sat in the dark corners of my house with a baby under each arm, waiting with nervous feet. When the sirens cried out to warn us of bombers, my neighbors and I jumped to our feet and scurried to the deep caves to hide like wild animals. But you can't stay in the dark for so long. Something inside of you starts to fade and you become like a starving person, crazy-hungry for light. Outside I could hear the bombing. Boom! Boom! And then the sound of raining rocks. And inside I was no longer hungry for the cabbage or the turnips of the hanging rock garden. I could only see the dripping bowels of an ancient hill that might collapse on top of me. Can you imagine how it is, to want to be neither inside nor outside, to want to be nowhere and disappear?

10   "So when the bombing sounds grew farther away, we would come back out like newborn kittens scratching our way back to the city. And always, I would be amazed to find the hills against the burning sky had not been torn apart.

11   "I thought up Joy Luck on a summer night that was so hot even the moths fainted to the ground, their wings were so heavy with the damp heat. Every place was so crowded there was no room for fresh air. Unbearable smells from the sewers rose up to my second-story window and the stink had nowhere else to go but into my nose. At all hours of the night and day, I heard screaming sounds. I didn't know if it was a peasant slitting the throat of a runaway pig or an officer beating a half-dead peasant for lying in his way on the sidewalk. I didn't go to the window to find out. What use would it have been? And that's when I thought I needed something to do to help me move.

12   "My idea was to have a gathering of four women, one for each corner of my mah jong table. I knew which women I wanted to ask. They were all young like me, with wishful faces. One was an army officer's wife, like myself. Another was a girl with very fine manners from a rich family in Shanghai. She had escaped with only a little money. And there was a girl from Nanking who had the blackest hair I have ever seen. She came from a low-class family, but she was pretty and pleasant and had married well, to an old man who died and left her with a better life.

13   "Each week one of us would host a party to raise money and to raise our spirits. The hostess had to serve special *dyansyin* foods to bring good fortune of all kinds—dumplings shaped like silver money ingots, long rice noodles for

long life, boiled peanuts for conceiving sons, and of course, many good-luck oranges for a plentiful, sweet life.

14   "What fine food we treated ourselves to with our meager allowances! We didn't notice that the dumplings were stuffed mostly with stringy squash and that the oranges were spotted with wormy holes. We ate sparingly, not as if we didn't have enough, but to protest how we could not eat another bite, we had already bloated ourselves from earlier in the day. We knew we had luxuries few people could afford. We were the lucky ones.

15   "After filling our stomachs, we would then fill a bowl with money and put it where everyone could see. Then we would sit down at the mah jong table. My table was from my family and was of a very fragrant red wood, not what you would call rose-wood, but *hong mu*, which is so fine there's no English word for it. The table had a very thick pad, so that when the mah jong *pai* were spilled onto the table the only sound was of ivory tiles washing against one another.

16   "Once we started to play, nobody could speak, except to say *'Pung!'* or *'Chr!'* when taking a tile. We had to play with seriousness and think of nothing else but adding to our happiness through winning. But after sixteen rounds, we would again feast, this time to celebrate our good fortune. And then we would talk into the night until the morning, saying stories about good times in the past and good times yet to come.

17   "Oh, what good stories! Stories spilling out all over the place! We almost laughed to death. A rooster that ran into the house screeching on top of dinner bowls, the same bowls that held him quietly in pieces the next day! And one about a girl who wrote love letters for two friends who loved the same man. And a silly foreign lady who fainted on a toilet when firecrackers went off next to her.

18   "People thought we were wrong to serve banquets every week while many people in the city were starving, eating rats and, later, the garbage that the poorest rats used to feed on. Others thought we were possessed by demons— to celebrate when even within our own families we had lost generations, had lost homes and fortunes, and were separated, husband from wife, brother from sister, daughter from mother. Hnnnh! How could we laugh, people asked.

19   "It's not that we had no heart or eyes for pain. We were all afraid. We all had our miseries. But to despair was to wish back for something already lost. Or to prolong what was already miserable. How much can you wish for a favorite warm coat that hangs in the closet of a house that burned down with your mother and father inside of it? How long can you see in your mind arms and legs hanging from telephone wires and starving dogs running down the streets with half-chewed hands dangling from their jaws? What was worse, we asked among ourselves, to sit and wait for our own deaths with proper somber faces? Or to choose our own happiness?

20   "So we decided to hold parties and pretend each week had become the new year. Each week we could forget past wrongs done to us. We weren't allowed to think a bad thought. We feasted, we laughed, we played games, lost and won, we told the best stories. And each week, we could hope to be lucky. That hope was our only joy. And that's how we came to call our little parties Joy Luck."

21   My mother used to end the story on a happy note, bragging about her skill at the game. "I won many times and was so lucky the others teased that I had learned the trick of a clever thief," she said. "I won tens of thousands of *yuan*. But I wasn't rich. No. By then paper money had become worthless. Even toilet paper was worth more. And that made us laugh harder, to think a thousand-*yuan* note wasn't even good enough to rub on our bottoms."

Descriptive Technique Questions

1. Sensory images are very important to effective description. List at least two textures (touch), sounds, sights, tastes, and smells in the story. How do these sensory images help the reader understand the physical and emotional environment of the story's setting?

   Possible answers: *touch* "slippery silks" (1) and "rub on our bottoms" (21); *sound* "fragile English" (2) and "the sirens cried out" (9); *sight* "quickly their eyes moved" (2) and "hanging rock gardens in the shapes and colors of cabbage, winter melons, turnips, and onions" (5); *taste* "eat the moss for food" (4) and "dumplings were stuffed mostly with stringy squash" (14); *smell* "everyone shared the same sidewalk to spit on and suffered the same fast-moving diarrhea. We all had the same stink" (8); and "My table was from my family and was of a very fragrant red wood" (15). The sensory descriptions mirror the physical and emotional states of the people as they remember the Japanese atrocities in China and the relative safety and peaceful environment of San Francisco.

2. The title of the selection is "The Joy Luck Club." How can the title be both a literal and ironic description of the women's situation?

   Possible answer: The women are lucky to be in San Francisco out of harm's way, and they can share in the joy of each other's company, as well. However, the reason they have great joy and luck in the present is a consequence of a previous painful and unhappy past experience.

3. A great variety of food is described at the meetings, as well as the process of eating it. What is the significance of the focus on food and how it's eaten?

   Possible answer: Humans need to be both physically and spiritually nourished. Food is the obvious physical means of getting nourishment, but the *process* of eating food can have both symbolic and functional meaning. The food in the story was a special *dyansyin* food that was to bring good fortune for those eating it: "dumplings shaped like silver money ingots, long rice noodles for long life, boiled peanuts for conceiving sons, and of course, many good-luck oranges for a plentiful, sweet life" (13).

Descriptive Writing Opportunities

1. Write an essay describing the food and table setting at your favorite family holiday feast. In your essay, focus on how these things describe your family.

2. Write an essay describing some important event from your childhood. Along with similes, metaphors, and other language devices, use sensory images to focus on the dominant impression you wish to convey.

NARRATION

FOR MY INDIAN DAUGHTER

Lewis Sawaquat

> Prejudice, cultural awareness, and ethnic pride are three basic elements involved in any racial minority's world. In this essay, the author focuses on the problems caused by ethnicity, ancestry, and heritage.

Vocabulary

Before you begin to read, look up the definitions of the following words that appear in the story. The numbers in parentheses after each word refers to the paragraph number of the essay.

affluent (5)	backlash (4)	comeuppance (7)
forge (9)	guttural (2)	iridescent (9)
masquerade (10)	mingling (1)	unbidden (1)

For My Indian Daughter

1   My little girl is singing herself to sleep upstairs, her voice mingling with the sounds of the birds outside in the old maple trees. She is two and I am nearly 50, and I am very taken with her. She came along late in my life, unexpected and unbidden, a startling gift.

2   Today at the beach my chubby-legged, brown-skinned daughter ran laughing into the water as fast as she could. My wife and I laughed watching her, until we heard behind us a low guttural curse and then an unpleasant voice raised in an imitation war whoop.

3   I turned to see a fat man in a bathing suit, white and soft as a grub, as he covered his mouth and prepared to make the Indian war cry again. He was middle-aged, younger than I, and had three little children lined up next to him, grinning foolishly. My wife suggested we leave the beach, and I agreed.

4   I knew the man was not unusual in his feelings against Indians. His beach behavior might have been socially unacceptable to more civilized whites, but his basic view of Indians is expressed daily in our small town, frequently on the editorial pages of the county newspaper, as white people speak out against Indian fishing rights and land rights, saying in essence, "Those Indians are taking our fish, our land." It doesn't matter to them that we were here first, that the U.S. Supreme Court has ruled in our favor. It matters to them that we have something they want, and they hate us for it. Backlash is the common

explanation of the attacks on Indians, the bumper stickers that say, "Spear an Indian, Save a Fish," but I know better. The hatred of Indians goes back to the beginning when white people came to this country. For me it goes back to my childhood in Harbor Springs, Mich.

5 *Theft.* Harbor Springs is now a summer resort for the very affluent, but a hundred years ago it was the Indian village of my Ottawa ancestors. My grandmother, Anna Showanessy, and other Indians like her, had their land there taken by treaty, by fraud, by violence, by theft. They remembered how whites had burned down the village at Burt Lake in 1900 and pushed the Indians out. These were the stories in my family.

6 When I was a boy my mother told me to walk down the alleys in Harbor Springs and not to wear my orange football sweater out of the house. This way I would not stand out, not be noticed, and not be a target.

7 I wore my orange sweater anyway and deliberately avoided the alleys. I was the biggest person I knew and wasn't really afraid. But I met my come-uppance when I enlisted in the U.S. Army. One night all the men in my barracks gathered together and, gang-fashion, pulled me into the shower and scrubbed me down with rough brushes used for floors, saying, "We won't have any dirty Indians in our outfit." It is a point of irony that I was cleaner than any of them. Later in Korea I learned how to kill, how to bully, how to hate Koreans. I came out of the war tougher than ever and, strangely, white.

8 I went to college, got married, lived in La Porte, Ind., worked as a surveyor and raised three boys. I headed Boy Scout groups, never thinking it odd when the Scouts did imitation Indian dances, imitation Indian lore.

9 One day when I was 35 or thereabouts I heard about an Indian powwow. My father used to attend them and so with great curiosity and a strange joy at discovering a part of my heritage, I decided the thing to do to get ready for this big event was to have my friend make me a spear in his forge. The steel was fine and blue and iridescent. The feathers on the shaft were bright and proud.

10 In a dusty state fairground in southern Indiana, I found white people dressed as Indians. I learned they were "hobbyists," that is, it was their hobby and leisure pastime to masquerade as Indians on weekends. I felt ridiculous with my spear, and I left.

11 It was years before I could tell anyone of the embarrassment of this weekend and see any humor in it. But in a way it was that weekend, for all its silliness, that was my awakening. I realized I didn't know who I was. I didn't have an Indian name. I didn't speak the Indian language. I didn't know the Indian customs. Dimly I remembered the Ottawa word for dog, but it was a baby word, *kahgee*, not the full word, *muhkaghee*, which I was later to learn. Even more hazily I remembered a naming ceremony (my own). I remembered legs dancing around me, dust. Where had that been? What had I been? "Sawaquat," my mother told me when I asked, "where the tree begins to grow."

12 That was 1968, and I was not the only Indian in the country who was feeling the need to remember who he or she was. There were others. They had powwows, real ones, and eventually I found them. Together we researched our past, a search that for me culminated in the Longest Walk, a march on Washington in 1978. Maybe because I now know what it means to be Indian, it surprises me that others don't. Of course there aren't very many of us left. The chances of an average person knowing an average Indian in an average lifetime are pretty slim.

13 *Circle.* Still, I was amused one day when my small, four-year-old neighbor looked at me as I was hoeing in my garden and said, "You aren't a real Indian, are you?" Scotty is little, talkative, likable. Finally I said, "I'm a real Indian." He looked at me for a moment and then said squinting into the sun, "Then where's your horse and feathers?" The child was simply a smaller, whiter ver-

sion of my own ignorant self years before. We'd both seen too much TV, that's all. He was not to be blamed. And so, in a way, the moronic man on the beach today is blameless. We come full circle to realize other people are like ourselves, as discomfiting as that may be sometimes.

14   As I sit in my old chair on my porch, in a light that is fading so the leaves are barely distinguishable against the sky, I can picture my girl asleep upstairs. I would like to prepare her for what's to come, take her each step of the way saying, there's a place to avoid, here's what I know about this, but much of what's before her she must go through alone. She must pass through pain and joy and solitude and community to discover her own inner self that is unlike any other and come through that passage to the place where she sees all people are one, and in so seeing may live her life in a brighter future.

Narrative Technique Questions

1. What do you think is the purpose behind Sawaquat writing this story?

   Possible answer: To help prepare his daughter for the racism she will no

   doubt encounter as she grows, even though he knows she must go

   through most of it alone.

2. The author writes about an event that involved his daughter. Why does his memory of her stir within him remembrances of his own identity crises?

   Possible answer: He realizes that in many ways he, too, when young, was

   as ignorant about different cultures as those who taunted him about his

   race when he was grown.

3. What does the author learn about himself after attending his first powwow?

   Possible answer: He realized he had no Indian identity. He had no Indian

   name, did not speak an Indian language, and did not know Indian customs.

Narrative Writing Opportunities

1. Write an essay about your own cultural heritage. What kinds of problems has it caused for you? Or has your culture been the cause of problems for others of different cultures?

2. Pretend you are living in a new country. Write an essay for your new neighbors explaining your identity and how your culture or ethnicity affects your life.

KUBOTA

Garrett Hongo

Many Japanese Americans had their possessions, property, and businesses taken away from them during World War II. In this essay, Hongo retells his grandfather's experiences from that period and, in so doing, expresses the feelings and experiences of an entire group.

Vocabulary

Before you begin reading, look up the definitions of the following words that appear in the essay. The number in parentheses after each word refers to the paragraph number of the essay.

auxiliary (6)	habitually (9)	ideograms (1)
idiom (10)	injunction (12)	interstices (19)
pidgin (11)	phalanx (15)	plangent (9)
querulous (21)	stigma (14)	

Kubota

1   On December 8, 1941, the day after the Japanese attack on Pearl Harbor in Hawaii, my grandfather barricaded himself with his family—my grandmother, my teenage mother, her two sisters and two brothers—inside of his home in La'ie, a sugar plantation village on Oahu's North Shore. This was my maternal grandfather, a man most villagers called by his last name, Kubota. It could mean either "Wayside Field" or else "Broken Dreams," depending on which ideograms he used. Kubota ran La'ie's general store, and the previous night, after a long day of bad news on the radio, some locals had come by, pounded on the front door, and made threats. One was said to have brandished a machete. They were angry and shocked, as the whole nation was in the aftermath of the surprise attack. Kubota was one of the few Japanese Americans in the village and president of the local Japanese language school. He had become a target for their rage and suspicion. A wise man, he locked all his doors and windows and did not open his store the next day, but stayed closed and waited for news from some official.

2   He was a *kibei*, a Japanese American born in Hawaii (a U.S. territory then, so he was thus a citizen) but who was subsequently sent back by his father for formal education in Hiroshima, Japan, their home province. *Kibei* is written with two ideograms in Japanese: one is the world for "return" and the other is the world for "rice." Poetically, it means one who returns from America, known as the Land of Rice in Japanese (by contrast, Chinese immigrants called their new home Mountain of Gold).

3   Kubota was graduated from a Japanese high school and then came back to Hawaii as a teenager. He spoke English—and a Hawaiian creole version of it at that—with a Japanese accent. But he was well liked and good at numbers, scrupulous and hard working like so many immigrants and children of immigrants. Castle & Cook, a grower's company that ran the sugarcane business along the North Shore, hired him on first as a stock boy and then appointed him to run one of its company stores. He did well, had the trust of management and labor—not an easy accomplishment in any day—married, had children, and had begun to exert himself in community affairs and excel in his own recre-

ations. He put together a Japanese community organization that backed a Japanese language school for children and sponsored teachers from Japan. Kubota boarded many of them, in succession, in his own home. This made dinners a silent affair for his talkative, Hawaiian-bred children, as their stern *sensei,* or teacher, was nearly always at table and their own abilities in the Japanese language were as delinquent as their attendance. While Kubota and the *sensei* rattled on about things Japanese, speaking Japanese, his children hurried through their suppers and tried to run off early to listen to the radio shows.

4   After dinner, while the *sensei* graded exams seated in a wicker chair in the spare room and his wife and children gathered around the radio in the front parlor, Kubota sat on the screened porch outside, reading the local Japanese newspapers. He finished reading about the same time as he finished the tea he drank for his digestion—a habit he'd learned in Japan—and then he'd get out his fishing gear and spread it out on the plank floors. The wraps on his rods needed to be redone, gears in his reels needed oil, and, once through with those tasks, he'd painstakingly wind on hundreds of yards of new line. Fishing was his hobby and his passion. He spent weekends camping along the North Shore beaches with his children, setting up umbrella tents, packing a rice pot and hibachi along for meals. And he caught fish. *Ulu'a* mostly, the huge surf-feeding fish known on the mainland as the jack crevalle, but he'd go after almost anything in its season. In Kawela, a plantation-owned bay nearby, he fished for mullet Hawaiian-style with a throw net, stalking the bottom-hugging, gray-backed schools as they gathered at the stream mouths and in the freshwater springs. In an outrigger out beyond the reef, he'd try for *aku*—the skipjack tuna prized for steaks and, sliced raw and mixed with fresh seaweed and cut onions, for *sashimi* salad. In Kahaluu and Ka'awa and on an offshore rock locals called Goat Island, he loved to go torching, stringing lanterns on bamboo poles stuck in the sand to attract *kumu'u,* the red goatfish, as they schooled at night just inside the reef. But in Lai'e on Laniloa Point near Kahuku, the northernmost tip of Oahu, he cast twelve-and fourteen-foot surf rods for the huge, varicolored, and fast-running *ulu'a* as they ran for schools of squid and baitfish just beyond the biggest breakers and past the low sand flats wadable from the shore to nearly a half mile out. At sunset, against the western light, he looked as if he walked on water as he came back, fish and rods slung over his shoulders, stepping along the rock and coral path just inches under the surface of a running tide.

5   When it was torching season, in December or January, he'd drive out the afternoon before and stay with old friends, the Tanakas or Yoshikawas, shopkeepers like him who ran stores near the fishing grounds. They'd have been preparing for weeks, selecting and cutting their bamboo poles, cleaning the hurricane lanterns, tearing up burlap sacks for the cloths they'd soak with kerosene and tie onto sticks they'd poke into the soft sand of the shallows. Once lit, touched off with a Zippo lighter, these would be the torches they'd use as beacons to attract the schooling fish. In another time, they might have made up a dozen paper lanterns of the kind mostly used for decorating the summer folk dances outdoors on the grounds of the Buddhist church during O-Bon, the Festival for the Dead. But now, wealthy and modern and efficient killers of fish, Tanaka and Kubota used rag torches and Colemans and cast rods with tips made of Tonkin bamboo and butts of American-spun fiberglass. After just one good night, they might bring back a prize bounty of a dozen burlap bags filled with scores of bloody, rigid fish delicious to eat and even better to give away as gifts to friends, family, and special customers.

6   It was Monday night, the day after Pearl Harbor, and there was a rattling knock at the front door. Two FBI agents presented themselves, showed identification, and took my grandfather in for questioning in Honolulu. He didn't return home for days. No one knew what had happened or what was wrong.

But there was a roundup going on of all those in the Japanese-American community suspected of sympathizing with the enemy and worse. My grandfather was suspected of espionage, and communicating with offshore Japanese submarines launched from the attack fleet days before war began. Torpedo planes and escort fighters, decorated with the insignia of the Rising Sun, had taken an approach route from northwest of Oahu directly across Kahuku Point and on toward Pearl. They had strafed an auxiliary air station near the fishing grounds my grandfather loved and destroyed a small gun battery there, killing three men. Kubota was known to have sponsored and harbored Japanese nationals in his own home. He had a radio. He had wholesale access to firearms. Circumstances and an undertone of racial resentment had combined with wartime hysteria in the aftermath of the tragic naval battle to cast suspicion on the loyalties of my grandfather and all other Japanese Americans. The FBI reached out and pulled hundreds of them in for questioning in dragnets cast throughout the West Coast and Hawaii.

7   My grandfather was lucky; he'd somehow been let go after only a few days. Others were not as fortunate. Hundreds, from small communities in Washington, California, Oregon, and Hawaii, were rounded up and, after what appeared to be routine questioning, shipped off under Justice Department orders to holding centers in Leuppe on the Navaho reservation in Arizona, in Fort Missoula in Montana, and on Sand Island in Honolulu Harbor. There were other special camps on Maui in Ha'iku and on Hawaii—the Big Island—in my own home village of Volcano.

8   Many of these men—it was exclusively the Japanese-American men suspected of ties to Japan who were initially rounded up—did not see their families again for more than four years. Under a suspension of due process that was only after the fact ruled as warranted by military necessity, they were, if only temporarily, "disappeared" in Justice Department prison camps scattered in particularly desolate areas of the United States designated as militarily "safe." These were grim forerunners of the assembly centers and concentration camps for the 120,000 Japanese-American evacuees that were to come later.

9   I am Kubota's eldest grandchild, and I remember him as a lonely habitually silent old man who lived with us in our home near Los Angeles for most of my childhood and adolescence. It was the fifties, and my parents had emigrated from Hawaii to the mainland in the hope of a better life away from the old sugar plantation. After some success, they had sent back for my grandparents who did the work of the household while my mother and father worked their salaried city jobs. My grandmother cooked and sewed, washed our clothes, and knitted in the front room under the light of a huge lamp with a bright three-way bulb. Kubota raised a flower garden, read up on soils and grasses in gardening books, and planted a zoysia lawn in front and a dichondra one in back. He planted a small patch near the rear block wall with green onions, eggplant, white Japanese radishes, and cucumber. While he hoed and spaded the loamless, clayey earth of Los Angeles, he sang particularly plangent songs in Japanese about plum blossoms and bamboo groves.

10   Once, in the mid-sixties, after a dinner during which, as always, he had been silent while he worked away at a meal of fish and rice spiced with dabs of Chinese mustard and catsup thinned with soy sauce, Kubota took his own dishes to the kitchen sink and washed them up. He took a clean jelly jar out of the cupboard—the glass was thick and its shape squatty like an old-fashioned. He reached around to the hutch below where he kept his bourbon. He made himself a drink and retired to the living room where I was expected to join him for "talk story," the Hawaiian idiom for chewing the fat.

11   I was a teenager and, though I was bored listening to stories I'd heard often enough before at holiday dinners, I was dutiful. I took my spot on the couch next to Kubota and heard him out. Usually, he'd tell me about his schooling

in Japan where he learned judo along with mathematics and literature. He'd learned the *soroban* there—the abacus, which was the original pocket calculator of the Far East—and that, along with his strong, judo-trained back, got him his first job in Hawaii. This was the moral. "Study *ha-ahd*," he'd say with pidgin emphasis. "Learn read good. Learn speak da kine *good* English." The message is the familiar one taught to any children of immigrants: success through education. And imitation. But this time, Kubota reached down into his past and told me a different story. I was thirteen by then, and I suppose he thought me ready for it. He told me about Pearl Harbor, how the planes flew in wing after wing of formations over his old house in La'ie in Hawaii, and how, the next day, after Roosevelt had made his famous "Day of Infamy" speech about the treachery of the Japanese, the FBI agents had come to his door and taken him in, hauled him off to Honolulu for questioning, and held him without charge for several days. I thought he was lying. I thought he was making up a kind of horror story to shock me and give his moral that much more starch. But it was true. I asked around. I brought it up during history class in junior high school, and my teacher, after silencing me and stepping me off to the back of the room, told me that it was indeed so. I asked my mother and she said it was true. I asked my schoolmates, who laughed and ridiculed me for being so ignorant. We lived in a Japanese-American community, and the parents of most of my classmates were the *nisei* who had been interned as teenagers all through the war. But there was a strange silence around all of this. There was a hush, as if one were invoking the ill powers of the dead when one brought it up. No one cared to speak about the evacuation and relocation for very long. It wasn't in our history books, though we were studying World War II at the time. It wasn't in the family albums of the people I knew and whom I'd visit staying over weekends with friends. And it wasn't anything that the family talked about or allowed me to keep bringing up either. I was given the facts, told sternly and pointedly that "it was war" and that "nothing could be done." "*Shikatta ga nai*" is the phrase in Japanese, a kind of resolute and determinist pronouncement on how to deal with inexplicable tragedy. I was to know it but not to dwell on it. Japanese Americans were busy trying to forget it ever happened and were having a hard enough time building their new lives after "camp." It was as if we had no history for four years and the relocation was something unspeakable.

12   But Kubota would not let it go. In session after session, for months it seemed, he pounded away at his story. He wanted to tell me the names of the FBI agents. He went over their questions and his responses again and again. He'd tell me how one would try to act friendly toward him, offering him cigarettes while the other, who hounded him with accusations and threats, left the interrogation room. Good cop, bad cop, I thought to myself, already superficially streetwise from stories black classmates told of the Watts riots and from my having watched too many episodes of *Dragnet* and *The Mod Squad*. But Kubota was not interested with my experiences. I was not made yet, and he was determined that his stories be part of my making. He spoke quietly at first, mildly, but once into his narrative and after his drink was down, his voice would rise and quaver with resentment and he'd make his accusations. He gave his testimony to me and I held it at first cautiously in my conscience like it was an heirloom too delicate to expose to strangers and anyone outside of the world Kubota made with his words. "I give you story now," he once said, "and you learn speak good, eh?" It was my job, as the disciple of his preaching I had then become, Ananda to his Buddha, to reassure him with a promise. "You learn speak good like the Dillingham," he'd say another time, referring to the wealthy scion of the grower family who had once run, unsuccessfully, for one of Hawaii's first senatorial seats. Or he'd then invoke a magical name, the name of one of his heroes, a man he thought particularly exemplary and

righteous. "Learn speak dah good Ing-rish like *Mistah Inouye*," Kubota shouted. "He *lick* dah Dillingham even in debate. I saw on *terre-bision* myself." He was remembering the debates before the first senatorial election just before Hawaii was admitted to the Union as its fiftieth state. "You *tell* the story," Kubota would end. And I had my injunction.

13   The town we settled in after the move from Hawaii is called Gardena, the independently incorporated city south of Los Angeles and north of San Pedro harbor. At its northern limit, it borders on Watts and Compton, black towns. To the southwest are Torrance and Redondo Beach, white towns. To the rest of L.A., Gardena is primarily famous for having legalized five-card draw poker after the war. On Vermont Boulevard, its eastern border, there is a dingy little Vegas-like strip of card clubs with huge parking lots and flickering neon signs that spell out "The Rainbow" and "The Horseshoe" in timed sequences of vari-colored lights. The town is only secondarily famous as the largest community of Japanese Americans in the United States outside of Honolulu, Hawaii. When I was in high school there, it seemed to me that every *sansei* kid I knew wanted to be a doctor, an engineer, or a pharmacist. Our fathers were gardeners or electricians or nurserymen or ran small businesses catering to other Japanese Americans. Our mothers worked in civil service for the city or as cashiers for Thrifty Drug. What the kids wanted was a good job, good pay, a fine home, and no troubles. No one wanted to mess with the law—from either side—and no one wanted to mess with language or art. They all talked about getting into the right clubs so that they could go to the right schools. There was a certain kind of sameness, an intensely enforced system of conformity. Style was all. Boys wore moccasin-sewn shoes from Flagg Brothers, black A–1 slacks, and Kensington shirts with high collars. Girls wore their hair up in stiff bouffants solidified in hairspray and knew all the latest dances from the slauson to the funky chicken. We did well in chemistry and in math, no one who was Japanese but me spoke in English class or in history unless called upon, and no one talked about World War II. The day after Robert Kennedy was assassinated, after winning the California Democratic primary, we worked on calculus and elected class coordinators for the prom, featuring the 5th Dimension. We avoided grief. We avoided government. We avoided strong feelings and dangers of any kind. Once punished, we tried to maintain a concerted emotional and social discipline and would not willingly seek to fall out of the narrow margin of protective favor again.

14   But when I was thirteen, in junior high, I'd not understood why it was so difficult for my classmates, those who were themselves Japanese American, to talk about the relocation. They had cringed, too, when I tried to bring it up during our discussions of World War II. I was Hawaiian-born. They were mainland-born. Their parents had been in camp, had been the ones to suffer the complicated experience of having to distance themselves from their own history and all things Japanese in order to make their way back and into the American social and economic mainstream. It was out of this sense of shame and a fear of stigma I was only beginning to understand that the *nisei* had silenced themselves. And, for their children, among whom I grew up, they wanted no heritage, no culture, no contact with a defiled history. I recall the silence very well. The Japanese-American children around me were burdened in a way I was not. Their injunction was silence. Mine was to speak.

15   Away at college, in another protected world in its own way as magical to me as the Hawaii of my childhood, I dreamed about my grandfather. Tired from studying languages, practicing German conjugations or scripting an army's worth of Chinese ideograms on a single sheet of paper, Kubota would come to me as I drifted off into sleep. Or I would walk across the newly mown

ball field in back of my dormitory, cutting through a street-side phalanx of ancient eucalyptus trees on my way to visit friends off campus, and I would think of him, his anger, and his sadness.

16   I don't know myself what makes someone feel that kind of need to have a story they've lived through be deposited somewhere, but I can guess. I think about *The Illiad, The Odyssey, The Peloponnesian Wars* of Thucydides, and a myraid of the works of literature I've studied. A character, almost a *topoi* he occurs so often, is frequently the witness who gives personal testimony about an event the rest of his community cannot even imagine. The sibyl is such a character. And Procne, the maid whose tongue is cut out so that she will not tell that she has been raped by her own brother-in-law, the king of Thebes. There are the dime novels, the epic blockbusters Hollywood makes into miniseries, and then there are the plain, relentless stories of witnesses who have suffered through horrors major and minor that have marked and changed their lives. I myself haven't talked to Holocaust victims. But I've read their survival stories and their stories of witness and been revolted and moved by them. My father-in-law, Al Thiessen, tells me his war stories again and again and I listen. A Mennonite who set aside the strictures of his own church in order to serve, he was a Marine codeman in the Pacific during World War II, in the Signal Corps on Guadalcanal, Morotai, and Bougainville. He was part of the island-hopping maneuver MacArthur had devised to win the war in the Pacific. He saw friends die from bombs which exploded not ten yards away. When he was with the 298th Signal Corps attached to the Thirteenth Air Force, he saw plane after plane come in and crash, just short of the runway, killing their crews, setting the jungle ablaze with oil and gas fires. Emergency wagons would scramble, bouncing over newly bulldozed land men used just the afternoon before for a football game. Every time we go fishing together, whether it's in a McKenzie boat drifting for salmon in Tillamook Bay or taking a lunch break from wading the riffles of a stream in the Cascades, he tells me about what happened to him and the young men in his unit. One was a Jewish boy from Brooklyn. One was a foul-mouthed kid from Kansas. They died. And he *has* to tell me. And I *have* to listen. It's a ritual payment the young owe their elders who have survived. The evacuation and relocation is something like that.

17   Kubota, my grandfather, had been ill with Alzheimer's disease for some time before he died. At the house he'd built on Kamehameha Highway in Hau'ula, a seacoast village just down the road from La'ie where he had his store, he'd wander out from the garage or greenhouse where he'd set up a workbench, and trudge down to the beach or up toward the line of pines he'd planted while employed by the Work Projects Administration during the thirties. Kubota thought he was going fishing. Or he thought he was back at work for Roosevelt, planting pines as a windbreak or soilbreak on the windward flank of the Ko'olau Mountains, emerald monoliths rising out of sea and cane fields from Waialua to Kaneohe. When I visited, my grandmother would send me down to the beach to fetch him. Or I'd run down Kam Highway a quarter mile or so and find him hiding in the cane field by the roadside, counting stalks, measuring circumferences in the claw of his thumb and forefinger. The look on his face was confused or concentrated, I didn't know which. But I guessed he was going fishing again. I'd grab him and walk him back to his house on the highway. My grandmother would shut him in a room.

18   Within a few years, Kubota had a stroke and survived it, then he had another one and was completely debilitated. The family decided to put him in a nursing home in Kahuku, just set back from the highway, within a mile or so of Kahuku Point and the Tanaka Store where he had his first job as a stock boy. He lived there three years, and I visited him once with my aunt. He was

like a potato that had been worn down by cooking. Everything on him—his eyes, his teeth, his legs and torso—seemed like it has been sloughed away. What he had been was mostly gone now and I was looking at the nub of a man. In a wheelchair, he grasped my hands and tugged on them—violently. His hands were still thick and, I believed, strong enough to lift me out of my own seat into his lap. He murmured something in Japanese—he'd long ago ceased to speak any English. My aunt and I cried a little, and we left him.

19   I remember walking out on the black asphalt of the parking lot of the nursing home. It was heat-cracked and eroded already, and grass had veined itself into the interstices. There were coconut trees around, a cane field I could see across the street, and the ocean I knew was pitching a surf just beyond it. The green Ko'olaus came up behind us. Somewhere nearby, alongside the beach, there was an abandoned airfield in the middle of the canes. As a child, I'd come upon it playing one day, and my friends and I kept returning to it, day after day, playing war or sprinting games or coming to fly kites. I recognize it even now when I see it on TV—it's used as a site for action scenes in the detective shows Hollywood always sets in the islands: helicopter chasing the hero racing away in a Ferrari, or gun dealers making a clandestine rendezvous on the abandoned runway. It was the old airfield strafed by Japanese planes the day the major flight attacked Pearl Harbor. It was the airfield the FBI thought my grandfather had targeted in his night fishing and signaling with the long surf poles he'd stuck in the sandy bays near Kahuku Point.

20   Kubota died a short while after I visited him, but not, I thought, without giving me a final message. I was on the mainland, in California studying for Ph.D. exams, when my grandmother called me with the news. It was a relief. He'd suffered from his debilitation a long time and I was grateful he'd gone. I went home for the funeral and gave the eulogy. My grandmother and I took his ashes home in a small, heavy metal box wrapped in a black *furoshiki*, a large silk scarf. She showed me the name the priest had given to him on his death, scripted with a calligraphy brush on a long, narrow talent of plain wood. Buddhist commoners, at death, are given priestly names, received symbolically into the clergy. The idea is that, in their next life, one of scholarship and leisure, they might meditate and attain the enlightenment the religion is aimed at. *"Shaku Sh[[umacron]]chi,"* the ideograms read. It was Kubota's Buddhist name, incorporating characters from his family and given names. It meant "Shining Wisdom of the Law." He died on Pearl Harbor Day, December 7, 1983.

21   After years, after I'd finally come back to live in Hawaii again, only once did I dream of Kubota, my grandfather. It was the same night I'd heard HR442, the redress bill for Japanese Americans, had been signed into law. In my dream that night Kabota was "torching," and he sang a Japanese song, a querulous and wavery folk ballad, as he hung paper lanterns on bamboo poles stuck into the sand in the shallow water of the lagoon behind the reef near Kahuku Point. Then he was at a work table, smoking a hand-rolled cigarette, letting it dangle from his lips Bogart-style as he drew, daintily and skillfully, with a narrow trim brush, ideogram after ideogram on a score of paper lanterns he had hung in a dark shed to dry. He had painted a talismanic mantra onto each lantern, the ideogram for the word "red" in Japanese, a bit of art blended with some superstition, a piece of sympathetic magic appealing to the magenta coloring on the rough skins of the schooling, night-feeding fish we wanted to attract to his baited hooks. He strung them from pole to pole in the dream then, hiking up his khaki worker's pants so his white ankles showed and wading through the shimmering black waters of the sand flats and then the reef. "The moon is leaving, leaving," he sang in Japanese. "Take me deeper in the savage sea." He turned and crouched like an ice racer then, leaning forward so that his

unshaven face almost touched the light film of water. I could see the light stubble of beard like a fine, gray ash covering the lower half of his face. I could see his gold-rimmed spectacles. He held a small wooden boat in his cupped hands and placed it lightly on the sea and pushed it away. One of his lanterns was on it and, written in small neat rows like a sutra scroll, it had been decorated with the silvery names of all our dead.

Narrative Technique Questions

1. Hongo begins with the Pearl Harbor attack and then moves backward in time to talk about earlier periods in Kubota's life. How does this nonchronological positioning of events add to the story?

   Possible answer: It juxtaposes the relatively peaceful life of Japanese

   Americans and how they wove their Japanese cultural background with

   the American lifestyle versus how they were treated during the war—as

   potential traitors and threats to the American way of life.

2. What introductory paragraph lead-in technique does the author use?

   Personal experience, in that Hongo has been told this family story.

3. Explain what the dream sequence in the last paragraph means. How does it relate to the rest of the story?

   Possible answer: The dream sequence suggests that the passing of HR442

   has a symbolic meaning for Japanese Americans. Like Kubota prior to

   the war, Japanese Americans can once again practice their ancestral her-

   itage with pride and honor. The dream also suggests that the dead have

   finally been honored, at least symbolically.

Narrative Writing Opportunities

1. Find out about some other ethnic group that was treated as disloyal during a national conflict, and write an essay about the events and consequences in that time and place.

2. Kubota's story represents that of an entire group. Write an essay about a friend, family member, or acquaintance and the events in that person's life that represent an entire group.

EXAMPLE

BELIEVERS IN SEARCH OF PIERCING INSIGHT

D. James Romero

Body piercing is currently the rage among America's young adults. Most people probably believe that body piercing is predominantly an act of "primitive" people. In this essay, the author pricks those balloons with a quick trip through history while commenting on just what the practice means to people today.

Vocabulary

Before you begin reading, look up the definitions of the following words that appear in the essay. The number in parentheses after each word refers to the paragraph number of the essay.

aesthetic (9)	authenticity (17)	chaste (18)
genitalia (1)	mecca (2)	nomads (1)
paradox (19)	relinquished (16)	septum (7)

Believers in Search of Piercing Insight

1   Here we are at the end of a century of scientific and technological advances so vast they may surpass the rest of humankind's history of knowledge—and cutting edge culture has some of us looking like tribal nomads ready to take some heads: barbells in our eyebrows. Studs in our chins. Hoops in our genitalia.

2   Many in California—this holy mecca of holes—say they pierce their bodies to fully realize their individuality. The body's landscape—for so long adorned with T-shirts-as-billboards, and clothing-labels-as-advertisements—becomes *their* own. Piercing is a return to flesh as fashion—and a revitalized rite of passage.

3   "If someone's under 18, it's normal behavior to get pierced," asserts pop culture expert Stuart Ewen. "It's when I see 50-year-old guys at the gym with nipple rings that I start to worry."

4   Indeed, there isn't much progressive about piercing anymore. Not when your yuppie uncle has enough hoops in his body to set off airport security. And not when state lawmakers are trying to make a note from Mom mandatory for under–18 piercing.

5   So what is a fashion-wary West Coaster to do?

6   Not to worry. There are youth cults busy at work devising new ways to anger parents and subvert the mainstream's black hole.

7   The cutting edge of piercing's "modern primitive" movement can be found at Nomad Body Piercing Studio in San Francisco. The shop specializes in tribal

and ancient piercings such as stretched-out lip holes (piercing the lower lip and stretching the hole), large septum jewelry and low-hanging earlobes.

8   The term "modern primitive" was coined by Fakir Musafar, a '70s pioneer of body modification who now publishes *Body Play* magazine. The phenomenon took off in 1989 with the publication of *Modern Primitives* (Re/Search), a book that featured photos of ancient and modern body art.

9   "It's a rejection of the modern aesthetic," says Nomad owner Kristian White. "Your body is yours. It's the one thing you have to express yourself with."

10   Extreme piercing can be found in underground pagan and gothic cults, too—sets that hang at L.A. nightclubs such as Sin-a-matic, Stigmata and Coven 13. Reports also abound of underground parties where piercing is performed and rites of pain are demonstrated as performance art.

11   Sexual piercings are the rage in L.A. body art, from the male Prince Albert (apparently, the old chap had a genital piercing—in Victorian times, no less) to the unisex nipple ring. *Body Modification E-Zine,* an online magazine, surveyed readers and found that half had their nipples pierced.

12   "It's a freaky subculture of people," says West Hollywood piercer Jennifer "Jeff" Middleton, who has square chrome hair, several piercings in her ears and one in her nose.

13   Earlier in the day, she was putting on latex gloves and preparing sterile instruments in a bright, clean second-floor room at the Gauntlet in West Hollywood. Customer Brian Lee had hoops in both ears and a tattoo on his back, so he felt the need to distinguish himself—with a pierced brow. "You want to show off what you're about," he said.

14   It took only about five minutes for Middleton to clean Lee's right eyebrow, mark it, pinch it with forceps and poke an ultra-sharp, inch-long needle through his skin: $30 please. Lee didn't flinch. Middleton explained the eight weeks of tedious healing and cleaning, but Lee just looked in the mirror and smiled when he saw the "barbell" protruding from his head.

15   "It does get trendy," said Lee, a 22-year-old club deejay. "But there will always be a new body to be pierced."

16   Culture watchers say there is something deeper going on here. The Nomad studio's White says organized religion has relinquished its grip on the minds and bodies of youth so that they may go back to pre-Christian rituals. And professor Ewen, chair of media studies at Hunter College in New York, says it is indeed a rejection of the neat, sleek, modern fashion aesthetic.

17   "This was a culture that was sold on the idea of progress since the turn of the century—clean lines, industrial aesthetic, mass-produced clothes," he says. "There's a sense of meaninglessness in this, so there's a search for meaning—a belief that other ways of life might have more authenticity than ours."

18   It is said that Roman warriors pierced body parts to show how tough they were, while Victorian women, otherwise notoriously chaste, pierced their nipples in acts of sensuality. Body modification has also been a staple of non-Western cultures for thousands of years.

19   But today, as teens and twenty-somethings try to stand out, they face the paradox of modern subculture: More people want it, more people want to make money off it, and rebellion becomes a uniform instead of a torch of individuality.

20   "Body art was an embrace against the packaged self," Ewen says. "Yet any attempt to marginalize one's self provides new grist for the style industries.

21   "The only way to battle it is to find an ideal and stick with it. At that point, you kill off the consumption process. My only solution is to buy five pairs of pants and five sweaters and never wear anything else."

22   Now that's a radical concept.

Example Technique Questions

1. Why do people get pierced, according to the author?

   For a variety of reasons: to realize their individuality, as a rite of passage, to anger parents and subvert the mainstream society, and to achieve sexual fulfillment.

2. A "nomad" is a wandering person, while a "studio" is a place. Why is "Nomad" an appropriate name for the piercing studio described in the essay?

   Possible answer: The term "nomad" usually describes a primitive, tribal people who do not stay in one place too long. The people getting body piercings are outside the mainstream, tend to move from job to job and place to place. In many ways, they resemble the nomads in other cultures.

3. What is paradoxical about piercing becoming a mainstream activity, instead of the mark of individuality that it was first intended to be?

   According to Romero, "more and more people want to do it, more people want to make money off it, and rebellion becomes a uniform instead of a torch of individuality" (19).

Example Writing Opportunities

1. If you have body piercings, write an example essay about why you decided to add to your personal appearance in this manner. If you haven't body pierced, interview some people who have, and write an essay giving specific examples of the kinds of piercings each person has had done and how that personifies something about their identity.

2. The author points out that body piercing is yet another attempt by young people to anger their parents and other older people. Write an essay opposing Romero's position by using other examples of why young people body pierce.

THE BAFFLING QUESTION

Bill Cosby

> Parents must go through a multitude of joys and difficulties raising children. In this essay, the great comedian uses humor to reflect on the challenges inherent in parenthood. Look for irony—it's one of the main techniques Cosby uses to set the tone of the essay.

Vocabulary

Before you begin reading, look up the definitions of the following words that appear in the essay. The number in parentheses after each word refers to the paragraph number of the essay.

batch (21)   brunch (21)   coping (1)

intimate (1)   paternal (15)   precious (21)

savored (1)

The Baffling Question

1   So you've decided to have a child. You've decided to give up quiet evenings with good books and lazy weekends with good music, intimate meals during which you finish whole sentences, sweet private times when you've savored the thought that just the two of you and your love are all you will ever need. You've decided to turn your sofas into trampolines and to abandon the joys of leisurely contemplating reproductions of great art for the joys of frantically coping with reproductions of yourselves.

2   Why?

3   Poets have said the reason to have children is to give yourself immortality; and I must admit I did ask God to give me a son because I wanted someone to carry on the family name. Well, God did just that and I now confess that there have been times when I've told my son not to reveal who he is.

4   "You make up a name," I've said. "Just don't tell anybody who you are."

5   Immortality? Now that I have had five children, my only hope is that they all are out of the house before I die.

6   No, immortality was not the reason why my wife and I produced these beloved sources of dirty laundry and ceaseless noise. And we also did not have them because we thought it would be fun to see one of them sit in a chair and stick out his leg so that another one of them running by was launched like Explorer I. After which I said to the child who was the launching pad, "Why did you do that?"

7   "Do what?" he replied.

8   "Stick out your leg."

9   "Dad, I didn't know my leg was going out. My leg, it does that a lot."

10   If you cannot function in a world where things like this are said, then you better forget about raising children and go for daffodils.

11   My wife and I also did not have children so they could yell at each other all over the house, moving me to say, "What's the problem?"

12   "She's waving her foot in my room," my daughter replied.

13   "And something like that *bothers* you?"

14   "Yes, I don't *want* her foot in my room."

15   "Well," I said, dipping into my storehouse of paternal wisdom, "why don't you just close the door?"

16   "Then I can't see what she's doing!"

17   Furthermore, we did not have the children because we thought it would be rewarding to watch them do things that should be studied by the Menninger Clinic.

18   "Okay," I said to all five one day, "go get into the car."

19   All five then ran to the same door, grabbed the same handle, and spent the next few minutes beating each other up. Not one of them had the intelligence to say, "Hey, *look.* There are three more doors." The dog, however, was already inside.

20   And we did not have the children to help my wife develop new lines for her face or because she had always had a desire to talk out loud to herself: "Don't tell *me* you're *not* going to do something when I tell you to move!" And we didn't have children so I could always be saying to someone, "Where's my change?"

21   Like so many young couples, my wife and I simply were unable to project. In restaurants we did not see the small children who were casting their bread on the water in the glasses the waiter had brought; and we did not see the mother who was fasting because she was both cutting the food for one child while pulling another from the floor to a chair that he would use for slipping to the floor again. And we did not project beyond those lovely Saturdays of buying precious little things after leisurely brunches together. We did not see that *other* precious little things would be coming along to destroy the first batch.

Example Technique Questions

1. What is the "baffling question" referred to in the title of the essay? What is the main point of the essay?

> **Why do people want to have children and, thereby, destroy "quiet**
>
> **evenings with good books and lazy weekends with good music, intimate**
>
> **meals during which you finish whole sentences, sweet private times**
>
> **when you've savored the thought that just the two of you and your love**
>
> **are all you will ever need" (1).**
>
> **Main point: Most people don't pay much attention to other people's children,**
>
> **so they don't anticipate the problems that having children might pose for**
>
> **their marriage.**

2. As a comedian, Cosby is expected to use humor. Point out some examples of humor in the essay, and explain how they support the overall tone of the essay.

> **Answers will vary, but all the incidents described in paragraphs 3–20 are**
>
> **humorous. The humor is not cruel or sarcastic. Rather, it is affectionate,**
>
> **and it does not describe serious problems softened by humor. Quite the**

contrary. It pokes gently at events that he remembers with fondness and

love.

3. According to Cosby, how do children change the life of a married couple? Point out specific examples.

Paragraphs 1 and 21 are packed with specific examples.

Example Writing Opportunities

1. Write an essay about your own or your parents' joys and difficulties raising children. Use specific examples to support the topic in each paragraph.

2. Your Childhood Education 101 instructor asks you to write an essay explaining the most effective techniques for raising a child. This might include subtopics such as toilet training, night crying, disciplining, or reading. Use specific examples to support your points.

CLASSIFICATION

SINGLE WHITE FEMALE

Viet D. Dinh

> Relationships are difficult enough without opposition from parents and friends because a partner is a different race. In this essay, Dinh expresses his dismay that race is often still an objection where marriage is concerned.

Vocabulary

Before you begin reading, look up the definitions of the following words that appear in the essay. The number in parentheses after each word refers to the paragraph number of the essay.

absolve (23)	bequeath (21)	conflagration (23)
innocuous (17)	opprobrium (16)	proxy (18)
talisman (21)	surreptitiously (12)	

Single White Female

1. Mary and I met in my senior year of high school at a weekend speech and debate tournament in northern California. By chance, I stopped at an afternoon storytelling competition and listened to her recite passages from *Jonathan*

Livingston Seagull. We fell in love—quickly, foolishly. Each day after watching each other compete, we'd sneak into San Francisco for dinner in Chinatown (my choice) or Ghiradelli Square (hers) and a stroll through North Beach to Coit Tower.

2   About a week later, Mary's mother asked about her new boyfriend on the drive to school.

3   "I hear you've met a new boy."

4   "Yes."

5   "Is he Catholic?"

6   "Yes."

7   "College?"

8   "Yes, he's going to Harvard."

9   Her mother smiled, "Well, good. What's his name?"

10   "Viet," Mary answered, wittily adding a pronunciation tip, "as in Vietnam."

11   "I'm sorry, Mary, tell him you can't see him anymore."

12   That was the end. I saw Mary only a few times after she told me this story, mostly to talk about what happened. She wondered why we didn't continue surreptitiously; I tried to understand what motivated her mother's response. Mary offered (inexplicably) that her mother was from Indiana, and argued that she really was not racist, that if I were to apply for a job at her real estate office she probably would hire me.

13   I met Mary's mother once, years later. I worked as a real estate developer and wanted to buy some land in the area. More as an excuse than out of necessity, I called up to schedule a tour of her listings. She never placed me, and after an hour in her car, I began to accept that Mary was right. Her mother was not a racist—at least not in the sense that I had imagined in high school. She was comfortable with me. Nothing in her manner betrayed nervousness or artificial cordiality.

14   That revelation only made my question harder to answer. What motivates an otherwise intelligent person to inflict such pain on such a seemingly irrational basis? She is not racist, yet cannot tolerate her daughter dating an Asian. Why is love, or sex, so special?

15   The question presents itself frequently. Open any magazine to the personal ads and one finds exposed on every page the impulse that Mary's mother displayed. Single White Female seeking same; Divorced Black Male, professional, seeking compatible companion; Gay White Male seeking mate; Asian Woman seeking a gentleman. The open invitation to judge based on race extends shamelessly across all social barriers, from *New York Review of Books* intellectuals to *Village Voice* bohemians to *Washingtonian* power brokers.

16   Such open reliance on racial qualifications is hard to reconcile with moral and social opprobrium accorded to racism and the suspicion of racial classifications in the post–Civil Rights era. In most cases, race cannot legally be a factor in hiring or firing, in buying or selling, in admission or rejection. Even an acknowledgment that one's friends or associates are only of a particular race gives pause and sometimes has derailed otherwise promising public careers. Yet romantic race-typing persists, explicitly and pervasively, not noticed and hardly questioned.

17   Maybe the designation of one's race in a personal ad is innocuous. The ad, after all, attempts to convey a full (maybe even inflated) picture of its owner, and race is simply part of the picture, like a glimpse of someone walking down the street or eating in a restaurant. But to offer race as part of that verbal picture is to recognize, and approve, that race matters when one judges a stranger for compatibility and attraction. Why?

18   For one thing, the racial designation may be shorthand for a number of cultural and ethnic traits that cannot be fully captured in a short ad or a quick

glimpse. But to accept race as proxy for personal characteristics is to succumb to exactly the impulse that one finds reprehensible in racism: the blind acceptance of generalized biases without regard to individual qualities. It is not justifiable (both factually and morally) to assume that a black man likes jazz or that an Asian woman is petite any more than to say that black men are muggers or Asian women are submissive.

19 Moreover, race is just one arbitrary level of generalization. If it is a "package" of personal characteristics that one is looking for, that mix need not be determined by race. Asian Male describes very little of who I am, the differences among Asian cultures being large. Southeast Asian is closer, but then why not Vietnamese, or South Vietnamese? Better yet, why not simply Male?

20 When I told my sister that I don't discriminate in my romantic decisions, she replied, "Maybe you're just not very discriminating." Race-typing, she argued, flows from the natural desire to preserve one's culture in a pluralistic society. She feared that in searching for an American, I would stop being Vietnamese.

21 But this argument assumes that culture is something timeless, a never-changing talisman that has been begotten and bequeathed and is to be passed on forever. That is hardly the case. Any immigrant who returns to his native country can readily observe the chasm that only a few years' absence has forged between him and the culture that he had nostalgically and unrequitedly loved. People change, traditions evolve, and institutions adapt. To assume that one's "culture" could remain unchanged is to ignore that what defines culture is simply a dynamic and complex process of human and natural interaction.

22 I do not deny that I am Vietnamese, that I have a distinct cultural heritage in which to take pride. It is precisely that pride which makes me willing to share my culture, not to lock it away in a tower of racial chastity. Whatever is lost in authenticity I hope is gained doubly in wider acceptance and deeper appreciation.

23 Perhaps romantic race-typing can be absolved as a Darwinian strategy to perpetuate one's genetic longevity. A friend confesses to having felt a tinge of alarm when her then-fiancé casually remarked that their children would look like him, since his Jamaican genes would dominate her recessive white ones. Such a reaction, natural as it may be, is only valid if the animating desire for racial purity is itself justifiable. At another time or in a different place, racial homogeneity may have been an effective means of preservation and survival. But in America's multiracial 1990s, where the danger is not of racial extinction but of ethnic conflagration, racial husbandry is as unwise as it is indefensible.

24 After my relationship with a Vietnamese woman ended when we could find little in common, I recently began seeing someone new, a white woman. Often when we walk hand in hand down Capitol Hill or through the Boston Common, we smile at the people who hold us in their stares. I think I will stop wondering about Mary's mother when I can be confident that the heads that turn do so because of my girlfriend's beauty or our apparent happiness together.

Classification Technique Questions

1. The author states that Mary's mother "was not a racist—at least not in the sense that I had imagined." How does he classify her as a racist?

She seems to be comfortable and accepting of him in a business situation.

It is in the marriage arena with her daughter that she seems to have a

racist attitude.

2. According to the author, in what areas of life is it no longer acceptable to use race as an issue?

Employment, business practices, college admissions, and holding pub-

lic office.

3. How does his sister defend choosing a partner using discriminatory practices?

She argues that race-typing "flows from the natural desire to preserve

one's culture in a pluralistic society." She fears that Vietnamese who

marry Americans will lose their cultural identity (20).

Classification Writing Opportunities

1. Write an essay in which you classify a group of people by their religious beliefs.

2. Write an essay in which you classify people by how they dress, or by the food they eat.

CONFESSIONS OF AN EX-SMOKER

Franklin Zimring

Addiction is an increasing problem in America. This includes addiction to heroin, sugar, caffeine, sex, food, and alcohol. But for many people, the addiction to nicotine seems harder to break than almost any other. Some heroin addicts have stated that it was easier for them to give up heroin than it was for them to stop smoking.

Vocabulary
Before you begin reading, look up the definitions of the following words that appear in the essay. The number in parentheses after each word refers to the paragraph number of the essay.

anecdotal (4)	brimstone (2)	nil (5)
excoriate (10)	fervor (3)	tenuous (3)
proselytizing (7)	recidivist (3)	watershed (1)
unmitigating (6)	vitriolic (4)	
zealots (1)	cessation (1)	

Confessions of an Ex-Smoker

1   Americans can be divided into three groups—smokers, nonsmokers and that expanding pack of us who have quit. Those who have never smoked don't know what they're missing, but former smokers, ex-smokers, reformed smokers can never forget. We are veterans of a personal war, linked by that watershed experience of ceasing to smoke and by the temptation to have just one more cigarette. For almost all of us ex-smokers, smoking continues to play an important part in our lives. And now that it is being restricted in restaurants around the country and will be banned in almost all indoor public places in New York State starting next month, it is vital that everyone understand the different emotional states cessation of smoking can cause. I have observed four of them; and in the interest of science I have classified them as those of the zealot, the evangelist, the elect and the serene. Each day, each category gains new recruits.

2   Not all antitobacco zealots are former smokers, but a substantial number of fire-and-brimstone opponents do come from the ranks of the reformed. Zealots believe that those who continue to smoke are degenerates who deserve scorn not pity and the penalties that will deter offensive behavior in public as well. Relations between these people and those who continue to smoke are strained.

3   One explanation for the zealot's fervor in seeking to outlaw tobacco consumption is his own tenuous hold on abstaining from smoking. But I think part of the emotional force arises from sheer envy as he watches and identifies with each lung-filling puff. By making smoking in public a crime, the zealot seeks reassurance that he will not revert to bad habits; give him strong social penalties and he won't become a recidivist.

4   No systematic survey has been done yet, but anecdotal evidence suggests that a disproportionate number of doctors who have quit smoking can be found among the fanatics. Just as the most enthusiastic revolutionary tends to make the most enthusiastic counterrevolutionary, many of today's vitriolic zealots include those who had been deeply committed to tobacco habits.

5   By contrast, the antismoking evangelist does not condemn smokers. Unlike the zealot, he regards smoking as an easily curable condition, as a social disease, and not a sin. The evangelist spends an enormous amount of time seeking and preaching to the unconverted. He argues that kicking the habit is not *that* difficult. After all, *he* did it; moreover, as he describes it, the benefits of quitting are beyond measure and the disadvantages are nil.

6   The hallmark of the evangelist is his insistence that he never misses tobacco. Though he is less hostile to smokers than the zealot, he is resented more. Friends and loved ones who have been the targets of his preachments frequently greet the resumption of smoking by the evangelist as an occasion for unmitigated glee.

7   Among former smokers, the distinctions between the evangelist and the elect are much the same as the differences between proselytizing and non-proselytizing religious sects. While the evangelists preach the ease and desirability of abstinence, the elect do not attempt to convert their friends. They think that virtue is its own reward and subscribe to the Puritan theory of predestination. Since they have proved themselves capable of abstaining from tobacco, they are therefore different from friends and relatives who continue to smoke. They feel superior, secure that their salvation was foreordained. These ex-smokers rarely give personal testimony on their conversion. They rarely speak about their tobacco habits, while evangelists talk about little else. Of course, active smokers find such blue-nosed behavior far less offensive than that

of the evangelist or the zealot, yet they resent the elect simply because they are smug. Their air of self-satisfaction rarely escapes the notice of those lighting up. For active smokers, life with a member of the ex-smoking elect is less stormy than with a zealot or evangelist, but it is subtly oppressive nonetheless.

8   I have labeled my final category of former smokers the serene. This classification is meant to encourage those who find the other psychic styles of ex-smokers disagreeable. Serenity is quieter than zealotry and evangelism, and those who qualify are not as self-righteous as the elect. The serene ex-smoker accepts himself and also accepts those around him who continue to smoke. This kind of serenity does not come easily nor does it seem to be an immediate option for those who have stopped. Rather it is a goal, an end stage in a process of development during which some former smokers progress through one or more of the less-than-positive psychological points en route. For former smokers, serenity is thus a positive possibility that exists at the end of the rainbow. But all former smokers cannot reach that promised land.

9   What is it that permits some former smokers to become serene? I think the key is self-acceptance and gratitude. The fully mature former smoker knows he has the soul of an addict and is grateful for the knowledge. He may sit up front in an airplane, but he knows he belongs in the smoking section in back. He doesn't regret that he quit smoking, nor any of his previous adventures with tobacco. As a former smoker, he is grateful for the experience and memory of craving a cigarette.

10   Serenity comes from accepting the lessons of one's life. And ex-smokers who have reached this point in their world view have much to be grateful for. They have learned about the potential and limits of change. In becoming the right kind of former smoker, they developed a healthy sense of self. This former smoker, for one, believes that it is better to crave (one hopes only occasionally) and not to smoke than never to have craved at all. And by accepting that fact, the reformed smoker does not need to excoriate, envy or disassociate himself from those who continue to smoke.

Classification Technique Questions

1. Into what classifications does the author divide all Americans?

Smokers, nonsmokers, and those that have quit.

2. Into what classifications does the author divide ex-smokers, and how does the author characterize each type?

The zealot, the evangelist, the elect, and the serene. Zealots believe that

smokers are degenerates; evangelists do not condemn smokers, but

believe smoking is a curable condition; elects do not attempt to convert

smokers, and they feel superior to smokers; the serene accept themselves

and all others for who they are, without judgment.

3. What is the essay's purpose, and how does classification help achieve the purpose?

> **Possible answer: The essay's purpose is to shed light on the various categories of ex-smokers and their feelings about those who continue to smoke. He seems to be making a statement that striving to be a "serene" ex-smoker will probably help ex-smokers remain ex-smokers and, at the same time, give hope to smokers and other ex-smokers that there is the possibility of inner peace somewhere in the difficult process of quitting smoking.**

Classification Writing Opportunities

1. Write an essay about things that you are addicted to. Whether you write about having a single addiction or multiple addictions, try to classify them by type, i.e., food, drug, behavior, etc. The classification should help identify, explain, and clarify the point you are trying to make about the addiction.

2. Write an essay explaining the consequences that can happen because of an addiction. Classify the consequences into categories (physical, psychological, social, etc.) to help you explain the points you make about the consequences.

PROCESS

COMING OUT: A PROCESS OF DILEMMA

Sean T. Wherley

> Deciding to share a deep, personal secret even with the closest of friends can be a nerve-testing and soul-searching endeavor. But sharing such a secret with the whole world can be a life-changing action with long-term consequences. In this essay, the author explains that the process of "coming out" never really ends.

Vocabulary
Before you begin reading, look up the definitions of the following words that appear in the essay. The number in parentheses after each word refers to the paragraph number of the essay.

advocate (1)	badger (16)	deplorable (3)
forge (2)	pinnacle (6)	rambunctious (11)
transgender (2)		

Coming Out: A Process of Dilemma

1   My sister Colleen is a college graduate and an aspiring liberal who needs time to understand the complexities of my being a gay man. I do not intend to single out Colleen because she is one of my strongest advocates. She regularly accompanies me to a family support group for lesbians and gay men, and willingly discusses issues related to my being a minority. But her attitude is probably reflective of many people who choose not to get too involved. For example, she compared my "coming out" process to a wedding. She noted the similarities of exhaustive planning, accommodating people's feelings, and recovering from the draining day. While I do appreciate comparing the "celebratory" aspect of both events, coming out is clearly no wedding.

2   Therefore, with Colleen's perspective as a basis, I want to clarify the coming out process. Coming out is the phrase used to encourage gay, lesbian, bisexual, and transgender people to announce their identity to friends, family members, co-workers, classmates, and neighbors. People are encouraged to come out in order to increase their visibility in the larger community, and to forge stronger relationships with those closest to them. To highlight this process, National Coming Out Day is celebrated each October 11 to commemorate the first Washington, DC, march for gay and lesbian rights in 1987.

3   With that in mind, let us return to the comparison of a wedding and coming out. Although a wedding is filled with happiness, it is deplorable to compare it to the coming out process. A wedding lasts one day. It usually includes a gathering of friends and family to mark the momentous occasion. Support of the union is rarely solicited and often overflowing. Guests are eager to attend and lavish the couple with gifts. Sometimes the event entails months of planning to determine a site, date, and accessories. Thousands of dollars are spent on invitations, meals, and entertainment. After the day ends, the couple begins life as a legally recognized couple. A smattering of conversation will follow the gala-filled day, but for the most part the day and its related discussion have concluded.

4   Meanwhile, coming out as a gay man also entails months of planning. Dilemmas include: "Do I tell both parents simultaneously? Where should I tell them? Dare I consider coming out to co-workers?"

5   Some money may be spent returning to hometowns to tell parents or friends, but otherwise the costs of coming out are psychological, not financial.

6   After those examples, however, the similarities between a wedding and coming out end. Where weddings last one day, the process of coming out never ends. The coming out pinnacle of the year may occur on National Coming Out Day, but it does not serve as the only time to come out. As much as I wish that one day could suffice in announcing my sexual orientation to everyone, that is far from a reality. National Coming Out Day does not account for the other 364 days and the events endured during that time. It is during those other 364 days that the joys of coming out are experienced. Situations continuously arise where I can choose to withhold my identity or speak proudly.

7   As a student, I am faced with coming out each quarter to classmates and professors. This does not mean announcing to them, "I'm gay." Rather, it means incorporating gay issues into class discussions or making reference to my group involvement and my partner (as straight students constantly do).

8   The workplace is another environment I must confront. As a prospective employee, I contemplate asking if the company's nondiscrimination policy includes sexual orientation, or if the benefits package is extended to same-sex domestic partners. After being hired, I could come out one day, but new employees are always arriving, thus rendering some unaware of my identity.

9 As a son and brother, I can tell my parents and siblings that I am gay, but what about grandparents, aunts, uncles, and cousins? I cannot tell them all on one day; that is impossible with the geographic distance separating us. And once the family members know I am gay, will they be accepting if I bring my partner to family gatherings?

10 Thankfully, my family was more supportive than most families when I came out; however, this is not the norm. Gay, lesbian, bisexual, and transgender people incessantly worry that parents will reject them upon learning of their identity, and sadly, some parents do.

11 In addition to the major settings of life (school, work, and family), coming out occurs in fleeting and casual situations. For example, last October I bought some flowers for my then-boyfriend, whom I had been dating for one month. While grasping the flowers and waiting to board the bus to his house, four rambunctious teenagers approached me. One of the teenagers turned to comment on my assortment of flowers.

12 "Your flowers are pretty, sir," he said.

13 "Thank you," I replied.

14 "Are they for your mom?" he asked.

15 "No," I said, growing restless and craning my neck for the next bus.

16 He continued badgering: "Are they for your girlfriend?"

17 My body immediately froze and I began sweating. I debated the risk of telling him the truth and possibly being harassed after we boarded the bus together.

18 "Yeah," I said in a whisper. "They're for my girlfriend."

19 Now, if coming out was a one-time event (like a wedding), I would have had no qualms about telling the boy who the recipient of my flowers was. That is a circumstance, however, enjoyed only in dreams. And if coming out was a celebration (like a wedding), my family members would be delighted that I am at peace with myself. They would insist upon telling friends and family, and holding a party.

20 That, too, however, is a dream, as my parents were outraged that I told my aunt before them.

Process Technique Questions

1. What are the difficulties in the coming out process?

Possible answer: The process of coming out never ends; gays have to raise gay issues in the classroom; gays have to find out if a potential employer's nondiscrimination policy includes gays, and whether the company's insurance extends to a gay's partner; it is often a difficult decision whether to tell aunts, uncles, cousins, nieces, and nephews.

2. The author's sister compares the coming out process to a wedding, but the author disagrees. What are the three reasons he suggests the analogy isn't a good one?

A wedding lasts one day, while coming out lasts forever; for a wedding, guests are eager to attend, and they lavish the couple with gifts—not so

at a coming out event; wedded couples are recognized legally, while gay

partners are not.

3. The writer lied about the flowers when accosted by the four teenagers. How do you think the encounter would have gone had he given a truthful answer?

Answers will vary, but the inference is that he may have been beaten or

roughed up had he told the truth.

Process Writing Opportunities

1. Wherley doesn't think the process of coming out and the wedding process have much in common. Write an essay describing a process that does have similarities to coming out.

2. Write an essay about something you think would be difficult to tell your parents. Describe the process you would use to make the secret known.

MANAGING YOUR TIME

Edwin Bliss

> The lack of good time-management skills probably is at the heart of most failures and jobs not well done. In this essay, the author lays out the steps necessary for using your time more effectively.

Vocabulary
Before you begin reading, look up the definitions of the following words that appear in the essay. The number in parentheses after each word refers to the paragraph number of the essay.

allocate (3)	chaotic (8)	constituent (1)
delegate (15)	differentiate (17)	invariably (4)
irretrievably (19)	isometric (5)	neurotic (9)
omission (9)	piecemeal (4)	procrastinate (11)

Managing Your Time

1   I first became interested in the effective use of time when I was an assistant to a U.S. Senator. Members of Congress are faced with urgent and conflicting demands on their time—for committee work, floor votes, speeches, interviews, briefings, correspondence, investigations, constituents' problems,

and the need to be informed on a wide range of subjects. The more successful Congressmen develop techniques for getting maximum benefit from minimum investments of time. If they don't, they don't return.

2   Realizing that I was not one of those who use time effectively, I began to apply in my own life some of the techniques I had observed. Here are ten I have found most helpful.

Plan.

3   You need a game plan for your day. Otherwise, you'll allocate your time according to whatever happens to land on your desk. And you will find your-self making the fatal mistake of dealing primarily with problems rather than opportunities. Start each day by making a general schedule, with particular emphasis on the two or three major things you would like to accomplish—including things that will achieve long-term goals. Remember, studies prove what common sense tells us: The more time we spend planning a project, the less total time is required for it. Don't let today's busywork crowd planning-time out of your schedule.

Concentrate.

4   Of all the principles of time management, none is more basic than con-centration. People who have serious time-management problems invariably are trying to do too many things at once. The amount of time spent on a pro-ject is not what counts: It's the amount of *uninterrupted* time. Few problems can resist an all-out attack; few can be solved piecemeal.

Take Breaks.

5   To work for longer periods without taking a break is not an effective use of time. Energy decreases, boredom sets in, and physical stress and tension accumulate. Switching for a few minutes from a mental task to something physical—isometric exercises, walking around the office, even changing from a sitting position to a standing position for a while—can provide relief.

6   Merely resting, however, is often the best course, and you should not think of a "rest" break as poor use of time. Not only will being refreshed increase your efficiency, but relieving tension will benefit your health. Anything that contributes to health is good time management.

Avoid Clutter.

7   Some people have a constant swirl of papers on their desks and assume that somehow the most important matters will float to the top. In most cases, however, clutter hinders concentration and can create tension and frustra-tion—a feeling of being "snowed under."

8   Whenever you find your desk becoming chaotic, take time out to reorga-nize. Go through all your papers (making generous use of the wastebasket) and divide them into categories: (1) Immediate action, (2) Low priority, (3) Pending, (4) Reading material. Put the highest priority item from your first pile in the center of your desk, then put everything else out of sight. Remember, you can think of only one thing at a time, and you can work on only one task at a time, so focus all your attention on the most important one. A final point: Clearing the desk completely, or at least organizing it, each evening should be standard practice. It gets the next day off to a good start.

Don't Be a Perfectionist.

9   There is a difference between striving for excellence and striving for per-fection. The first is attainable, gratifying and healthy. The second is often unat-tainable, frustrating and neurotic. It's also a terrible waste of time. The stenographer who retypes a lengthy letter because of a trivial error, or the boss who demands such retyping, might profit from examining the Declaration of

Independence. When the inscriber of that document made two errors of omission, he inserted the missing letters between the lines. If this is acceptable in the document that gave birth to American freedom, surely it would be acceptable in a letter that will be briefly glanced at en route to someone's file cabinet or wastebasket.

Don't Be Afraid to Say No.

10   Of all the time-saving techniques ever developed, perhaps the most effective is frequent use of the word *no*. Learn to decline, tactfully but firmly, every request that does not contribute to your goals. If you point out that your motivation is not to get out of work but to save your time to do a better job on the really important things, you'll have a good chance of avoiding unproductive tasks. Remember, many people who worry about offending others wind up living according to other people's priorities.

Don't Procrastinate.

11   Procrastination is usually a deeply rooted habit. But we can change our habits provided we use the right system. William James, the father of American psychology, discussed such a system in his famous *Principles of Psychology,* published in 1890. It works as follows:

1. Decide to start changing as soon as you finish reading this article, while you are motivated. Taking that first step promptly is important.

2. Don't try to do too much too quickly. Just force yourself right now to do one thing you have been putting off. Then, beginning tomorrow morning, start each day by doing the most unpleasant thing on your schedule. Often it will be a small matter: an overdue apology; a confrontation with a fellow worker; an annoying chore you know you should tackle. Whatever it is, do it before you begin your usual morning routine. This simple procedure can well set the tone for your day. You will get a feeling of exhilaration from knowing that although the day is only 15 minutes old, you have already accomplished the most unpleasant thing you have to do all day.

12   There is one caution: Do not permit any exceptions. William James compared it to rolling up a ball of string; a single slip can undo more than many turns can wind up. Be tough with yourself, for the first few minutes of each day, for the next two weeks, and I promise you a new habit of priceless value.

Apply Radical Surgery.

13   Time-wasting activities are like cancers. They drain off vitality and have a tendency to grow. The only cure is radical surgery. If you are wasting your time in activities that bore you, divert you from your real goals, and sap your energy, cut them out, once and for all.

14   The principle applies to personal habits, routines, and activities as much as to ones associated with your work. Check your appointment calendar, your extracurricular activities, your reading list, your television viewing habits, and ax everything that doesn't give you a feeling of accomplishment or satisfaction.

Delegate.

15   An early example of failure to delegate is found in the Bible. Moses, having led his people out of Egypt, was so impressed with his own knowledge and authority that he insisted on ruling personally on every controversy that arose in Israel. His wise father-in-law, Jethro, recognizing that this was poor use of a leader's time, recommended a two-phase approach: First, educate the people concerning the laws; second, select capable leaders and give them full authority over routine matters, freeing Moses to concentrate on major decisions. The advice is still sound.

16   You don't have to be a national leader or a corporate executive to delegate, either. Parents who don't delegate household chores are doing a disservice to themselves and their children. Running a Boy Scout troop can be as time-consuming as running General Motors if you try to do everything yourself. One caution: Giving subordinates jobs that neither you nor anyone else wants to do isn't delegating, it's assigning. Learn to delegate the challenging and rewarding tasks, along with sufficient authority to make necessary decisions. It can help to free your time.

Don't Be a "Workaholic."

17   Most successful executives I know work long hours, but they don't let work interfere with the really important things in life, such as friends, family and fly fishing. This differentiates them from the workaholic who becomes addicted to work just as people become addicted to alcohol. Symptoms of work addiction include refusal to take a vacation, inability to put the office out of your mind on weekends, a bulging briefcase, and a spouse, son or daughter who is practically a stranger.

18   Counseling can help people cope with such problems. But for starters, do a bit of self-counseling. Ask yourself whether the midnight oil you are burning is adversely affecting your health. Ask where your family comes in your list of priorities, whether you are giving enough of yourself to your children and spouse, and whether you are deceiving yourself by pretending that the sacrifices you are making are really for them.

19   Above all else, good time management involves an awareness that today is all we ever have to work with. The past is irretrievably gone, the future is only a concept. British art critic John Ruskin had the word "TODAY" carved into a small marble block that he kept on his desk as a constant reminder to "Do It Now." But my favorite quotation is by an anonymous philosopher:

> Yesterday is a canceled check.
> Tomorrow is a promissory note.
> Today is ready cash. Use it!

Process Technique Questions

1. In your own words, explain the ten-step process for achieving effective time-management skills. Limit each explanation to no more than two sentences.

Answers will vary.

_____

_____

_____

2. At the end of the essay, the author gives his favorite quotation. Explain how the quotation supports his point about time-management.

Possible answer: The focus of time-management is on what you can

accomplish easily and effectively in the present, not the past or the future.

_____

_____

_____

3. In your opinion, which of the steps is the most important? Explain.

Answers will vary.

_____

_____

_____

_____

Process Writing Opportunities

1. Since you are a college student, write an essay describing a process that would help you become a more effective student.

2. Write a humorous essay describing the steps in a process designed to make you a terrible student.

COMPARE AND CONTRAST

A BATTLE OF CULTURES

K. Connie Kang

America is a multicultural nation, yet people from varying backgrounds still find it hard to communicate with each other even though we speak a common language. In this essay, Kang suggest that for a multicultural nation to work, we need "cultural insight."

Vocabulary

Before you begin reading, look up the definitions of the following words that appear in the essay. The number in parentheses after each word refers to the paragraph number of the essay.

bicultural (3)	bilingual (3)	brusque (4)
chided (10)	ethnic (5)	ethos (16)
gregarious (9)	inclination (10)	orientation (15)
prestigious (12)	retort (10)	sporadic (4)
volatile (1)		

A Battle of Cultures

1   A volatile inner-city drama is taking place in New York where blacks have been boycotting Korean groceries for four months.

2   The recent attack on three Vietnamese men by a group of blacks who mistook them for Koreans has brought this long-simmering tension between two minority groups to the world's attention. Korean newspapers from San Francisco to Seoul have been running front-page stories. Non-Asian commentators

around the country, whose knowledge of Korea may not be much more than images from the Korean war and the ridiculous television series *M.A.S.H.*, are making all sorts of comments.

3   As I see it, the problem in the Flatbush area of Brooklyn started with cultural misunderstanding and was compounded by a lack of bilingual and bicultural community leaders to intervene quickly.

4   Frictions between Korean store owners in New York and blacks had been building for years. Korean merchants have been complaining about thefts. On the other hand, their black customers have been accusing immigrant store owners of making money in their neighborhoods without putting anything back into the community. They have also complained about store owners being brusque. Over the past eight years, there have been sporadic boycotts but none has lasted as long as the current one, which stemmed from an accusation by a black customer in January that she had been attacked by a store employee. In defense, the store owner has said the employee caught the woman stealing.

5   The attack on the Vietnamese on May 13 wasn't the first time one group of Asians has been mistaken for another in America. But the publicity surrounding the case has made this unfortunate situation a case study in interethnic tension.

6   What's missing in this inner-city drama is cultural insight.

7   What struck me more than anything was a recent remark by a black resident: "The Koreans are a very, very rude people. They don't understand you have to smile."

8   I wondered whether her reaction would have been the same had she known that Koreans don't smile at Koreans either without a reason. To a Korean, a smile is not a facial expression he can turn on and off mechanically. Koreans have a word for it—mu-ttuk-ttuk-hada" (stiff). In other words, the Korean demeanor is "myu-po-jung"—lack of expression.

9   It would be an easy thing for blacks who are naturally friendly and gregarious to misunderstand Korean ways.

10   As a Korean American I've experienced this many times. Whenever I'm in Korea, which is often, I'm chided for smiling too much. "Why do you smile so easily? You act like a Westerner," people tell me. My inclination is to retort: "Why do you always have to look like you've got indigestion?" But I restrain myself because I know better.

11   In our culture, a smile is reserved for people we know and for a proper occasion. Herein lies a big problem when newcomers from Korea begin doing business in America's poor inner-city neighborhoods.

12   Culturally and socially, many newcomers from Korea, like other Asian immigrants, are ill-equipped to run businesses in America's inner cities. But because they are denied entry into mainstream job markets, they pool resources and open mom-and-pop operations in the only places where they can afford it. They work 14 and 15 hours a day, seven days a week, dreaming of the day when their children will graduate from prestigious schools and make their sacrifices worthwhile.

13   From the other side, inner-city African Americans must wonder how these new immigrants find the money to run their own businesses, when they themselves can't even get a small loan from a bank. Their hope of getting out of the poverty cycle is grim, yet they see newcomers living in better neighborhoods and driving new cars.

14   "They ask me, 'Where do you people get the money to buy a business?'" Bong-jae Jang, owner of one of the grocery stores being boycotted, told me. "How can I explain to my neighbors in my poor English the concept of our family system, the idea of 'kye' (uniquely Korean private money-lending system), our way of life?"

15   I think a little learning is in order on both sides. Korean immigrants, like other newcomers, need orientation before they leave their country as well as when they arrive in the United States. It's also important for Korean immigrants, like other Asians who live in the United States, to realize that they are indebted to blacks for the social gains won by their civil rights struggle. They face less discrimination today because blacks have paved the way. Instead of looking down on their culture, it would be constructive to learn their history, literature, music, and values and see our African American brothers and sisters in their full humanity.

16   I think it is also important to remind ourselves that while the Confucian culture has taught us how to be good parents, sons and daughters and how to behave with people we know, it has not prepared us for living in a democracy. The Confucian ethos lacks the value of social conscience, which makes democracy work.

17   It isn't enough that we think of educating our children and send them to the best schools. We need to think of other peoples' children, too. Most of all, we need to be more tolerant of other peoples' cultures. We need to celebrate our similarities as well as our differences.

18   Jang, the grocer, told me this experience has been painful but he has learned an important lesson. "We Koreans must learn to participate in this society," he said. "When this is over, I'm going to reach out. I want to give part-time work to black youths."

19   He also told me that he has been keeping a journal. "I'm not a writer but I've been keeping a journal," he said. "I want to write about this experience someday. It may help someone."

20   By reaching out, we can make a difference. The Korean grocer's lesson is a reminder to us all that making democracy work in a multicultural society is difficult but we have no choice but to strive for it.

Compare and Contrast
Technique Questions

1. What is the essay's purpose?

Possible answer: The essay suggests that people from different cultures

need to try to understand those from different cultures.

2. Point out several cultural differences that make it difficult for African Americans and Korean Americans to get along.

Possible answer: In the Korean culture, smiles are reserved for special

friends and special occasions, while African Americans are more naturally

friendly and gregarious in their demeanor. They see Koreans as being

rude because they do not smile. African Americans wanting to start a small business often find it next to impossible to get loans from banks

and the government. In the Korean culture, families loan money to family

members to start businesses. Without knowing of this practice, African

Americans often think that Koreans are being given preferential treatment

by banks and the government.

3. Why are Korean Americans indebted to African Americans? How does Kang suggest that comparing the two cultures would help the two communities get along better?

Possible answer: Kang suggests that Koreans should be grateful that

African Americans fought for decades during the civil rights movement

to bring about antidiscriminatory practices against *all* minorities. African

Americans should remember their roots and appreciate that other minori-

ties, like the Koreans, are going through similar experiences.

Compare and Contrast
Writing Opportunities

1. Write an essay comparing the similarities and contrasting the differences between your ethnic background and that of another ethnic group living in your community. As you write, comment on how those similarities and differences affect relationships within the community.

2. If your family is composed of more than one ethnic background, write an essay comparing the similarities and contrasting the differences of the cultural characteristics within your own family. As you write, comment on how the similarities and differences cause harmony and dissension between the family members.

TWO WAYS TO BELONG IN AMERICA

Bharati Mukherjee

Like much of her writing, this essay by Mukherjee involves immigrants. As you read the essay, notice how she engages your interest by moving from particular events to the general as she relates personal observations and universal beliefs.

Vocabulary

Before you begin reading, look up the definitions of the following words that appear in the essay. The number in parentheses after each word refers to the paragraph number of the essay.

ancestral (12)   curtailing (8)   expatriate (11)

hysteria (10)   looming (6)   mongrelization (5)

mythic (7)   opting (5)   quota (5)

referendum (13)   renouncing (5)   scrutiny (7)

subtext (9)

Two Ways to Belong in America

1   This is a tale of two sisters from Calcutta, Mira and Bharati, who have lived in the United States for some 35 years, but who find themselves on different sides in the current debate over the status of immigrants. I am an American citizen and she is not. I am moved that thousands of long-term residents are finally taking the oath of citizenship. She is not.

2   Mira arrived in Detroit in 1960 to study child psychology and pre-school education. I followed her a year later to study creative writing at the University of Iowa. When we left India, we were almost identical in appearance and attitude. We dressed alike, in saris; we expressed identical views on politics, social issues, love and marriage in the same Calcutta convent-school accent. We would endure our two years in America, secure our degrees, then return to India to marry the grooms of our father's choosing.

3   Instead, Mira married an Indian student in 1962 who was getting his business administration degree at Wayne State University. They soon acquired the labor certifications necessary for the green card of hassle-free residence and employment.

4   Mira still lives in Detroit, works in the Southfield, Mich., school system, and has become nationally recognized for her contributions in the fields of pre-school education and parent-teacher relationships. After 36 years as a legal immigrant in this country, she clings passionately to her Indian citizenship and hopes to go home to India when she retires.

5   In Iowa City in 1963, I married a fellow student, an American of Canadian parentage. Because of the accident of his North Dakota birth, I bypassed labor-certification requirements and the race-related "quota" system that favored the applicant's country of origin over his or her merit. I was prepared for (and even welcomed) the emotional strain that came with marrying outside my ethnic community. In 33 years of marriage, we have lived in every part of North America. By choosing a husband who was not my father's selection, I was opting for fluidity, self-invention, blue jeans and T-shirts, and renouncing 3,000 years (at least) of caste-observant, "pure culture" marriage in the Mukherjee family. My books have often been read as unapologetic (and in some quarters overenthusiastic) texts for cultural and psychological "mongrelization." It's a word I celebrate.

6   Mira and I have stayed sisterly close by phone. In our regular Sunday morning conversations, we are unguardedly affectionate. I am her only blood relative on this continent. We expect to see each other through the looming crises of aging and ill health without being asked. Long before Vice President Gore's "Citizenship U.S.A." drive, we'd had our polite arguments over the ethics of retaining an overseas citizenship while expecting the permanent protection and economic benefits that come with living and working in America.

7   Like well-raised sisters, we never said what was really on our minds, but we probably pitied one another. She, for the lack of structure in my life, the erasure of Indianness, the absence of an unvarying daily core. I, for the narrowness of her perspective, her uninvolvement with the mythic depths or the superficial pop culture of this society. But, now, with the scapegoating of "aliens" (documented or illegal) on the increase, and the targeting of long-term legal immigrants like Mira for new scrutiny and new self-consciousness, she and I find ourselves unable to maintain the same polite discretion. We were always unacknowledged adversaries, and we are now, more than ever, sisters.

8   "I feel used," Mira raged on the phone the other night. "I feel manipulated and discarded. This is such an unfair way to treat a person who was invited to stay and work here because of her talent. My employer went to the I.N.S. and petitioned for the labor certification. For over 30 years, I've invested my creativity and professional skills into the improvement of *this* country's pre-school system. I've obeyed all the rules, I've paid my taxes, I love my work, I love my students, I love the friends I've made. How dare America now change its rules in midstream? If America wants to make new rules curtailing benefits of legal immigrants, they should apply only to immigrants who arrive after those rules are already in place."

9   To my ears, it sounded like the description of a long-enduring, comfortable yet loveless marriage, without risk or recklessness. Have we the right to demand, and to expect, that we be loved? (That, to me, is the subtext of the arguments by immigration advocates.) My sister is an expatriate, professionally generous and creative, socially courteous and gracious, and that's as far as her Americanization can go. She is here to maintain an identity, not to transform it.

10   I asked her if she would follow the example of others who have decided to become citizens because of the anti-immigration bills in Congress. And here, she surprised me. "If America wants to play the manipulative game, I'll play it too," she snapped. "I'll become a U.S. citizen for now, then change back to Indian when I'm ready to go home. I feel some kind of irrational attachment to India that I don't to America. Until all this hysteria against legal immigrants, I was totally happy. Having my green card meant I could visit any place in the world I wanted to and then come back to a job that's satisfying and that I do very well."

11   In one family, from two sisters alike as peas in a pod, there could not be a wider divergence of immigrant experience. America spoke to me—I embraced the demotion from expatriate aristocrat to immigrant nobody, surrendering those thousands of years of "pure culture," the saris, the delightfully accented English. She retained them all. Which of us is the freak?

12   Mira's voice, I realize, is the voice not just of the immigrant South Asian community but of an immigrant community of the millions who have stayed rooted in one job, one city, one house, one ancestral culture, one cuisine, for the entirety of their productive years. She speaks for greater numbers than I possibly can. Only the fluency of her English and the anger, rather than fear, born of confidence from her education, differentiate her from the seamstresses, the domestics, the technicians, the shop owners, the millions of hard-working but effectively silenced documented immigrants as well as their less fortunate "illegal" brothers and sisters.

13   Nearly 20 years ago, when I was living in my husband's ancestral homeland of Canada, I was always well-employed but never allowed to feel part of the local Quebec or larger Canadian society. Then, through a Green Paper that invited a national referendum on the unwanted side effects of "nontraditional" immigration, the Government officially turned against its immigrant communities, particularly those from South Asia.

14   I felt then the same sense of betrayal that Mira feels now. I will never forget the pain of that sudden turning, and the casual racist outbursts the Green

Paper elicited. That sense of betrayal had its desired effect and drove me, and thousands like me, from the country.

15   Mira and I differ, however, in the ways in which we hope to interact with the country that we have chosen to live in. She is happier to live in America as expatriate Indian than as an immigrant American. I need to feel like a part of the community I have adopted (as I tried to feel in Canada as well). I need to put roots down, to vote and make the difference that I can. The price that the immigrant willingly pays, and that the exile avoids, is the trauma of self-transformation.

Compare and Contrast Technique Questions

1. What is the essay's thesis?

Possible answer: The immigrant experience has two forms represented

by the two sisters. They both should be shown respect by the government,

but Mukherjee's view is the one that will actually transform individuals in

a dramatic fashion so they can actually become citizens in practice and

spirit.

2. How is the essay organized, point-by-point or block?

Both. In paragraphs 3, 4, 5, 8, 9, 10,12, 13, and 14 she uses the block

method; in paragraphs 1, 2, 6, 7, 11, and 15 she uses the point-by-point

method.

3. What are the two ways to belong in America? Are the two ways being compared or contrasted?

As an expatriate Indian or an immigrant American. Although the two sisters'

similarities are discussed in the opening, their lifestyles and choices are

contrasted for most of the essay.

Compare and Contrast Writing Opportunities

1. Write an essay comparing or contrasting American culture from the perspective of a native and from the perspective of an immigrant.

2. Pretend your job forces you to move to another country for a long period of time. Write a comparison or contrast essay describing whether you would be more like Mukherjee or her sister.

DEFINITION

WHO'S A HILLBILLY?

Rebecca Thomas Kirkendall

People worldwide, in any culture you can identify, have names for various groups within their own country. Often these names are meant as a negative comment. The names may identify an ethnic group, a religious sect, or social class. As Kirkendall points out in this essay, sometimes the negative name can be associated with people from a particular region.

Vocabulary
Before you begin reading, look up the definitions of the following words that appear in the essay. The number in parentheses after each word refers to the paragraph number of the essay.

agrarian (9)	ambivalent (9)	belittle (2)
condescension (8)	derision (8)	egalitarianism (4)
foil (2)	gibe (11)	juxtaposed (7)
self-effacing (2)	stigma (4)	tolerance (2)

Who's a Hillbilly?

1   I once dated a boy who called me a hillbilly because my family has lived in the Ozarks in southern Missouri for several generations. I took offense, not realizing that as a foreigner to the United States he was unaware of the insult. He had meant it as a term of endearment. Nonetheless, it rankled. I started thinking about the implications of the term to me, my family, and my community.

2   While growing up I was often surprised at the way television belittled "country" people. We weren't offended by the self-effacing humor of *The Andy Griffith Show* and *The Beverly Hillbillies* because, after all, Andy and Jed were the heroes of these shows, and through them we could comfortably laugh at ourselves. But as I learned about tolerance and discrimination in school, I wondered why stereotypes of our lifestyle went unexamined. Actors playing "country" people on TV were usually comic foils or objects of ridicule. Every sitcom seemed to have an episode where country cousins, wearing high-water britches and carrying patched suitcases, visited their city friends. And movies like *Deliverance* portrayed country people as backward and violent.

3   As a child I laughed at the exaggerated accents and dress, never imagining that viewers believed such nonsense. Li'l Abner and the folks on *Hee Haw* were amusing, but we on the farm knew that our work did not lend itself to bare feet, gingham bras, and revealing cutoff jeans.

4   Although our nation professes a growing commitment to cultural egalitarianism, we consistently oversimplify and misunderstand our rural culture.

Since the 1960s, minority groups in America have fought for acknowledgment, appreciation, and above all, respect. But in our increasingly urban society, rural Americans have been unable to escape from the hillbilly stigma, which is frequently accompanied by labels like "white trash," "redneck" and "hayseed." These negative stereotypes are as unmerciful as they are unfounded.

5   When I graduated from college, I traveled to a nearby city to find work. There I heard wisecracks about the uneducated rural folk who lived a few hours away. I also took some ribbing about the way I pronounced certain words, such as "tin" instead of "ten" and "agin" for "again." And my expressed desire to return to the country someday was usually met with scorn, bewilderment, or genuine concern. Co-workers often asked, "But what is there to *do?*" Thoreau may have gone to Walden Pond, they argued, but he had no intention of staying there.

6   With the revival of country music in the early 1980s, hillbillyness was again marketable. Country is now big business. Traditional country symbols—Minnie Pearl's hat tag and Daisy Mae—have been eclipsed by the commercially successful Nashville Network, Country Music Television, and music theaters in Branson, MO. Many "country" Americans turned the negative stereotype to their advantage and packaged the hillbilly legacy.

7   Yet with successful commercialization, the authentic elements of America's rural culture have been juxtaposed with the stylized. Country and Western bars are now chic. While I worked in the city, I watched with amazement as my Yuppie friends hurried from their corporate desks to catch the 6:30 line-dancing class at the edge of town. Donning Ralph Lauren jeans and ankle boots, they drove to the trendiest country bars, sat and danced together, and poked fun at the local "hicks," who arrived in pickup trucks wearing Wrangler jeans and roper boots.

8   Every summer weekend in Missouri the freeways leading out of our cities are clogged with vacationers. Minivans and RVs edge toward a clear river with a campground and canoe rental, a quiet lake resort, or craft show in a remote Ozark town. Along these popular vacation routes, the rural hosts of convenience stores, gift shops, and corner cafés accept condescension along with personal checks and credit cards. On a canoeing trip not long ago, I recall sitting on the transport bus and listening, heartbroken, as a group of tourists ridiculed our bus driver. They yelled, "Hey, plowboy, ain't ya got no terbacker fer us?" They pointed at the young man's sweat-stained overalls as he, seemingly unaffected by their insults, singlehandedly carried their heavy aluminum canoes to the water's edge. That "plowboy" was one of my high-school classmates. He greeted the tourists with a smile and tolerated their derision because he knew tourism brings dollars and jobs.

9   America is ambivalent when it comes to claiming its rural heritage. We may fantasize about Thomas Jefferson's agrarian vision, but there is no mistaking that ours is an increasingly urban culture. Despite their disdain for farm life—with its manure-caked boots, long hours, and inherent financial difficulties—urbanites rush to imitate a sanitized version of this lifestyle. And the individuals who sell this rendition understand that the customer wants to experience hillbillyness without the embarrassment of being mistaken for one.

10   Through it all, we Ozarkians remind ourselves how fortunate we are to live in a region admired for its blue springs, rolling hills, and geological wonders. In spite of the stereotypes, most of us are not uneducated. Nor are we stupid. We are not white supremacists, and we rarely marry our cousins. Our reasons for living in the hills are as complex and diverse as our population. We have a

unique sense of community, strong family ties, a beautiful environment, and a quiet place for retirement.

11   We have criminals and radicals, but they are the exception. Our public-education system produces successful farmers, doctors, business professionals, and educators. Country music is our favorite, but we also like rock and roll, jazz, blues and classical. We read Louis L'Amour, Maya Angelou and the *Wall Street Journal.* And in exchange for living here, many of us put up with a lower standard of living and the occasional gibe from those who persist in calling us "hillbillies."

Definition Technique Questions

1. What is the definition of the stereotypical "hillbilly" presented in the essay, and why does the author take exception to the term?

> **Possible answer: Hillbillies are usually portrayed as having exaggerated accents and dress, having bare feet, gingham bras, and revealing cutoff jeans, and answering to a variety of pejorative labels, such as "white trash," "redneck," and "hayseed." The author argues that people living in rural areas are just as diverse in their demographics as city dwellers. Paragraphs 10–11 clarify this point.**

2. How does the author define "Ozarkian"?

> **See paragraphs 10–11.**

3. Why do Ozarkians prefer to live beyond the city and suburbs?

> **Possible answer: Ozarkians have a unique sense of community, strong family ties, a beautiful environment, and a quiet place for retirement.**

Definition Writing Opportunities

1. Write an essay defining the type of people who live in your area. Use the labels others give them, and explain the negative meanings of those labels.

2. While others use "hillbilly" negatively, Kirkendall points out that those living in rural Missouri can think of the term positively. Write an essay defining how the terms you used in question number one might be used positively by the groups given those labels.

A MAGIC CIRCLE OF FRIENDS

Elvira M. Franco

You might think that a forty-year-old returning to school would stand out like a sore thumb amid the twenty-somethings. But the author of this essay found a group of students her own age with similar backgrounds and with similar fears. Instead of forcing their new school environment to conform to their own experiences, the group allows their experience to help establish new ideas about life and friendships.

Vocabulary

Before you begin reading, look up the definitions of the following words that appear in the essay. The number in parentheses after each word refers to the paragraph number of the essay.

abrading (9)	bolstered (12)	brash (7)
cajole (14)	camaraderie (7)	depleted (3)
exhilarating (7)	ignited (5)	multifaceted (11)
orthopedic (5)	pangs (15)	prominent (5)
unique (1)		

A Magic Circle of Friends

1   Older than forty and starting from scratch: I thought I was a unique item, but as soon as I peeked out of my shell I found a sea of women in similar positions.

2   The little child in us has grown mature and middle-aged, almost to our surprise. We share a fear that sits in the back of the mind like a spider ready to pounce, but we've also developed determination, almost like a religion.

3   We know we have friends; at least, I know my friends are with me, if not always, at least most of the time. And most of the time I need them, and they me. We reach over the phone lines for that word of comfort, the encouragement we need to go on when our own store of willpower has become depleted.

4   Returning to school, I found my friends were my best fans. In spite of their own insecurities, they never failed to offer me the cheering I often needed to rewrite a paper one more time or to stay up one last half-hour to re-read a difficult chapter.

5   After classes we would go to a diner, a bunch of over-forty class-mates. Working together on a project that we felt strongly about ignited a part of us we did not know existed. While we were quite far from orthopedic shoes, bifocals were prominent. Underneath the artful makeup, we would measure the wrinkles on each other's cheeks across the table, almost as if these lines could form a cord to link us.

6   It was a good time. For years, in a locked-up corner of our minds, we had held the unspoken fear that we might actually be brain-dead. We were finally giving ourselves permission to celebrate our minds.

7   For some, it was a return to the carefree years of college. For others, a first-time discovery that learning can be both fun and exhilarating. Besides the intellectual surprises, we found joy in each other's company, and we delved in this new-found camaraderie with an intensity we did not know we could achieve outside of love and pregnancies. We were, and are, proud of our ages.

The only woman in the group who was under thirty struck most of us as brash, angry, and, frankly, quite inappropriate. We were probably insensitive to her needs, but somehow we failed to find out how she felt in our midst and were almost relieved when she found excuses for not joining our study sessions.

8 We ended up treating her almost like a daughter, and doing for her what most of us have been doing for our own daughters: that is, picking up the slack. The hidden bonus was that now we could continue to do things our way, which, we all knew, was the best anyway. Things were smoother when she was not around: the rest of us would always agree, and even our disagreements were somehow smooth and enjoyable.

9 We had, in fact, created a sort of bubble around us, a magic circle that follows us still and says we are bright, successful, caring, ambitious, and, finally, ready to change the world. We will not do it, as we might have been ready to do at twenty, pushing and fighting and abrading.

10 We will do it instead at a slower pace, because, along the way, we have learned lessons both small and big: for example, that the world is in no hurry to be changed and that we will have a better shot at it after a good night's sleep. We may not complete our plans by tomorrow, or even by the end of the week, because the details of our lives may interfere, such as a child home from college, or a neighbor's emergency.

11 Our goals may not even be achieved exactly as originally planned, and that is fine, too, because time has also brought us a sense of flexibility and an appreciation for the serendipitous properties of practically any action. The end product could turn out to be infinitely more complex, and in its way more perfect, more multifaceted and rich, than what we had first envisioned. The process is in itself an achievement.

12 They call us "late bloomers," they call us "returnees." We are sought by schools, thanks to the sheer numbers we represent, not to mention the life experience and the common sense that even the least bright among us brings to the classroom. We feel flattered and surprised, and our ego is bolstered by the realization that we are indeed quite capable.

13 There are fears, too ("Will it all make sense at some point?" "What if I'll never be able to get a decent job?"), but they are kept for only a few pairs of ears, where we know we will find support and understanding.

14 Graduation comes: the last papers have been handed in with trepidation, the test booklets carrying in their pages the very essence of our knowledge closed for the last time. Goodbyes, with promises and some tears, even a photograph to keep as souvenir. We've made it: watch out world, here come the mothers and the grandmothers, ready to push, cajole, smile, and negotiate to achieve those goals we did not have a chance to effect the first time around.

15 We may just be beginning to feel a few arthritic pangs in our toes and fingers, but with our hair neatly streaked and some expensive dental work, we know we still look good. We know we are still strong, smart, vital, and, most especially, ready to work. This time around we will make a big difference. We know, because, for sure, we already are different.

Definition Technique Questions

1. What is the simile in paragraph 2? What is the fear the author shares with her friends?

The simile is "We share a fear that sits in the back of the mind like a spider

ready to pounce." The fear encompasses fear of failure, fear of looking foolish, the fear of looking out of place, and the fear that after so many years they might be brain-dead.

2. Why does Franco define her group as a "magic circle"?

Possible answer: Franco says that she and her friends "created a sort of bubble around us, a magic circle that follows us still and says we are bright, successful, caring, ambitious, and, finally, ready to change the world" (9).

3. Why didn't Franco and her group of forty-year-olds have a chance to reach their goals earlier in life? How will their education help them achieve their goals this time around?

Students will have to call on their own experiences and assumptions to answer these questions. If you have some "returning" students, you might have them lead the discussion. Some lively discussions and comments should ensue.

Definition Writing Opportunities

1. What age group do you belong to? Write an essay defining your group as opposed to another age group that you have to compete with, either in school or on the job.

2. Write an essay about your circle of friends. What were the circumstances under which you met? How have you supported each other during crises? Is your group still together, or has it broken up? Why?

CAUSE AND EFFECT

HALFWAY TO DICK AND JANE

Jack Agueros

In this essay, the author, of Puerto Rican descent, relates some of the problems people of non-European ancestry have growing up and becoming a part of American society. He sets up the cause and effect part of the essay with a long introduction in which he talks about his family, home, and neighborhood.

Vocabulary

Before you begin reading, look up the definitions of the following words that appear in the essay. The number in parentheses after each word refers to the paragraph number of the essay.

chenille (3)	compensation (2)	declaim (2)
dismantle (2)	immaculate (3)	pathetically (7)
pathologically (7)	skewer (6)	sole (1)
stoops (3)	Victrola (2)	zip gun (7)

Halfway to Dick and Jane

1   I am an only child. My parents and I always talked about my becoming a doctor. The law and politics were not highly regarded in my house. Lawyers, my mother would explain, had to defend people whether they were guilty or not, while politicians, my father would say, were all crooks. A doctor helped everybody, rich and poor, white and black. If I became a doctor, I could study hay fever and find a cure for it, my godmother would say. Also, I could take care of my parents when they were old. I like the idea of helping, and for nineteen years my sole ambition was to study medicine.

2   My house had books, not many, but my parents encouraged me to read. As I became a good reader they bought books for me and never refused me money for their purchase. My father once built a bookcase for me. It was an important moment, for I had always believed that my father was not too happy about my being a bookworm. The atmosphere at home was always warm. We seemed to be a popular family. We entertained frequently, with two standing parties a year—at Christmas and for my birthday. Parties were always large. My father would dismantle the beds and move all the furniture so that the full two rooms could be used for dancing. My mother would cook up a storm, particularly at Christmas. *Pasteles, lechon asado, arroz con gandules,* and a lot of *coquito* to drink (meat-stuffed plantain, roast pork, rice with pigeon peas, and coconut nog). My father always brought in a band. They played without compensation and were guests at the party. They ate and drank and danced while a Victrola covered the intermissions. One year my father brought home a whole pig and hung it in the foyer doorway. He and my mother prepared it by rubbing it down with oil, orègano, and garlic. After preparation, the pig was taken down and carried over to a local bakery where it was cooked and returned home. Parties always went on till daybreak, and in addition to the band, there were always volunteers to sing and declaim poetry.

3   My mother kept an immaculate household. Bedspreads (chenille seemed to be very in) and lace curtains, washed at home like everything else, were hung up on huge racks with rows of tight nails. The racks were assembled in the living room, and the moisture from the wet bedspreads would fill the apartment. In a sense, that seems to be the lasting image of that period of my life. The house was clean. The neighbors were clean. The streets, with few cars, were clean. The buildings were clean and uncluttered with people on the stoops. The park was clean. The visitors to my house were clean, and the relationships that my family had with other Puerto Rican families, and the Italian families that my father had met through baseball and my mother through the garment center, were clean. Second Avenue was clean and most of the apartment windows had awnings. There was always music, there seemed to be no

rain, and snow did not become slush. School was fun, we wrote essays about how grand America was, we put up hunchbacked cats at Halloween, we believed Santa Claus visited everyone. I believed everyone was Catholic. I grew up with dogs, nightingales, my godmother's guitar, rocking chair, cat, guppies, my father's occasional roosters, kept in a cage on the fire escape. Laundry delivered and collected by horse and wagon, fruits and vegetables sold the same way, windowsill refrigeration in winter, iceman and box in summer. The police my friends, likewise the teachers.

4   In short, the first seven or so years of my life were not too great a variation on Dick and Jane, the schoolbook figures who, if my memory serves me correctly, were blond Anglo-Saxons, not immigrants, not migrants like the Puerto Ricans, and not the children of either immigrants or migrants.

5   My family moved in 1941 to Lexington Avenue into a larger apartment where I could have my own room. It was a light, sunny, railroad flat on the top floor of a well-kept building. I transferred to a new school, and whereas before my classmates had been mostly black, the new school had few blacks. The classes were made up of Italians, Irish, Jews, and a sprinkling of Puerto Ricans. My block was populated by Jews, Italians, and Puerto Ricans.

6   And then a whole series of different events began. I went to junior high school. We played in the backyards, where we tore down fences to build fires to cook stolen potatoes. We tore up whole hedges, because the green tender limbs would not burn when they were peeled, and thus made perfect skewers for our stolen "mickies." We played tag in the abandoned buildings, tearing the plaster off the walls, tearing the wire lath off the wooden slats, tearing the wooden slats themselves, good for fires, for kites, for sword fighting. We ran up and down the fire escapes playing tag and over and across many rooftops. The war ended and the heavy Puerto Rican migration began. The Irish and the Jews disappeared from the neighborhood. The Italians tried to consolidate east of Third Avenue.

7   What caused the clean and open world to end? Many things. Into an ancient neighborhood came pouring four to five times more people than it had been designed to hold. Men who came running at the promise of jobs were jobless as the war ended. They were confused. They could not see the economic forces that ruled their lives as they drank beer on the corners, reassuring themselves of good times to come while they were hell-bent toward alcoholism. The sudden surge in numbers caused new resentments, and prejudice was intensified. Some were forced to live in cellars, and were then characterized as cave dwellers. Kids came who were confused by the new surroundings; their Puerto Rican-ness forced us against a mirror asking, "If they are Puerto Ricans, what are we?" and thus they confused us. In our confusion we were sometimes pathetically reaching out, sometimes pathologically striking out. Gangs. Drugs. Wine. Smoking. Girls. Dances and slow-drag music. Mambo. Spics, Spooks, and Wops. Territories, brother gangs, and war councils establishing rules for right of way on blocks and avenues and for seating in the local theater. Pegged pants and zip guns. Slang.

8   Dick and Jane were dead, man. Education collapsed. Every classroom had ten kids who spoke no English. Black, Italian, Puerto Rican relations in the classroom were good, but we all knew we couldn't visit one another's neighborhoods. Sometimes we could not move too freely within our own blocks. On 109th, from the lamp post west, the Latin Aces, and from the lamp post east, the Senecas, the "club" I belonged to. The kids who spoke no English became known as Marine Tigers, picked up from a popular Spanish song. (The Marine Tiger and the Marine Shark were two ships that sailed from San Juan to New York and brought over many, many migrants from the island.)

9   The neighborhood had its boundaries. Third Avenue and east, Italian. Fifth Avenue and west, black. South, there was a hill on 103rd Street known locally as

Cooney's Hill. When you got to the top of the hill, something strange happened: America began, because from the hill south was where the "Americans" lived. Dick and Jane were not dead: they were alive and well in a better neighborhood.

10   When, as a group of Puerto Rican kids, we decided to go swimming to Jefferson Park Pool, we knew we risked a fight and a beating from the Italians. And when we went to La Milagrosa Church in Harlem, we knew we risked a fight and a beating from the blacks. But when we went over Cooney's Hill, we risked dirty looks, disapproving looks, and questions from the police like, "What are you doing in this neighborhood?" and "Why don't you kids go back where you belong?"

11   Where we belonged! Man, I had written compositions about America. Didn't I belong on the Central Park tennis courts, even if I didn't know how to play? Couldn't I watch Dick play? Weren't these policemen working for me too?…

Cause and Effect Technique Questions

1. Who are Dick and Jane, and why does the author choose them for his title?

   Paragraph 4: "In short, the first seven or so years of my life were not too

   great a variation on Dick and Jane, the schoolbook figures who, if my

   memory serves me correctly, were blond Anglo-Saxons, not immigrants,

   not migrants like the Puerto Ricans, and not the children of either immi-

   grants or migrants." Possible answer: He uses Dick and Jane as images

   that help set up the first part of his childhood on Second Avenue and that

   of his later, more difficult childhood, when his family moved to Lexington

   Avenue.

2. In which paragraph does the cause and effect technique begin? What tipped you off?

   Paragraph 7. The second word in the first sentence is "caused." It is also

   repeated in line 7.

3. Why does the author write with so much detail in the lengthy introduction? Does it help clarify the cause and effect being discussed in the essay?

   Possible answer: The detail regarding his "Dick and Jane" life on Second

   Avenue becomes part of the cause for his spiritual and psychological

change (the effects) at the end of the essay when Agueros goes into great

detail about life around Lexington Avenue. As he intones in the first sen-

tence of paragraph 8, "Dick and Jane were dead, man."

Cause and Effect Writing Opportunities

1. Write an essay about your childhood neighborhood. How did the environment and the people affect your maturing into adulthood?

2. Write an essay about the causes and effects of prejudice.

WHY WE CRAVE HORROR MOVIES

Stephen King

For the most part, people's lives are filled with fears about their jobs, paying the bills, their children, and a variety of crimes against people and property. Yet society doesn't respond well to those making their fears public. They are often seen as unbalanced, or troublemakers, or social misfits. Where do people go to release their pent up fears? In this essay, the master of the macabre reveals his thoughts about why people are drawn to accounts of horror.

Vocabulary
Before you begin reading, look up the definitions of the following words that appear in the essay. The number in parentheses after each word refers to the paragraph number of the essay.

anarchistic (11)	asylum (1)	depleted (3)
exalted (9)	innately (4)	menaced (6)
morbidity (12)	mythic (7)	normality (4)
penchant (7)	province (3)	remonstrance (10)
sanctions (10)	squinch (1)	status quo (9)
voyeur (6)		

Why We Crave Horror Movies

1   I think that we're all mentally ill; those of us outside the asylums only hide it a little better—and maybe not all that much better, after all. We've all known people who talk to themselves, people who sometimes squinch their faces into horrible grimaces when they believe no one is watching, people who have some hysterical fear—of snakes, the dark, the tight place, the long drop … and, of course, those final worms and grubs that are waiting so patiently underground.

2   When we pay our four or five bucks and seat ourselves at tenth-row center in a theater showing a horror movie, we are daring the nightmare.

3   Why? Some of the reasons are simple and obvious. To show that we can, that we are not afraid, that we can ride this roller coaster. Which is not to say that a really good horror movie may not surprise a scream out of us at some point, the way we may scream when the roller coaster twists through a complete 360 or plows through a lake at the bottom of the drop. And horror movies, like roller coasters, have always been the special province of the young; by the time one turns 40 or 50, one's appetite for double twists or 360-degree loops may be considerably depleted.

4   We also go to reestablish our feelings of essential normality; the horror movie is innately conservative, even reactionary. Freda Jackson as the horrible melting woman in *Die, Monster, Die!* confirms for us that no matter how far we may be removed from the beauty of a Robert Redford or a Diana Ross, we are still light-years from true ugliness.

5   And we go to have fun.

6   Ah, but this is where the ground starts to slope away, isn't it? Because this is a very peculiar sort of fun, indeed. The fun comes from seeing others menaced—sometimes killed. One critic has suggested that if pro football has become the voyeur's version of combat, then the horror film has become the modern version of the public lynching.

7   It is true that the mythic, "fairy-tale" horror film intends to take away the shades of gray…. It urges us to put away our more civilized and adult penchant for analysis and to become children again, seeing things in pure blacks and whites. It may be that horror movies provide psychic relief on this level because this invitation to lapse into simplicity, irrationality, and even outright madness is extended so rarely. We are told we may allow our emotions a free rein … or no rein at all.

8   If we are all insane, then sanity becomes a matter of degree. If your insanity leads you to carve up women, like Jack the Ripper or the Cleveland Torso Murderer, we clap you away in the funny farm (but neither of those two amateur-night surgeons was ever caught, heh-heh-heh); if, on the other hand, your insanity leads you only to talk to yourself when you're under stress or to pick your nose on your morning bus, then you are left alone to go about your business … though it is doubtful that you will ever be invited to the best parties.

9   The potential lyncher is in almost all of us (excluding saints, past and present; but then, most saints have been crazy in their own ways), and every now and then, he has to be let loose to scream and roll around in the grass. Our emotions and our fears form their own body, and we recognize that it demands its own exercise to maintain proper muscle tone. Certain of these emotional muscles are accepted—even exalted—in civilized society; they are, of course, the emotions that tend to maintain the status quo of civilization itself. Love, friendship, loyalty, kindness—these are all the emotions that we applaud, emotions that have been immortalized in the couplets of Hallmark cards and in the verses (I don't dare call it poetry) of Leonard Nimoy.

10   When we exhibit these emotions, society showers us with positive reinforcement; we learn this even before we get out of diapers. When, as children, we hug our rotten little puke of a sister and give her a kiss, all the aunts and uncles smile and twit and cry, "Isn't he the sweetest little thing?" Such coveted treats as chocolate-covered graham crackers often follow. But if we deliberately slam the rotten little puke of a sister's fingers in the door, sanctions follow—angry remonstrance from parents, aunts and uncles; instead of a chocolate-covered graham cracker, a spanking.

11   But anticivilization emotions don't go away, and they demand periodic exercise. We have such "sick" jokes as, "What's the difference between a truckload of bowling balls and a truckload of dead babies?" (You can't unload a truckload of bowling balls with a pitchfork … a joke, by the way, that I heard originally from a ten-year-old.) Such a joke may surprise a laugh or a grin out of us even as we recoil, a possibility that confirms the thesis: If we share a brotherhood of man, then we also share an insanity of man. None of which is intended as a defense of either the sick joke or insanity, but merely as an explanation of why the best horror films, like the best fairy tales, manage to be reactionary, anarchistic, and revolutionary all at the same time.

12   The mythic horror movie, like the sick joke, has a dirty job to do. It deliberately appeals to all that is worst in us. It is morbidity unchained, our most base instincts let free, our nastiest fantasies realized …, and it all happens, fittingly enough, in the dark. For those reasons, good liberals often shy away from horror films. For myself, I like to see the most aggressive of them—*Dawn of the Dead,* for instance—as lifting a trap door in the civilized forebrain and throwing a basket of raw meat to the hungry alligators swimming around in that subterranean river beneath.

13   Why bother? Because it keeps them from getting out, man. It keeps them down there and me up here. It was Lennon and McCartney who said that all you need is love, and I would agree with that.

14   As long as you keep the gators fed.

Cause and Effect Technique Questions

1. In King's opinion, why do people enjoy being scared by watching horror movies?

> **Answers may vary. Some answers are found in paragraphs 3 (to show**
>
> **that we are not afraid), 4 (to reestablish our feeling of normality), 5 (to**
>
> **have fun), 7 (to become children once again), and 11 (to periodically exer-**
>
> **cise our anticivilization emotions).**

2. Point out one metaphor and one simile wherein King compares horror movies to something else.

> **Paragraph 2: a horror movie is a nightmare (metaphor); paragraph 3:**
>
> **movies are like roller coasters (simile); paragraph 6: a movie is a public**
>
> **lynching (metaphor); paragraph 12: a movie is like a sick joke (simile) and**
>
> **a movie is morbidity unchained (metaphor).**

3. In the last line of the essay, King says, "As long as you keep the gators fed." What does he mean by this?

> **Possible answer: A gator is a dangerous, evil, scary creature that can sur-**
>
> **face at any moment to attack its victim. In that sense, it becomes a**

metaphor for that part of the human psyche that wants, from time to time,

to be scared, in jeopardy, and to face danger (at least in the relative safety

of a movie seat).

Cause and Effect Writing Opportunities

1. Horror movies are not the only type of film in which murder and mayhem take place. Choose another type of film and show the cause and effect relationship that exists between it and the viewing public.

2. King states that there is a certain amount of insanity in the American population. Write an essay pointing out the causes and effects of an insane society.

PERSUASION

HONEY, I WARPED THE KIDS

Carl Cannon

> The effects of television on American society have been the subject of a raging debate for more than four decades. Former FCC Chairman Newton Minnow, for example, called television a "vast wasteland." Carl Cannon's essay and the one that follows by John Leonard are clearly persuasive as they speak to the positive and negative aspects of television in society.

Vocabulary
Before you begin reading, look up the definitions of the following words that appear in the essay. The number in parentheses after each word refers to the paragraph number of the essay.

accost (6)	anecdotal (16)	cathartic (5)
cynical (16)	depiction (4)	desensitizes (14)
empathy (15)	implore (1)	innuendo (14)
jaundiced (23)	mock (15)	socioeconomic (13)

Honey, I Warped the Kids

1   Tim Robbins and Susan Sarandon implore the nation to treat Haitians with AIDS more humanely. Robert Redford works for the environment. Harry Belafonte marches against the death penalty. Actors and producers seem to be constantly speaking out for noble causes far removed from their lives. But in the one area over which they have control—the excessive violence in the entertainment industry—Hollywood activists remain silent.

2   The first congressional hearings on the effects of TV violence took place in 1954. Although television was still relatively new, its extraordinary marketing power was already evident. The tube was teaching Americans what to buy and how to act, not only in advertisements, but in dramatic shows, too.

3   Everybody from Hollywood producers to Madison Avenue ad men would boast about this power—and seek to use it on dual tracks: to make money and to remake society along better lines.

4   Because it seemed ludicrous to assert that there was only one area—the depiction of violence—where television did not influence behavior, the TV industry came up with this theory: Watching violence is cathartic. A violent person might be sated by watching a murder.

5   The notion intrigued social scientists, and by 1956 they were studying it in earnest. Unfortunately, watching violence turned out to be anything but cathartic.

6   In the 1956 study, one dozen 4-year-olds watched a "Woody Woodpecker" cartoon that was full of violent images. Twelve other preschoolers watched "Little Red Hen," a peaceful cartoon. Afterward, the children who watched "Woody Woodpecker" were more likely to hit other children, verbally accost their classmates, break toys, be disruptive, and engage in destructive behavior during free play.

7   For the next 30 years, researchers in all walks of the social sciences studied the question of whether television causes violence. The results have been stunningly conclusive.

8   "There is more published research on this topic than on almost any other social issue of our time," University of Kansas Professor Aletha C. Huston, chair of the American Psychological Association's Task Force on Television and Society, told Congress in 1988. "Virtually all independent scholars agree that there is evidence that television can cause aggressive behavior."

9   There have been some 3,000 studies of this issue—85 of them major research efforts—and they all say the same thing. Of the 85 major studies, the only one that failed to find a causal relationship between TV violence and actual violence was paid for by NBC. When the study was subsequently reviewed by three independent social scientists, all three concluded that it actually did demonstrate a causal relationship.

10   Some highlights from the history of TV violence research:

11   • In 1973, when a town in mountainous western Canada was wired for TV signals, University of British Columbia researchers observed first- and second-graders. Within two years, the incidence of hitting, biting, and shoving increased 160 percent.

12   • Two Chicago doctors, Leonard Eron and Rowell Heusmann, followed the viewing habits of a group of children for 22 years. They found that watching violence on television is the single best predictor of violent or aggressive behavior later in life, ahead of such commonly accepted factors as parents' behavior, poverty, and race.

13   • "Television violence affects youngsters of all ages, of both genders, at all socioeconomic levels and all levels of intelligence," they told Congress in 1992. "The effect is not limited to children who are already disposed to being aggressive and is not restricted to this country."

14   • In 1988, researchers Daniel G. Linz and Edward Donnerstein of the University of California, Santa Barbara, and Steven Penrod of the University of Wisconsin studied the effects on young men of horror movies and "slasher" films. They found that depictions of violence, not sex, are what desensitizes people. They divided male students into four groups. One

group watched no movies, a second watched nonviolent X-rated movies, a third watched teenage sexual-innuendo movies, and a fourth watched the slasher films *Texas Chainsaw Massacre, Friday the 13th, Part 2, Maniac,* and *Toolbox Murders.*

15   All the young men were placed on a mock jury panel and asked a series of questions designed to measure their empathy for an alleged female rape victim. Those in the fourth group measured lowest in empathy for the specific victim in the experiment—and for rape victims in general.

16   The anecdotal evidence is often more compelling than the scientific studies. Ask any homicide cop from London to Los Angeles to Bangkok if TV violence induces real-life violence and listen carefully to the cynical, knowing laugh.

17   Ask David McCarthy, police chief in Greenfield, Massachusetts, why 19-year-old Mark Branch killed himself after stabbing an 18-year-old female college student to death. When cops searched his room they found 90 horror movies, as well as a machete and a goalie mask like those used by Jason, the grisly star of *Friday the 13th.*

18   Or ask Sergeant John O'Malley of the New York Police Department about a 9-year-old boy who sprayed a Bronx office building with gunfire. The boy explained to the astonished sergeant how he learned to load his Uzi-like firearm: "I watch a lot of TV."

19   Numerous groups have called, over the years, for curbing TV violence: the National Commission on the Causes and Prevention of Violence (1969), the U.S. Surgeon General (1972), the National Institute of Mental Health (1982), and the American Psychological Association (1992) among them.

20   During that time, cable television and movie rentals have made violence more readily available while at the same time pushing the envelope for network television. But even leaving aside cable and movie rentals, a study of TV programming from 1967 to 1989 showed only small ups and downs in violence, with the violent acts moving from one time slot to another but the overall violence rate remaining pretty steady—and pretty similar from network to network.

21   "The percent of prime-time programs using violence remains more than seven out of ten, as it has been for the entire 22-year period," researchers George Gerbner of the University of Pennsylvania Annenberg School of Communication and Nancy Signorielli of the University of Delaware wrote in 1990. For the past 22 years, they found, adults and children have been entertained by about 16 violent acts, including two murders, in each evening's prime-time programming.

22   They also discovered that the rate of violence in children's programs is three times the rate in prime-time shows. By the age of 18, the average American child has witnessed at least 18,000 simulated murders on television.

23   But all of the scientific studies and reports, all of the wisdom of cops and grief of parents have run up against Congress's quite proper fear of censorship. For years, Democratic Congressman Peter Rodino of New Jersey chaired the House Judiciary Committee and looked at calls for some form of censorship with a jaundiced eye. At a hearing five years ago, Rodino told witnesses that Congress must be a "protector of commerce."

24   "Well, we have children that we need to protect," replied Frank M. Palumbo, a pediatrician at Georgetown University Hospital and a consultant to the American Academy of Pediatrics. "What we have here is a toxic substance in the environment that is harmful to children."

25   "Arnold Fege of the national PTA added, "Clearly, this committee would not protect teachers who taught violence to children. Yet why would we condone children being exposed to a steady diet of TV violence year after year?"

WHY BLAME TV

John Leonard

Vocabulary

Before you begin reading, look up the definitions of the following words that appear in the essay. The number in parentheses after each word refers to the paragraph number of the essay.

agnosticism (10)	catatonic (15)	claustrophobic (8)
daubed (1)	druidic (3)	gaudy (6)
lolling (5)	mantras (5)	mimetic (6)
per capita (6)	pikers (6)	snippets (10)
triffid (3)	ziggurat (1)	

Why Blame TV

1   Like a warrior-king of Sumer, daubed with sesame oil, gorged on goat, hefting up his sword and drum, Senator Ernest Hollings looked down November 23 from a ziggurat to intone, all over the op-ed page of the *New York Times:* "If the TV and cable industries have no sense of shame, we must take it upon ourselves to stop licensing their violence-saturated programming."

2   Hollings, of course, is co-sponsor in the Senate, with Daniel Inouye, of a ban on any act of violence on television before, say, midnight. Never mind whether this is constitutional, or what it would do to the local news. Never mind, either, that in Los Angeles last August, in the International Ballroom of the Beverly Hilton, in front of 600 industry executives, the talking heads—a professor here, a producer there, a child psychologist and a network veep for program standards—couldn't even agree on a definition of violence. (Is it only violent if it hurts or kills?) And they disagreed on which was worse, a "happy" violence that sugarcoats aggressive behavior or a "graphic" violence that at least suggests consequences. (How, anyway, does television manage somehow simultaneously to *desensitize* and to *incite?*) Nor were they really sure what goes on in the dreamy heads of our children as they crouch in the dark to commune with the tube while their parents, if they have any, aren't around. (*Road Runner?* Beep-beep.) Nor does the infamous scarlet V "parent advisory" warning even apply to cartoons, afternoon soaps, or Somalias.

3   Never mind, because everybody agrees that watching television causes anti-social behavior, especially among the children of the poor; that there seems to be more violent programming on the air now than there ever was before; that *Beavis and Butt-head* inspired an Ohio 5-year-old to burn down the family trailer; that in the blue druidic light of television we will have spawned generations of toadstools and triffids.

4   In fact, there is less violence on network television than there used to be; because of ratings, it's mostly sitcoms. The worst stuff is the Hollywood splatterflicks; they're found on premium cable, which means the poor are less likely to be watching. Everywhere else on cable, not counting the court channel or home shopping and not even to think about blood sports and Pat Buchanan, the fare is innocent to the point of stupefaction (Disney, Discovery, Family, Nickelodeon). That Ohio trailer wasn't even wired for cable, so the littlest firebird must have got his MTV elsewhere in the dangerous neighborhood. (And kids have been playing with matches since, at least, Prometheus. I recall burn-

ing down my very own bedroom when I was 5 years old. The fire department had to tell my mother that the evidence pointed to me.) Since the '60s, according to statistics cited by Douglas Davis in *The Five Myths of Television Power*, more Americans than ever before are going out to eat in restaurants, see films, plays, and baseball games, visit museums, travel abroad, jog, even *read*. Watching television, everybody does *something else* at the same time. While our children are playing with their Adobe Illustrators and Domark Virtual Reality Toolkits, the rest of us eat, knit, smoke, dream, read magazines, sign checks, feel sorry for ourselves, think about Hillary, and plot shrewd career moves or revenge.

5   Actually watching television, unless it's C-Span, is usually more interesting than the proceedings of Congress. Or what we read in hysterical books like Jerry Mander's *Four Arguments for the Elimination of Television*, or George Gilder's *Life After Television*, or Marie Winn's *The Plug in Drugs* or Neal Postman's *Amusing Ourselves to Death*, or Bill McKibben's *The Age of Missing Information*. Or what we'll hear at panel discussions on censorship, where right-wingers worry about sex and left-wingers worry about violence. Or just lolling around an academic deepthink-tank, trading mantras like "violence profiles" (George Gerbner), "processed culture" (Richard Hoggart), "narcoleptic joys" (Michael Sorkin), and "glass teat" (Harlan Ellison).

6   Of *course* something happens to us when we watch television; networks couldn't sell their millions of pairs of eyes to advertising agencies, nor would ad agencies buy more than $21 billion worth of commercial time each year, if speech (and sound, and motion) didn't somehow modify action. But what happens is far from clear and won't be much clarified by lab studies, however longitudinal, of habits and behaviors isolated from the larger feedback loop of a culture full of gaudy contradictions. The only country in the world that watches more television than we do is Japan, and you should see its snuff movies and pornographic comic books; but the Japanese are pikers compared with us when we compute per capita rates of rape and murder. Some critics in India tried to blame the recent rise in communal violence there on a state-run television series dramatizing the *Mahabharata*, but not long ago they were blaming Salman Rushdie, as in Bangladesh they have decided to blame the writer Taslima Nasrin. No Turk I know of attributes skinhead violence to German TV. It's foolish to pretend that all behavior is mimetic, and that our only model is Spock or Brokaw. Or Mork and Mindy. Why, after so many years of *M*A*S*H*, weekly in prime time and nightly in reruns, aren't all of us out there hugging trees and morphing dolphins? Why, with so many sitcoms, aren't all of us comedians?

7   But nobody normal watches television the way congressmen, academics, symposiasts, and Bill McKibben do. We are less thrilling. For instance:

8   On March 3, 1993, a Wednesday, midway through the nine-week run of *Homicide* on NBC, in an episode written by Tom Fontana and directed by Martin Campbell, Baltimore detectives Bayliss (Kyle Secor) and Pembleton (Andre Braugher) had 12 hours to wring a confession out of "Arab" Tucker (Moses Gunn) for the strangulation and disemboweling of an 11-year-old girl. In the dirty light and appalling intimacy of a single claustrophobic room, with a whoosh of wind sound like some dread blowing in from empty Gobi spaces, among maps, library books, diaries, junk food, pornographic crime-scene photographs, and a single black overflowing ashtray, these three men seemed as nervous as the hand-held cameras—as if their black coffee were full of jumping beans, amphetamines, and spiders; as if God himself were jerking them around.

9   Well, you may think the culture doesn't really need another cop show. And, personally, I'd prefer a weekly series in which social problems are solved through creative nonviolence, after a Quaker meeting, by a collective of vegetarian carpenters. But in a single hour, for which Tom Fontana eventually won an Emmy,

I learned more about the behavior of fearful men in small rooms than from any number of better-known movies, plays, and novels on the topic by the likes of Don DeLillo, Mary McCarthy, Alberto Moravia, Heinrich Böll, and Doris Lessing.

10   This, of course, was an accident, as it usually is when those of us who watch television like normal people are startled in our expectations. We leave home expecting, for a lot of money, to be exalted, and almost never are. But staying put, slumped in an agnosticism about sentience itself, suspecting that our cable box is just another bad-faith credit card enabling us to multiply our opportunities for disappointment, we are ambushed in our lethargy. And not so much by "event" television, like Ingmar Bergman's *Scenes from a Marriage,* originally a six-hour miniseries for Swedish television; or Marcel Ophuls' *The Sorrow and the Pity,* originally conceived for French television; or Rainer Werner Fassbinder's *Berlin Alexanderplatz,* commissioned by German television; or *The Singing Detective;* or *The Jewel in the Crown.* On the contrary, we've stayed home on certain nights to watch television, the way on other nights we'll go out to a neighborhood restaurant, as if on Mondays we ordered in for laughs, as on Fridays we'd rather eat Italian. We go to television—message center, mission control, Big Neighbor, electronic Elmer's glue-all—to look at Oscars, Super Bowls, moon shots, Watergates, Pearlygates, ayatollahs, dead Kings, dead Kennedys; and also, perhaps, to experience some "virtual" community as a nation. But we also go because we are hungry, angry, lonely, or tired, and television is always there for us, a 24-hour user-friendly magic box grinding out narrative, novelty, and distraction, news and laughs, snippets of high culture, remedial seriousness and vulgar celebrity, an incitement and a sedative, a place to celebrate and a place to mourn, a circus and a wishing well.

11   And suddenly Napoleon shows up, like a popsicle, on *Northern Exposure,* while Chris on the radio is reading Proust. Or *Roseanne* is about lesbianism instead of bowling. Or *Picket Fences* has moved on, from serial bathers and elephant abuse to euthanasia and gay-bashing.

12   Kurt Vonnegut on Showtime! David ("Masturbation") Mamet on TNT! Norman Mailer wrote the TV screenplay for *The Executioner's Song,* and Gore Vidal gave us *Lincoln* with Mary Tyler Moore as Mary Todd. In just the past five years, if I hadn't been watching television, I'd have missed *Tanner '88,* when Robert Altman and Garry Trudeau ran Michael Murphy for president of the United States; *My Name Is Bill W.,* with James Woods as the founding father of Alcoholics Anonymous; *The Final Days,* with Theodore Bikel as Henry Kissinger; *No Place Like Home,* where there wasn't one for Christine Lahti and Jeff Daniels, as there hadn't been for Jane Fonda in *The Dollmaker* and Mare Winningham in *God Bless the Child; Eyes on the Prize,* a home movie in two parts about America's second civil war; *The Last Best Year,* with Mary Tyler Moore and Bernadette Peters learning to live with their gay sons and HIV; *Separate but Equal,* with Sidney Poitier as Thurgood Marshall; and *High Crimes and Misdemeanors,* the Bill Moyers special on Irangate and the scandal of our intelligence agencies; Graham Green, John Updike, Philip Roth, Gloria Naylor, Arthur Miller, and George Eliot, plus Paul Simon and Stephen Sondheim. Not to mention—guiltiest of all our secrets—those hoots without which any popular culture would be as tedious as a John Cage or an Anaïs Nin, like Elizabeth Taylor in *Sweet Bird of Youth* and the Redgrave sisters in a remake of *Whatever Happened to Baby Jane?*

13   What all this television has in common is narrative. Even network news—which used to be better than most newspapers before the bean counters started closing down overseas bureaus and the red camera lights went out all over Europe and Asia and Africa—is in the storytelling business. And so far no one in Congress has suggested banning narrative.

14   Because I watch all those despised network TV movies, I know more about racism, ecology, homelessness, gun control, child abuse, gender confusion, date

rape, and AIDS than is dreamt of by, say, Katie Roiphe, the Joyce Maynard of Generation X, or than Hollywood has ever bothered to tell me, especially about AIDS. Imagine, Jonathan Demme's *Philadelphia* opened in theaters around the country well after at least a dozen TV movies on AIDS that I can remember without troubling my hard disk. And I've learned something else, too:

15   We were a violent culture before television, from Wounded Knee to the lynching bee, and we'll be one after all our children have disappeared by video game into the pixels of cyberspace. Before television, we blamed public schools for what went wrong with the Little People back when classrooms weren't over-crowded in buildings that weren't falling down in neighborhoods that didn't resemble Beirut, and whose fault is that? *The A-Team?* We can't control guns, or drugs, and each year two million American women are assaulted by their male partners, who are usually in an alcoholic rage, and whose fault is that? *Miami Vice?* The gangs that menace our streets aren't home watching Cinemax, and neither are the sociopaths who make bonfires, in our parks, from our homeless, of whom there are at least a million, a supply-side migratory tide of the deindustrialized and dispossessed, of angry beggars, refugee children, and catatonic nomads, none of them traumatized by *Twin Peaks.* So cut Medicare, kick around the Brady Bill, and animadvert Amy Fisher movies. But children who are loved and protected long enough to grow up to have homes and respect and lucky enough to have jobs don't riot in the streets. Ours is a tantrum culture that measures everyone by his or her ability to produce wealth, and morally condemns anybody who fails to prosper, and now blames Burbank for its angry incoherence. Why not recessive genes, angry gods, lousy weather? The mafia, the zodiac, the *Protocols of the Elders of Zion?* Probability theory, demonic possession, Original Sin? George Steinbrenner? Sunspots?

Persuasion Technique Questions

1. Who is the audience for the Cannon essay and for the Leonard essay? How do they differ from one another?

    Possible answer: Cannon's essay is directed at those who wish to reduce or remove violence from television programming. Leonard's audience consists of those who do not see television violence as the cause for violent behavior in children and adults. Cannon's audience is made up of parents who are conservative and consider themselves religious. Leonard's audience consists of liberal, college-educated (usually in the humanities) adults.

2. Both Cannon and Leonard use evidence to support their points of view. Which essay's evidence seems the most convincing? Why?

    Answers will vary.

3. Even though these two essays are on different sides of the issue, can you suggest a way that they can achieve a compromise?

Answers will vary.

Persuasive Writing Opportunities

1. Write a persuasive essay defending or attacking television violence.

2. Write a persuasive essay supporting or rejecting the idea that Congress should regulate the amount of violence on television and in the movies.

WHY I HUNT

Dan Sisson

> This essay by Dan Sisson and the one that follows by Steve Ruggeri are clearly persuasive and representative of groups on either side of the gun issue. As you read each writer's position, notice that they concede points to the other side, yet these concessions actually make their own positions stronger. Being fair to your opponent can be an effective technique in persuasive writing.

Vocabulary
Before you begin reading, look up the definitions of the following words that appear in the essay. The number in parentheses after each word refers to the paragraph number of the essay.

aesthetic (13)	anachronism (4)	articulate (11)
banal (7)	clichés (1)	corollary (6)
leper (3)	ponder (17)	

Why I Hunt

1   Hunting implies a relationship between man and animal, and as in any relationship, the layers of meaning that make it unique cannot be reduced to a single proposition or a simple-minded set of clichés.

2   Yet that is what has happened in the United States, where the debate between hunters and anti-hunters has been reduced to one question: How can anyone justify killing any animal?

3   As a hunter, I have felt hostility from people I know and respect who are anti-hunters. I have been told that killing any animal, except in self-defense, is immoral; and I have been characterized as a social leper who belongs to a more primitive age.

4   But this view of the hunter as an anachronism ignores the histories of science and of humankind. It conveniently blots out the fact that in nature every species, no matter how big or small, is either predator or prey, the hunter or the hunted. This—not the preservation of all life at any cost—is the dynamic of existence on our planet.

5   In all predator relationships there is an inequality between the hunter and the hunted. The belief that all creatures have an equal right to life, and that therefore all killing is immoral, is a fallacy without precedent in science or the natural world.

6   The conviction of the anti-hunter that killing any animal is wrong may be based on the misguided concept that equality between hunter and hunted is the corollary of equality before the law. The equality of men and their right to life are *artificial* constructs of constitutional government and hold true only in the most civilized nations.

7   For me the essence of hunting is not the indulgence of the instinct to kill, nor is it to be found in the instant one kills. In fact, killing is no more necessary to a successful hunt than catching a fish is to a good fishing trip. If every hunt ended in a successful kill, hunting would be both boring and banal.

8   The essence of hunting for me is to pursue the animal ethically and in a manner that makes the possibility of killing or capturing it a genuine challenge. There is no certainty of killing when I hunt. Indeed, the *uncertainty* is what makes the sport interesting.

9   I accept limits on my ability to kill. The hunting seasons are carefully constructed so as to make the wit of the hunter and the cunning of the animal more truly competitive.

10   That is why we limit seasons to several days or weeks a year, limit the use of baits to lure unwary animals and birds, and limit the number of animals we kill, their size and age and sex. We limit our behavior by law in order to pursue game ethically and to make the challenge even more difficult. These odds I take on happily, knowing the elk herds will continue to flourish. Those who refuse to accept the odds—the poachers—are not hunters, they are outlaws.

11   Hunting is a complex activity involving undercurrents that are rarely articulated, but that nevertheless form the basis for one's actions. One of these unstated values is the attempt to establish a strong ethical position in life. Few activities in this world test ethical standards as does hunting.

12   There are no witnesses in the wilderness. The hunter knows in his conscience whether he has compromised the sportsman's standards. For an ethical hunter, hypocrisy and hunting are incompatible.

13   I have asserted that hunting involves much more than the act of killing. I hunt to nourish my aesthetic appreciation of nature; being in the field six months a year allows me to experience, personally, the most beautiful parts of America.

14   I hunt for food, and I do not choose to delegate my right to obtain it to a slaughterhouse. My friends go to supermarkets and buy packaged beef and lamb. I go into the wilderness and kill elk, venison, and wildfowl. Is there a moral difference between a cow being killed for market and a deer for my freezer?

15   I hunt because it deepens my relationship with my son. We have literally spent years in duck blinds, on deer stands, and around campfires—talking. I would not trade those conversations for anything on Earth.

16   I hunt because I can contribute to conservation directly. Last year I raised 5,000 valley quail. I killed 49 of them. This reflects a traditional value of giving more to the land and the environment than you take from it. How many anti-hunters can make a similar claim?

17   I hunt to simplify my life, away from the noise and the pollution of urban environments. What better way to ponder John Muir's axiom that every star is connected to every other star in the universe than by starlight after a day in the wilderness?

18   All this is why I hunt.

WHY I DON'T HUNT

Steve Ruggeri

Vocabulary

Before you begin reading, look up the definitions of the following words that appear in the essay. The number in parentheses after each word refers to the paragraph number of the essay.

compunction (4)	credo (7)	diversion (2)
rigors (2)	solicitous (5)	visceral (4)
wantonly (9)		

Why I Don't Hunt

1   Why did I hunt? From the time I was 12 until shortly after my 18th birthday, I pumped lead at the furred and feathered from Maine to Pennsylvania. I was the youngest member of the Newport Rifle Club in Rhode Island, where I was trained and disciplined as a small-bore competitive shooter. I was tutored by masters of the art, and I was given numerous opportunities to engage in my sport.

2   Despite my enthusiasm, I sought diversion from the rigors of competitive shooting. Trap and skeet shooting introduced me to moving targets, but I was anxious to sight down a barrel at animate ones. I looked forward to the pleasure of seeing birds plummet earthward. I knew I would delight in the contortions of small game, the end-over-end tumbling after the rabbit felt the sting of my .22. And I was confident that I would shrug and say, "Better luck, next buck," should I miscalculate shot placement and merely blow the lower jaw completely off a deer.

3   I didn't disappoint myself. I reveled in killing, maiming, bloodletting, and gutting. Never did I have the slightest thought regarding carrying capacity, overbrowsing, population dynamics, or any other game-management concept. The arguments that hunters advanced in defense of their sport were alien to me. I hunted in order to kill; I did not kill in order to have "the hunting experience."

4   Why did I stop? Social expedience: My pastime was deemed unacceptable by a circle of high-school mates from whom I sought acceptance. Would I have ever experienced an after-kill crisis of conscience of such emotional magnitude that I would hurl my weapon into the nearest lake? No, I was incapable of the

visceral compunction that has triggered the moral rebirth of many who formerly exploited animals.

5   A couple of years after my guns had been silenced by peer pressure, I was dining on a hamburger so rare that the blood still appeared to be coursing through the animal tissue. While hurrying to finish so as not to be late for my cat's appointment with the vet, I was seized by the realization of how utterly inconsistent it was for me to be so solicitous of a cat, yet have no regard for the cow I was devouring.

6   Pain is pain, I reasoned, whether felt by the family feline or by the unknown steer shackled and hoisted above the killing-room floor. It became morally imperative for me to end my complicity in the infliction of any gratuitous pain and suffering upon either wild or domesticated animals. This ethical awakening led to extensive research and reading that enlightened me further as to the magnitude of our exploitation of nonhuman animals, and reaffirmed my resolve to embrace an ethic of moral consideration for all animal species. I recognized that my decision to stop hunting years earlier had been correct, though made for the wrong reason.

7   Why don't I hunt? I could allude to the fruits of exhaustive research into the ecological and biological consequences of hunting, and to the collective insight of biologists, ecologists, and naturalists who challenge the prevailing wildlife-management dogma. Yet, fundamentally, the answer can be expressed in simple moral terms: Hunting is wrong, and should be acknowledged to be so not only by those who espouse the strict precepts of the animal-rights credo, but by those who hold a common sense of decency, respect, and justice. When we have exposed the specious reasoning of the hunters' apologists and stripped their sport of its counterfeit legitimacy, the naked brutality of hunting defines itself: killing for the fun of it.

8   Although my current occupation requires attention to a wide array of animal issues, the subject of hunting is the predominant focus of my work. If I find my energy or motivation waning during the course of a day's work, I merely conjure up the image of my former self as a slayer of wildlife. The memory of stalking targets on the hoof or wing infuses me with renewed vigor in my labor against blood sports.

9   But obviously, no amount of dedication or energy expanded will atone for the suffering and death I visited upon the scores of animals I wantonly killed.

Persuasion Technique Questions

1. Identify the thesis sentence in each essay. What are the main differences?

Answers will vary. A good candidate is the first paragraph of Sisson's

essay: "Hunting implies a relationship between man and animal, and as

in any relationship, the layers of meaning that make it unique cannot be

reduced to a single proposition or a simple-minded set of clichés." In

Ruggeri's, a good candidate is in paragraph 6: "It became morally imper-

ative for me to end my complicity in the infliction of any gratuitous pain

and suffering upon either wild or domesticated animals." Sisson argues that the reasons behind hunting are multifaceted and multidimensional, while Ruggeri reduces the entire argument to a single ethical position.

2. Which essay contains the most persuasive evidence based on how it is organized? Explain.

Answers will vary.

3. What logical fallacies can you find in each essay? Explain how you think they detract from each essay's effectiveness.

Some examples of fallacies from Sisson are paragraph 4—either/or; 5—false premise; 6—false analogy; 7—hasty generalization; 13—non sequitur; and some might consider paragraphs 14–17 stacked evidence.

Examples from Ruggeri are paragraphs 2–3—exaggerated emotional language; 2 & 4—ad hominem; 5—false analogy; and 7—ad populum and non sequitur.

Persuasive Writing Opportunities

1. Write an essay defending why you either hunt or do not hunt.

2. Hunting is only one activity that impacts the environment. Write a persuasive essay about how another activity adversely affects the environment: off-road racing including motorcross biking, snow mobiling, camping, canoeing, or skiing are just a few examples.

Limited Answer Key

Chapter 3

PRACTICE 1

1. Reading a newspaper each day is important because it keeps you informed about current events.

3. Working while going to school should teach young people responsibility.

5. The Beatles remain popular, even after their breakup decades ago, because of their versatile musical style.

PRACTICE 2

2. Getting older, talented newcomers, and constant travel make maintaining a sports career a difficult lifestyle.

4. A successful career often hinges upon hard work, dedication, and intelligence.

PRACTICE 3

1. Fruits are a good source for vitamin C. (The essay map is missing.)

3. Many students make college a worthwhile experience by joining fraternities and sororities, playing intramural sports, and participating in student government.

5. Styling, construction, and value make the Breitling a popular wristwatch for collectors.

7. Skydiving and bungee jumping are dangerous activities. (The essay map is missing.)

9. *Star Trek* has been a long-running television series because of special effects, interesting characters, and fascinating stories.

PRACTICES 4–7
Answers will vary.

Chapter 4
Answers will vary in all the Practices.

Chapter 5
Answers will vary.

Chapter 6
Answers will vary in all the Practices.

Chapter 7
Answers will vary in all the Practices.

Chapter 8
Answers will vary in all the Practices.

Chapter 9

PRACTICE 1

Answers will vary.

PRACTICE 2

1. <u>Cybersex</u> <u>is becoming a popular activity</u>.

3. <u>Binge drinking at parties</u> <u>is increasing</u>.

5. <u>A positive attitude</u> <u>can help fight illness</u>.

Chapter 10

Answers will vary in all the Practices.

Chapter 11

Answers will vary in all the Practices.

Chapter 12

Answers will vary in all the Practices.

Chapter 13

Answers will vary in all the Practices.

Chapter 14

PRACTICE 1

Answers will vary.

PRACTICE 2

2. The problem is one of *coincidence*. The problem may have nothing to do with overeating or being exposed to cold weather on a walk. It would be unusual for the person never to have overeaten on other holidays. Did the person become sick then? Most likely the person is exposed to cold weather during the winter months on other occasions, such as playing in the snow with family or friends, waiting for a bus, or walking the dog. Did illness occur after these events? If the answer is no, then the cause lies elsewhere. A good candidate would be an allergy to a specific food such as turkey, cranberries, or pumpkin pie, foods that are commonly eaten on holidays.

Chapter 15

PRACTICE 1

Answers will vary, but sample responses are provided.

1. Pro: Selling cigarettes to teens under eighteen years of age should be legalized.

Con: Teens under eighteen years of age should not be permitted to buy cigarettes.

3. Pro: Organized prayer should be permitted in public schools to promote morality.

Con: To ensure the separation of church and state, organized prayer should not be allowed in public schools.

5. Pro: All eighteen-year-olds should be drafted into the armed services.

Con: Eighteen-year-olds should not be drafted into military service.

7. Pro: The government should require periodic safety inspections for automobiles.

Con: The government should not require periodic safety inspections for automobiles.

9. Pro: The income tax must be increased.

Con: The income tax must not be increased.

PRACTICE 4

2. Either-or

5. Red herring

Chapter 17

PRACTICE

Essay responses will vary. Key terms:

2. evaluate

4. contrast

Chapter 18

Answers will vary in all the Practices.

Glossary

Absolute phrase: a group of words consisting of a noun or pronoun and a **participle** (not the regular verb form) plus any other completing words. Absolute phrases modify the entire sentence and cannot be punctuated as a complete sentence.

Abstract language: general words that refer to ideas or concepts that cannot be perceived through the senses.

Action verb: a verb that states what a subject does (in the past, present, or future tense).

Active voice: a verb form in which the subject of the sentence does the acting (using an action verb or a transitive verb).

Adjective: a word that modifies (or describes) a noun or pronoun. Adjectives usually come before the nouns they describe, but they can also follow the noun (in the predicate of the sentence).

Adverb: a word that modifies (describes) a verb, an adjective, or another adverb. Often adverbs end in *–ly*. Many adverbs answer the question *where, how,* or *when*.

Adverbial conjunction: a word that often follows a semicolon to explain how or in what way the two clauses joined by the semicolon are logically related.

Antecedent: the **noun** to which a **pronoun** refers in a sentence.

Apostrophe: a punctuation mark used to indicate contractions (isn't) or possession/ownership (Anna's papers).

Appositive: a word or phrase that renames the preceding word or phrase. Appositive phrases are often called noun phrases.

Argument: developing a topic by persuading the audience to agree with, or be convinced by, a particular point of view.

Article: a type of word that introduces a noun and indicates whether it is specific or countable. Frequently used articles are *a, an, the*.

Background character: a character that serves as part of the scene or setting but is not developed.

Block citation: a quotation of 5 or more typed lines separated from the text by being indented ten spaces from the left margin and followed with parenthetical citation of the source.

Body paragraphs: the central section of an essay that explains the thesis statement of the essay.

Brackets: punctuation marks used in quoted material to set apart editorial explanations. (The dean wrote, "All faculty must teach sumer [sic] school.")

Brainstorming: a form of freewriting in which the writer lists thoughts freely, at random.

Causal chain: a series of events that can develop; the relationships that exist between events.

Causal relationship: the connection between cause and effect.

Cause-effect: an organization system that examines why something happens or the consequences stemming from causes.

Central character: a character presented as complicated, multidimensional (round), and essential to the plot and theme of a literary work.

Chronological order: an organization system for events according to how they occur in order of time. This order is used most often in narratives, process analysis, and cause-effect essays.

Chronological plot: a story line of events presented in order of time (chronological order).

Class definition: the indication of a word's meaning by its placement in a broad class of similar things that readers will readily understand. A class definition usually includes a specific detail that distinguishes the original term or word from the others in the class.

Classification: an organization system that divides the subject matter into categories determined by one criterion or basis for grouping.

Clause: a group of related words containing both a subject and a verb. Clauses are either **independent** or **dependent.** They also can be **restrictive** or **non-restrictive.**

Climax: the point at which the protagonist learns a truth that forever changes the character or the action of the plot; the moment of highest tension that soon leads to falling action.

Clustering: a type of prewriting in which the writer explores and organizes thoughts in a chart that begins with putting the main topic in a circle in the center of the page, then connecting related ideas (in smaller circles) with lines (branches).

Coherence: a quality in which the relationship between ideas is clear throughout a paragraph or essay.

Coincidence: two or more events that occur around the same time but with no direct cause-effect relationship.

Colon: a punctuation mark most often used to show that a list or explanation will follow. (Eat plenty of green vegetables: broccoli, spinach, and cabbage for example.)

Comma: a punctuation mark used for separating ideas, independent clauses, and items in a list, and for enclosing descriptive phrases.

Comma splice: a sentence containing two independent clauses incorrectly joined by a comma.

Comparison-contrast: an organization system showing similarities (comparisons) and differences (contrasts) between two or more subjects or topics. The organization can be blocked by topic, or point by point by criteria.

Complex sentence: a sentence that contains an independent clause and a dependent clause.

Complication: a plot element that introduces a problem or conflict to stimulate a reader's interest.

Compound verb (predicate): a predicate (the part of the sentence containing the verb) containing two or more verbs.

Compound sentence: a sentence consisting of two or more independent clauses.

Compound subject: two or more simple subjects joined by a coordinating conjunction.

Concluding paragraph: the paragraph that ends an essay and gives a sense of completeness.

Conclusion: the last sentence of a paragraph or the last paragraph of an essay that ties together the preceding ideas.

Concrete language: particular, specific words used to portray the unique complex nature of the real world.

Conjunction: a joining word or phrase (see **coordinating conjunction, adverbial conjunction,** and **subordinating conjunction**).

Connotative language: use of words which have (or develop) associations and implications apart from their explicit sense.

Controlling idea or attitude: the focus concerning the topic or how the author feels about the topic.

Coordinating conjunction: a word that joins grammatically equal structures. The most frequently used are *and, but, or, yet, for, nor, so.*

Coordination: joining two or more grammatically equal structures, most often with a coordinating conjunction or a semicolon.

Countable nouns: nouns that can be either singular or plural.

Criterion: the standard used to classify things (basis for grouping, evaluating, comparing, and contrasting).

Dangling modifier: a descriptive phrase or clause that does not modify (describe) any word or phrase in a sentence.

Dash: a punctuation mark used to set apart parenthetical information that needs more emphasis than would be indicated by parentheses. (Irina's professor—a dynamic sociology teacher—helped her understand American society.)

Definition: an organization system that explains the meaning of a term or concept using a variety of strategies (examples, contrast, description, etc.)

Definition by negation: saying what a given word or term *is not* before saying what the word or term *actually is*.

Demonstrative pronoun: a pronoun used to point out or specify certain people, places, or things (*this, that, these, those*).

Denotative language: use of words in their accepted, dictionary-defined sense.

Dependent clause: a group of words with a subject and verb but which cannot stand alone and must be joined to an independent clause to complete its meaning. Most dependent clauses begin with subordinating conjunctions or relative pronouns.

Description: the mode of writing which develops a topic through the use of vivid sensory detail.

Developing character: a character that undergoes change during the course of a literary work.

Direct object: the word or words (usually nouns or pronouns) following and receiving the action of an action verb.

Directional process: the explanation of how to do something. The intent of directional process writing is to enable the readers to do something (to duplicate some process) after they have followed the directions.

Dominant impression: the overall feeling or emotional response the writer wants the reader to take away from descriptive writing.

Editing: one of the final steps in the writing process during which the writer checks the draft of the essay for misspelled words, grammatical errors, missing words, and other errors.

Essay: an organized written work on a topic in a series of paragraphs, including an introduction that attracts the reader's attention and states the thesis of the essay, body paragraphs that present the supporting points of the thesis and develop them with facts, details, and examples, and a conclusion that summarizes the ideas and coherently ends the work.

Essay map: in the thesis sentence of an essay, the indication of the subtopics that the essay will cover.

Example: an instance or case used to illustrate or explain a point.

Exposition: informative writing. In a literary work, it introduces the audience to the universe of the fictional work, the characters and their inter-relationships, and the narrator's point of view.

Expository writing (exposition): informative writing, the primary purpose of which is to explain a concept.

Extended definition: a definition explained in several sentences or a paragraph by means of any one mode of development or any combination of the modes of development: description, narration, example, classification, process, comparison and contrast, and cause and effect.

Fact: a statement that can be proven to be true.

Falling action: in the plot line, the diminishing of tension and release of emotion following the climax.

Figurative language: the device of describing a person or thing in terms usually associated with something very different.

Flashback: a plot device that interrupts the chronological sequence to introduce a past episode.

Flat character: a character portrayed as representative, incomplete, or not complex—a type rather than an individual.

Foreshadowing: a hint or suggestion of what will come later.

Fragment: an incomplete sentence because it is missing a subject or verb or the verb is incomplete; a dependent clause not attached to an independent clause.

Frame: an introduction to or explanation for a quotation. The frame states the name of the person quoted, the person's title or expertise, or a brief comment on the quotation's content. This information can be placed before the quotation, after the quotation, or in the middle of the quotation.

Freewriting: writing that is used to explore ideas without concern for grammar, spelling, or organization.

Future tense: a tense used to indicate action or being that has not yet occurred.

Gerund: the –*ing* form of a verb that functions as a noun in a sentence.

Gerund phrase: a **gerund** and its completing words.

Helping verb: a part of the verb before the main verb, conveying information about tense. Helping verbs usually are forms of *have, be, do, will.*

Hyphen: a punctuation mark used to join descriptive adjectives before a noun, to join compound words, to attach some prefixes, or to separate syllables at the end of a line.

Image/imagery: a word, phrase, or figure of speech (such as a simile or metaphor) addressing the senses, suggesting sounds, smells, sights, feelings, tastes, or actions.

Indefinite pronoun: a pronoun used to refer to general or indeterminate people, places, or things (*everyone, everybody, someone, somebody, everything, something, nothing, anyone*).

Independent clause: a clause that can stand alone as a sentence, containing a complete subject and verb.

Indirect object: a noun or pronoun following a verb that receives a direct object. (Jane gave *her* the book.)

Infinitive phrase: a group of words consisting of *to* plus a verb and its completing words. An infinitive phrase can function as a noun, adjective, or adverb.

Informational process: the explanation of how something was made, how an event occurred, or how something works.

Interrupter: a clause or phrase that clarifies or provides additional meaning.

In-text citation: quoted material of no more than three or four typed lines incorporated into the text of the paper rather than set apart in block form. This material should be followed by parentheses containing the author's name and the page number of the source.

Introductory paragraph: the paragraph that introduces the reader to the topic of an essay.

Introductory sentence: the sentence that often precedes the thesis sentence. The purpose of introductory sentences is to catch the reader's attention and clarify your **tone.**

Inverted plot: a plot pattern in which events are portrayed out of sequence.

Irony: a verbal device that expresses a contrast between what is said and what is meant.

Irregular verb: a verb that does not form the past tense by adding –*ed*, or –*d*. Some verbs do not change forms at all, or they form the past tense by changing the spelling of the entire word (stem-changing verbs).

Linking verb: a verb that does not express action but links the subject to the word or words that describe the subject. The most common linking verbs are forms of *be.*

Literary analysis: an interpretation or discussion of one or more works of literature. Literary analysis often takes a persuasive approach; the writer takes a position about some aspect of the work and defends it.

Main verb: the most important word in a verb phrase, usually conveying the action of the sentence.

Metaphor: a way to describe a topic in terms of another concept (love is *a rose*).

Modes of development: the different viewpoints from which to write about a topic: description, narration, example, classification, process, comparison and contrast, definition, cause and effect, persuasion.

Modifier: a word or group of words which functions as an adjective or adverb (providing description).

Motif: a recurring thematic element in an artistic or literary work.

Narration: a story, usually told in chronological order, usually building to a climax and then resolving.

Nonrestrictive clause: a clause that is not essential to complete the meaning of a sentence. If you remove a nonrestrictive clause from a sentence, the basic meaning of the sentence will remain clear.

Noun: a word that stands for a person, place, or thing. It can be singular or plural.

Noun clause: a clause functioning as a noun, usually beginning with *a, the, what, where, why,* or *when.*

Object: a word or words (usually nouns or pronouns) following prepositions, action verbs, and words formed from verbs (participles, infinitives).

Objective description: factual description, using sensory details of what is seen, heard, tasted, smelled, or touched without any emotional response or interpretation.

Oxymoron: a verbal device in which two contradictory words are used together to enhance meaning ("sweet sorrow"); a condensed form of **paradox.**

Paradox: a statement that at first appears to be a contradiction but upon study makes sense.

Paragraph: a group of sentences that discuss or develop a topic.

Parallel construction (parallelism): the repetition of the same grammatical structure for coherence or emphasis.

Paraphrase: restating someone's ideas in your own words and sentence structure (not directly quoting the other person's words).

Parenthesis: a mark of punctuation used to set off specific details giving additional information, explanations, or qualifications of the main idea in a sentence. *Many students name famous athletes as heroes (Sammy Sosa and Mark McGwire, for example).*

Participial phrase: a group of words consisting of a participle and its completing words.

Participle: a verb form ending in *–ed* or *–ing* that is used as an adjective or used with helping verbs to form present perfect or past perfect forms. See **past participle** and **present participle**.

Passive voice: a verb form chosen when the actor of the sentence is not important or when the writer wishes to avoid naming the subject. In the passive voice, the object of an active verb becomes the subject of a passive verb (*be* + past participle).

Past participle: a verb form used to help form the present perfect and past perfect tenses and the passive voice. Past participles usually end with *–d, –ed,* or *–en.*

Past perfect tense: a tense used to describe past action or events occurring prior to a later time in the past. The past perfect is formed from *had* and the verb's past participle form.

Past tense: a tense used to discuss completed past actions. All **regular verbs** in the past-tense end in *–ed.*

Period: a punctuation mark that is used to end a complete statement or is included in an abbreviation.

Personal pronoun: a pronoun that refers to a specific person or thing (*I, me, you, he, him, she, her, it, we, us, they, them).* There are three forms, depending on how the personal pronoun is used in a sentence: subjective (used as a subject), objective (used as an object), or possessive (used to indicate possession or ownership).

Personification: a form of metaphor in which non-human things are given human characteristics.

Persuasion: argument that seeks to convince others of the rightness of a belief, point of view, or course of action.

Phrase: a group of related words missing a subject or verb, or both. Phrases are used in sentences to complete thoughts or add descriptive detail; they may be restrictive or nonrestrictive. See **prepositional phrase, participial phrase, gerund phrase, infinitive phrase,** and **absolute phrase.**

Phrasal verb: a two-word or three-word expression that combines a verb with another word, changing the meaning (such as *pick it up).*

Plagiarism: presenting someone else's ideas or words as if they were your own.

Point of the story: in narrative writing, what is interesting about the subject.

Predicate: the part of the sentence containing the verb, making a statement or asking a question about the subject.

Preposition: a word that connects a noun or pronoun to the rest of the sentence, often showing location or time. Frequently used prepositions are *in, on, over, before, after.*

Prepositional phrase: a phrase that contains a preposition and its object (e.g., *in the car* or *on the table*).

Present participle: a verb form ending in *–ing* that is used to help form the **progressive tenses** and that may be used as an adjective.

Present perfect tense: a tense used to describe an action or condition that started in the past and continues up to the present. The tense is formed by combining *has* or *have* and the past participle.

Present tense: a tense used to discuss habitual actions, facts, or conditions that are true of the present.

Prewriting: the step in the writing process in which the writer thinks about the topic, purpose, and audience and explores ideas for development through **brainstorming, clustering,** or **freewriting.**

Process: a series of actions leading to a concluding point.

Process analysis: an organizational structure that explains how to do something or how something works.

Progressive tense: a tense that discusses actions that are or were happening or are planned for the future. This tense is formed by adding a form of the verb *be* (*is, am, are*) to a verb ending in *–ing.*

Pronoun: a word that takes the place of, or refers to, a noun. The word or phrase that the pronoun refers to is the **antecedent** of the pronoun. See **personal pronoun, relative pronoun, demonstrative pronoun, indefinite pronoun,** and **reflexive pronoun.**

Question mark: the punctuation mark that ends a direct question.

Reflexive pronoun: a pronoun ending in *–self* or *–selves* that is used to indicate action performed to or on the antecedent.

Regular verb: a verb ending in *–ed* in the past tense or past participle, or forming its third-person singular form by adding *–s* or *–es.*

Relative clause: a clause that functions as an adjective and begins with a **relative pronoun** (*who, whom, which, that*).

Relative pronoun: a pronoun used to introduce a qualifying or explanatory clause (*who, whom, which, that, whoever, whichever*).

Resolution (*denouement*): the section of the plot line in which the complications are resolved, but not necessarily in a satisfactory way when compared to the traditional legal or moral values of society.

Restrictive clause: a clause that is essential to identify nouns or to complete the meaning. These clauses follow the nouns or ideas they modify. No commas are used to offset restrictive clauses.

Rising action: a plot element in which increased emotional effect is created by additional events or ramifications from the original action, creating complications for the protagonist.

Round character: a character presented as a complicated, multidimensional individual.

Run-on sentence: a sentence containing two or more independent clauses with nothing that joins them together (a serious grammatical error).

Semicolon: a mark of punctuation that usually joins two independent clauses; it occasionally is used to separate items in a series containing internal commas.

Sensory image: descriptive writing utilizing or evoking the five senses: sight, touch, smell, sound, and taste.

Sentence: a complete statement or question containing a subject and a verb and expressing a complete thought.

Setting: the location within a literary work, consisting of both spatial (house, community, region, country) and cultural qualities (social, moral, economic, political, psychological). The setting can create an atmosphere, playing on our feelings about certain locations.

Simile: a comparison using *like* or *as* (My love is *like a rose*).

Simple definition: a brief explanation such as found in a dictionary. There are three types of simple definition: definition by synonym, class, and negation.

Static character: a character that remains essentially unchanged throughout a literary work.

Subject: the topic (who or what) about which a clause makes a statement or asks a question. Usually the subject is a noun or pronoun, and usually the subject precedes the verb.

Subjective description: description that creates an easily identifiable emotion or impression. This type of description communicates the writer's emotional response to what he or she encounters.

Subject-verb agreement: Subjects and verbs should agree in number. Thus, singular subjects require verbs with singular endings, and plural subjects require verbs with plural endings.

Subordinating conjunction: a word that joins two clauses by making one clause dependent on the other (independent) clause. (Examples: *although, after, because, while*.)

Subordination: joining a dependent clause to an independent clause.

Support sentence: a sentence that explains, clarifies, or defines the subject stated in the topic sentence.

Supporting character: a character who is not the main protagonist but who supports the main characters and may be round or complex.

Symbol: an object, person, image, word, or event that represents more than the literal significance of the term, often evoking complex ideas or themes in literary works.

Synonym: a word with the same, or close to the same, meaning as another word.

Synonym definition: defines a word by supplying another (often simpler) word that means the same thing.

Tense: the form of the verb that shows when in time an action occurred (present, past, future).

Theme: the central meaning, purpose, or dominant idea of a literary work.

Thesis sentence: the sentence, usually included in the introduction, that states the main idea of an essay and often outlines the subtopics of the essay (**essay map**).

Three-item essay map: three items listed in a thesis sentence that will support the thesis.

Tone: the author's implied attitude toward the reader or the places, people, and events in a literary work, revealed by the style and word choice.

Topic: the subject or focus of a paragraph or essay.

Topic sentence: a sentence stating the main idea of a paragraph.

Transitional expression: a word or phrase explaining how or in what way two ideas are related. These are often **adverbial conjunctions.**

Uncountable nouns: nouns that represent an idea or concept that cannot be counted (water, air) and cannot be made plural.

Unity: a clearness, coherence, and consistency in the purpose, theme, or organization of a literary work.

Verb: a word indicating action, feeling, or being. The form of the verb can indicate the time of the action: present, past, or future (**tense**).

Works cited: a listing of the reference works referred to in a research paper and cited parenthetically in MLA form.

Credits

Text Credits

Mario Suarez, "La Hoya" is reprinted from *Arizona Quarterly* 47.2(1947), by permission of the Regents of The University of Arizona.

Eric Kim, "Have You Ever Met an Asian Man You Thought Was Sexy?" *Glamour*, March 1995.

"Joy Luck Club", from THE JOY LUCK CLUB by Amy Tan, copyright © 1989 by Amy Tan. Used by permission of G.P. Putnam's Sons, a division of Penguin Putnam, Inc.

Tania Nyman, "I Have a Gun" *Times Picayune* 4/21/90.

Lewis Sawaquat, "For My Indian Daughter," *Newsweek*, September 5, 1983.

"Kubota" by Garrett Hongo is reprinted by permission of the author.

Harold Krents, "Darkness at Noon," *New York Times*, May 26, 1976. Copyright © 1976 by the New York Times Company. Reprinted by permission.

D. James Romero, "Belivers in Search of Piercing Insight" *Los AngelesTimes* January 29, 1997. Copyright 1997. Reprinted by permission.

From FATHERHOOD by Bill Cosby, copyright © 1986 by William H. Cosby, Jr., Used by permission of Doubleday, a division of Random House.

Judy Brady, "Why I Want a Wife" is reprinted by permission of the author.

Viet D. Dinh, "Single White Female," *Reconstruction*, Vol. 2, No. 3. Copyright © 1994. Reprinted by permission of Viet D. Dinh.

Franklin Zimring, "Confessions of an Ex-Smoker," *Newsweek*, April 20, 1987.

Meneka Ghandi, "You Are Sure You Want to Do This?" *Baltimore Sun*, November 20, 1989.

Sean T. Wherley, "Coming Out: A Process of Dilemnas," *The Minnesota Daily*, October 9, 1995. Copyright 1995. Reprinted by permission.

Reprinted with the permission of Scribner, a division of Simon & Schuster from GETTING THINGS DONE: THE ABC'S OF TIME MANAGEMENT by Edwin C. Bliss. Copyright © 1976 by Edwin C. Bliss.

Charisse Jones, "Light Versus Dark Skin," *Glamour*, October 1995.

Photo Credits

Page 2: John Henley/The Stock Market

Page 8: Erik Viktor/Science Photo Library/Photo Researchers, Inc.

Page 26: David Hamilton/The Imagebank

Page 39: Tommy Hindley/The Image Works

Page 70: Wesley Frank/Woodfin Camp & Associates

Page 84 (left): James Shaffer/PhotoEdit; (middle): Mary Kate Denny/PhotoEdit; (right): David Young-Wolit/PhotoEdit

Page 96: John Henley/The Stock Market

Page 109 (left): Scott Fischer/Woodfin Camp & Associates; (top right): Dugald Bremner/ Stone Images; (bottom right): Vandystadt/Woodfin Camp & Associates

Page 124: Bob Daemmrich/The Image Works

Page 143 (left): Whitford & Hughes, London, UK/Bridgeman Art Library; (right): Musee Picasso, Paris, France/Peter Willi/Bridgeman Art Library. ©2001 Estate of Pablo Picasso/Artists Rights Society, New York

Page 158: Michael Yarish/CBS Photo Archive

Page 176: Richard Hutchings/Photo Researchers, Inc.

Index